'Bankers are born no greedier than the rest of us. That assertion alone makes Joseph Stiglitz's comprehensive postmortem stand out from the reams of books published so far about the financial crisis'
Barbara Kiviat, *Time*

'Mr Stiglitz uses his experience teaching to give the lay reader a lucid account of how overleveraged banks, a shoddy mortgage industry, predatory lending and unregulated trading contributed to the meltdown, and how, in his opinion, ill-conceived rescue efforts may have halted the freefall but have failed to grapple with more fundamental problems. His prescience lends credibility to his trenchant analysis of the causes of the fiscal meltdown'
Michiko Kakutani, *New York Times*

'*Freefall* is a spirited attack on Wall Street, the free market and the Washington consensus' David Smith, *The Times*

'[Stiglitz] has managed to clarify deftly and intelligently almost all the relevant and perplexing issues that have arisen from the crisis'
Jeff Madrick, *New York Review of Books*

'If anyone is going to produce a bold new economic theory and vision to guide the centre left beyond the financial crisis, it's going to be Joe . . . It is to Stiglitz's lasting credit that, while other economists have already moved back into the realm of algebra and Greek letters, he has remained in the trenches of policy'
Paul Mason, *New Statesman*

'*Freefall* is a must-read for anyone seeking to understand the roots of the financial crisis. Stiglitz brilliantly analyzes the economic reasons behind the banking collapse, but he goes much further, digging down to the wrongheaded national faith in the power of free markets to regulate themselves and provide wealth for all'
Chuck Leddy, *Boston Globe*

FREEFALL

*Free Markets and the
Sinking of the Global Economy*

JOSEPH E. STIGLITZ

PENGUIN BOOKS

PENGUIN BOOKS

Published by the Penguin Group
Penguin Books Ltd, 80 Strand, London WC2R 0RL, England
Penguin Group (USA), Inc., 375 Hudson Street, New York, New York 10014, USA
Penguin Group (Canada), 90 Eglinton Avenue East, Suite 700, Toronto, Ontario, Canada M4P 2Y3
(a division of Pearson Penguin Canada Inc.)
Penguin Ireland, 25 St Stephen's Green, Dublin 2, Ireland (a division of Penguin Books Ltd)
Penguin Group (Australia), 250 Camberwell Road, Camberwell, Victoria 3124, Australia
(a division of Pearson Australia Group Pty Ltd)
Penguin Books India Pvt Ltd, 11 Community Centre, Panchsheel Park, New Delhi – 110 017, India
Penguin Group (NZ), 67 Apollo Drive, Rosedale, North Shore 0632, New Zealand
(a division of Pearson New Zealand Ltd)
Penguin Books (South Africa) (Pty) Ltd, 24 Sturdee Avenue, Rosebank,
Johannesburg 2196, South Africa

Penguin Books Ltd, Registered Offices: 80 Strand, London WC2R 0RL, England

www.penguin.com

First published in the USA by W. W. Norton & Company, Inc., 2009
First published in Great Britain by Allen Lane 2009
Published with updated material in Penguin Books 2010

4

Copyright © Joseph E. Stiglitz, 2009, 2010

The moral right of the author has been asserted

Printed in Great Britain by Clays Ltd, St Ives plc

A CIP catalogue record for this book is available from the British Library

978–0–141–04512–2

www.greenpenguin.co.uk

Mixed Sources
Product group from well-managed
forests and other controlled sources
www.fsc.org Cert no. SA-COC-1592
© 1996 Forest Stewardship Council

Penguin Books is committed to a sustainable future
for our business, our readers and our planet.
The book in your hands is made from paper
certified by the Forest Stewardship Council.

TO MY STUDENTS,
FROM WHOM I HAVE LEARNED SO MUCH,
IN THE HOPE THAT THEY WILL LEARN
FROM OUR MISTAKES.

CONTENTS

PREFACE

I N THE GREAT RECESSION THAT BEGAN IN 2008, MILLIONS of people in America and all over the world lost their homes and jobs. Many more suffered the anxiety and fear of doing so, and almost anyone who put away money for retirement or a child's education saw those investments dwindle to a fraction of their value. A crisis that began in America soon turned global, as tens of millions lost their jobs worldwide—20 million in China alone—and tens of millions fell into poverty.[1]

This is not the way things were supposed to be. Modern economics, with its faith in free markets and globalization, had promised prosperity for all. The much-touted New Economy—the amazing innovations that marked the latter half of the twentieth century, including deregulation and financial engineering—was supposed to enable better risk management, bringing with it the end of the business cycle. If the combination of the New Economy and modern economics had not eliminated economic fluctuations, at least it was taming them. Or so we were told.

The Great Recession—clearly the worst downturn since the Great Depression seventy-five years earlier—has shattered these illusions. It is forcing us to rethink long-cherished views. For a quarter century, certain free market doctrines have prevailed: Free and unfettered markets are efficient; if they make mistakes, they quickly correct them. The best government is a small government, and regulation only impedes innovation. Central banks should be independent and only focus on keeping inflation low. Today, even the high priest of that ideology, Alan Greenspan, the chairman of the Federal Reserve Board during the period in which these views prevailed, has admitted that there was a flaw in this reasoning—but his confession came too late for the many who have suffered as a consequence.

This book is about a battle of ideas, about the ideas that led to the failed policies that precipitated the crisis and about the lessons that we take away from it. In time, every crisis ends. But no crisis, especially one of this severity, passes without leaving a legacy. The legacy of 2008 will include new perspectives on the long-standing conflict over the kind of economic system most likely to deliver the greatest benefit. The battle between capitalism and communism may be over, but market economies come in many variations and the contest among them rages on.

I believe that markets lie at the heart of every successful economy but that markets do not work well on their own. In this sense, I'm in the tradition of the celebrated British economist John Maynard Keynes, whose influence towers over the study of modern economics. Government needs to play a role, and not just in rescuing the economy when markets fail and in regulating markets to prevent the kinds of failures we have just experienced. Economies need a balance between the role of markets and the role of government—with important contributions by nonmarket and nongovernmental institutions. In the last twenty-five years, America lost that balance, and it pushed its unbalanced perspective on countries around the world.

This book explains how flawed perspectives led to the crisis, made it difficult for key private-sector decision makers and public-sector policymakers to see the festering problems, and contributed to policymakers' failure to handle the fallout effectively. The length of the crisis will depend on the policies pursued. Indeed, mistakes already made will result in the downturn being longer and deeper than it otherwise would have been. But managing the crisis is only my first concern; I am also concerned about the world that will emerge after the crisis. We won't and can't go back to the world as it was before.

Before the crisis, the United States, and the world generally, faced many problems, not the least of which was that of adapting to climate change. The pace of globalization was forcing rapid changes in economic structure, stretching the coping capacity of many economies. These challenges will remain, in magnified form, after the crisis, but the resources that we have to deal with them will be greatly diminished.

The crisis will, I hope, lead to changes in the realm of policies *and* in the realm of ideas. If we make the right decisions, not merely the politically or socially expedient ones, we will not only make another crisis less likely, but perhaps even accelerate the kinds of real innovations that would improve the lives of people around the world. If we make the wrong decisions, we will emerge with a society more divided and an economy more vulnerable to another crisis and less well equipped to meet the challenges of the twenty-first century. One of the purposes of this book is to help us understand better the post-crisis global order that eventually will arise and how what we do today will help shape it for better or for worse.

✦   ✦   ✦

ONE MIGHT have thought that with the crisis of 2008, the debate over market fundamentalism—the notion that unfettered markets by themselves can ensure economic prosperity and growth—would be over. One might have thought that no one ever again—or at least until memories of this crisis have receded into the distant past—would argue that markets are self-correcting and that we can rely on the self-interested behavior of market participants to ensure that everything works well.

Those who have done well by market fundamentalism offer a different interpretation. Some say our economy suffered an "accident," and accidents happen. No one would suggest that we stop driving cars just because of an occasional collision. Those who hold this position want us to return to the world before 2008 as quickly as possible. The bankers did nothing wrong, they say.[2] Give the banks the money they ask for, tweak the regulations a little bit, give a few stern lectures to the regulators not to let the likes of Bernie Madoff get away with fraud again, add a few more business school courses on ethics, and we will emerge in fine shape.

This book argues that the problems are more deep-seated. Over the past twenty-five years this supposedly self-regulating apparatus, our financial system, has repeatedly been rescued by the government. From the system's survival, we drew the wrong lesson—that it was working on its own. Indeed, our economic system hadn't been working so well for most Americans before the crisis. Somebody was doing well, but it was not the average American.

An economist looks at a crisis in the same way a doctor approaches disease pathology: both learn much about how things work normally by seeing what happens when things are not normal. As I approached the crisis of 2008, I felt I had a distinct advantage over other observers. I was, in a sense, a "crisis veteran," a crisologist. This was not the first major crisis in recent years. Crises in developing countries have occurred with an alarming regularity—by one count, 124 between 1970 and 2007.[3] I was chief economist at the World Bank at the time of the last global financial crisis, in 1997–1998. I watched a crisis that began in Thailand spread to other countries in East Asia and then to Latin America and Russia. It was a classic example of contagion—a failure in one part of the global economic system spreading to other parts. The full consequences of an economic crisis may take years to manifest themselves. In the case of Argentina, the crisis began in 1995, as part of the fallout from Mexico's own crisis, and was exacerbated by the East Asian crisis of 1997 and the Brazilian crisis of 1998, but the full collapse didn't take place until late 2001.

Economists might feel proud about the advances in economic science over the seven decades since the Great Depression, but that doesn't mean that there has been unanimity about how crises should be handled. Back in 1997, I watched in horror as the U.S. Treasury and the International Monetary Fund (IMF) responded to the East Asian crisis by proposing a set of policies that harkened back to the misguided policies associated with President Herbert Hoover during the Great Depression and were bound to fail.

There was, then, a sense of déjà vu as I saw the world slipping once again into a crisis in 2007. The similarities between what I saw then and a decade earlier were uncanny. To mention but one, the initial public denial of the crisis: ten years earlier, the U.S. Treasury and the IMF had at first denied that there was a recession / depression in East Asia. Larry Summers, then Undersecretary of Treasury and now President Obama's chief economic adviser, went ballistic when Jean-Michel Severino, then the World Bank's vice president for Asia, used the R-word (Recession) and the D-word (Depression) to describe what was happening. But how else would one describe a downturn that left 40 percent of those in Indonesia's central island of Java unemployed?

So too in 2008, the Bush administration at first denied there was any serious problem. We had just built a few too many houses, the president suggested.[4] In the early months of the crisis, the Treasury and the Federal Reserve veered like drunk drivers from one course to another, saving some banks while letting others go down. It was impossible to discern the principles behind their decision making. Bush administration officials argued that they were being pragmatic, and to be fair, they were in uncharted territory.

As the clouds of recession began to loom over the U.S. economy in 2007 and early 2008, economists were often asked whether another depression, or even deep recession, was possible. Most economists instinctively replied, NO! Advances in economic science—including knowledge about how to manage the global economy—meant that such a catastrophe seemed inconceivable to many experts. Yet, ten years ago, when the East Asian crisis happened, we had failed, and we had failed miserably.

Incorrect economic theories not surprisingly lead to incorrect policies, but, obviously, those who advocated them thought they would work. They were wrong. Flawed policies had not only brought on the East Asian crisis of a decade ago but also exacerbated its depth and duration and left a legacy of weakened economies and mountains of debt.

The failure ten years ago was also partly a failure of global politics. The crisis struck in the developing countries, sometimes called the "periphery" of the global economic system. Those running the global economic system were not so much worried about protecting the lives and livelihoods of those in the affected nations as they were in preserving Western banks that had lent these countries money. Today, as America and the rest of the world struggle to restore their economies to robust growth, there is again a failure of policy *and* politics.

Freefall

When the world economy went into freefall in 2008, so too did our beliefs. Long-standing views about economics, about America, and about our heroes have also been in freefall. In the aftermath of the last great financial crisis, *Time* magazine on February 15, 1999, ran a cover picture of Federal Reserve Chairman Alan Greenspan and Treasury Secretary Robert Rubin, who were long given credit for the boom in the 1990s, together with their protégé Larry Summers. They were labeled the "Committee to Save the World," and in the popular mindset they were thought of as supergods. In 2000, the best-selling investigative journalist Bob Woodward wrote a Greenspan hagiography entitled *Maestro*.[5]

Having seen firsthand the handling of the East Asian crisis, I was less impressed than *Time* magazine or Bob Woodward. To me, and to most of those in East Asia, the policies foisted on them by the IMF and the U.S. Treasury at the behest of the "Committee to Save the World" had made the crises far worse than they otherwise would have been. The policies showed a lack of understanding of the fundamentals of modern macroeconomics, which call for expansionary monetary and fiscal policies in the face of an economic downturn.[6]

As a society, we have now lost respect for our long-standing economic gurus. In recent years, we had turned to Wall Street as a whole—not just the demigods like Rubin and Greenspan—for advice on how to run the complex system that is our economy. Now, who is there to turn to? For the most part, economists have been no more helpful. Many of them had provided the intellectual armor that the policymakers invoked in the movement toward deregulation.

Unfortunately, attention is often shifted away from the battle of ideas toward the role of individuals: the villains that created the crisis, and the heroes that saved us. Others will write (and in fact have already written) books that point fingers at this policymaker or another, this financial executive or another, who helped steer us into the current crisis. This book has a different aim. Its view is that essentially all the critical policies, such as those related to deregulation, were the consequence of political and economic "forces"—interests, ideas, and ideologies—that go beyond any particular individual.

When President Ronald Reagan appointed Greenspan chairman of the Federal Reserve in 1987, he was looking for someone committed to deregulation. Paul Volcker, who had been the Fed chairman previously, had earned high marks as a central banker for bringing the U.S. inflation rate down from 11.3 percent in 1979 to 3.6 percent in 1987.[7] Normally, such an accomplishment would have earned automatic reappointment. But Volcker understood the importance of regulations, and Reagan wanted someone who would work to strip them away. Had Greenspan not been available for the job, there were plenty of others able and willing to assume the deregulation mantle. The problem was not so much Greenspan as the deregulatory ideology that had taken hold.

While this book is mostly about economic beliefs and how they affect policies, to see the link between the crisis and these beliefs, one has to unravel what happened. This book is not a "whodunit," but there are important elements of the story that are akin to a good mystery: How did the largest economy in the world go into freefall? What policies and what events triggered the great downturn of 2008? If we can't agree on the answers to these questions, we can't agree on what to do, either to get us out of the crisis or to prevent the next one. Parsing out the relative role of bad behavior by the banks, failures of the regulators, or loose monetary policy by the Fed is not easy, but I will explain why I put the onus of responsibility on financial markets and institutions.

Finding root causes is like peeling back an onion. Each explanation gives rise to further questions at a deeper level: perverse incentives may have encouraged shortsighted and risky behavior among bankers, but why did they have such perverse incentives? There is a ready answer: problems in corporate governance, the manner in which incentives and pay get determined. But why didn't the market exercise discipline on bad corporate governance and bad incentive structures? Natural selection is supposed to entail survival of the fittest; those firms with the governance and incentive structures best designed for long-run performance should have thrived. That theory is another casualty of this crisis. As one thinks about the problems this crisis revealed in the financial sector, it becomes obvious that they are more general and that there are similar ones in other arenas.

What is also striking is that when one looks beneath the surface, beyond the new financial products, the subprime mortgages, and the collateralized debt instruments, this crisis appears so similar to many that have gone before it, both in the United States and abroad. There was a bubble, and it broke, bringing devastation in its wake. The bubble was supported by bad bank lending, using as collateral assets whose value had been inflated by the bubble. The new innovations had allowed the banks to hide much of their bad lending, to move it off their balance sheets, to increase their effective leverage—making the bubble all the greater, and the havoc that its bursting brought all the worse. New instruments (credit default swaps), allegedly for managing risk but in reality as much designed for deceiving regulators, were so complex that they amplified risk. The big question, to which much of this book is addressed, is, How and why did we let this happen *again*, and on such a scale?

While finding the deeper explanations is difficult, there are some simple explanations that can easily be rejected. As I mentioned, those who worked on Wall Street wanted to believe that individually they had done nothing wrong, and they wanted to believe that the *system* itself was fundamentally right. They believed they were the unfortunate victims of a once-in-a-thousand-year storm. But the crisis was not something that just happened to the financial markets; it was man-made—it was something that Wall Street did to itself and to the rest of our society.

For those who don't buy the "it just happened" argument, Wall Street advocates have others: The government made us do it, through its encouragement of homeownership and lending to the poor. Or, the government should have stopped us from doing it; it was the fault of the regulators. There is something particularly unseemly about these attempts of the U.S. financial system to shift the blame in this crisis, and later chapters will explain why these arguments are unpersuasive.

Believers in the system also trot out a third line of defense, the same one used a few years earlier at the time of the Enron and World-Com scandals. Every system has its rotten apples, and, somehow, our "system"—including the regulators and investors—simply didn't do a good enough job protecting itself against them. To the Ken Lays (the CEO of Enron) and Bernie Ebbers (the CEO of WorldCom) of the early years of the decade, we now add Bernie Madoff and a host of others (such as Allen Stanford and Raj Rajaratnam) who are now facing charges. But what went wrong—then and now—did not involve just a few people. The defenders of the financial sector didn't get that it was their barrel that was rotten.[8]

Whenever one sees problems as persistent and pervasive as those that have plagued the U.S. financial system, there is only one conclusion to reach: the problems are systemic. Wall Street's high rewards and single-minded focus on making money might attract more than its fair share of the ethically challenged, but the universality of the problem suggests that there are fundamental flaws in the system.

Difficulties in interpretation

In the policy realm, determining success or failure presents a challenge even more difficult than ascertaining to whom or to what to give credit (and who or what to blame). But what is success or failure? To observers in the United States and Europe, the East Asian bailouts in 1997 were a success because the United States and Europe had not been harmed. To those in the region who saw their economies wrecked, their dreams destroyed, their companies bankrupted, and their countries saddled with billions in debt, the bailouts were a dismal failure. To the critics, the policies of the IMF and U.S. Treasury had made things worse. To their supporters, they had prevented disaster. And there is the rub. The questions are, What would things have been like if other policies had been pursued? Had the actions of the IMF and U.S. Treasury prolonged and deepened the downturn, or shortened it and made it shallower? To me, there is a clear answer: the high interest rates and cutbacks in expenditures that the IMF and Treasury pushed—just the opposite of the policies that the United States and Europe followed in the current crisis—made things worse.[9] The countries in East Asia eventually recovered, but it was in spite of those policies, not because of them.

Similarly, many who observed the long expansion of the world economy during the era of deregulation concluded that unfettered markets worked—deregulation had enabled this high growth, which would be sustained. The reality was quite different. The growth was based on a mountain of debt; the foundations of this growth were shaky, to say the least. Western banks were repeatedly saved from the follies of their lending practices by bailouts—not just in Thailand, Korea, and Indonesia, but in Mexico, Brazil, Argentina, Russia . . . the list is almost endless.[10] After each episode the world continued on, much as it had before, and many concluded that the markets were working fine by themselves. But it was government that repeatedly saved markets from their own mistakes. Those who had concluded that all was well with the market economy had made the wrong inference, but the error only became "obvious" when a crisis so large that it could not be ignored occurred *here*.

These debates over the effects of certain policies help to explain how bad ideas can persist for so long. To me, the Great Recession of 2008 seemed the inevitable consequence of policies that had been pursued over the preceding years.

That those policies had been shaped by special interests—of the financial markets—is obvious. More complex is the role of economics. Among the long list of those to blame for the crisis, I would include the economics profession, for it provided the special interests with arguments about efficient and self-regulating markets—even though advances in economics during the preceding two decades had shown the limited conditions under which that theory held true. As a result of the crisis, economics (both theory and policy) will almost surely change as much as the economy, and in the penultimate chapter, I discuss some of these changes.

I am often asked how the economics profession got it so wrong. There are always "bearish" economists, those who see problems ahead, predicting nine out of the last five recessions. But there was a small group of economists who not only were bearish but also shared a set of views about *why* the economy faced these inevitable problems. As we got together at various annual gatherings, such as the World Economic Forum in Davos every winter, we shared our diagnoses and tried to explain why the day of reckoning that we each saw so clearly coming had not yet arrived.

We economists are good at identifying underlying forces; we are not good at predicting precise timing. At the 2007 meeting in Davos, I was in an uncomfortable position. I had predicted looming problems, with increasing forcefulness, during the preceding annual meetings. Yet, global economic expansion continued apace. The 7 percent global growth rate was almost unprecedented and was even bringing good news to Africa and Latin America. As I explained to the audience, this meant that either my underlying theories were wrong, or the crisis, when it hit, would be harder and longer than it otherwise would be. I obviously opted for the latter interpretation.

◆   ◆   ◆

THE CURRENT crisis has uncovered fundamental flaws in the capitalist system, or at least the peculiar version of capitalism that emerged in the latter part of the twentieth century in the United States (sometimes called American-style capitalism). It is not just a matter of flawed individuals or specific mistakes, nor is it a matter of fixing a few minor problems or tweaking a few policies.

It has been hard to see these flaws because we Americans wanted so much to believe in our economic system. "Our team" had done so much better than our arch enemy, the Soviet bloc. The strength of our system allowed us to triumph over the weaknesses of theirs. We rooted for our team in all contests: the United States vs. Europe, the United States vs. Japan. When U.S. Secretary of Defense Donald Rumsfeld denigrated "Old Europe" for its opposition to our war in Iraq, the contest he had in mind—between the sclerotic European social model and U.S. dynamism—was clear. In the 1980s, Japan's successes had caused us some doubts. Was our system really better than Japan, Inc.? This anxiety was one reason why some took such comfort in the 1997 failure of East Asia, where so many countries had adopted aspects of the Japanese model.[11] We did not publicly gloat over Japan's decade-long malaise during the 1990s, but we did urge the Japanese to adopt our style of capitalism.

Numbers reinforced our self-deception. After all, our economy was growing so much faster than almost everyone's, other than China's—and given the problems we thought we saw in the Chinese banking system, it was only a matter of time before it collapsed too.[12] Or so we thought.

This is not the first time that judgments (including the very fallible judgments of Wall Street) have been shaped by a misguided reading of the numbers. In the 1990s, Argentina was touted as the great success of Latin America—the triumph of "market fundamentalism" in the south. Its growth statistics looked good for a few years. But like the United States, its growth was based on a pile of debt that supported unsustainable levels of consumption. Eventually, in December 2001, the debts became overwhelming, and the economy collapsed.[13]

Even now, many deny the magnitude of the problems facing our market economy. Once we are over our current travails—and every recession does come to an end—they look forward to a resumption of robust growth. But a closer look at the U.S. economy suggests that there are some deeper problems: a society where even those in the middle have seen incomes stagnate for a decade, a society marked by increasing inequality; a country where, though there are dramatic exceptions, the statistical chances of a poor American making it to the top are lower than in "Old Europe,"[14] and where average performance in standardized education tests is middling at best.[15] By all accounts, several of the key economic sectors in the United States *besides finance* are in trouble, including health, energy, and manufacturing.

But the problems that have to be addressed are not just within the borders of the United States. The global trade imbalances that marked the world before the crisis will not go away by themselves. In a globalized economy, one cannot fully address America's problems without viewing those problems broadly. It is *global* demand that will determine global growth, and it will be difficult for the United States to have a robust recovery—rather than slipping into a Japanese-style malaise—unless the world economy is strong. And it may be difficult to have a strong global economy so long as part of the world continues to produce far more than it consumes, and another part—a part which should be saving to meet the needs of its aging population—continues to consume far more than it produces.

+   +   +

WHEN I began writing this book, there was a spirit of hope: the new president, Barack Obama, would right the flawed policies of the Bush administration, and we would make progress not only in the immediate recovery but also in addressing longer-run challenges. The country's fiscal deficit would temporarily be higher, but the money would be well spent: on helping families keep their homes, on investments that would increase the country's long-run productivity and preserve the environment, and, in return for any money that was given to the banks, there would be a claim on future returns that would compensate the public for the risk it bore.

Writing this book has been painful: my hopes have only partially been fulfilled. Of course, we should celebrate the fact that we have been pulled back from the brink of disaster that so many felt in the fall of 2008. But some of the giveaways to the banks were as bad as any under President Bush; the help to homeowners was less than I would have expected. The financial system that is emerging is less competitive, with too-big-to-fail banks presenting an even greater problem. Money that could have been spent restructuring the economy and creating new, dynamic enterprises has been given away to save old, failed firms. Other aspects of Obama's economic policy have been decidedly movements in the right direction. But it would be wrong to have criticized Bush for certain policies and not raise my voice when those same policies are carried on by his successor.

Writing this book has been hard for another reason. I criticize—some might say, vilify—the banks and the bankers and others in the financial market. I have many, many friends in that sector—intelligent, dedicated men and women, good citizens who think carefully about how to contribute to a society that has rewarded them so amply. They not only give generously but also work hard for the causes they believe in. They would not recognize the caricatures that I depict here, and I don't recognize these caricatures in them. Indeed, many of those in the sector feel that they are as much victims as those outside. They have lost much of their life savings. Within the sector, most of the economists who tried to forecast where the economy was going, the dealmakers who tried to make our corporate sector more efficient, and the analysts who tried to use the most sophisticated techniques possible to predict profitability and to ensure that investors get the highest return possible were not engaged in the malpractices that have earned finance such a bad reputation.

As seems to happen so often in our modern complex society, "stuff happens." There are bad outcomes that are the fault of no single individual. But this crisis was the result of actions, decisions, and arguments by those in the financial sector. The system that failed so miserably didn't just happen. It was created. Indeed, many worked hard—and spent good money—to ensure that it took the shape that it did. Those who played a role in creating the system and in managing it—including those who were so well rewarded by it—must be held accountable.

✦ ✦ ✦

IF WE can understand what brought about the crisis of 2008 and why some of the initial policy responses failed so badly, we can make future crises less likely, shorter, and with fewer innocent victims. We may even be able to pave the way for robust growth based on solid foundations, not the ephemeral debt-based growth of recent years; and we may even be able to ensure that the fruits of that growth are shared by the vast majority of citizens.

Memories are short, and in thirty years, a new generation will emerge, confident that it will not fall prey to the problems of the past. The ingenuity of man knows no bounds, and whatever system we design, there will be those who will figure out how to circumvent the regulations and rules put in place to protect us. The world, too, will change, and regulations designed for today will work imperfectly in the economy of the mid-twenty-first century. But in the aftermath of the Great Depression, we did succeed in creating a regulatory structure that served us well for a half century, promoting growth and stability. This book is written in the hope that we can do so again.

in many countries, large and small, developed and developing (including the United Kingdom, the United States, Iceland, France, Germany, South Africa, Portugal, Spain, Australia, India, China, Argentina, Malaysia, Thailand, Greece, Italy, Nigeria, Tanzania, and Ecuador).

I have been writing on the subject of financial regulation since the savings and loan debacle in the United States in the late 1980s, and the influence of my coauthors in this area, both at Stanford University and at the World Bank, should be apparent: Kevin Murdock, Thomas Hellmann, Gerry Caprio (now at Williams College), Marilou Uy, and Patrick Honohan (now governor of the Central Bank of Ireland).

I am indebted to Michael Greenberger, now professor of law at the University of Maryland and director of the Division of Trading and Markets of the Commodity Futures Trading Commission during the critical period in which there was an attempt to regulate derivatives, and to Randall Dodd, now of the IMF but formerly of the Financial Policy Forum and Derivatives Study Center, for enhancing my understanding of what happened in the derivatives market. To mention a few others who have helped shape my views: Andrew Sheng, formerly of the World Bank and former head of the Hong Kong Securities and Futures Commission; Dr. Y. V. Reddy, former governor of the Reserve Bank of India; Arthur Levitt, former chairman of the U.S. Securities and Exchange Commission; Leif Pagrotsky, who played a central role in solving the Swedish banking crisis; Governor Zeti Aziz of Malaysia's central bank, who played a central role in managing Malaysia's economy during its financial crisis; Howard Davies, former head of the U.K. Financial Services Administration and now at the London School of Economics; Jamie Galbraith of the University of Texas, Austin; Richard Parker and Kenneth Rogoff of Harvard; Andrew Crockett and Bill White, both formerly with the Bank for International Settlements; Mar Gudmundsson, who as chief economist of its Central Bank first brought me to Iceland, and now serves as the governor; Luigi Zingales of the University of Chicago; Robert Skidelsky of the University of Warwick; Yu Yongding of Beijing's Institute of World Economics and Politics; David Moss of the Tobin Project and Harvard Law School; Elizabeth Warren and David Kennedy, also of Harvard Law School; Damon Silver, director of policy of the AFL-CIO; Ngaire Woods of Oxford; Jose Antonio Ocampo, Perry Merhing, Stephany Griffith-Jones, Patrick Bolton, and Charles Calomiris, all of Columbia University; and Keith Leffler of the University of Washington.

Luckily there are some excellent, and courageous, journalists who have helped ferret out what was going on in the financial sector and exposed it to light. I have particularly benefitted from the writings and, in some cases extended conversations with, Gretchen Morgenson, Floyd Norris, Martin Wolf, Joe Nocera, David Wessel, Gillian Tett, and Mark Pittman.

While I am critical of Congress, kudos have to be given to Congresswoman Carolyn Maloney, co-chair of the Joint Economic Committee, for her efforts, and I am indebted to her for discussions of many of the issues here. Whatever legislation is passed will bear the stamp of Congressman Barney Frank, chair of the House Financial Services Committee, and I have valued the many conversations with him and his chief economist, David Smith, as well as the opportunities to testify before his committee. And while this book is critical of some of the approaches of the Obama administration, I am indebted to their economic team (including Timothy Geithner, Larry Summers, Jason Furman, Austan Goolsbee, and Peter Orszag) for sharing their perspectives and helping me to understand their strategy. I also want to thank Dominique Strauss-Kahn, the managing director of the IMF, not only for numerous conversations over the years but also for his efforts at reshaping that institution.

Two individuals should be singled out for their influence in shaping my views on the subject at hand: Rob Johnson, a former Princeton student, brought distinct perspectives to the crisis, having straddled the private and public sectors, serving as chief economist of the Senate Banking Committee during the savings and loan travails as well as working on Wall Street. And Bruce Greenwald, my coauthor for a quarter century, and professor of finance at Columbia University, who, as always, provided deep and creative insights into every subject on which I touch in this book—from banking, to global reserves, to the history of the Great Depression.

Earlier versions of portions of this book have appeared in *Vanity Fair,* and I am especially grateful for my editor there, Cullen Murphy, for his role in helping shape and edit these articles ("Wall Street's Toxic Message," *Vanity Fair,* July 2009, and "Reversal of Fortune," *Vanity Fair,* October 2008).

In the production of this book I have been particularly fortunate ben- efitting from the assistance of a first-rate team of research assistants— Jonathan Dingel, Izzet Yildiz, Sebastian Rondeau, and Dan Choate; and editorial assistants, Deidre Sheehan, Sheri Prasso, and Jesse Berlin. Jill Blackford not only oversaw the whole process but also made invaluable contributions at every stage, from research to editorial.

Once again, I have been lucky to work with W. W. Norton and Penguin: Detailed comments and editing from Brendan Curry, Drake McFeely, and Stuart Proffitt were invaluable. Mary Babcock did a superb job of copyediting under an extraordinarily tight deadline.

Finally, as always, I owe my biggest debt to Anya Schiffrin, from the discussion of the ideas in their formative stage to the editing of the manuscript. This book would not be possible without her.

FREEFALL

CHAPTER ONE

THE MAKING OF
A CRISIS

THE ONLY SURPRISE ABOUT THE ECONOMIC CRISIS OF 2008 was that it came as a surprise to so many. For a few observers, it was a textbook case that was not only predictable but also predicted. A deregulated market awash in liquidity and low interest rates, a global real estate bubble, and skyrocketing subprime lending were a toxic combination. Add in the U.S. fiscal and trade deficit and the corresponding accumulation in China of huge reserves of dollars—an unbalanced global economy—and it was clear that things were horribly awry.

What *was* different about this crisis from the multitude that had preceded it during the past quarter century was that this crisis bore a "Made in the USA" label. And while previous crises had been contained, this "Made in the USA" crisis spread quickly around the world. We liked to think of our country as one of the engines of global economic growth, an exporter of sound economic policies—not recessions. The last time the United States had exported a major crisis was during the Great Depression of the 1930s.[1]

The basic outlines of the story are well known and often told. The United States had a housing bubble. When that bubble broke and housing prices fell from their stratospheric levels, more and more homeowners found themselves "underwater." They owed more on their mortgages than what their homes were valued. As they lost their homes, many also lost their life savings and their dreams for a future—a college education for their children, a retirement in comfort. Americans had, in a sense, been living in a dream.

The richest country in the world was living beyond its means, and the strength of the U.S. economy, and the world's, depended on it. The global economy needed ever-increasing consumption to grow; but how could this continue when the incomes of many Americans had been stagnating for so long?[2] Americans came up with an ingenious solution: borrow and consume as if their incomes *were* growing. And borrow they did. Average savings rates fell to zero—and with many rich Americans saving substantial amounts, that meant poor Americans had a large negative savings rate. In other words, they were going deeply into debt. Both they and their lenders could feel good about what was happening: they were able to continue their consumption binge, not having to face up to the reality of stagnating and declining incomes, and lenders could enjoy record profits based on ever-mounting fees.

Low interest rates and lax regulations fed the housing bubble. As housing prices soared, homeowners could take money out of their houses. These mortgage equity withdrawals—which in one year hit $975 billion, or more than 7 percent of GDP[3] (gross domestic product, the standard measure of the sum of all the goods and services produced in the economy)—allowed borrowers to make a down payment on a new car and still have some equity left over for retirement. But all of this borrowing was predicated on the risky assumption that housing prices would continue to go up, or at least not fall.

The economy was out of kilter: two-thirds to three-quarters of the economy (of GDP) was housing related: constructing new houses or buying contents to fill them, or borrowing against old houses to finance consumption. It was unsustainable—and it wasn't sustained. The breaking of the bubble at first affected the worst mortgages (the subprime mortgages, lent to low-income individuals), but soon affected all residential real estate.

When the bubble popped, the effects were amplified because banks had created complex products resting on top of the mortgages. Worse still, they had engaged in multibillion-dollar bets with each other and with others around the world. This complexity, combined with the rapidity with which the situation was deteriorating and the banks' high leverage (they, like households, had financed their investments by heavy borrowing), meant that the banks didn't know whether what they owed to their depositors and bondholders exceeded the value of their assets. And they realized accordingly that they couldn't know the position of any other bank. The trust and confidence that underlie the banking system evaporated. Banks refused to lend to each other—or demanded high interest rates to compensate for bearing the risk. Global credit markets began to melt down.

At that point, America and the world were faced with both a financial crisis and an economic crisis. The economic crisis had several components: There was an unfolding residential real estate crisis, followed not long after by problems in commercial real estate. Demand fell, as households saw the value of their houses (and, if they owned shares, the value of those as well) collapse and as their ability—and willingness—to borrow diminished. There was an inventory cycle—as credit markets froze and demand fell, companies reduced their inventories as quickly as possible. And there was the collapse of American manufacturing.

There were also deeper questions: What would replace the unbridled consumption of Americans that had sustained the economy in the years before the bubble broke? How were America and Europe going to manage their restructuring, for instance, the transition toward a service-sector economy that had been difficult enough during the boom? Restructuring was inevitable—globalization and the pace of technology demanded it—but it would not be easy.

THE STORY IN SHORT

While the challenges going forward are clear, the question remains: How did it all happen? This is not the way market economies are *supposed* to work. Something went wrong—badly wrong.

There is no natural point to cut into the seamless web of history. For purposes of brevity, I begin with the bursting of the tech (or dot-com) bubble in the spring of 2000—a bubble that Alan Greenspan, chairman of the Federal Reserve at that time, had allowed to develop and that had sustained strong growth in the late 1990s.[4] Tech stock prices fell 78 percent between March 2000 and October 2002.[5] It was hoped that these losses would not affect the broader economy, but they did. Much of investment had been in the high-tech sector, and with the bursting of the tech stock bubble this came to a halt. In March 2001, America went into a recession.

The administration of President George W. Bush used the short recession following the collapse of the tech bubble as an excuse to push its agenda of tax cuts for the rich, which the president claimed were a cure-all for any economic disease. The tax cuts were, however, not designed to stimulate the economy and did so only to a limited extent. That put the burden of restoring the economy to full employment on monetary policy. Accordingly, Greenspan lowered interest rates, flooding the market with liquidity. With so much excess capacity in the economy, not surprisingly, the lower interest rates did not lead to more investment in plant and equipment. They worked—but only by replacing the tech bubble with a housing bubble, which supported a consumption and real estate boom.

The burden on monetary policy was increased when oil prices started to soar after the invasion of Iraq in 2003. The United States spent hundreds of billions of dollars importing oil—money that otherwise would have gone to support the U.S. economy. Oil prices rose from $32 a barrel in March 2003 when the Iraq war began to $137 per barrel in July 2008. This meant that Americans were spending $1.4 billion per day to import oil (up from $292 million per day before the war started), instead of spending the money at home.[6] Greenspan felt he could keep interest rates low because there was little inflationary pressure,[7] and without the housing bubble that the low interest rates sustained and the consumption boom that the housing bubble supported, the American economy would have been weak.

In all these go-go years of cheap money, Wall Street did not come up with a good mortgage product. A good mortgage product would have low transaction costs and low interest rates and would have helped people manage the risk of homeownership, including protection in the event their house loses value or borrowers lose their job. Homeowners also want monthly payments that are predictable, that don't shoot up without warning, and that don't have hidden costs. The U.S. financial markets didn't look to construct these better products, even though they are in use in other countries. Instead, Wall Street firms, focused on maximizing their returns, came up with mortgages that had high transaction costs and variable interest rates with payments that could suddenly spike, but with no protection against the risk of a loss in home value or the risk of job loss.

Had the designers of these mortgages focused on the ends—what we actually wanted from our mortgage market—rather than on how to maximize *their* revenues, then they might have devised products that would have *permanently* increased homeownership. They could have "done well by doing good." Instead their efforts produced a whole range of complicated mortgages that made them a lot of money in the short run and led to a slight *temporary* increase in homeownership, but at great cost to society as a whole.

The failings in the mortgage market were symptomatic of the broader failings throughout the financial system, including and especially the banks. There are two core functions of the banking system. The first is providing an efficient payments mechanism, in which the bank facilitates transactions, transferring its depositors' money to those from whom they buy goods and services. The second core function is assessing and managing risk and making loans. This is related to the first core function, because if a bank makes poor credit assessments, if it gambles recklessly, or if it puts too much money into risky ventures that default, it can no longer make good on its promises to return depositors' money. If a bank does its job well, it provides money to start new businesses and expand old businesses, the economy grows, jobs are created, and at the same time, it earns a high return—enough to pay back the depositors with interest and to generate competitive returns to those who have invested their money in the bank.

The lure of easy profits from transaction costs distracted many big banks from their core functions. The banking system in the United States and many other countries did not focus on lending to small- and medium-sized businesses, which are the basis of job creation in any economy, but instead concentrated on promoting securitization, especially in the mortgage market.

It was this involvement in mortgage securitization that proved lethal. In the Middle Ages, alchemists attempted to transform base metals into gold. Modern alchemy entailed the transformation of risky subprime mortgages into AAA-rated products safe enough to be held by pension funds. And the rating agencies blessed what the banks had done. Finally, the banks got directly involved in gambling—including not just acting as middlemen for the risky assets that they were creating, but actually holding the assets. They, and their regulators, might have thought that they had passed the unsavory risks they had created on to others, but when the day of reckoning came—when the markets collapsed—it turned out that they too were caught off guard.[8]

PARSING OUT BLAME

As the depth of the crisis became better understood—by April 2009 it was already the longest recession since the Great Depression—it was natural to look for the culprits, and there was plenty of blame to go around. Knowing who, or at least what, is to blame is essential if we are to reduce the likelihood of another recurrence and if we are to correct the obviously dysfunctional aspects of today's financial markets. We have to be wary of too facile explanations: too many begin with the excessive greed of the bankers. That may be true, but it doesn't provide much of a basis for reform. Bankers acted greedily because they had incentives and opportunities to do so, and that is what has to be changed. Besides, the basis of capitalism is the pursuit of profit: should we blame the bankers for doing (perhaps a little bit better) what everyone in the market economy is supposed to be doing?

In the long list of culprits, it is natural to begin at the bottom, with the mortgage originators. Mortgage companies had pushed exotic mortgages on to millions of people, many of whom did not know what they were getting into. But the mortgage companies could not have done their mischief without being aided and abetted by the banks and rating agencies. The banks bought the mortgages and repackaged them, selling them on to unwary investors. U.S. banks and financial institutions had boasted about their clever new investment instruments. They had created new products which, while touted as instruments for managing risk, were so dangerous that they threatened to bring down the U.S. financial system. The rating agencies, which should have checked the growth of these toxic instruments, instead gave them a seal of approval, which encouraged others—including pension funds looking for safe places to put money that workers had set aside for their retirement—in the United States and overseas, to buy them.

In short, America's financial markets had failed to perform their essential societal functions of managing risk, allocating capital, and mobilizing savings while keeping transaction costs low. Instead, they had created risk, misallocated capital, and encouraged excessive indebtedness while imposing high transaction costs. At their peak in the years before the crisis, the bloated financial markets absorbed 40 percent of profits in the corporate sector.[9]

One of the reasons why the financial system did such a poor job at managing risk is that the market mispriced and misjudged risk. The "market" badly misjudged the risk of defaults of subprime mortgages, and made an even worse mistake trusting the rating agencies and the investment banks when they repackaged the subprime mortgages, giving a AAA rating to the new products. The banks (and the banks' investors) also badly misjudged the risk associated with high bank leverage. And risky assets that normally would have required substantially higher returns to induce people to hold them were yielding only a small risk premium. In some cases, the seeming mispricing and misjudging of risk was based on a smart bet: they believed that if troubles arose, the Federal Reserve and the Treasury would bail them out, and they were right.[10]

The Federal Reserve, led first by Chairman Alan Greenspan and later by Ben Bernanke, and the other regulators stood back and let it all happen. They not only claimed that they couldn't tell whether there was a bubble until after it broke, but also said that even if they had been able to, there was nothing they could do about it. They were wrong on both counts. They could have, for instance, pushed for higher down payments on homes or higher margin requirements for stock trading, both of which would have cooled down these overheated markets. But they chose not to do so. Perhaps worse, Greenspan aggravated the situation by allowing banks to engage in ever-riskier lending and encouraging people to take out variable-rate mortgages, with payments that could—and did—easily explode, forcing even middle-income families into foreclosure.[11]

Those who argued for deregulation—and continue to do so in spite of the evident consequences—contend that the costs of regulation exceed the benefits. With the global budgetary and real costs of this crisis mounting into the trillions of dollars, it's hard to see how its advocates can still maintain that position. They argue, however, that the real cost of regulation is the stifling of innovation. The sad truth is that in America's financial markets, innovations were directed at circumventing regulations, accounting standards, and taxation. They created products that were so complex they had the effect of both increasing risk and information asymmetries. No wonder then that it is impossible to trace any sustained increase in economic growth (beyond the bubble to which they contributed) to these financial innovations. At the same time, financial markets did not innovate in ways that would have helped ordinary citizens with the simple task of managing the risk of homeownership. Innovations that would have helped people and countries manage the other important risks they face were actually resisted. Good regulations could have redirected innovations in ways that would have increased the efficiency of our economy and security of our citizens.

Not surprisingly, the financial sector has attempted to shift blame elsewhere—when its claim that it was just an "accident" (a once-in-a-thousand-years storm) fell on deaf ears.

Those in the financial sector often blame the Fed for allowing interest rates to remain too low for too long. But this particular attempt to shift blame is peculiar: what other industry would say that the reason why its profits were so low and it performed so poorly was that the costs of its inputs (steel, wages) were too low? The major "input" into banking is the cost of its funds, and yet bankers seem to be complaining that the Fed made money too cheap! Had the low-cost funds been used well, for example, if the funds had gone to support investment in new technology or expansion of enterprises, we would have had a more competitive and dynamic economy.

Lax regulation without cheap money might not have led to a bubble. But more importantly, cheap money with a well-functioning or well-regulated banking system could have led to a boom, as it has at other times and places. (By the same token, had the rating agencies done their job well, fewer mortgages would have been sold to pension funds and other institutions, and the magnitude of the bubble might have been markedly lower. The same might have been true even if rating agencies had done as poor a job as they did, if investors themselves had analyzed the risks properly.) In short, it is a combination of failures that led the crisis to the magnitude that it reached.

Greenspan and others, in turn, have tried to shift the blame for the low interest rates to Asian countries and the flood of liquidity from their excess savings.[12] Again, being able to import capital on better terms should have been an advantage, a blessing. But it is a remarkable claim: the Fed was saying, in effect, that it can't control interest rates in America anymore. Of course, it can; the Fed *chose* to keep interest rates low, partly for reasons that I have already explained.[13]

In what might seem an outrageous act of ingratitude to those who rescued them from their deathbed, many bankers blame the government—biting the very hand that was feeding them. They blame the government for not having stopped them—like the kid caught stealing from the candy store who blamed the storeowner or the cop for looking the other way, leading him to believe he could get away with his misdeed. But the argument is even more disingenuous because the financial markets had *paid* to get the cops off the beat. They successfully beat back attempts to regulate derivatives and restrict predatory lending. Their victory over America was total. Each victory gave them more money with which to influence the political process. They even had an argument: deregulation had led them to make more money, and money was the mark of success. Q.E.D.

Conservatives don't like this blaming of the market; if there is a problem with the economy, in their hearts, they know the true cause must be government. Government wanted to increase household ownership, and the bankers' defense was that they were just doing their part. Fannie Mae and Freddie Mac, the two private companies that had started as government agencies, have been a particular subject of vilification, as has the government program called the Community Reinvestment Act (CRA), which encourages banks to lend to underserved communities. Had it not been for these efforts at lending to the poor, so the argument goes, all would have been well. This litany of defenses is, for the most part, sheer nonsense. AIG's almost $200 billion bailout (that's a big amount by any account) was based on derivatives (credit default swaps)—banks gambling with other banks. The banks didn't need any push for egalitarian housing to engage in excessive risk-taking. Nor did the massive overinvestment in commercial real estate have anything to do with government homeownership policy. Nor did the repeated instances of bad lending around the world from which the banks have had to be repeatedly rescued. Moreover, default rates on the CRA lending were actually comparable to other areas of lending—showing that such lending, if done well, does not pose greater risks.[14] The most telling point though is that Fannie Mae and Freddie Mac's mandate was for "conforming loans," loans to the middle class. The banks jumped into subprime mortgages—an area where, at the time, Freddie Mac and Fannie Mae were not making loans—without any incentives from the government. The president may have given some speeches about the ownership society, but there is little evidence that banks snap to it when the president gives a speech. A policy has to be accompanied by carrots and sticks, and there weren't any. (If a speech would do the trick, Obama's repeated urging of banks to restructure more mortgages and to lend more to small businesses would have had some effect.) More to the point, advocates of homeownership meant permanent, or at least long-term, ownership. There was no point of putting someone in a home for a few months and then tossing him out after having stripped him of his life savings. But that was what the banks were doing. I know of no government official who would have said that lenders should engage in predatory practices, lend beyond people's ability to pay, with mortgages that combined high risks and high transaction costs. Later on, years after the private sector had invented the toxic mortgages (which I discuss at greater length in chapter 4), the privatized and under-regulated Fannie Mae and Freddie Mac decided that they too should join in the fun. Their executives thought, Why couldn't they enjoy bonuses akin to others in the industry? Ironically, in doing so, they helped save the private sector from some of its own folly: many of the securitized mortgages wound up on their balance sheet. Had they not bought them, the problems in the private sector arguably would have been far worse, though by buying so many securities, they may also have helped fuel the bubble.[15]

As I mentioned in the preface, figuring out what happened is like "peeling an onion": each explanation raises new questions. In peeling back the onion, we need to ask, Why did the financial sector fail so badly, not only in performing its critical social functions, but even in serving shareholders and bondholders well?[16] Only executives in financial institutions seem to have walked away with their pockets lined— less lined than if there had been no crash, but still better off than, say, the poor Citibank shareholders who saw their investments virtually disappear. The financial institutions complained that the regulators didn't *stop* them from behaving badly. But aren't firms supposed to behave well on their own? In later chapters I will give a simple explanation: flawed incentives. But then we must push back again: Why were there flawed incentives? Why didn't the market "discipline" firms that employed flawed incentive structures, in the way that standard theory says it should? The answers to these questions are complex but include a flawed system of corporate governance, inadequate enforcement of competition laws, and imperfect information and an inadequate understanding of risk on the part of the investors.

While the financial sector bears the major onus for blame, regulators didn't do the job that they should have done—ensuring that banks don't behave badly, as is their wont. Some in the less regulated part of the financial markets (like hedge funds), observing that the worst problems occurred in the highly regulated part (the banks), glibly conclude that regulation is the problem. "If only they were unregulated like us, the problems would never have occurred," they argue. But this misses the essential point: The reason why banks are regulated is that their failure can cause massive harm to the rest of the economy. The reason why there is less regulation needed for hedge funds, at least for the smaller ones, is that they can do less harm. The regulation did not cause the banks to behave badly; it was deficiencies in regulation and regulatory enforcement that failed to prevent the banks from imposing costs on the rest of society as they have repeatedly done. Indeed, the one period in American history when they have not imposed these costs was the quarter century after World War II when strong regulations were effectively enforced: it can be done.

Again, the failure of regulation of the past quarter century needs to be explained: the story I tell below tries to relate those failures to the political influence of special interests, particularly of those in the financial sector who made money from deregulation (many of their economic investments had turned sour, but they were far more acute in their political investments), and to ideologies—ideas that said that regulation was not necessary.

MARKET FAILURES

Today, after the crash, almost everyone says that there is a need for regulation—or at least for more than there was before the crisis. Not having the necessary regulations has cost us plenty: crises would have been less frequent and less costly, and the cost of the regulators and regulations would be a pittance relative to these costs. Markets on their own evidently fail—and fail very frequently. There are many reasons for these failures, but two are particularly germane to the financial sector: "agency"—in today's world scores of people are handling money and making decisions on behalf of (that is, as agents of) others—and the increased importance of "externalities."

The agency problem is a modern one. Modern corporations with their myriad of small shareholders are fundamentally different from family-run enterprises. There is a separation of ownership and control in which management, owning little of the company, may run the corporation largely for its own benefit.[17] There are agency problems too in the process of investment: much was done through pension funds and other institutions. Those who make the investment decisions—and assess corporate performance—do so not on their behalf but on behalf of those who have entrusted their funds to their care. All along the "agency" chain, concern about performance has been translated into a focus on *short-term returns*.

With its pay dependent not on long-term returns but on stock market prices, management naturally does what it can to drive up stock market prices—even if that entails deceptive (or creative) accounting. Its short-term focus is reinforced by the demand for high quarterly returns from stock market analysts. That drive for short-term returns led banks to focus on how to generate more fees—and, in some cases, how to circumvent accounting and financial regulations. The innovativeness that Wall Street ultimately was so proud of was dreaming up new products that would generate more income in the short term for its firms. The problems that would be posed by high default rates from some of these innovations seemed matters for the distant future. On the other hand, financial firms were not the least bit interested in innovations that might have helped people keep their homes or protect them from sudden rises in interest rates.

In short, there was little or no effective "quality control." Again, in theory, markets are supposed to provide this discipline. Firms that produce excessively risky products would lose their reputation. Share prices would fall. But in today's dynamic world, this market discipline broke down. The financial wizards invented highly risky products that gave about normal returns for a while—with the downside not apparent for years. Thousands of money managers boasted that they could "beat the market," and there was a ready population of shortsighted investors who believed them. But the financial wizards got carried away in the euphoria—they deceived themselves as well as those who bought their products. This helps explain why, when the market crashed, they were left holding billions of dollars' worth of toxic products.

Securitization, the hottest financial-products field in the years leading up to the collapse, provided a textbook example of the risks generated by the new innovations, for it meant that the relationship between lender and borrower was broken. Securitization had one big advantage, allowing risk to be spread; but it had a big disadvantage, creating new problems of imperfect information, and these swamped the benefits from increased diversification. Those buying a mortgage-backed security are, in effect, lending to the homeowner, about whom they know nothing. They trust the bank that sells them the product to have checked it out, and the bank trusts the mortgage originator. The mortgage originators' incentives were focused on the quantity of mortgages originated, not the quality. They produced massive amounts of truly lousy mortgages. The banks like to blame the mortgage originators, but just a glance at the mortgages should have revealed the inherent risks. The fact is that the bankers *didn't want to know*. Their incentives were to pass on the mortgages, and the securities they created backed by the mortgages, as fast as they could to others. In the Frankenstein laboratories of Wall Street, banks created new risk products (collateralized debt instruments, collateralized debt instruments squared, and credit default swaps, some of which I will discuss in later chapters) without mechanisms to manage the monster they had created. They had gone into the moving business—taking mortgages from the mortgage originators, repackaging them, and moving them onto the books of pension funds and others—because that was where the fees were the highest, as opposed to the "storage business," which had been the traditional business model for banks (originating mortgages and then holding on to them). Or so they thought, until the crash occurred and they discovered billions of dollars of the bad assets on their books.

Externalities

The bankers gave no thought to how dangerous some of the financial instruments were to the rest of us, to the large externalities that were being created. In economics, the technical term *externality* refers to situations where a market exchange imposes costs or benefits on others who aren't party to the exchange. If you are trading on your own account and lose your money, it doesn't really affect anyone else. However, the financial system is now so intertwined and central to the economy that a failure of one large institution can bring down the whole system. The current failure has affected everyone: millions of homeowners have lost their homes, and millions more have seen the equity in their homes disappear; whole communities have been devastated; taxpayers have had to pick up the tab for the losses of the banks; and workers have lost their jobs. The costs have been borne not only in the United States but also around the world, by billions who reaped no gains from the reckless behavior of the banks.

When there are important agency problems and externalities, markets typically fail to produce efficient outcomes—contrary to the widespread belief in the efficiency of markets. This is one of the rationales for financial market regulation. The regulatory agencies were the last line of defense against both excessively risky and unscrupulous behavior by the banks, but after years of concentrated lobbying efforts by the banking industry, the government had not only stripped away existing regulations but also failed to adopt new ones in response to the changing financial landscape. People who didn't understand why regulation was necessary—and accordingly believed that it was unnecessary—became regulators. The repeal in 1999 of the Glass-Steagall Act, which had separated investment and commercial banks, created ever larger banks that were too big to be allowed to fail. Knowing that they were too big to fail provided incentives for excessive risk-taking.

In the end, the banks got hoisted by their own petard: The financial instruments that they used to exploit the poor turned against the financial markets and brought them down. When the bubble broke, most of the banks were left holding enough of the risky securities to threaten their very survival—evidently, they hadn't done as good a job in passing the risk along to others as they had thought. This is but one of many ironies that have marked the crisis: in Greenspan and Bush's attempt to minimize the role of government in the economy, the government has assumed an unprecedented role across a wide swath—becoming the owner of the world's largest automobile company, the largest insurance company, and (had it received in return for what it had given to the banks) some of the largest banks. A country in which socialism is often treated as an anathema has socialized risk and intervened in markets in unprecedented ways.

These ironies are matched by the seeming inconsistencies in the arguments of the International Monetary Fund (IMF) and the U.S. Treasury before, during, and after the East Asian crisis—and the inconsistencies between the policies then and now. The IMF might claim that it believes in market fundamentalism—that markets are efficient, self-correcting, and accordingly, are best left to their own devices if one is to maximize growth and efficiency—but the moment a crisis occurs, it calls for massive government assistance, worried about "contagion," the spread of the disease from one country to another. But contagion is a quintessential externality, and if there are externalities, one can't (logically) believe in market fundamentalism. Even after the multibillion-dollar bailouts, the IMF and U.S. Treasury resisted imposing measures (regulations) that might have made the "accidents" less likely and less costly—because they believed that markets fundamentally worked well on their own, even when they had just experienced repeated instances when they didn't.

The bailouts provide an example of a set of inconsistent policies with potentially long-run consequences. Economists worry about incentives—one might say it is their number-one preoccupation. One of the arguments put forward by many in the financial markets for not helping mortgage owners who can't meet their repayments is that it gives rise to "moral hazard"—that is, incentives to repay are weakened if mortgage owners know that there is some chance they will be helped out if they don't repay. Worries about moral hazard led the IMF and the U.S. Treasury to argue vehemently against bailouts in Indonesia and Thailand—

setting off a massive collapse of the banking system and exacerbating the downturns in those countries. Worries about moral hazard played into the decision not to bail out Lehman Brothers. But this decision, in turn, led to the most massive set of bailouts in history. When it came to America's big banks in the aftermath of Lehman Brothers, concerns about moral hazard were shunted aside, so much so that the banks' officers were allowed to enjoy huge bonuses for record losses, dividends continued unabated, and shareholders and bondholders were protected. The repeated rescues (not just bailouts, but ready provision of liquidity by the Federal Reserve in times of trouble) provide part of the explanation of the current crisis: they encouraged banks to become increasingly reckless, knowing that there was a good chance that if a problem arose, they would be rescued. (Financial markets referred to this as the "Greenspan/Bernanke put.") Regulators made the mistaken judgment that, because the economy had "survived" so well, markets worked well on their own and regulation was not needed—not noting that they had survived *because* of massive government intervention. Today, the problem of moral hazard is greater, by far, than it has ever been.

Agency issues and externalities mean that there is a role for government. If it does its job well, there will be fewer accidents, and when the accidents occur, they will be less costly. When there are accidents, government will have to help in picking up the pieces. But how the government picks up the pieces affects the likelihood of future crises—and a society's sense of fairness and justice. Every successful economy—every successful society—involves both government and markets. There needs to be a balanced role. It is a matter not just of "how much" but also of "what." During the Reagan and both Bush administrations, the United States lost that balance—doing too little then has meant doing too much now. Doing the wrong things now may mean doing more in the future.

Recessions

One of the striking aspects of the "free market" revolutions initiated by President Ronald Reagan and Prime Minister Margaret Thatcher of the

United Kingdom was that perhaps the most important set of instances when markets fail to yield efficient outcomes was forgotten: the repeated episodes when resources are not fully utilized. The economy often operates below capacity, with millions of people who would like to find work not being able to do so, with episodic fluctuations in which more than one out of twelve can't find jobs—and numbers that are far worse for minorities and youth. The official unemployment rate doesn't provide a full picture: Many who would like to work full-time are working part-time because that's the only job they could get, and they are not included in the unemployment rate. Nor does the rate include those who join the rolls of the disabled but who would be working if they could only get a job. Nor does it include those who have been so discouraged by their failure to find a job that they give up looking. This crisis though is worse than usual. With the broader measure of unemployment, by September, 2009, more than one in six Americans who would have liked to have had a full-time job couldn't find one, and by October, matters were worse.[18] While the market is self-correcting—the bubble eventually burst—this crisis shows once again that the correction may be slow and the cost enormous. The cumulative gap between the economy's actual output and potential output is in the trillions.

WHO COULD HAVE
FORESEEN THE CRASH?

In the aftermath of the crash, both those in the financial market and their regulators claimed, "Who could have foreseen these problems?" In fact, many critics had—but their dire forecasts were an inconvenient truth: too much money was being made by too many people for their warnings to be heard.

I was certainly not the only person who was expecting the U.S. economy to crash, with global consequences. New York University economist Nouriel Roubini, Princeton economist and *New York Times* columnist Paul Krugman, financier George Soros, Morgan Stanley's Stephen Roach, Yale University housing expert Robert Shiller, and former Clinton Council of Economic Advisers/National Economic Council staffer Robert Wescott all issued repeated warnings. They were all Keynesian economists, sharing the view that markets were not self-correcting. Most of us were worried about the housing bubble; some (such as Roubini) focused on the risk posed by global imbalances to a sudden adjustment of exchange rates.

But those who had engineered the bubble (Henry Paulson had led Goldman Sachs to new heights of leverage, and Ben Bernanke had allowed the issuance of subprime mortgages to continue) maintained their faith in the ability of markets to self-correct—until they *had* to confront the reality of a massive collapse. One doesn't have to have a Ph.D. in psychology to understand why they wanted to pretend that the economy was going through just a minor disturbance, one that could easily be brushed aside. As late as March 2007, Federal Reserve Chairman Bernanke claimed that "the impact on the broader economy and financial markets of the problems in the subprime market seems likely to be contained."[19] A year later, even after the collapse of Bear Stearns, with rumors swirling about the imminent demise of Lehman Brothers, the official line (told not only publicly but also behind closed doors with other central bankers) was that the economy was already on its way to a robust recovery after a few blips.

The real estate bubble that had to burst was the most obvious symptom of "economic illness." But behind this symptom were more fundamental problems. Many had warned of the risks of deregulation. As far back as 1992, I worried that the securitization of mortgages would end in disaster, as buyers and sellers alike underestimated the likelihood of a price decline and the extent of correlation.[20]

Indeed, anyone looking closely at the American economy could easily have seen that there were major "macro" problems as well as "micro" problems. As I noted earlier, our economy had been driven by an unsustainable bubble. Without the bubble, aggregate demand—the sum total of the goods and services demanded by households, firms, government, and foreigners—would have been weak, partly because of the growing inequality in the United States and elsewhere around the world, which shifted money from those would have spent it to those who didn't.[21]

For years, my Columbia colleague Bruce Greenwald and I had drawn attention to the further problem of a *global* lack of aggregate demand—the total of all the goods and services that people throughout the world want to buy. In the world of globalization, global aggregate demand is what matters. If the sum total of what people around the world want to buy is less than what the world can produce, there is a problem—a weak global economy. One of the reasons for weak global aggregate demand is the growing level of reserves—money that countries set aside for a "rainy day."

Developing countries put aside hundreds of billions of dollars in reserves to protect themselves from the high level of global volatility that has marked the era of deregulation, and from the discomfort they feel at turning to the IMF for help.[22] The prime minister of one of the countries that had been ravaged by the global financial crisis of 1997 said to me, "We were in the class of '97. We learned what happens if you don't have enough reserves."

The oil-rich countries too were accumulating reserves—they knew that the high price of crude was not sustainable. For some countries, there was another reason for reserve accumulation. Export-led growth had been lauded as the best way for developing countries to grow; after new trade rules under the World Trade Organization took away many of the traditional instruments developing countries used to help create new industries, many turned to a policy of keeping their exchange rates competitive. And this meant buying dollars, selling their own currencies, and accumulating reserves.

These were all good reasons for accumulating reserves, but they had a bad consequence: there was insufficient global demand. A half trillion dollars, or more, was being set aside in these reserves every year in the years prior to the crisis. For a while, the United States had come to the rescue with debt-based profligate consumption, spending well beyond its means. It became the world's consumer of last resort. But that was not sustainable.

The global crisis

This crisis quickly became global—and not surprisingly, as nearly a quarter of U.S. mortgages had gone abroad.[23] Unintentionally, this helped the United States: had foreign institutions not bought as much of its toxic instruments and debt, the situation here might have been far worse.[24] But first the United States had exported its deregulatory philosophy—without that, foreigners might not have bought so many of its toxic mortgages.[25] In the end, the United States also exported its recession. This was, of course, only one of several channels through which the American crisis became global: the U.S. economy is still the largest, and it is hard for a downturn of this magnitude not to have a global impact. Moreover, global financial markets have become closely interlinked—evidenced by the fact that two of the top three beneficiaries of the U.S. government bailout of AIG were foreign banks.

In the beginning, many in Europe talked of decoupling, that they would be able to maintain growth in their economies even as America went into a downturn: the growth in Asia would save them from a recession. It should have been apparent that this too was just wishful thinking. Asia's economies are still too small (the entire consumption of Asia is just 40 percent of that of the United States),[26] and their growth relies heavily on exports to the United States. Even after a massive stimulus, China's growth in 2009 was some 3 to 4 percent below what it had been before the crisis. The world is too interlinked; a downturn in the United States could not but lead to a global slowdown. (There is an asymmetry: because of the immense internal and not fully tapped market in Asia, it might be able to return to robust growth even though the United States and Europe remain weak—a point to which I return in chapter 8.)

While Europe's financial institutions suffered from buying toxic mortgages and the risky gambles they had made with American banks, a number of European countries grappled with problems of their own design. Spain too had allowed a massive housing bubble to develop and is now suffering from the near-total collapse of its real estate market. In contrast to the United States, however, Spain's strong banking regulations have allowed its banks to withstand a much bigger trauma with better results—though, not surprisingly, its overall economy has been hit far worse.

The United Kingdom too succumbed to a real estate bubble. But worse, under the influence of the city of London, a major financial hub, it fell into the trap of the "race to the bottom," trying to do whatever it could to attract financial business. "Light" regulation did no better there than in the United States. Because the British had allowed the financial sector to take on a greater role in their economy, the cost of the bailouts was (proportionately) even greater. As in the United States, a culture of high salaries and bonuses developed. But at least the British understood that if you give taxpayer money to the banks, you have to do what you can to make sure they use it for the purposes intended—for more loans, not for bonuses and dividends. And at least in the U.K., there was some understanding that there had to be accountability—the heads of the bailed-out banks were replaced—and the British government demanded that the taxpayers get fair value in return for the bailouts, not the giveaways that marked both the Obama and Bush administrations' rescues.[27]

Iceland is a wonderful example of what can go wrong when a small and open economy adopts the deregulation mantra blindly. Its well-educated people worked hard and were at the forefront of modern technology. They had overcome the disadvantages of a remote location, harsh weather, and depletion of fish stocks—one of their traditional sources of income—to generate a per capita income of $40,000. Today, the reckless behavior of their banks has put the country's future in jeopardy.

I had visited Iceland several times earlier in this decade and warned of the risks of its liberalization policies.[28] This country of 300,000 had three banks that took on deposits and bought assets totaling some $176 billion, eleven times the country's GDP.[29] With a dramatic collapse of Iceland's banking system in the fall of 2008, Iceland became the first developed country in more than thirty years to turn to the IMF for help.[30] Iceland's banks had, like banks elsewhere, taken on high leverage and high risks. When financial markets realized the risk and started pulling money out, these banks (and especially Landsbanki) lured money from depositors in the U.K. and Netherlands by offering them "Icesaver" accounts with high returns. The depositors foolishly thought that there was a "free lunch": they could get higher returns without risk. Perhaps they also foolishly thought their own governments were doing their regulatory job. But, as everywhere, regulators had largely assumed that markets would take care of themselves. Borrowing from depositors only postponed the day of reckoning. Iceland could not afford to pour hundreds of billions of dollars into the weakened banks. As this reality gradually dawned on those who had provided funds to the bank, it became only a matter of time before there would be a run on the banking system; the global turmoil following the Lehman Brothers collapse precipitated what would in any case have been inevitable. Unlike the United States, the government of Iceland knew that it could not bail out the bondholders or shareholders. The only questions were whether the government would bail out the Icelandic corporation that insured the depositors, and how generous it would be to the foreign depositors. The U.K. used strong-arm tactics—going so far as to seize Icelandic assets using anti-terrorism laws—and when Iceland turned to the IMF and the Nordic countries for assistance, they insisted that Icelandic taxpayers bail out U.K. and Dutch depositors even beyond the amounts the accounts had been insured for. On a return visit to Iceland in September 2009, almost a year later, the anger was palpable. Why should Iceland's taxpayers be made to pay for the failure of a private bank, especially when foreign regulators had failed to do their job of protecting their own citizens? One widely held view for the strong response from European governments was that Iceland had exposed a fundamental flaw in European integration: "the single market" meant that any European bank could operate in any country. Responsibility for regulation was put on the "home" country. But if the home country failed to do its job, citizens in other countries could lose billions. Europe didn't want to think about this and its profound implications; better to simply make little Iceland pick up the tab, an amount some put at as much as 100 percent of the country's GDP.[31]

As the crisis worsened in the United States and Europe, other countries around the world suffered from the collapse in global demand.

Developing countries suffered especially, as remittances (transfers of money from family members in developed countries) fell and capital that had flowed into them was greatly diminished—and in some cases reversed. While America's crisis began with the financial sector and then spread to the rest of the economy, in many of the developing countries—including those where financial regulation is far better than in the United States—the problems in the "real economy" were so large that they eventually affected the financial sector. The crisis spread so rapidly partly because of the policies, especially of capital and financial market liberalization, the IMF and the U.S. Treasury had foisted on these countries—based on the same free market ideology that had gotten the United States into trouble.[32] But while even the United States finds it difficult to afford the trillions in bailouts and stimulus, corresponding actions by poorer countries are well beyond their reach.

The big picture

Underlying all of these symptoms of dysfunction is a larger truth: the world economy is undergoing seismic shifts. The Great Depression coincided with the decline of U.S. agriculture; indeed, agricultural prices were falling even before the stock market crash in 1929. Increases in agricultural productivity were so great that a small percentage of the population could produce all the food that the country could consume. The transition from an economy based on agriculture to one where manufacturing predominated was not easy. In fact, the economy only resumed growing when the New Deal kicked in and World War II got people working in factories.

Today the underlying trend in the United States is the move away from manufacturing and into the service sector. As before, this is partly because of the success in increasing productivity in manufacturing, so that a small fraction of the population can produce all the toys, cars, and TVs that even the most materialistic and profligate society might buy. But in the United States and Europe, there is an additional dimension: globalization, which has meant a shift in the locus of production and comparative advantage to China, India, and other developing countries.

Accompanying this "microeconomic" adjustment are a set of macroeconomic imbalances: while the United States should be saving for the retirement of its aging baby-boomers, it has been living beyond its means, financed to a large extent by China and other developing countries that have been producing more than they have been consuming. While it is natural for some countries to lend to others—some to run trade deficits, others surpluses—the pattern, with poor countries lending to the rich, is peculiar and the magnitude of the deficits appear unsustainable. As countries get more indebted, lenders may lose confidence that the borrower can repay—and this can be true even for a rich country like the United States. Returning the American and global economy to health will require the restructuring of economies to reflect the new economics and correcting these global imbalances.

We can't go back to where we were before the bubble broke in 2007. Nor should we want to. There were plenty of problems with that economy—as we have just seen. Of course, there is a chance that some new bubble will replace the housing bubble, just as the housing bubble replaced the tech bubble. But such a "solution" would only postpone the day of reckoning. Any new bubble could pose dangers: the oil bubble helped pushed the economy over the brink. The longer we delay in dealing with the underlying problems, the longer it will be before the world returns to robust growth.

There is a simple test of whether the United States has made sufficient strides in ensuring that there will not be another crisis: If the proposed reforms had been in place, could the current crisis have been avoided? Would it have occurred anyway? For instance, giving more power to the Federal Reserve is key to the proposed Obama regulatory reform. But as the crisis began, the Federal Reserve had more powers than it used. In virtually every interpretation of the crisis, the Fed was at the center of the creation of this and the previous bubble. Perhaps the Fed's chairman has learned his lesson. But we live in a country of laws, not of men: should we have a system requiring that the Fed first be burned by fire to ensure that another won't be set? Can we have confidence in a system that can depend so precariously on the economic philosophy or understanding of one person—or even of the seven members of the Board of Governors of the Fed? As this book goes to press, it is clear that the reforms have not gone far enough.

We cannot wait until *after the crisis*. Indeed, the way we have been dealing *with* the crisis may be making it all the more difficult to address these deeper problems. The next chapter outlines what we should have done to address the crisis—and why what we did fell far short.

CHAPTER TWO

FREEFALL AND ITS AFTERMATH

IN OCTOBER 2008 AMERICA'S ECONOMY WAS IN FREE-fall, poised to take down much of the world economy with it. We had had stock market crashes, credit crunches, housing slumps, and inventory adjustments before. But not since the Great Depression had all of these come together. And never before had the storm clouds moved so quickly over the Atlantic and Pacific oceans, gathering strength as they went. But while everything seemed to be falling apart at the same time, there was a common source: the reckless lending of the financial sector, which had fed the housing bubble, which eventually burst. What was unfolding was the predictable and predicted consequences of the bursting of the bubble. Such bubbles and their aftermath are as old as capitalism and banking itself. It was just that the United States had been spared such bubbles for decades after the Great Depression because of the regulations the government had put in place after that trauma. Once deregulation had taken hold, it was only a matter of time before these horrors of the past would return. The so-called financial innovations had just enabled the bubble to become bigger before it burst, and had made it more difficult to untangle the messes after it burst.[1]

The need for drastic measures was clear as early as August 2007. In that month the difference between interest rates on interbank loans (the interest rate at which banks lend to each other) and T-bills (the interest rate at which government can borrow money) spiked drastically. In a "normal" economy, the two interest rates differ little. A large difference means that banks didn't trust each other. The credit markets were at risk of freezing—and for good reason. Each knew the enormous risks they faced on their own balance sheets, as the mortgages they held were going sour and other losses mounted. They knew how precarious their own conditions were—and they could only guess how precarious the position of other banks was.

The collapse of the bubble and the tightening of credit had inevitable consequences. They would not be felt overnight; it would take months, but no amount of wishful thinking could stop the process. The economy slowed. As the economy slowed, the number of foreclosures mounted. The problems in real estate first surfaced in the subprime market but soon became manifest in other areas. If Americans couldn't make their house payments, they would also have trouble making their credit card payments. With real estate prices plunging, it was only a matter of time before problems in prime residential and commercial real estate appeared. As consumer spending dried up, it was inevitable that many businesses would go bankrupt—and that meant the default rate on commercial loans would also rise.

President Bush had maintained that there was only a little ripple in the housing market and that few homeowners would be hurt. As the housing market fell to a fourteen-year low, he reassured the nation on October 17, 2007: "I feel good about many of the economic indicators here in the United States." On November 13, he reassuringly said, "The underpinnings of our economy are strong, and we're a resilient economy." But conditions in the banking and real estate sectors continued to worsen. As the economy went into recession in December 2007, he began to admit that there might be a problem: "There's definitely some storm clouds and concerns, but the underpinning is good."[2]

As the calls for action from economists and the business sector increased, President Bush turned to his usual cure for all economic ills and passed a $168 billion tax cut in February 2008. Most Keynesian economists predicted that the medicine would not work. Americans were saddled with debt and suffering from tremendous anxiety, so why would they spend, rather than save, the small tax rebate? In fact, they saved more than half, which did little to stimulate an already slowing economy.[3]

But even though the president supported a tax cut, he refused to believe that the economy was headed for recession. Indeed, even when the country had been in a recession for a couple months, he refused to recognize it, declaring on February 28, 2008, "I don't think we're headed to a recession." When, shortly thereafter, the Federal Reserve and Treasury officials brokered the shotgun marriage of investment giant Bear Stearns to JPMorgan Chase for a mere two dollars a share (later revised to ten dollars a share), it was clear that the bursting of the bubble had caused more than a ripple in the economy.[4]

When Lehman Brothers faced bankruptcy that September, those same officials abruptly changed course and allowed the bank to fail, setting off in turn a cascade of multibillion-dollar bailouts. After that, the recession could no longer be ignored. But the collapse of Lehman Brothers was the consequence of the economic meltdown, not its cause; it accelerated a process that was well on its way.

Despite mounting job losses (in the first nine months of 2008, a loss of some 1.8 million jobs, with 6.1 million Americans working part-time because they could not get a full-time job) and a decrease of 24 percent in the Dow Jones average since January 2008, President Bush and his advisers insisted that things were not as bad as they appeared. Bush stated in an address on October 10, 2008, "We know what the problems are, we have the tools we need to fix them, and we're working swiftly to do so."

But, in fact, the Bush administration turned to a limited set of tools—and even then couldn't figure out how to make them work. The administration refused to help homeowners, it refused to help the unemployed, and it refused to stimulate the economy through standard measures (increasing expenditures, or even its "instrument of choice," further tax cuts). The administration focused on throwing money at the banks but floundered as it struggled to devise an effective way of doing so, one that would quickly restart lending.

Following the demise of Lehman Brothers, the nationalization of Fannie Mae and Freddie Mac, and the bailout of AIG, Bush rushed to help the banks with a massive $700 billion bailout, under a euphemistically titled program, "Troubled Asset Relief Program" (TARP). Bush's policy in the fall of 2008 of helping the banks but ignoring the millions of homes going into foreclosure was akin to giving a massive blood transfusion to a patient dying from internal bleeding. It should have been obvious: unless something was done about the underlying economy and the flood of mortgages going into foreclosure, pouring money into the banks might not save them. At most, the cash infusion would be a temporary palliative. One bailout followed another, with even the same bank (such as Citibank, America's largest bank at the time) having to be rescued more than once.[5]

THE RECOVERY DEBATE AND THE PRESIDENTIAL CAMPAIGN

As the presidential election of November 2008 approached, it was clear to almost everyone (except, evidently, President Bush) that more had to be done to get the economy out of recession. The administration hoped that, beyond the bank bailouts, low interest rates would suffice. While flawed monetary policies may have played a central role in bringing on the Great Recession, they wouldn't get the country out of it. John Maynard Keynes had once explained the impotence of monetary policy in a recession by comparing it to pushing on a string. When sales are plummeting, lowering the interest rate from 2 percent to 1 percent will not induce firms to build a new factory or buy new machines. Excess capacity typically increases markedly as the recession gains momentum. Given these uncertainties, even a zero interest rate might not be able to resuscitate the economy. Moreover, the central bank can lower the interest rate the government pays, but it doesn't determine the interest rate firms pay or even whether banks will be willing to lend. The most that could be hoped for from monetary policy was that it wouldn't make things worse—as the Fed and Treasury had done in their mismanagement of the Lehman Brothers' collapse.

Both presidential candidates, Barack Obama and John McCain, agreed that a basic three-pronged strategy was needed: stemming the flood of bad mortgages, stimulating the economy, and resuscitating banking. But they disagreed on what should be done in each area. Many of the old economic, ideological, and distributive battles that had been waged over the preceding quarter century reappeared. McCain's proposed stimulus focused on a tax cut that would encourage consumption. Obama's plan called for increased government expenditures and especially for investment, including "green investments" that would help the environment.[6] McCain had a strategy for dealing with foreclosures—the government would in effect pick up the banks' losses from bad lending. In this area, McCain was the big spender; Obama's program was more modest but focused on helping homeowners. Neither candidate had a clear vision of what to do with the banks, and both were afraid of "roiling" the markets by even hinting at criticism of President Bush's bailout efforts.

Curiously, McCain sometimes took a more populist stand than Obama and seemed more willing to criticize Wall Street's outrageous behavior. He could get away with it: the Republicans were known as the party of big business, and McCain had a reputation as an iconoclast. Obama, like Bill Clinton before him, struggled to distance himself from the antibusiness reputation of the Old Democrats, though during the primary he had made a forceful speech at Cooper Union explaining why the day had come for better regulation.[7]

Neither candidate wanted to risk delving into the deeper causes of the crisis. Criticizing Wall Street's greed might be acceptable, but discussing the problems in corporate governance that gave rise to flawed incentive structures and in turn encouraged bad behavior would have been too technical. Talking about the suffering of ordinary Americans was acceptable, but linking this to the insufficiency of aggregate demand would have risked going beyond the standard campaign dictum to "keep it simple." Obama would push for strengthening the right to unionize, but only as a basic right, not as part of a strategy that might be linked to economic recovery or even the more modest goal of reducing inequality.

When the new president took office, there was a collective sigh of relief. At last *something* would be done. In the chapters that follow I will explore what the Obama administration faced when it came into power, how it responded to the crisis, and what it should have done to get the economy going and to prevent another crisis from occurring. I will try to explain why policymakers took certain approaches—including what they were thinking or hoping might happen. Ultimately, Obama's team opted for a *conservative* strategy, one that I describe as "muddling through." It was, perhaps counterintuitively, a highly risky strategy. Some of the downside risks inherent in President Obama's plan may be apparent even as this book is published; others will become apparent only over the years. But the question remains: why did Obama and his advisers choose to muddle through?

THE EVOLVING ECONOMY

Figuring out what to do in an economy in freefall is not easy. Realizing that every downturn comes to an end provides little comfort.

The bursting of the housing bubble in mid-2007 led—as I and others had predicted—to recession shortly thereafter. While credit conditions had been bad even before the bankruptcy of Lehman Brothers, they became worse afterward. Faced with high costs of credit—if they could get credit at all—and declining markets, firms responded quickly by cutting back inventories. Orders dropped abruptly—well out of proportion to the decline in GDP—and the countries that depended on investment goods and durables, expenditures that could be postponed, were particularly hard hit. (From mid-2008 to mid-2009, Japan saw its exports fall by 35.7 percent, Germany by 22.3 percent.)[8] The best bet was that the "green shoots" seen in the spring of 2009 indicated a recovery in some of the areas hit hardest at the end of 2008 and the beginning of 2009, including a rebuilding of some of the inventories that had been excessively depleted.

A close look at the fundamentals Obama had inherited on taking office should have made him deeply pessimistic: millions of homes were being foreclosed upon, and in many parts of the country, real estate prices were still falling. This meant that millions more home mortgages were underwater—future candidates for foreclosure. Unemployment was on the rise, with hundreds of thousands of people reaching the end of recently extended unemployment benefits. States were being forced to lay off workers as tax revenues plummeted.[9] Government spending under the stimulus bill that was one of Obama's first achievements helped—but only to prevent things from becoming worse.

The banks were being allowed to borrow cheaply from the Fed, on the basis of poor collateral, and to take risky positions. Some of the banks reported earnings in the first half of 2009, mostly based on accounting and trading profits (read: speculation). But this kind of speculation wouldn't get the economy going again quickly. And if the bets didn't pay off, the cost to the American taxpayer would be even larger.

By taking advantage of these low-cost funds and lending them at much higher interest rates—reduced competition in banking meant that they had more power to raise lending rates—the banks would gradually get recapitalized, provided they weren't first overwhelmed by losses on mortgages, commercial real estate, business loans, and credit cards. If nothing untoward happened, the banks might make it through without another crisis. In a few years (so it was hoped), the banks would be in better shape and the economy would return to normal. Of course, the high interest rates that the banks charged as they struggled to recapitalize would impair the recovery—but this was part of the price for avoiding nasty political debates.

The banks (including many of the smaller banks on which so many small and medium-sized businesses rely for funds) faced stresses in almost every category of lending—commercial and residential real estate, credit cards, consumer and commercial loans. In the spring of 2009 the administration put the banks through a stress test (which was in fact not very stressful) to see how they would withstand a period of higher unemployment and falling real estate prices.[10] But even if the banks were healthy, the deleveraging process—bringing down the debt that was pervasive in the economy—made it likely that the economy would be weak for an extended period of time. Banks had taken their small amount of equity (their basic "capital" or "net worth") and borrowed heavily against it, to have a large asset base—sometimes thirty times larger than their equity. Homeowners, too, had borrowed heavily against what little equity they had in their homes. It was clear that there was too much debt resting on too little equity, and debt levels would have to be reduced. This would be hard enough. But as this happened, asset prices, which had been sustained by all the borrowing, would likely fall. The loss in wealth would induce stress in many parts of the economy; there would be bankruptcies, but even the firms or people that didn't go bankrupt would cut back on spending.

It was possible, of course, that Americans might continue to live as they had before, with zero savings, but to bet on that was reckless, and data showing the savings rate rising to 5 percent of household income suggested otherwise.[11] A weak economy meant, more likely than not, more bank losses.

Some hoped that exports might save the U.S. economy—they had helped soften the decline during 2008. But in a world of globalization, problems in one part of the system quickly reverberate elsewhere. The crisis of 2008 was a synchronous global downturn. That meant that it was unlikely that the United States could export its way out of the crisis—as East Asia had done a decade earlier.

As the United States entered the first Gulf War in 1990, General Colin Powell articulated what came to be called the Powell doctrine, one element of which included attacking with decisive force. There should be something analogous in economics, perhaps the Krugman-Stiglitz doctrine. When an economy is weak, very weak as the world economy appeared in early 2009, attack with overwhelming force. A government can always hold back the extra ammunition if it has it ready to spend, but not having the ammunition ready can have long-lasting effects. Attacking the problem with insufficient ammunition was a dangerous strategy, especially as it became increasingly clear that the Obama administration had underestimated the strength of the downturn, including the increase in unemployment. Worse, as the administration continued its seemingly limitless support to the banks, there didn't seem to be a vision for the future of the American economy and its ailing financial sector.

VISION

Franklin Roosevelt's New Deal had shaped economic life in the United States for a half century, until we forgot the lessons of the Great Depression. In 2008, with the U.S. financial system in tatters and the economy undergoing a wrenching transformation, we needed a vision for what kind of financial markets and economy we wanted to emerge from the crisis. Our actions could or would affect the shape of our economy for decades to come. We needed a new vision not just because our old model had failed but also because we had learned with great pain that the assumptions underlying the old model were wrong. The world was changing, and we weren't keeping pace.

One of Obama's great strengths was engendering a sense of hope, a *feeling* about the future and the possibility of change. And yet, in a more fundamental sense, "no drama" Obama was conservative: he didn't offer an alternative vision of capitalism. Apart from the justly famous Cooper Union speech mentioned earlier and adding his voice to the chorus of criticism about bailout bonuses, Obama had little to say about the new financial system that might emerge from the ashes of the meltdown or how that system might function.

What he did offer was a broader, pragmatic plan for the future—ambitious programs for fixing America's health care, education, and energy sectors—and a Reagan-like attempt to change the mood of the country from despair to hope at a time when despair was the natural consequence of a seemingly endless stream of bad economic news. Obama had another vision too, of a country less divided than it had been under George W. Bush and less polarized by ideological divides.

It's possible that the new president avoided any deep discussion of what had gone wrong in America's economy—specifically the wrongs committed by members of the financial sector—because he feared doing so would provoke conflict at a time when we needed unity. Would a thorough discussion lead to social cohesion or exacerbate social conflict? If, as some observers argued, the economy and society had suffered only a minor bruise, it might be best to let them heal on their own. The risk, however, was that the problems were more like festering wounds that could be healed only by exposing them to the antiseptic effects of sunlight.

While the risks of formulating a vision were clear, so were the risks of not having one. Without a vision, the whole "reform" process might be seized by those in the financial sector, leaving the country with a financial system that was even more fragile than the one that had failed, and less able to manage risk and efficiently deliver funds to where they should be going. We needed to have more money going into America's high-tech sectors, to create new businesses and expand old. We had been channeling too much money into real estate—too much money, to people beyond their ability to repay. The financial sector was supposed to ensure that funds went to where the returns to society were highest. It had clearly failed.

The financial sector had its own vision, centered on more profits and, so far as possible, going back to the world as it had been before 2007. Financial firms had come to see their business as an end in itself and prided themselves on its size and profitability. But a financial system should be a means to an end, not an end in itself. An outsized financial sector's profits may come at the expense of the prosperity and efficiency of the rest of the economy. The outsized financial sector had to be downsized—even as some parts of it, such as those lending to small and medium-sized businesses, might be strengthened.

The Obama administration also didn't have (or at least didn't articulate) a clear view of why the U.S. financial system failed. Without a vision of the future and an understanding of the failures of the past, its response floundered. At first, it offered little more than the usual platitudes of better regulation and more responsible banking. Instead of redesigning the system, the administration spent much of the money on reinforcing the existing, failed system. "Too big to fail" institutions repeatedly came to the government for bailouts, but the public money flowing to the big banks at the center of the failures actually strengthened the part of the system that had repeatedly run into trouble. At the same time, government wasn't spending proportionately as much on strengthening those parts of the financial sector that were supplying capital to the dynamic parts of the economy, new ventures and small and medium-sized enterprises.

THE BIG GAMBLE: MONEY AND FAIRNESS

Some might describe the Obama administration's approach as pragmatic, a realistic compromise with existing political forces, even a sensible approach to fixing the economy.

Obama faced a dilemma in the days following his election. He wanted to calm the storms on Wall Street, but he needed to address its fundamental failings and address the concerns of America. He began on a high note: almost everyone wanted him to succeed. But he should have known that he couldn't please everyone in the midst of a major economic war between Main Street and Wall Street. The president was caught in the middle.

During the Clinton years, these tensions simmered just below the surface. Clinton had appointed a diversity of economic advisers, with Robert Reich, his old friend from his Oxford days, on the left (as Secretary of Labor); Robert Rubin and Larry Summers on the right; and Alan Blinder, Laura Tyson, and me at the Council of Economic Advisers in the center. It was truly a cabinet reflecting rival sets of ideas, and the debates were intense, though mostly civil.

We fought battles over priorities—deciding whether to focus on deficit reduction or on investment and the provision of basic needs (humane welfare reform and health care reform that extended the provision of care). While I always believed that Clinton's heart was with the left and the center, the realities of politics and money led to different outcomes: the right won on many issues, especially after the 1994 congressional election in which the Republicans seized power in Congress.

One of the issues that raised blood pressures the most entailed the attack on corporate welfare, the mega-payments to America's companies in the form of subsidies and tax preferences. Rubin not only didn't like the term *corporate welfare*, he thought it smacked of class warfare. I sided with Reich: it wasn't a matter of class warfare; it was a matter of economics. Resources are scarce, and the role of government is to make the economy more efficient and to help the poor and those who can't fend for themselves. These payments to companies made the economy less efficient. The redistributions were going the wrong way, and especially in an era of fiscal stringency, it meant money that should be going to poor Americans or to high-return investments in infrastructure and technology was instead heading to already rich corporations. For the country as a whole, there was little to show for this money that was bleeding out of Washington.

In the waning days of the Bush administration, corporate welfare reached new heights—the amounts spent were beyond the imagination of anyone in any prior administration. The corporate safety net was extended from commercial banks to investment banks and then to an insurance company—to firms that not only had paid no insurance premium for the risks against which the taxpayer was protecting them, but also had gone to great lengths to avoid taxation. As Obama took office, the question was, would he continue with this corporate welfarism, or would he seek a new balance? If he gave more money to the banks, would he insist on some sense of accountability, and would he ensure that the taxpayer got value in return? Wall Street would have demanded nothing less if it had come to the rescue of some hapless firm facing the threat of bankruptcy.

Obama's administration decided, especially in the key area of bank restructuring, to take a big gamble by largely staying the course that President Bush had laid out, avoiding, so far as possible, playing by the usual rules of capitalism: When a firm can't pay its debts, it goes into bankruptcy (or receivership), where typically shareholders lose every-thing and the bondholders/creditors become the new shareholders. Similarly, when a bank can't pay what it owes, it is forced into "conser-vatorship." To placate Wall Street—and perhaps to speed its recovery —he decided to risk the wrath of Main Street. If the Obama strategy worked, it meant the deep ideological battles might be avoided. If the economy quickly recovered, Main Street might forgive the largesse bestowed on Wall Street. There were, however, major risks inherent in staying the course—risks to the economy in the short run, risks to the country's fiscal position in the medium term, and risks to our sense of fairness and social cohesion in the long run. Every strategy involves risks, but it was not clear that this strategy would minimize those risks over the long run. The strategy also risked alienating even many in the financial markets, for they saw the policies as being driven by the big banks. The playing field was already tilted toward these mega-institu-tions, and it looked like it was being tilted farther, toward the parts of the financial system that had caused the problems in the first place.

Dribbling money out to the banks would be costly and might com-promise the agenda for which Obama had run for office. He had not aspired to the presidency to become the banking system's emergency doctor. Bill Clinton had sacrificed much of his presidential ambitions on the altar of deficit reduction. Obama ran the risk of losing his on the even less satisfying altar of bank recapitalization, bringing the banks back to health so that they could engage in the same reckless behavior that had gotten the economy into trouble in the first place.

Obama's gamble of continuing the course on bank bailouts set by the Bush administration had many dimensions. If the economic downturn turned out to be deeper or longer lasting than he thought, or if the banks' problems were greater than they claimed, the cost of cleaning them up would be greater. Obama might not have enough money to solve the problem. More money might be needed for a second round of stimulus. Unhappiness over squandering of the money on the banks would make it difficult to get funds from Congress. And inevitably, spending on the banks would come at the expense of his other priori-ties. His moral authority might even be put into doubt, given that the

should have had a twenty-first-century Electronic Funds Transfer System, with the low transaction costs that modern technology allows, and there was no excuse for the failure of American banks to provide it. America should have had a mortgage system that was at least as good as that of Denmark or any other country, but it did not. Why should these financial institutions that were saved by American taxpayers be allowed to continue to prey on ordinary Americans with deceptive credit card practices and predatory lending? Even asking these questions would be interpreted by the big banks as hostile.

I noted earlier that during the Clinton administration the response from some members of the cabinet to those of us (myself and Robert Reich, for instance) who labeled the billions of dollars of subsidies given to America's wealthy companies as "corporate welfare" was that we were waging class warfare. If our quiet attempts to curb what seem like from today's perspective mild excesses met with such opprobrium, what might we expect from a direct attack on the unprecedented transfer of money to America's financial sector?

A *familiar pattern begins to play out*

As the United States slipped into crisis, I worried that what I had seen so often in developing countries would happen here. Bankers, who had in large part precipitated the problem, took advantage of the panic that resulted to redistribute wealth—to take from the public purse to enrich their own. In each instance, taxpayers were told that the government had to recapitalize the banks if the economy was to recover. In these earlier crises, the government gave billions to the banks under sweetheart terms, and the economy eventually recovered. (Every downturn comes to an end, and in many of the cases, it is not clear whether the bailouts accelerated or retarded the recovery.)[15] With the recovery, a grateful country would give a sigh of relief but would pay little attention to what had happened beneath the surface. The cost of Mexico's bank rescue of 1994–1997 was estimated to be equal to 15 percent of its GDP, and a substantial part of that went to the wealthy owners of banks.[16] In spite of that enormous capital infusion, the banks didn't really resume lending, and the reduced supply of credit contributed to Mexico's slow growth over the ensuing decade. A decade later, wages of Mexican workers, adjusted for inflation, were lower, while inequality was higher.[17]

Just as the Mexican crisis did little to diminish the power of Mexican bankers, the U.S. crisis did not mean the end of the financial sector's influence. Wealth in the sector may have been diminished, but somehow the political capital survived. Financial markets were still the single most important factor in American politics, especially in the realm of economics. Their influence was both direct and indirect.

Firms involved in the financial markets had made hundreds of millions of dollars in campaign contributions to both political parties over a decade.[18] They had reaped good returns—far better returns on these political investments than the returns on what was supposed to be their areas of expertise, investing in markets and making loans. They got their *initial* returns through the deregulation movement. They had reaped even better returns through the massive government bailouts. They hope, I am sure, to reap still more returns from these "investments" in preventing a return to regulation.

Revolving doors in Washington and New York also stoked the movement to prevent new regulatory initiatives. A number of officials with direct or indirect ties to the financial industry were called in to frame the rules *for their own industry*. When the officials who have responsibility for designing the policies for the financial sector come from the financial sector, why would one expect them to advance perspectives that are markedly different from those the financial sector wants? In part, it's a matter of narrow mindsets, but one can't totally dismiss the role of personal interests. Individuals whose fortunes or future job prospects depend on the performance of the banks are more likely to agree that what is good for Wall Street is good for America.[19]

If America needed evidence of the overarching influence of financial markets, the contrast between the treatment of the banks and the auto industry provided it.

The auto bailout

The banks were not the only firms that had to be bailed out. As 2008 came to a close, two of the Big Three automakers, GM and Chrysler, were on the edge of collapse. Even well-managed car companies faced problems as a result of the precipitous collapse of sales, and no one would claim that either of these two companies was well managed. The worry was that there would be a cascade effect: their suppliers would go bankrupt, unemployment would soar, and the economic downturn would worsen. It was remarkable how, even in public, some of the financiers who had run to Washington for help argued that it was one thing to bail out banks—they were the lifeblood of the economy—but quite another to start bailing out companies that actually produced things. It would be the end of capitalism as we know it.

President Bush wavered—and postponed the problem to his successor, extending a lifeline that would keep the companies going for a short while. The condition for more assistance was that they develop a viable survival plan. The Obama administration articulated a clear double standard: contracts for AIG executives were sacrosanct, but wage contracts for workers in the firms receiving help had to be renegotiated. Low-income workers who had worked hard all their life and had done nothing wrong would have to take a wage cut, but not the million-dollar-plus financiers who had brought the world to the brink of financial ruin. They were so valuable that they had to be paid retention bonuses, even if there was no profit from which to pay them a bonus. The bank executives could continue with their high incomes; the car company executives had to show a little less hubris. However, scaling down their hubris wasn't enough; the Obama administration forced the two companies into bankruptcy.

The standard rules of capitalism described earlier applied: shareholders lost everything while bondholders and other claimants (union health funds and the governments that helped save the companies) became the new shareholders. America had entered into a new phase of government intervention in the economy. It may have been necessary, but what puzzled many was, Why the double standard? Why had banks been treated so differently from car companies?

It further highlighted the deeper problem facing the country's restructuring: done in a rush, there was little confidence that the $50 billion Band-Aid that the government provided in the summer of 2009 would work, that the companies, largely with old management (though the head of GM was changed), that had failed to compete against Japanese and European automakers for a quarter century would suddenly rise to the top of the class. If the plan didn't work, the U.S. national deficit would be $50 billion larger, but the task of restructuring the economy would be little farther along.

Resistance to change

As the financial storm grew, neither the bankers nor the government wanted to engage in philosophical discussions of what a good financial system should look like. The bankers just wanted to have money pumped into the system. As discussion of the possibility of new regulations was raised, they quickly sounded the alarm bells. At a meeting of business titans in Davos as the crisis loomed in January 2007, one of the concerns expressed most forcefully was the worry that there would be "overreaction," a code word for more regulation. Yes, they admitted, there had been some excesses, but they contended that they had now learned the lesson. Risk is part of capitalism. The real risk, they argued, was that excessive regulation would stifle innovation.

But just giving the banks more money would not be enough. They had lost the trust of the American people—and deservedly so. Their "innovations" had neither led to higher sustained growth nor helped ordinary Americans manage the risk of homeownership; they had only led to the worst recession since the Great Depression and to massive bailouts. Giving the banks more money, without changing their incentives or the constraints they faced, would simply allow them to go on as before. And indeed, to a large extent that was what happened.

The strategy of players in the financial markets was clear: let the advocates for real change in the banking sector talk and talk; the crisis will be over before an agreement is reached—and with the end of the crisis, momentum for reform will disappear.[20]

Moving chairs on the Titanic

The hardest challenge facing a new president is the choice of his team. While appointees are supposed to reflect and implement the president's vision, in an area of great complexity like the economy, they really shape the program. The new president faced a major quandary: Would he opt for continuity or change—in personnel as well as policy? How much of his political capital would he spend in overcoming the resistance to change?

Bush's team consisted of Ben Bernanke, the Federal Reserve chairman the president appointed in 2006; Timothy Geithner, head of the New York Federal Reserve; and Henry (Hank) Paulson, Secretary of Treasury.

While Ben Bernanke inherited a bubble in the making, he did little to deflate it.[21] It was perhaps understandable: Wall Street was enjoying record profits, based on the bubble. They would not be happy if he took actions that would have burst the bubble, or even if he deflated it gradually. Even if he had recognized that there was a bubble, he would face a quandary: if he blew the whistle—if, for instance, he tried to stop some of the reckless real estate lending and the complex securitization that was built upon it—he would be blamed for deflating the bubble and bringing down the economy; there would be all those unfavorable comparisons to Alan Greenspan, the maestro who preceded him, who (it would be argued) would have known how to deflate the bubble gradually or keep it going forever!

But there were other reasons why Bernanke may have let the bubble continue. Perhaps he took Greenspan's rhetoric seriously: perhaps he really believed that there was no bubble, just a little froth; perhaps he believed that, in any case, one couldn't be sure that there was a bubble until after it popped.[22] Perhaps he believed, with Greenspan, that the Fed didn't have the instruments to deflate the bubble gradually and that it would be easier to fix things after it popped.

Still, it's hard to see how any serious economist wouldn't be worried—so worried that he would *have* to blow the whistle. In either case, it isn't a pretty picture: one central banker who created a bubble and a successor who let it continue, blowing up out of all proportions.

Tim Geithner had had a longer-term role. He had been a deputy to Larry Summers and Robert Rubin, two of the architects of the Clinton-era deregulation movement. More importantly, he was the chief regulator of New York banks—including the biggest of the big, Citibank, with assets of nearly $2.36 trillion in 2007.[23] He had been its chief regulator since 2003, when he was appointed president of the New York Federal Reserve. Evidently, as their regulator, Geithner saw nothing wrong with what the New York banks were doing—even though they would soon need hundreds of billions of dollars in government assistance. Of course, he gave speeches warning of the dangers of excessive risk-taking. But he was meant to be a regulator, not a preacher.

The third member of the Bush crisis team was Hank Paulson who, like Clinton's Treasury Secretary, Robert Rubin, had moved to Washington after a stint as head of Goldman Sachs. Having made his fortune, he was turning to public service.

Remarkably, President Obama, who had campaigned on the promise of "Change You Can Believe In," only slightly rearranged the deck chairs on the *Titanic*. Those on Wall Street had used their usual instrument—fear of "roiling" the markets—to get what they wanted, a team that had already demonstrated a willingness to give banks ample money on favorable terms. Geithner replaced Paulson as Secretary of Treasury. Bernanke stayed in place—his term as chairman would not end until the beginning of 2010, but Obama announced in August 2009 that he would give him a second term, through 2014.

To coordinate the economic team, Obama installed Rubin's former deputy, Larry Summers, who proclaimed that one of his great achievements as Secretary of Treasury in 1999–2001 was ensuring that the explosive derivatives would remain unregulated. Obama chose this team in spite of the fact that he must have known—he certainly was advised to that effect—that it would be important to have new faces at the table who had no vested interests in the past, either in the deregulatory movement that got us into the problem or in the faltering rescues that had marked 2008, from Bear Stearns through Lehman Brothers to AIG.

A fourth member of the Obama team was another Bush holdover, Sheila Bair, head of the Federal Deposit Insurance Corporation (FDIC), the agency that insures deposits. Even as Bush had sat idly by as foreclosures mounted, she had become a vocal advocate for doing something to help homeowners by restructuring mortgages, and ironically, as disillusionment with some members of Obama's new team grew, she looked like the one person on the economic team with both the heart and willingness to stand up to the big banks. Many of the "smoke and mirrors" attempts to finance the banks without going back to Congress involved the magic of the FDIC, which was supposed to be protecting small depositors, not guaranteeing bank bonds or lending money to help hedge funds buy the banks' toxic assets at overinflated prices.

As the *New York Times* put it, the question was "whether they [the Obama economic team] have learned from their mistakes, and if so, what."[24] Obama had chosen a team of honest public servants, dedicated to serving the country well. That wasn't the problem. It was a question of how they saw the world and how Americans would see them. We needed a new vision for the financial markets, and it was going to take all the political and economic skills of Obama and his economic team to formalize, articulate, and realize that vision. Were these people, so involved in the mistakes of the past, the right people to put forward that new vision and make the tough decisions? When they looked to history or the experiences of other countries, would they draw the right lessons? Many of the officials tasked with making critical decisions about regulation had long-established positions on the topics at issue. In psychology, there is a phenomenon called escalating commitment. Once one takes a position, one feels compelled to defend it. Economics offers a contrasting perspective: bygones are bygones. One should always be forward looking, evaluating whether an earlier position worked, and if it didn't, moving on to a new position. Not surprisingly, the psychologists are right, the economists wrong. The champions of deregulation had a vested interest in making sure that their ideas prevailed—even in the face of overwhelming evidence to the contrary. Now, when it appeared as though they might have to cave in to the demands for regulation, at least in some instances, there was a worry that they would strive to make these new regulations as consonant with their previous ideas as possible. When they would say that the regulations (for instance, on the explosive derivatives) they proposed were the "right" regulations—not too tough, not too soft, but the golden mean in between—would their statements be viewed as credible?

There was another reason for concern about keeping so much of the old team. The crisis had shown that its economic analyses, models, and judgments had been badly flawed. Inevitably, though, the economic team would want to believe otherwise. Rather than quickly realizing that there had been a lot of bad lending based on bubble prices, it would want to believe that the market was just temporarily depressed, and if it could just restore "confidence," housing prices would be restored, and the economy would go on as before. Basing economic policy on this hope was risky—as reckless as the bank lending that preceded the crisis. The consequences would unfold over the ensuing months.

It was, however, not just a matter of views about economics. Somebody would have to bear the losses. Would it be the American taxpayer or Wall Street? When Obama's advisers, so closely linked with the financial sector and the failures of the past, claimed that they had pushed the banks as hard as they could and made them take as many sacrifices as possible, without impairing the banks' ability to lend, would they be believed? Would Americans believe that they were working for them, or for Wall Street?

Economic principles (which require making firms pay for the consequences of their actions) and fairness suggested that the banks should pay at least for the full direct costs of fixing the financial system—even if they didn't have to pay for all the damage they had wrought. But the banks claimed that making them pay would impede their recovery. The banks that survived would claim that making them pay for the costs of those that failed was "unfair"—even if their own survival had depended at some critical juncture on government assistance. The Obama administration sided with the banks. It might claim that in doing so it was not because Obama wanted to give the banks a gift but that the administration had no alternatives in order to save the economy. Americans were rightly suspicious: as I argue in the chapters that follow, there *were* alternatives that would have preserved and strengthened the financial system and done more to restart lending, alternatives that in the long run would have left the country with a national debt that was hundreds and hundreds of billions of dollars smaller and with a larger sense of fair play. But these alternatives would have left the banks' shareholders and bondholders poorer. To the critics of Obama's rescue package, it was no surprise that Obama's team, so tightly linked to Wall Street, had not pushed for these alternatives.

Keeping so much of the old team in place also exposed the president to blame for decisions that were taken by the Fed—or at least seemed to be. The Fed and Treasury seemed to be acting in tandem under Bush, and the coziness continued with Obama. No one was really sure who was making the calls; the seamlessness of the transition suggested nothing had changed. Paulson's throwing an $89 billion lifeline to AIG, with his old firm Goldman Sachs the single largest beneficiary, was bad enough. But then this was almost doubled to $180 billion (part of which occurred under Obama). Even worse was the way the obligations of AIG were settled—the $13 billion handed over to Goldman Sachs being among the most unconscionable. If an insurance company decides to cancel a fire insurance policy held by an ordinary American, that person is left to scramble to find another insurance firm willing to provide the insurance coverage. But when the government decided to cancel AIG's policies with Goldman Sachs, it paid them off as if the house had completely burned down. There was no justification for such largesse: other credit default swaps had been settled for thirteen cents on the dollar.[25]

These and other episodes raised concerns about the motives behind other decisions—both what was done and what was not done—during the crisis. How could the administration say, for instance, that the banks are too big to fail—indeed so big that the ordinary rules of capitalism are suspended to protect their bondholders and shareholders—and yet not propose to break them up or to tax them or impose additional restrictions on them so that they would no longer be too big to fail?[26] Similarly, one had to wonder how the administration, after talking about the importance of mortgage restructuring, could design such an ineffective package. There was a disquieting, but obvious, answer (discussed further in chapter 4): what should have been done would have forced banks to recognize losses from their bad lending, and they didn't want that.

A new version of an old conflict

America has long had a suspicion of banks, especially big banks, reflected in the controversies over the proposals of the first Secretary of Treasury, Alexander Hamilton, for the establishment of a national bank. Regulations on interstate banking (finally repealed under President Clinton) were designed to limit the power of the big banks in New York and other large cities. Main Street depended on banks for funds; the banks' profits came from lending to Main Street. It was a symbiotic relationship, but there was often a lack of trust.

The battle between Wall Street and Main Street may be a caricature of complex conflicts among different economic groups; there are, nonetheless, real conflicts of interests and perspectives that the Great Recession of 2008 brought to the fore. In this new variant of the old conflict between Wall Street and the rest of the country, the banks held a gun to the heads of the American people: "If you don't give us more money, you will suffer." There were no alternatives, so they said. If you impose constraints—if you stop us from paying dividends or bonuses, or if you hold our executives accountable (as the government did in the case of GM), we will never be able to raise capital in the future. Maybe they were right, and if they were, no politician wanted to take the rap for the demise of the American economy. Wall Street used the fear of an economic collapse to extract enormous amounts of money, quickly, from American taxpayers. Amazingly, complaints swirled on Wall Street. Why hadn't they gotten more money? Why did they have to call it a bailout? If they could only figure out a better name, perhaps a "recovery" or "investment" program, then maybe there wouldn't be such opposition. Veterans of other crises knew what lay ahead: losses had been created, and battles would be fought about who would pay for them.

No one was surprised when Bush sided with Wall Street and gave in to its blackmail. Many had hoped that Obama would take a more balanced approach. Wherever Obama's heart might lie, his actions at least appeared to side too closely with the interests of Wall Street. A president who was supposed to bring all groups together inside a big tent seemed, by the choice of his team, to have chosen sides even before he took office.

Even the way success of the bailouts was measured seemed biased: as successive approaches to providing assistance to the banks were tried (some of which are described in chapter 5), attention centered around how Wall Street responded and what happened to bank share prices. But a sweeter deal for the banks, reflected in higher bank share prices, typically meant a worse deal for the taxpayer. What Main Street wanted was for lending to be rekindled—and almost none of the efforts at bank resuscitation did well on that score.

Wall Street made Obama's task of national reconciliation all the more difficult through its political insensitivity—paying out billions in dividends and bonuses as American taxpayers poured billions into the banks, allegedly to recapitalize them so that they would lend.[27]

As the bonus scandal reached a crescendo in February 2009, Obama had to speak out. But in criticizing the bonuses, he got caught in a vise: the favor that he had curried from Wall Street quickly dissipated, and yet he still didn't have a team with Main Street's confidence.

These mistakes colored the political environment and indeed may have shaped the political constraints that the Obama administration faced as it tried to resuscitate the banks, stabilize the mortgage market, and stimulate the economy. Investors were reluctant to participate in some government-sponsored programs, fearful that if they delivered the profits that they were designed to deliver, Congress might change the rules of the game and take the profits away or impose other penalties or restrictions. Though it was impossible to tell how much money the banks would need, the increasing unpopularity of the bank bailout meant that if more funds were needed, it would be very hard to get them from Congress.

This situation forced a strategy involving increasing complexity and lack of transparency. Congress was supposed to approve all government expenditures, but subterfuges through the Federal Reserve and FDIC became the rule of the day, providing funds in ways free from the kind of scrutiny that Americans have come to expect as an essential part of their democracy.[28] The Fed claimed the Freedom of Information Act didn't extend to it, at least in key respects. Bloomberg, a financial information news company, challenged that claim. In August 2009, a U.S. district court ruled against the Federal Reserve. Even then, the Fed refused to accept that it was subject to the kind of transparency expected in our democracy from a public institution, and it appealed.[29]

The banks had gotten into trouble by putting so much of what they were doing "off balance sheet"—in an attempt to deceive their investors and regulators—and now these financial wizards were helping the administration to do the same, perhaps in an attempt to deceive taxpayers and voters.[30]

Economic prospects

Nine months into his presidency, it was still not clear whether the gambles Obama had taken would pay off. The economy may have been off life support and pulled back from the brink of disaster. The best that could be said for the economy was that by the fall of 2009 it seemed to be at the end of a *freefall*, a decline without an end in sight. But the end of freefall is not the same as a return to normalcy.

By the fall of 2009, the economy had had a few months of strong growth as inventories that had been excessively depleted were replenished.[31] But even that growth did little to close the gap between the economy's actual output and its potential, and it did not mean that either the global or the American economy was in for a robust recovery any time soon. Indeed, most forecasters saw growth slowing toward the end of 2009 and into 2010, and further problems ahead in 2011.

The resumption of growth meant that in a technical sense, the recession was over. Economists define a recession as two or more quarters of negative growth—and so when growth turns positive, no matter how anemic, they declare the end of the recession. To workers, the economy is still in recession when unemployment is high, and especially when it is growing. To businesses, the economy is in recession so long as they see excess capacity, which means the economy is operating below its potential. As long as there is excess capacity, they won't invest.

As this book goes to press, the prospects of the economy returning to producing at its potential even within a year or two are dim. Focusing on the economic fundamentals—putting aside wishful thinking—suggests it will be long before the unemployment rate returns to normal. The bounce back from the bottom will thus not bring the economy back to where it should be, and the likelihood is that the economy will level out into a Japanese-style malaise long before full employment is restored. (America's growth might be slightly stronger than that of Japan during its long period of stagnation, simply because Japan's labor force is stagnant, while America's has been growing at 1 percent per year. But we shouldn't let this difference fool us.) There may be wiggles along the way, as the economy faces one or another shock: a sudden collapse of another financial institution, problems in commercial real estate, or even simply the end of the stimulus package in 2011. As I explain later, to get unemployment back to normal levels will require sustained growth in excess of 3 percent, and that's nowhere on the horizon.

It is natural that both the administration and those who sell stocks try to convey a sense of optimism. A restoration of confidence would, it is hoped, encourage consumption and investment; it might even restore housing prices. And if that happened, the Great Recession of 2008 would quickly pass into history—a bad dream the memory of which would rapidly fade.

The recovery of stock prices from their lows is often taken as a barometer of the restoration of economic health. Unfortunately, an increase in stock market prices may not necessarily indicate that all is well. Stock market prices may rise because the Fed is flooding the world with liquidity, and interest rates are low, so stocks look much better than bonds. The flood of liquidity coming from the Fed will find some outlet, hopefully leading to more lending to businesses, but it could also result in a mini-asset price or stock market bubble. Or rising stock market prices may reflect the success of firms in cutting costs—firing workers and lowering wages. If so, it's a harbinger of problems for the overall economy. If workers' incomes remain weak, so will consumption, which accounts for 70 percent of GDP.

As I noted earlier, this downturn is complex—a financial crisis compounding and interacting with an economic downturn. Recent recessions had been small, temporary aberrations. Most seemed to be caused by the Fed stepping on the brake too hard—sometimes because the government had previously stepped on the accelerator too strongly.[32] Recovery was easy: the Fed recognized the mistake, took its foot off the brake, and put it on the accelerator, and growth resumed. Other recessions were caused by excessive inventory accumulations. As soon as the excesses were corrected—normally within a year—again growth resumed. The Great Depression was different: the financial system collapsed. Experience with other recessions associated with financial crises has shown that the recovery in these circumstances is far more difficult, and takes much longer.[33]

We should celebrate that the banks that were on the verge of bankruptcy may not look so close to the edge. Despite the thawing of financial markets and a strengthening of bank balance sheets, there is still a myriad of shadows on the horizon. There are, for instance, looming problems in the financial markets posed by the collapse in commercial real estate and the lingering problems in residential real estate and credit card debt. Persistently high unemployment will pose renewed problems for home mortgages and credit cards. New measures to allow banks to keep on their books at face value mortgages that are not fully performing have undermined the ability to judge the health of the banking system. Bad loans can be rolled over, postponing the day of reckoning. But many of the commercial real estate loans have been securitized, and have to be rolled over in the next few years. The stage is set for a new wave of bankruptcies and foreclosures. Both commercial and residential real estate markets have been propped up by the usual measures taken by the Fed, which lowered long-term interest rates. What will happen when the Fed exits the extraordinary interventions in financial markets? And what will happen if the Fed *doesn't* exit, as promised, because it realizes the risks of taking away these life supports?

But even if the financial system were restored to perfect health, there are problems with the *real economy*. As we look at each of the components of aggregate demand, there is little basis for optimism. Even if banks were fully repaired, they would not want to lend as recklessly as they had before; and even if they were willing to lend, most Americans would not want to borrow. They have learned a costly lesson; they will surely save more, and probably substantially more, than they did when banks were pouring money out to them willy-nilly. Even if there were no uncertainties about increasing unemployment, the wealth of a large fraction of Americans has been badly eroded: home equity was their major asset, and, even those who have not seen it totally disappear realize that it is greatly diminished, not to be restored for years, if ever.

Looked at another way, the deleveraging process—reducing, for instance, the abnormal level of household debt that was 1.3 times disposable income—requires higher-than-*normal* savings, which means lower levels of household spending.

A robust recovery for the other elements of aggregate demand also appears problematic. With so many other countries facing problems of their own, the United States can't count on an export boom. Certainly, as I have noted, the entire world cannot export its way to growth. In the Great Depression, countries tried to protect themselves at the expense of their neighbors. These were called beggar-thy-neighbor policies, and included protectionism (imposing tariffs and other trade barriers) and competitive devaluations (making one's currency cheaper, which makes one's exports cheaper and imports less attractive). These are no more likely to work today than they did then; they are likely to backfire.

China's growth has been strong, but its consumption is still so much smaller than U.S. consumption that an increase in China's spending can't make up for the reductions in the United States—and only a small fraction of China's increase in spending will show up as increased American exports. And given how badly the global crisis has affected many in the developing world, those countries that can will continue to set aside substantial sums in reserves—weakening global demand.

Without a strong recovery of consumption or exports, it is hard to see how investment can recover, at least until the excess capacity in the economy expires or fades into obsolescence. Meanwhile, the forthcoming withdrawal of stimulus spending and cutbacks in state and local spending as a result of shortfalls in tax revenues are likely to exert further downward pressures on the American economy.

What had sustained the American economy—and to a large extent the global economy—before the crisis was a debt-financed consumption binge supported by a housing bubble. People could live beyond their income because they believed house prices would rise forever. No one believes that now. The "model" on which American growth was based had come to an end, but there was nothing on the horizon to replace it.

In short, there was relief that the economy had pulled back from the precipice that it seemed to be on in the fall of 2008, but no one would claim that it had returned to health. The rising debt was putting at risk President Obama's other programs. Anger at the bank bailout also had spilled over into other arenas. But while the banks were still tight in their lending, their executives were receiving near record bonuses (one survey in early November 2009 suggested that the typical trader would reap a $930,000 windfall),[34] and their shareholders were pleased as their shares increased in market value. Obama had learned that he couldn't please everyone. But had he pleased the right people?

What may have been viewed as a low-risk strategy, muddling through, avoiding conflicts, was proving to be a high-risk one, economically and politically: Confidence in government risked being undermined, conflict between the big banks and the rest of the country risked becoming more pronounced, the economy faced a risk of a slower recovery, and the costly open and hidden bailouts put at risk the fiscal position of the government—and put in jeopardy other government programs so necessary for the future of the nation.

Obama could have taken alternative actions, and there are still many options available, though the decisions already made have substantially circumscribed them. In the next four chapters I describe how the government went about stimulating the economy (chapter 3), how it helped or failed to save homeowners (chapter 4), and how it attempted to resurrect the financial system and re-regulate it (chapters 5 and 6). What worries me is that because of the choices that have already been made, not only will the downturn be far longer and deeper than necessary, but also we will emerge from the crisis with a much larger legacy of debt, with a financial system that is less competitive, less efficient, and more vulnerable to another crisis, and with an economy less prepared to meet the challenges of this century.

CHAPTER THREE

A FLAWED
RESPONSE

WHEN BARACK OBAMA AND HIS ADVISERS TOOK THE helm in January 2009, they confronted a crisis of unprecedented proportions. Thankfully they recognized that they couldn't restore the banking system to health without doing something about the real economy. They had to breathe life back into it, and they had to stem the flood of mortgage foreclosures. America had not had a crisis of this severity for three-quarters of a century. But elsewhere, crises had become all too common. From history and experiences abroad, there was a wealth of available information about how to treat economic crises, including those created by the bursting of real estate bubbles. Obama's team could have drawn upon theory, empirical evidence, and common sense to design a package that would stimulate the economy in the short run and strengthen the country for the future. But politics is not always so analytic.

The single most important idea in dealing with the aftermath of a crisis is a simple one: crises don't destroy the assets of an economy. The banks may be bankrupt. Many firms and households may be bankrupt. But the *real* assets are much as they were before—the same buildings, factories, and people; the same human, physical, and natural capital. What happens in a crisis is that confidence and trust erode, the institutional fabric of a society weakens as banks and firms go into or approach bankruptcy, and the market economy jumbles ownership claims. It is not always clear who owns and controls particular assets, as ownership, for instance, is transferred from shareholders to bondholders in the normal process of bankruptcy. In the run-up to a crisis, resources are wasted—putting money into building houses, for instance, rather than to more productive uses. But this is water over the dam—or, as it is sometimes put, bygones are bygones. The key question is, how will resources be used after the bubble is broken? This is typically when most of the losses occur, as resources fail to be used efficiently and fully and as unemployment soars. This is the real market failure, and one that is avoidable if the right policies are put into place. What is striking is how often the right policies are not put into place, and the losses during the bubble are compounded by the losses after it bursts.

THE STIMULUS

The big debate in the Depression era occurred between fiscal conservatives, who wanted to rein in the deficit, and Keynesians, who thought the government should run deficits to stimulate the economy. In 2008 and 2009, while everyone had suddenly become devout Keynesians (for the moment), there was disagreement about the exact shape the government's response to the crisis should take. By the time Obama took office, the downward momentum was so solidly in place that there was nothing he could do to reverse it immediately. But the design of the stimulus and its magnitude would determine how quickly the economy stabilized. Regrettably, the Obama administration didn't present a clear view of what was needed. Instead it largely left it to Congress to craft the size and shape of the stimulus. What emerged was not fully what the economy needed.

A well-designed stimulus program should reflect seven principles:

1. It should be fast. President George W. Bush's delay had been costly. Economic policies take months to be fully effective. It is therefore imperative to get money into the economy quickly.

2. It should be effective. Effectiveness means a big bang for the buck—every dollar spent should give rise to a large increase in employment and output. The amount by which national income increases for every dollar spent is called the multiplier: in standard Keynesian analysis, a dollar of government spending gives rise to more than a dollar's increase in national output. If the government spends money on a construction project, then the workers spend their pay to buy things, and others, in turn, spend their money. Each stage in the chain boosts national income, making the total increase in national income far greater than the initial amount spent by the government.

On average, the short-run multiplier for the U.S. economy is around 1.5.[1] If the government spends a billion dollars now, GDP this year will go up by $1.5 billion. Long-run multipliers are larger—some of the benefits of today's spending are felt next year or even the year after; because the current recession is likely to be a long-term one, policymakers also should care about the benefits realized two or three years from now.

Not all spending has the same multiplier: spending on foreign contractors working in Iraq has a low multiplier, because much of their consumption takes place outside the United States; so do tax cuts for the rich—who save much of what they receive. Increased unemployment benefits have a high multiplier, because those who find themselves suddenly short of income are going to spend almost every dollar they receive.[2]

3. It should address the country's long-term problems. Low national savings, huge trade deficits, long-term financial problems for Social Security and other programs for the elderly, decaying infrastructure, and global warming all cloud the country's long-term outlook. An effective stimulus would target them, or at the very least not make them worse.

4. It should focus on investment. A stimulus package will inevitably increase a country's deficit, but a country's debt only measures one side of the balance sheet—what it owes. Assets are equally important. If stimulus money is invested in assets that increase the country's long-run productivity, the country will be in a better shape *in the long run* as a result of the stimulus—even as short-run output and employment are increased. This concern about improving the balance sheet is particularly important today, with the United States borrowing so much money abroad. If a country stimulates its economy through debt-financed consumption, standards of living in the future will be lower when the time comes to pay back the debt or even just to pay interest on it. If a country stimulates the economy through investment, future output is higher—with good investments, by more than enough to pay the interest. Such investments not only improve standards of living today but also improve those of the next generation.

5. It should be fair. Middle-class Americans have fared far worse in recent years compared to those at the top.[3] Any stimulus should be designed with that in mind. Fairness means that the kinds of tax cuts George W. Bush had enacted in 2001 and 2003—with most of the benefits going to the rich—would be out of the question.

6. It should deal with the short-run exigencies created by the crisis. In a downturn, states often run out of money and have to start cutting jobs. The jobless are left without health care insurance. People struggling to make mortgage payments could go under if they lose their job or someone in their family gets sick. A well-designed stimulus should deal with as many of these issues as possible.

7. The stimulus should be targeted at areas of job loss. If the job losses are likely to be permanent, the stimulus should be directed at retraining workers with the skills they will need for their future job.

Sometimes these objectives are in conflict, and sometimes they are complementary. Much of the spending to meet the short-run exigencies is very effective—the multiplier is large—but it does not create an asset. Spending money to bail out the auto companies may be pouring money down a hole, even though it temporarily saves jobs. Investing money in roads may contribute to global warming, one of the world's most important long-term problems; it would be far better to create a modern high-speed public transportation system. Spending money to bail out the banks without getting something in return gives money to the richest Americans and has almost no multiplier.[4]

Automatic stabilizers—expenditures that go up automatically when the economy weakens—are one of the most effective forms of stimulus because they "titrate" the level of spending to the needs of the economy, giving more money as needed. These include, for instance, the increased unemployment benefits that get paid out automatically as unemployment rates increase. If the economy recovers more quickly than expected, then spending on unemployment benefits automatically gets cut back.

WHAT WAS DONE AND WHAT SHOULD HAVE BEEN DONE

These principles give considerable guidance for the size of the stimulus and how it should have been designed. A few countries, in particular Australia, designed a stimulus consistent with these principles; its downturn was modest, and it was the first of the advanced industrial countries to resume growth.

In the end, the Obama administration's stimulus made a big difference—but it should have been bigger and better designed. It was too small, too much of it (about a third) went to tax cuts, too little went to help states and localities and those that were falling through the holes in the safety nets, and the investment program could have been more effective.

Size

The almost $800 billion cost of the stimulus package sounded like a lot of money at first. It was to be spent over more than two years, and in a $14 trillion economy, the amount was less than 3 percent per year of GDP. About a fourth of the money would go out the first year, but that $200 billion was hardly enough to offset the cutbacks in spending at the state and local levels. In short, in 2009, subtracting the state cutbacks from the increased federal "stimulus" package resulted in almost no stimulus.

The administration's own numbers highlight the inadequacy. The president and his advisers said the stimulus would create 3.6 million new jobs—or prevent the loss of that number.[5] (They were aware there might not be any *net* job creation over the two-year period of the stimulus.) But that 3.6 million number needs to be put in perspective. In a normal year, almost 1.5 million *net* new entrants join the labor force, and the economy produces jobs for them. Between the start of the recession, in December 2007, and October 2009, the economy lost 8 million jobs.[6] Including new entrants into the labor force, this means that by the fall of 2009 the jobs deficit, the number of jobs that would need to be created to restore the economy to full employment, had grown to more than 12 million.[7]

In economics, you have to run to stay still. The difficulty of achieving the goal of full employment should be clear. With the labor force growing at its normal pace and productivity growing at its normal rate of 2 to 3 percent, in order for unemployment *not* to increase, the GDP has to grow by 3 to 4 percent. To reduce unemployment from the levels it reached in 2009, the economy needs to grow *faster* than that baseline. But the "consensus forecasts"—representing neither the most optimistic nor the most pessimistic of economists—saw cumulative growth in 2009 and 2010, *with* the stimulus, was under 1.5 percent,[8] and that is a big shortfall.

A closer look at the numbers casts even a darker cloud over what was happening. The numbers the government and media focus on are "seasonally corrected." They take account of the fact that normally there are new entrants into the labor force in June and July, as students leave school, and that sales go up around Christmas. However, these "seasonal" corrections don't work well in recessions. They describe the "normal" adjustments, but recessions are abnormal events. So when the government reported that some 492,000 jobs were lost between June and August, there was a collective sigh of relief—the pace of job destruction had slowed down. But the reality was otherwise: the true number of jobs destroyed was three times as high, 1.622 million. These were the number of jobs that would have had to be newly created if the economy was to return to "normal." In two months, the economy had destroyed half as many jobs as the entire Obama program had hoped to create over two years. The stimulus program, even if it is as fully successful as the Obama administration has claimed it will be, won't be able to do the trick of even approaching full employment by the end of 2011.

Of course, those trying to manage expectations, to keep things upbeat, talk about the "lag" between job growth and economic growth. Jobs would recover, they admit, slowly. These calculations show how difficult it is going to be to create enough jobs *even without lags*. If there is a lag—and almost surely there will be, as employers hesitate to hire more workers until they are confident that the recovery is real—matters will be even worse.

In fact, the "advertised" unemployment rate—in October 2009, it was *only* 10.2 percent—masked the true weaknesses in the labor force. I noted earlier that this official unemployment rate doesn't include the millions who had dropped out of the labor force, too discouraged even to keep looking (if workers aren't looking for a job, they aren't called unemployed, even though, quite obviously, they are not employed) and the millions who had had to accept part-time employment because they couldn't get a full-time job. A broader measure of unemployment that includes these "involuntary" part-time workers and discouraged workers had soared from 10.8 percent before the crisis, in August 2008, to 17.5 percent by October 2009, the highest on record.[9] The fraction of the working-age population that was employed, at 58.5 percent, was the lowest since 1947.

These are, of course, "average" numbers. In some places and for some groups the numbers were not this bad, but for others they were much worse. By October, 2009, while the official unemployment rate in Michigan had reached 15.1 percent, the broader measure stood at

20.9 percent—more than one out of five couldn't find a full-time job. In California the broader measure was almost 20 percent. Teenage unemployment had grown to a (record) 27.6 percent, while unemployment among African-Americans soared to 15.7 percent.[10]

There was another reason why the unemployment rate underestimated how bad things were. Many of the unemployed chose to go on disability—which pays better and for longer. In the first eight months of 2009, the number of applicants for disability increased 23 percent. No wave of disease had spread over America. In 2008, disability payments reached a record $106 billion, 4 percent of the government's budget. The Social Security Administration estimates that by the end of 2011, 1 million more people will have applied for disability *because* of the recession, and about 500,000 will receive it. And a large fraction of these will be on disability for the rest of their lives.[11]

With the downturn stretching on for more than a year and a half, the number of the long-term unemployed (those unemployed more than six months) reached levels not seen since the Great Depression. The average duration of unemployment was close to half a year (24.9 weeks).[12]

Some looked at the unemployment rate and noted it was not (yet) as bad as it had been in the Reagan recession of 1981–1982, when the unemployment rate reached 10.8 percent, and much lower than that in the Great Depression. Such comparisons have to be taken with a grain of salt. The structure of the economy has changed, as it has moved from manufacturing (20 percent of the economy in 1980, to 11.5 percent today) to services.[13] Then there were fewer part-time jobs. Moreover, the structure of the labor force has changed markedly as well. Unemployment is normally higher in young workers, and in the 1980s there were many more of these. Adjusting for these demographic changes adds 1 percent or more to today's unemployment rate.[14]

The absence of jobs increased anxiety—even those who had jobs worried that they might get a pink slip, and they knew if they did, getting another job would be nigh impossible. By mid-2009, there were six unemployed workers for every vacancy—a record, and twice the number at the peak of the previous recession.[15] Those with jobs were working shorter weeks—down to thirty-three hours—the lowest since the data began to be collected in 1964.[16] And the weaknesses in the job market also put downward pressures on wages.

The collapse of the housing market interacted with the weak labor market in two further ways to enhance anxieties. America's labor market is among the most dynamic in the world. It has been one of the country's strengths. It ensures that workers are used in the most efficient way. But this dynamism is facing major obstacles. First, traditionally, people who lose their jobs in one place are willing to move thousands of miles to find a job in another. But for most Americans, their home is their most important asset, and even those who still have *some* equity in their home (that is, whose home mortgage is not underwater) have lost a very large fraction of it—so much that many won't be able to make a 20 percent down payment on a house of comparable size. Their ability to move has been reduced. People with jobs are not going to be leaving for better jobs. People without jobs will likely remain unemployed longer—moving is a less attractive option.

Moreover, many older Americans are facing a second problem, which also affects unemployment. Most retirement programs used to be what were called defined benefit programs—where the retirees knew what they got when they retired. In the last twenty years, however, there has been a shift to "defined contribution programs," where the employer contributes a certain amount, which is then invested in the market—and much of it was invested in the stock market.[17] The collapse of the stock market, combined with that of the housing market, has meant that many Americans are rethinking their retirement.[18] With fewer people leaving the labor force, there will be fewer new openings—unless employment expands.

In short, within a few months of the passage of the stimulus bill, it became obvious that it had not been big enough; but that should have been apparent at the time the administration was designing it.[19] The contraction in consumption as savings increased from the non-sustainable level of zero, combined with cutbacks in state and local spending, meant that $800 billion stretched over two years just wouldn't do the trick.

Assisting states

In a crisis, without federal assistance states and localities will contract their expenditures, which make up about a third of all government spending. States have balanced-budget frameworks, and they must limit spending to revenues. When property values and profits decrease, tax revenues also drop. The combined budget gaps for the fiscal years 2010 and 2011 are estimated to total at least $350 billion.[20] In 2009, California alone had to cut expenditures and raise taxes by $42 billion.[21] Just offsetting the state revenue shortfall would require *federal* stimulus spending greater than 1 percent of GDP per year.

While the stimulus bill passed in February 2009 did contain some help for states and localities, it wasn't enough. Cutbacks in state and local government programs hit the poor particularly hard; as the administration was touting its stimulus, newspapers were describing the suffering of many of the innocent victims of this crisis. The first priority should have been to make up for the shortfall in state revenues. It makes little economic sense to hire new workers to build bridges and at the same time lay off teachers and nurses. The administration was sensitive to these concerns, and in its first report on the jobs created by the stimulus, in October 2009, it pointed out that of the 640,000 jobs saved or created by the first round of stimulus spending, over half were in education, and only 80,000 were in construction.[22] But the stimulus was still not big enough to stop layoffs and furloughs among teachers, and even shovel-ready projects take time to get going. The job losses contributed to the loss of morale, and they occurred far faster than new jobs could be created. In September 2009 alone, government employment went down by 40,000.[23]

A simple formula—making up for the lost revenue on a state-by-state basis—would have been fair and would have deployed the money quickly. This money would have had high multipliers and would have been directed at the people who needed help the most. And it would have acted as an automatic stabilizer: if, magically, the economy recovered faster, the spending wouldn't occur. If in the more likely event the downturn proved deeper and longer than expected, there would be more money.

Filling in the holes in the safety net

The next priority should have been filling in the holes in the safety net. The bill that passed did a little of this, but not enough. Congress approved three extensions of federally funded unemployment benefits to a maximum of 73 weeks (many states provide benefits for only a third that amount of time),[24] but as the recession continued, it became clear that this would not be enough.[25] For the first time, though, the government did do something about the fact that because we have an employer-based health insurance system, individuals lose their health coverage when they lose their jobs. Earlier reforms had ensured that they could *buy* insurance (COBRA) *if they could afford it*, but increasingly those without a job could not afford insurance. Without assistance, the ranks of the uninsured—already large—would be increased further. Part of the Obama stimulus package was a provision to pay 65 percent of the cost of health insurance as part of the extended unemployment benefits (but only for workers who lost their jobs after September 1, 2008, and before the end of 2009).

Perhaps most tellingly, the government didn't do enough to help on an issue that went to the heart of the crisis: the unemployed can't make mortgage payments. Many of the unemployed lost their homes soon after they lost their jobs—all through no fault of their own. The Obama administration should have provided a new kind of "mortgage insurance" that, in these circumstances, would pick up the mortgage payments—allowing most of them to be deferred until the homeowner is back at work. It is not only a matter of fairness, but also one of national interest: as more houses went into foreclosure, prices fell, exacerbating the downward cycle.

Investments

It would have made sense to give priority to investments that strengthen our future—especially high-return investments in people and in technology. With private universities' endowments savaged by collapsing markets and huge state budget shortfalls, such spending was hard hit.

Much of the stimulus money went into shovel-ready projects, followed by green investments that could be put in place relatively quickly. It should have been clear that there was a high risk that in two years, the economy would still be in need of more stimulus. A longer-term stimulus package would have allowed going beyond the shovel-ready projects to higher-return public investments—one of the few advantages of a long downturn.

The country's most important investment shortages are in the public sector, but there are limits to that sector's ability to install more investment *quickly*. Tax cuts that spur investment would accelerate the flow of funds into the economy—and yield long-term benefits. A program to provide tax incentives for homeowners to insulate existing homes would, for instance, have employed some of the construction workers who lost their jobs as the real estate sector sank to a fifty-year low.

In a downturn, most firms are not willing to take the risk of investing. A temporary investment tax credit can provide them with the appropriate incentive. In effect, a tax cut makes it cheaper to invest now, when the national benefits are large—rather than later, when the economy has returned to normal. It's like a sale of capital goods. An incremental temporary investment tax credit is even better. Even in a downturn, some firms are going to invest, and it makes little sense to reward them for doing what they would have done anyway. Giving credit only to investments that exceed, say, 80 percent of a company's investment dollars over the last couple of years increases the bang for the buck.

Ineffective tax cuts

It wasn't just the size and timing of the stimulus program that didn't fully meet the mark. With almost a third of the stimulus devoted to tax cuts, there was a risk that much of it would be very ineffective. President Bush's February 2008 tax cut didn't work because so much of it was saved, and there was every reason to believe that matters would be little different with this tax cut, even if it was designed to encourage more spending.

Americans were faced with an overhang of debt, as well as anxieties about their jobs and the future. Even those most willing to take on debt would understand that in a toughening credit environment they might not be able to turn to their credit card in time of need. As a result, they would likely decide to save much of the money they receive in the short term. This sort of behavior is understandable but undermines the purpose of the stimulus, which is to *increase* spending. The tax cut would increase the national debt, but there would be little to show for it, either in the short run or in the long.[26]

Other parts of the stimulus program were borrowing against the future: the cash-for-clunkers program helped stimulate demand for cars, but cars bought because of the program are cars that will not be bought in the future—a strategy that might make sense if the downturn lasted only six months but far riskier given the uncertain length of this crisis. The fears proved justified: the program boosted car purchases in the summer of 2009, but at the expense of purchases in the fall. The cash-for-clunkers program also exemplifies poorly targeted spending— there were ways of spending the money that would have stimulated the economy more in the short run and helped the economy to restructure in the ways that were needed for the long run.

There was, besides, something peculiar about both the tax cuts and the cash-for-clunkers program: the problem was not that Americans were consuming too little before the crisis; they were consuming too much. Yet the response to the crisis was to encourage people to consume more. It was understandable, given the precipitous fall in consumption, but the focus should have been less on trying to encourage more consumer spending when what was needed for long-run growth was more investment.

THE CONSEQUENCES

As the spring of 2009 rolled into summer and the number of unemployed continued to grow, a chorus was raised: the stimulus hadn't worked. But the true measure of the success of the stimulus is not the actual level of unemployment, but what unemployment would have been without the stimulus. The Obama administration was always clear that it would create some three million jobs *more than what would otherwise be the case.* The problem is that the shock to the economy from the financial crisis was so bad that even Obama's seemingly huge fiscal stimulus has not been enough.

While most economists were convinced that a stimulus was necessary and that it was working—even though a bigger stimulus would have been desirable—there were a few naysayers. Some conservatives have even been trying to rewrite history to suggest that government spending didn't work in the Great Depression.[27] Of course it didn't pull the country out of the Great Depression—the United States didn't really emerge from the Depression until World War II. But the reason was that Congress and the Roosevelt administration vacillated. The stimulus was not consistently strong enough. As in this crisis, cutbacks in state spending partially offset increases in federal spending. Large-scale peace-time Keynesian economics had never really been tried—the rhetoric to the contrary. Government wartime spending did succeed in getting the economy back to full employment—and very quickly. After Obama's stimulus, critics again argued that Keynesian economics had been proved wrong now that it had been put to the test.[28] But it hadn't been—and all the evidence showed that the stimulus had made things better.

There are three reasons why a stimulus might not work—one often raised by academic economists shows how out of touch with reality they are; but the other two raise real concerns. Some economists have suggested that if the government runs a deficit, households will be spurred to save, knowing that at some time in the future they will have to pay the debt back through higher taxes. In this view the increased government spending is *fully* offset by reduced household spending. Ricardian equivalence, as it's known to economists, is taught in every graduate school in the country. It is also sheer nonsense. When President Bush cut taxes in the early years of the decade, savings rates actually fell. Of course, in the world of economics, things are never as they seem. The defenders of Ricardian equivalence would argue that perhaps they would have fallen even more without the tax cut. That would mean that America's savings rates before the crisis would have been solidly negative, by several percentage points.

Conservatives invoke Ricardian equivalence more often as an argument against expenditure increases than as an argument against tax decreases. Indeed, the theory suggests that nothing matters much. If the government increases taxes, people adjust; they spend exactly as much money today as they would otherwise, knowing that they will have to pay less taxes in the future.

These theories are based on simple assumptions that have come to be accepted in the schools of economics that played such a large part in precipitating the current crisis. Two of the assumptions are commonplace but obviously wrong: markets and information are perfect. In this scenario, everyone can borrow as much as they want. If the government raises taxes, those who want to increase spending in an offsetting way have no trouble going to a bank and borrowing the money—at the same rate that the government can borrow (adjusted appropriately for the risk of default). Two of the assumptions are peculiar: individuals live forever, and redistributions don't matter. If people live forever, they simply can't escape paying for today's borrowing; but in reality, this generation can pass the burden of today's borrowing onto future generations, enabling the older generation to consume more than it otherwise would. In this peculiar theory, even though poor elderly people might spend a larger fraction of their limited income than the rich middle-aged, redistributing income from the rich to the poor would have no effect on total consumption. In reality, household savings are likely to increase in this recession whether the government increases the deficit or not; and the savings rate is not likely to be affected much by the size of the deficit.

A more serious concern is that as the government borrows more, those who lend the money will worry about whether the government will be able to pay it back. As their worry increases, they may demand a higher interest rate. This concern is well known to developing countries, because they are caught between a rock and a hard place. If they don't spend money on a stimulus, their economy weakens and creditors demand high interest rates. If they do spend money on a stimulus, their indebtedness increases and creditors demand high interest rates. America, fortunately, is not (yet) at this critical juncture. In my judgment, the current benefits of a stimulus are so strong that it outweighs these longer-term risks.

A closely related concern is that investors will become more worried about future inflation. Countries that lend the United States money are already expressing the worry that there will be an incentive to "inflate the huge debt away," that is, decrease its *real* value by inflation. Furthermore, they worry that investors, seeing this debt, will think the dollar is at risk, and the value of the dollar (in terms of other currencies) will diminish. Whether these anxieties are rational or not, if they are there, longer-term interest rates will rise, and this can decrease investment, diminishing the net increase in aggregate demand.

Through monetary policy, the Federal Reserve can largely offset any tendency of increased government borrowing to cause an increase in at least short-term interest rates. But in the current crisis, the unprecedented magnitude and character of its measures[29] have led to worries about its ability to "unwind" the actions at just the right time. The Fed has tried to convince the market that it can do so, ensuring that inflation will not rise by appropriately tightening monetary policy at exactly the right time. As I note in chapter 5, there are good reasons for a lack of confidence in the Fed's response. Again, whether justified or not, if these beliefs are widespread, they put the Fed in a bind: if it does return to its "normal" policy of focusing on the short-term interest rates, then long-term interest rates may rise, even if it keeps short-term interest rates low, dampening the recovery.

If, however, the stimulus money is spent on investments, these adverse effects are less likely to occur, because markets should realize that the United States is actually in a stronger economic position as a result of the stimulus, not a weaker position. If the stimulus spending is for investment, then the asset side of the nation's balance sheet increases in tandem with the liabilities, and there is no reason for lenders to be worried, no reason for an increase in interest rates.[30]

Anxieties about the deficit growing out of hand lead to the real source of concern: the political risk that America will not be able to stay the course, just as it failed to do so during the Great Depression and just as Japan failed to do so after the bursting of its bubble in the early 1990s. Will the government continue to provide a stimulus if the economy fails to achieve a robust recovery after the first dose of medicine? Will those who never believed in Keynesian economics ally themselves with deficit hawks in Congress to urge a cutback in government spending? I worry that they will, and if they do, a return to strong growth may be delayed.

THE WAY FORWARD

The Bush and Obama administrations underestimated the severity of the recession. They believed that providing money to the banks would restore the economy to health, reignite the flow of credit, and resurrect the real estate market. The Obama stimulus was designed to get the country through the interim while all this happened. Each of these hypotheses was wrong: restoring the banks' balance sheet would not automatically bring lending back to "normal." The underlying debt-based consumption model of the American economy broke when the real estate bubble broke, and would not be so easily repaired. Even an arrest in the decline in real estate prices does not mean that they will return to where they had been. And that means that the major source of wealth for most Americans—the equity in their home—has been greatly diminished if not totally eradicated.

We need to be prepared for a second round of stimulus spending as the current round of stimulus spending comes to an end—which, by itself, will contribute to "negative" growth. Some of what should have been included in the first round (such as making up for the shortfall in state taxes) should be included in the next round. We need to be ready for more investment spending in 2011. It may not be necessary, but if we don't begin preparing now, we won't be ready when the time comes. If we prepare now, we can cut back if it turns out to be unnecessary. Unfortunately, the choices made by the Obama and Bush administrations have made the chances of passing another stimulus package difficult at best. Some of the untoward consequences of Obama's risky strategy of muddling through are already unfolding.

In the end, deficit-financed stimulus spending alone remains a temporary palliative, especially as pressures mount in many countries, including the United States, over the growing debt. Critics argue that the country has simply gone from debt-financed private consumption to debt-financed public consumption. While such spending can help spur the restructuring of the economy that is necessary to ensure long-term growth, too little of the money is directed at that goal—and too much has been spent in ways that preserve the status quo.

There are other policies that could help sustain the economy—and replace the debt-financed consumption bubble. For total American consumption to be restored on a sustainable basis, there would have to be a large redistribution of income, from those at the top who can afford to save, to those below who spend every penny they can get. More progressive taxation (taxing those at the top more heavily, reducing taxes at the bottom) would not only do that but also help stabilize the economy. If the government raises taxes on upper-income Americans to finance an expansion of government spending, especially on investment, the economy will expand—this is called a "balanced budget multiplier." Supply-side economists, popular in the Reagan days, argued that such taxes will discourage work and savings and thus lower GDP. But their analysis (if correct at all) applies only to situations where production is limited by supply; now there is excess capacity, and production is limited by demand.

If global consumption is to be strengthened, there will have to be a new global reserve system so that developing countries can spend more and save less.[31] The international community will have to provide more help to poor countries, and China will have to have more success in reducing its savings rate than it has had in recent years. If the world committed itself to a high price of carbon (what firms and households have to pay for emissions of greenhouse gases), there would be large incentives to retrofit the economy. It would inspire innovations and investments in more energy-efficient housing, plant, and equipment.

None of these suggestions are likely to happen quickly, but so far most of the issues are not even under discussion.

Three challenges now face the United States and the world: the restoration of sustainable aggregate demand, strong enough to ensure global full employment; the reconstructing of the financial system so that it performs the functions that a financial system is supposed to, rather than the reckless risk-taking that was undertaken prior to the crisis; and the restructuring of the U.S. and other world economies— to reflect, for instance, shifts in global comparative advantages and changes in technology. As of this writing, we are failing on all three accounts. Indeed, there is too little discussion of any of these underlying problems as we focus on our immediate worries. A central concern of this book is that the measures we have taken to save us from going over the brink into the abyss may, at the same time, inhibit our return to robust growth. Just as the banks were shortsighted in their lending, we have been shortsighted in our rescue—with consequences that may be felt long into the future.

These are particularly apparent in the financial sector, which was at the heart of the storm. The next three chapters focus on the attempts to rescue and resuscitate the financial system. The next chapter looks at the mortgage market. While President Obama recognized that it would be difficult to restore the economy to full health so long as millions of Americans faced the threat of foreclosure, too little was done: foreclosures continue, almost unabated. The contrast between what was done and what should have been done is far starker than in the case of the stimulus. The stimulus may not have been all that was needed, but it was, nonetheless, a success. One can't give such a high grade to what was done for the mortgages. And when it comes to the banks—the subject of chapters 5 and 6—the disappointment is all the greater.

ments were made in the United States, she thought they were good investment for her clients. "The American mortgage market is so big. We never thought it would have problems," she told me.

Excessive risk coupled with excessive leverage had created what *seemed* like high returns—and they were high for a while. Wall Street thought that by repackaging the mortgages and passing them on to numerous investors, they were sharing the risk and protecting themselves. With risk widely shared, it could easily be absorbed. But securitizing the mortgages actually made them more risky. The bankers who precipitated the problems are now saying it was not completely their fault. Dick Parsons, the chairman of Citigroup, exemplifies the bankers' view: "Besides banks, there was reduced regulatory oversight, loans to unqualified borrowers were encouraged and people took out mortgages or home-equity loans they couldn't afford."[3]

Executives like Parsons are blaming the borrowers for buying houses they could not afford, but many of these borrowers were financially illiterate and did not understand what they were getting into. This was especially true in the subprime mortgage market, which became the epicenter of the crisis. Subprime mortgages were mortgages given to individuals who were less qualified than those given "conventional" mortgages, for example, because of low or unstable income. Other homeowners were encouraged by lenders to treat their houses as ATMs, repeatedly borrowing against their value. For instance, Doris Canales's home was threatened with foreclosure after she refinanced her home thirteen times in six years with "no-doc" mortgages, which required low or no documentation of income or assets. "They'd just call and say, 'Hey, do you need money in the bank?' And I was like, 'Yeah, I need money in the bank,'" Ms. Canales said. Many of the forms submitted by brokers on her behalf belied Ms. Canales's true income.[4] In some cases, the results were literally quite deadly.[5] Suicides and broken marriages resulted as borrowers across the country found that their homes were sold out from under them. Even some people who had kept up on their payments and taxes found their houses put up for auction without their knowledge. The dramatic stories that filled the newspapers may have been the exception, but they touched a raw nerve: America now faces a social tragedy alongside an economic one. Millions of poor Americans have lost or are losing their homes—by one estimate, 2.3 million in 2008 alone. (In 2007, there were foreclosure actions against almost 1.3 million properties.)[6] Moody's *Economy.com* projected that a total of 3.4 million homeowners would default on their mortgages in 2009, and 2.1 million would lose their homes. Millions more are expected to go into foreclosure by 2012.[7] Banks jeopardized the life savings of millions of people when they persuaded them to live beyond their means—though in some cases it undoubtedly did not take that much persuasion. With the loss of their homes, many Americans are losing their life savings and their dreams of a better future, of an education for their children, of a retirement in modest comfort.

At times it appeared that only the foot soldiers—the mortgage originators who sold the subprime mortgages—had any direct sense of culpability, and even they could claim they were just doing their job. They had incentive structures that encouraged them to write as many mortgages as they could. They trusted their bosses to only approve mortgages if they made sense. Still, some of the lower-level employees knew that danger was ahead. California mortgage lender Paris Welch wrote to U.S. regulators in January 2006: "Expect fallout, expect foreclosures, expect horror stories." One year later, the housing implosion cost her her job.[8]

Ultimately, the financial instruments that banks and lenders used to exploit the poor were also their undoing. The fancy instruments were designed to extract as much money as possible from the borrower. The securitization process supported never-ending fees, the never-ending fees supported unprecedented profits, and the unprecedented profits generated unheard-of bonuses, and all of this blinded the bankers. They may have suspected it was too good to be true—and it was. They may have suspected that it was unsustainable—hence the rush to get as much as they could as quickly as they could—and it was unsustainable. Some weren't aware of the casualties until the system collapsed. While the bank accounts of many top executives in the financial industry have been greatly diminished, many have profited from the mess with millions of dollars—in some cases, hundreds of millions of dollars.

But even the collapse of the system did not curb their avarice. As the government provided the banks with money to recapitalize and ensure a flow of credit, they instead used the money in part to pay themselves record bonuses—for the record losses! Nine lenders that combined had nearly $100 billion in losses received $175 billion in bailout money through TARP and paid out nearly $33 billion in bonuses, including more than $1 million apiece to nearly five thousand employees.[9] Other money was used to pay dividends, which are supposed to be a sharing of profits with shareholders. In this case, though, there were no profits, just government handouts.

In the years preceding the crisis, the Federal Reserve had kept interest rates low. But cheap money can lead to an investment boom in plants and equipment, strong growth, and sustained prosperity. In the United States, and in much of the rest of the world, it led to a housing bubble. That's not the way the market is *supposed* to behave. Markets are *supposed* to allocate capital to its most productive use. But historically, there have been repeated instances of banks using other people's money to engage in excessive risk-taking and to lend to those who can't repay. There have been repeated instances of such lending giving rise to housing bubbles. It's one of the reasons for regulation.

Yet, in the deregulatory frenzy of the 1980s, 1990s, and the early years of this decade, even attempts to restrict the worst lending practices—such as the predatory lending in the subprime market— were beaten back.[10] Regulations serve many purposes. One is to stop the banks from exploiting poor or poorly educated people. Another is to ensure the stability of the financial system.[11] U.S. deregulators stripped away both kinds of regulations and, in so doing, paved the way for the bankers to figure out new ways to exploit homeowners, many of whom were poor and buying a house for the first time. America's subprime financial institutions created an array of subprime mortgages—innovations all designed to maximize the fees they might generate. Good financial markets are supposed to do what they do *efficiently*, and that means at low transaction costs, that is, *low fees*. But while most people in the economy dislike transaction costs, those in the mortgage game (and finance more broadly) love them. They are what they live off of, so they strive to maximize fees, not to minimize them.

TRADITIONAL BANKING

Before the arrival of modern innovations in finance, lenders lived in a simple world. They assessed creditworthiness, made loans, monitored the loans to make sure that those who borrowed from them spent the money in the way promised, and collected the money back, with interest. Bankers, and banking, were boring. That's exactly what the people who entrusted their money to them wanted. Ordinary citizens didn't want someone to take their hard-earned money and gamble with it. It was a relationship based on trust—trust that the money given to the bank would be returned. But over the past hundred years there have been numerous bank runs, episodes in which people rush to the banks to pull out their money because they are afraid the bank didn't have the funds to cover their deposits.

In the midst of the Great Depression, in 1933, the government stepped in and set up the Federal Deposit Insurance Corporation (FDIC) to insure deposits so that people would feel that their money was protected even if there were rumors that a bank was facing difficulties. Once the government provided this insurance, it had to make sure that it was not exposed to undue risks, just as a fire insurance company looks to reduce the likelihood of loss in a fire by insisting that a building have sprinklers. The government did this by regulating the banks, ensuring that they did not undertake excessive risk.

Because banks held on to the loans they originated, they had to be careful. They had an incentive to make sure that the borrower could repay. To do that, they had to verify the income of the borrower and build in an incentive for repayment. If the money the banks lent accounted for only, say, 80 percent of the value of the house and the borrower didn't repay the loan, he stood to lose not just his house but also the money (the 20 percent) he had put into his house, his equity—a considerable sum. Moreover, the likelihood that an 80 percent mortgage would wind up exceeding the value of the house was small—prices would have to drop by 20 percent. Bankers understood rightly that a mortgage that was "underwater" had a large risk of nonpayment, especially given America's peculiar system of nonrecourse loans, where if a borrower fails to repay the loan, the worst that can happen is that he loses his house.[12] The lender can't get anything more. The system worked pretty well. Homeowners' aspirations for a large home were dampened by the reality that they had to put up 20 percent of its value to get a loan.

The "innovative" U.S. financial system managed to forget these long-learned and elementary lessons of banking. There were many reasons for their amnesia. In fact, the lessons were forgotten periodically—the world has been marked by frequent real estate bubbles and crashes; banks around the world have repeatedly had to be bailed out. The only extended period in which that was not the case was the quarter century after World War II when there were strong regulations that were effectively enforced. Government-backed deposit insurance may have provided further impetus (as if the banks needed any) for bad lending and other forms of excessive risk-taking. It meant that if the bank undertook risk and lost, the government picked up the cost; if the bank won, it kept the extra returns. (This is another example of "moral hazard.") When deposit insurance was first proposed in the wake of the Depression, President Franklin Roosevelt was so worried about the moral hazard involved that he was hesitant to support the idea. He was persuaded, however, that if the insurance were accompanied by strong-enough regulation, the risk could be controlled.[13] Supporters of the current rush to deregulation forgot not only that financial markets had frequently been guilty of excessive risky lending, but also that with deposit insurance, the incentives and opportunities for bad behavior had been multiplied. Remarkably, the rush to deregulation occurred at a time when the dangers of excessive risk-taking were increasing because of new financial products.

There are other reasons behind the banks' decisions to start making extremely risky loans and to engage in other excessive risk-taking. Especially after the repeal of the Glass-Steagall Act in 1999, which had separated commercial and investment banking, the biggest banks had become bigger and bigger—too big to fail, and they knew it. They knew that if they got into trouble, the government would rescue them. This was true even of the banks that did not have deposit insurance, like the investment banks. Second, the decision makers—bankers—had perverse incentives that encouraged shortsighted behavior and excessive risk-taking. Not only did they know the bank would be rescued if it got into trouble, but they knew that they would still be well-off even if the bank was allowed to fail. And they were right.

These problems were compounded by the fact that the risk-management models banks used were badly flawed—the so-called experts in risk management didn't really realize the risks they were undertaking. In today's complex world, "sophisticated" banks try to be more precise about the risks they face; they don't want to rely on seat-of-the-pants judgments. They wanted to know the probability of, say, a bundle of mortgages (or enough of their loan portfolio) going sour, sufficiently so that it would put the bank into jeopardy. If a few had problems, that could easily be managed. The likelihood that *many* would simultaneously have difficulties would depend on a number of different but often related risks: the chances that the unemployment rate or interest rates would be high or that housing prices would fall. If one knew the probabilities of each, and their interrelationships, one could estimate the risk that a particular mortgage might default; but of even greater importance, one could estimate the chances that, say, more than 5 percent would go bad. These models could then go on to forecast how much the bank could recover from the mortgage in default—what the house would sell for. And on the basis of that, one could estimate the chances that the bank would be in trouble, that it would lose so much that it couldn't repay depositors. (Similar models could be used to estimate the losses on any group of mortgages that were bundled together into securities, or the losses of the complex securities that the investment banks constructed on the basis of the mortgage-backed securities.) But the predictions of a model are only as good as the assumptions that go into it; if one wrongly estimates the probabilities of, say, a decrease in housing prices, all of the conclusions of the model will be wrong.

The banks relied on these models not only to evaluate the financial products they bought and sold, but also to manage their overall risk. By "financial engineering," they believed they could make sure that their capital was better used—allowing them to take on as much risk as regulators would allow. The irony was that the attempt to use financial capital more efficiently contributed to the crisis, which resulted in the massive underutilization of *real* capital—both physical and human capital.

These flawed models may not have been just an accident: distorted compensation schemes undermined incentives to develop sound risk-management models. Besides, many of those in charge of the markets, though they might pride themselves on their business acumen and ability to appraise risk, simply didn't have the ability to judge whether the models were good or not. Many were lawyers, untrained in the subtle mathematics of the models.

There was one other important difference between the good old days and modern banking, and that is how the banks generated their profits. In the old days, banks made most of their money from the difference in the interest rate that they received from the borrowers and the interest they had to pay depositors. The difference, or spread, was often not very large and made normal commercial banking comfortably, but not wildly, lucrative. But as regulations were loosened and the culture of banking changed, they began to look for new ways to generate profits. They found the answer in a simple word: fees.

Indeed, many of the new "innovative" products based on mortgages had some critical factors in common: while they may not have helped borrowers manage risk, they were designed to shift as much risk away from the bank as possible and to generate as many fees as possible—often in ways that the borrower was never fully aware of. The products were also designed, where necessary, to get around regulatory and accounting restraints that might restrict lending and risk-taking.

New innovations that were designed to help manage risk were, when misused, capable of amplifying risk—and whether through incompetence or flawed incentives, that's what happened. And some of the new innovations helped the bankers circumvent the regulations that were trying to prevent them from misbehaving: they helped hide what was going on, moving risks off balance sheet; they were complex and obscure, so that even if the regulators had wanted to do their job—even if they had believed that regulation was necessary to maintain the stability of the economy—they would have found it increasingly difficult to do so.

INNOVATION GONE AWRY: A PLETHORA OF BAD PRODUCTS

There is not enough space to describe the details of the myriad types of mortgages that were in use during the boom, but let's take one example: the 100 percent mortgage in which banks would lend 100 percent, or more, of the value of the house. A 100 percent nonrecourse mortgage is what economists call an option. If the price of the house goes up, the homeowner keeps the difference. If it goes down, he has nothing to lose; the borrower can just turn his keys over to the creditor and walk away at any time. This meant that the larger the house, the more potential money the borrower can make. The result was that homeowners were tempted to buy houses more expensive than what they could afford. And because bankers and mortgage originators collected fees regardless, they had little incentive to curb this profligacy.

Mortgages with teaser rates (temporarily low rates that exploded after a few years) and balloon payments (a short-term mortgage taking advantage of currently low interest rates that had to be refinanced in five years) were particularly advantageous *to the lenders*. They entailed repeated refinancing. At each refinancing, with the borrower facing a new set of fees, the mortgage originator had a new source of profits. When the teaser period ended and the rates jumped, families who borrowed all they could would be hard pressed to make their payments. But if they asked the lenders about this potential danger, many were told not to worry since the price of their home would rise before the teaser rate expired, allowing them to easily refinance—and take out some money to buy a car or enjoy a vacation.

There were even mortgages that allowed the borrower to choose how much he paid back—he didn't even have to pay the full amount of interest he owed each month. These mortgages are said to have negative amortization—that is, at the end of the year, the borrower owed more than at the beginning. But again the borrower was told that while he might owe more money, the rise in value of the house would exceed the additional amount he owed, and he would end up richer. Just as the regulators and investors should have been suspicious of 100 percent mortgages, they should have been suspicious of mortgages that left the borrower increasingly in debt and those that forced him to refinance and refinance.

"Liar loans," so called because individuals were not required to prove their income to get one, were among the most peculiar of the new products. In many cases borrowers were encouraged to overstate their income. In others, loan officers did the overstating, and the borrower only discovered the "mistake" at the closing.[14] As with other innovations, this was all in service of a simple mantra: the larger the house, the larger the loan, the greater the fees. No matter that there might be a problem down the line.

All of these "innovative" mortgages had several flaws. The first was the assumption that it would be easy to refinance because house prices would continue to rise at the rapid rate that they had been rising. This was a near economic impossibility. Real income (adjusted for inflation) of most Americans has been stagnating—in 2005 the median household (the household such that half of those had higher incomes, half lower) income was nearly 3 percent lower than in 1999.[15] Meanwhile home prices had been rising far faster than inflation or real income. From 1999 to 2005, home prices increased by 62 percent.[16] The result was that for the median family, the ratio of housing prices to income increased from 3.72 in 1999 to 5.29 in 2005, the highest level since records were kept (in 1991).[17]

Moreover, the exotic mortgage market operated on the assumption that when it came time to refinance a given mortgage, the banks would be willing to do so. Perhaps they would—but perhaps they wouldn't. Interest rates could increase, credit conditions could tighten, unemployment could increase—and each of these represented risks to the borrower looking to refinance.

If many individuals had to sell their homes at the same time, say, because of a jump in unemployment, this would drive down house prices and burst the bubble. And it was here that the various mistakes in mortgages interacted: if the lenders had issued a 100 percent mortgage (or if the value of what was owed had grown to 100 percent as a result of negative amortization), there was no way to sell the house and repay the mortgage. There was no way, short of default, of downsizing to a house that the family could afford.

Federal Reserve Chairman Alan Greenspan, the man who was supposed to be protecting the country from excessive risk-taking, actually encouraged it. In 2004, Greenspan gave a now-infamous speech in which he noted that homeowners "might have saved tens of thousands of dollars had they held adjustable-rate mortgages [where rates adjust when interest rates change] rather than fixed-rate mortgages during the past decade."[18] In the past, most Americans had taken out long-term (twenty- to thirty-year) fixed-rate mortgages, where payments do not change over the life of the mortgage. This has a big advantage. Households, knowing what the mortgage payments will be, can plan the family budget. But Greenspan advised them otherwise. The reason why they would have done better with a variable-rate mortgage than with a fixed-rate mortgage was obvious. Typically, long-term interest rates reflect the average value of the (expected) interest rates going forward. And typically, markets project interest rates to remain roughly where they have been—except in unusual periods. But in 2003, Greenspan had done something unprecedented—he brought interest rates down to 1 percent. It's no wonder the markets had not anticipated this. It's also no wonder that those who had gambled on variable-rate mortgages did better than those stuck with the fixed-rate mortgages. But with interest rates at 1 percent, there was only one way for them to go—up. That meant that anyone who had a variable-rate mortgage was almost sure to see his interest payments rise in the future, and perhaps by a great deal. And rise they did, as the short-term interest rate went from 1 percent in 2003 to 5.25 percent in 2006.

Those who had followed the dictum of taking out the largest mortgage they could afford suddenly faced payments that exceeded their budget. When they all tried to sell their homes, house prices plummeted. For those with 100 percent mortgages, this meant that they could not refinance, could not repay what was owed, and could not afford to stay where they were. As house prices fell, this became true even for borrowers who had taken out a 90 percent, or sometimes even an 80 percent mortgage. Defaulting on their mortgage was the only option for millions.

Greenspan had, in effect, advised the country to take an extraordinarily risky course. Other countries like Turkey simply did not allow variable-rate mortgages. In the United Kingdom, many of the variable-rate mortgages still keep a fixed payment, so individuals aren't forced into foreclosure. Instead, banks lengthen the amount of time over which the mortgage is repaid, though this obviously won't work for mortgages that are already at 100 percent of the value of the property and in which the borrower is already not paying all of the interest due.

When the various mortgage innovations were used in combination—for instance, negative amortization mortgages combined with 100 percent "liar" mortgages—it created a particularly explosive potential for mischief. As I noted, the borrower had apparently nothing to lose in getting as big a mortgage as the bank would allow. Since the mortgage originators got a larger fee the larger the mortgage was, but typically didn't bear any risk if the borrower did not repay, the incentives of the mortgage originator and of the homeowner were aligned in a most peculiar way. They both wanted the largest house and the largest mortgage that they could get away with. This meant lying all around—lying about what the family could afford and lying about the value of the house.

If the mortgage originator could get an appraiser to value a house worth $300,000 for $350,000, he could sell a mortgage for, say, $325,000. Under this scenario, the seller gained, the real estate broker gained, the mortgage originator gained, and the homeowner seemed to have little to lose. Indeed, to make sure the homeowner thought he had nothing to lose, he could even get a kickback—in effect *a negative down payment*.[19] Unfortunately, at least from the perspective of the mortgage originators, some real estate appraisers took a professional attitude and refused to give bloated appraisals. There was an easy solution: create your own real estate appraisal company. This had the further advantage of a new way of generating fee revenues. For instance, Wells Fargo had its own subsidiary appraisal management company, called Rels Valuation.[20] Proving in any particular case that there was a deliberate overvaluation is difficult at best, especially in a bubble when prices are rising rapidly. But what is clear is that there was a *conflict of interest*: there were incentives for bad behavior. Regulators should have recognized this and put a stop to it.[21]

Many home buyers turned to mortgage brokers to get the lowest interest rate possible. They were *supposed* to be working for the borrower, but they often received kickbacks from the lender—an obvious conflict of interest. Brokers soon became a vital part of America's predatory lending system. Subprime borrowers fared worse when they went through brokers than when they went directly to lenders: additional interest payments for those who went through brokers ranged from $17,000 to $43,000 for every $100,000 they borrowed.[22] This was, of course, in addition to the 1 to 2 percent of the loan value that they received *from the borrower* for (supposedly) getting him a good deal. Worse, the brokers got the biggest rewards for steering borrowers into the riskiest mortgages, adjustable-rate loans with prepayment penalties, and even got kickbacks when the borrower refinanced. They got big kickbacks too when the broker steered a borrower into a higher-rate mortgage than he was qualified for.

WARNING SIGNS IGNORED

It was well known that the financial sector was engaged in all of these shenanigans, and it should have been a warning to borrowers, to the investors who bought the mortgages, and to the regulators. They all should have seen that mortgage origination was fee-driven: the borrowers had to constantly refinance, and at the point of financing there were new fees—large prepayment penalties in settling the old mortgage and further charges at the issuance of the new mortgage. The fees could be recorded as profits, and high profits generate high share values for the mortgage originators and others in the financial sector. (Even if the mortgage originators had held on to their mortgages, standard accounting procedures would have worked to their benefit. While to any rational individual, there was a high likelihood that many of these "novel" mortgages would eventually not be repaid, no note of future losses would have to be made until the mortgage actually went into delinquency.) Innovation responds to incentives, and the incentives were to create products that generated more fees *now*, not products that managed risks better. The high fees and profits should also have been a sign that something was awry. For mortgage originators, including the banks, one more innovation—securitization—made their life sweet, for it enabled them to enjoy the rewards of high fees, with *seemingly* almost no risk.

SECURITIZATION

As I noted, in the old days (before securitization became fashionable in the 1990s) when banks were banks, they kept the mortgages that they issued. If a borrower defaulted, the bank bore the consequences. If a borrower had trouble—say, he lost his job—the bank could help him along. Banks knew when it paid to extend credit and when it was necessary to foreclose, something they did not do lightly. With securitization, a group of mortgages would be bundled together and sold to investors anywhere. The investors might never have even visited the communities in which the houses were located.

Securitization offered one big advantage—it diversified and shared risks. Community banks lent mostly to members of the community, so if a factory in town shut down, many in the community would be unable to meet their mortgage payments and the bank might risk going bankrupt. With securitization, investors could buy shares in bundles of mortgages, and investment banks could even combine multiple bundles of mortgages, making diversification even easier for the investor. It was unlikely, so the logic went, that mortgages from disparate geographic regions would experience problems at the same time. But there were dangers too. There are many circumstances in which diversification works imperfectly—as indicated earlier in the chapter, an increase in interest rates would pose problems throughout the country.[23] Moreover, securitization created several new problems. One was that it created information *asymmetries*: the buyer of the security typically knew less than the bank or firm that had originated the mortgage. And because the originator didn't bear the consequences of his mistakes (except in the long run—through the loss of reputation), his incentives for doing a good job at credit assessment were greatly attenuated.

The securitization process involved a long chain. Mortgage origina-tors created the mortgages that were bundled together by investment banks, which then repackaged and converted them into new securities. The banks kept some of these securities in special investment vehicles off their balance sheets, but most were passed on to investors, including pension funds. To buy the securities, managers of pension funds had to be sure the securities they were buying were safe, and the credit rating agencies played a vital role by certifying their safety. Financial markets created an incentive structure which ensured that each of those in this chain played their role in the grand deception with enthusiasm.

The whole securitization process depended on the greater fool theory—that there were fools who could be sold the toxic mortgages and the dangerous pieces of paper that were based on them. Globaliza-tion had opened up a whole world of fools; many investors abroad did not understand America's peculiar mortgage market, especially the idea of nonrecourse mortgages. This ignorance did little to stop them from snapping up these securities though. We should be thankful. Had for-eigners not bought so many of our mortgages, the problems facing our financial system almost surely would have been worse.[24]

Perverse incentives and flawed models—
accelerated by a race to the bottom

The rating agencies should have recognized the risk of the products whose safety they were being asked to certify. Had they been doing their job, they would have thought about the perverse incentives of both the mortgage originators and the investment banks and bankers, and this would have made them particularly wary.

Some have expressed surprise at how poorly the rating agencies performed. I was more surprised at the surprise. After all, the rating agencies have a long track record of poor performance—going back well before the Enron and WorldCom scandals in the early 2000s. During the 1997 East Asian crisis, the agencies were blamed for contributing to the bubble that preceded it. They had given the debt of countries like Thailand a high rating until days before the crisis. When they withdrew their high rating—moving Thailand down two notches and placing it below investment grade—they forced pension funds and other "fiduciaries" to sell off Thai bonds, contributing to the crash in their markets and their currency. In both the East Asian and the recent American crises, the rating agencies were clearly behind the ball. Rather than providing information that would help the market to make good investment decisions, they figured out that something was wrong at just about the same time that the market did—and too late to prevent the pension funds' money from going where it shouldn't have gone.

To explain the rating agencies' poor performance, we have to go back to incentives: like everyone else in the sector, their incentives were distorted; they had their own conflicts of interest. They were being paid by the banks that originated the securities they were asked to rate. Moody's and Standard & Poor's, among others, might not have understood risk, but they did understand incentives. They had an incentive to please those who were paying them. And competition among the rating agencies just made matters worse: if one rating agency didn't give the grade that was wanted, the investment banks could turn to another. It was a race to the bottom.[25]

Compounding the problem, the rating agencies had discovered a new way to enhance their income: provide consulting services, such as on how to get better ratings, including the coveted AAA rating. They raked in fees as they told the investment houses how to get good ratings and then made still more money when they assigned the grades. Smart investment bankers soon figured out how to extract the highest mix of ratings from any set of securities. Initially, mortgage bundles were just sliced up into tranches. Any money received in payment first went to the "safest" (or highest) tranche. After that tranche got paid what it was owed, money would go to the second tranche, and so forth. The lowest tranche would get paid back only after higher tranches got all of their money. But then the financial wizards discovered that the highest tranche would still get a AAA rating if it provided some income to the lowest tranche in some unlikely situation, say, where greater than 50 percent of the loans in the pool went into default. Because the likelihood of the event was considered so remote, this "insurance" didn't affect the higher tranche's AAA rating, but if structured right, it could help the rating of the lower tranche. The different tranches were soon joined in a complicated web, so that when the (supposedly) once-in-a-thousand-years event actually occurred, the supposedly AAA-rated upper tranche didn't get all the money that was promised. In short, there were losses all around, not just in the lowest tranches.

There is another reason why the rating agencies did so badly: they used the same bad models that the investment bankers used. They assumed, for instance, that there would almost never be a housing price decline and certainly not a price decline in many parts of the country at the same time. If there were foreclosures, so the model predicted, they would not be correlated. As I noted, the premise of securitization was diversification, but diversification only works if the loans that make up the security are not correlated. Their thinking ignored the common elements creating the housing bubble throughout the economy: low interest rates, lax regulations, and close to full employment. A change in any of these factors could and would affect markets throughout the country—and indeed throughout the world. Even if the financial wizards didn't understand this, it was common sense, and because it was common sense, there was a high risk of a bubble burst in one part of

A new world with old data

Advocates of the new financial products—all those who were making money from them, from the mortgage originators who were producing the toxic mortgages, to investment banks that were slicing and dicing them into new securities, to the rating agencies that were certifying their safety—argued that they were fundamentally transforming the economy; it was one way to justify the high incomes they were receiving. The products that resulted were so complicated that analysts needed technical computer models to evaluate them. But to really assess the risks, they had to know the likelihood, say, of prices going down by more than 10 percent. In another example of the intellectual inconsistencies that were pervasive, to make those assessments, they relied on past data—which meant that while they claimed that their new products had transformed the market, they implicitly assumed nothing had changed. But consistent with their shortsightedness, they didn't go very far into the past. If they had, they would have realized that real estate prices do fall, and can fall simultaneously in many parts of the country. They should have realized *something* had changed, but for the worse—new asymmetries of information had been created, and neither the investment banks nor the rating agencies took these asymmetries into account in their modeling. They should have realized that the newly minted "innovative" mortgages would have much higher default rates than traditional loans.

New impediments to renegotiation

As if these problems with securitization were not enough, one more important problem has played out with a vengeance over the past couple of years. Banks with long-standing relations with the community had an incentive to treat borrowers who got into trouble well; if there was a good chance that borrowers would catch up on their payments if they were given some time, then the bank would give them the time they needed. But the distant holders of the mortgages had no interest in the community and no concern about having a reputation as a good lender. The result is illustrated by a story the *New York Times* ran on the front page of the Business section about a couple in Arkansas who borrowed $10 million to expand the fitness center they owned.[29] When they got behind in their payments, their mortgage was resold to a speculator who paid just thirty-four cents on the dollar. He demanded full repayment in ten days or he would foreclose on their property. They had offered $6 million, with an additional $1 million as soon as they sold their gym. But the speculator was not interested: he saw an opportunity for an even larger return through foreclosure. A situation like this is bad for the lender, bad for the borrower, and bad for the community. Only the mortgage speculator gains.

But securitization also made it more difficult to renegotiate mortgages when problems arose—as they often did, especially with the perverse incentives that had led to such bad lending practices.[30] As mortgages got sold and resold and the friendly local banker disappeared, responsibility for managing the mortgages (collecting the payments and distributing the money to the disparate holders) was assigned to a new player, the mortgage servicers. The holders of the mortgages were worried that these mortgage servicers might be too soft on the borrowers. As a result, investors put in restrictions making renegotiation more difficult.[31] The result has been a shocking waste of money and an unnecessary toll on communities.

America's litigiousness makes matters still worse. Whatever the renegotiation, someone will complain. Whoever did the renegotiation will surely be sued for not squeezing more from the hapless borrower. And America's financial sector had compounded these problems by creating still further conflicts of interests. Typically, highly indebted homeowners had a first mortgage (say, for 80 percent of the value of the house) and a second mortgage (say, for the next 15 percent). If there had been a *single* mortgage for 95 percent of the value of the house, and if house prices fell by 20 percent, it might make sense to write down the mortgage to reflect this—to give the borrower a fresh start. But with two separate mortgages, doing so would typically wipe out the holder of the second mortgage. For him, it might be preferable to refuse to restructure the loan; there might be an admittedly small chance that the market would recover and that he would at least get back some of what he lent. The interest in restructuring—and the terms at which they would be willing to do so—differed markedly between the holders of the first and second mortgages. Into this mess the financial system added one more complication: the mortgage servicer—who was in charge of any restructuring—was often the holder of the second mortgage, so responsibility for renegotiating was often given to one of the interested parties. But this meant that a lawsuit was almost inevitable; with the only recourse for ensuring fair treatment in such an entangled world being the courts, it was no wonder that proposals to give the mortgage servicers legal immunity met with resistance. Even in this most elementary of financial products, mortgages, our financial wizards had created such a tangled web that sorting it out was no easy matter.

If all of this weren't bad enough, in responding to the crisis the government gave banks incentives *not* to restructure mortgages: restructuring would, for instance, have forced them to recognize losses that bad accounting allowed them to ignore for the moment. It was no wonder that the Bush and Obama administrations' half-hearted attempts to have mortgages restructured met with such little success.[32]

RESUSCITATING THE MORTGAGE MARKET

Given that the troubles in the financial sector originated with mortgages, one might have thought that the people charged with fixing the problem would start with these mortgages. But they did not, and as the meltdown continued in late 2008 and early 2009, the number of anticipated foreclosures continued to mount. What once seemed like high estimates—that a fifth of all home mortgages would be underwater—turned out to be conservative.[33]

Foreclosures result from two groups of borrowers: those who can't pay, and those who choose not to pay. It is not always easy to distinguish the two. Some people could pay, but only with a great deal of financial pain. Economists like to believe in rational individuals. For many Americans, the best option when the home mortgage is underwater is default. Since most U.S. mortgages are nonrecourse, the borrower can just turn his keys over to the creditor with no further consequences. If George Jones lives in a $300,000 house, with a $400,000 mortgage, on which he pays $30,000 a year, he can move into the neighboring $300,000 house that's identical to his own and reduce his payments by a quarter. In the midst of the crisis, he wouldn't be able to get a mortgage, but he could rent. (With his home equity wiped out, he probably couldn't make the down payment in any case.) Rents in most places have fallen too; and even if he had the savings for a down payment, renting might make sense until the markets settled down. He might hesitate, worrying about what walking away would do to his credit reputation. But with everyone going into default, the stigma was likely to be muted—blame the banks for bad lending, not the borrower. In any case, everyone has a price; when the sacrifice to make the payments becomes too large, the homeowner will default.

President Obama finally came forward with a proposal to deal with the foreclosure problem in February 2009. It was an important step in the right direction but likely not enough to prevent large numbers of foreclosures from occurring. His plan provided a little help in reducing payments, but nothing was done about the write-down of the principal (what people owed) of underwater mortgages at private banks—for good reason.[34] If the mortgages were restructured, the banks would have to recognize the fact that they had made bad loans; they would have to do something to fill the hole in their balance sheet. (The largest holders of mortgages were Fannie Mae and Freddie Mac, which had been nationalized by the Bush administration. This meant that any write-down of principal—as opposed to simply stretching out payments over time—would come at taxpayers' expense.)[35]

One of the complexities in dealing with mortgages was the concern about fairness: taxpayers who hadn't engaged in profligate borrowing felt that they should not be made to pay for those who had. That was why many argued that the burden of adjustment should be placed on the lenders: as I noted earlier, a loan is a voluntary transaction between a borrower and a lender, the lenders are supposed to be financially savvy in risk assessment, they failed to do the job for which they were

well compensated, and now they should bear the brunt of the consequences, though the borrowers, in seeing most of their equity in their
home wiped out, might *relatively* be paying an even higher price.

But this was not the approach taken. The banks' influence dominated almost every decision the U.S. Treasury made. In this case, however, *both* the banks and the Treasury had a common interest: writing
down the principal of the mortgage would mean that the banks would
have to recognize a loss. In turn, making the hole in the banks' balance sheets more transparent would have forced them to come up with
more equity. Since it would be difficult for banks to do this privately,
it would require more government money. But the government didn't
have the money, and given the myriad mistakes in the bank restructuring program, it would be difficult to get Congress to approve any more
spending.

So, after Obama's forceful words saying that we had to deal with the
mortgage problem, he instead kicked the can a little farther down the
road. Reports on the program were not encouraging: only 651,000 (20
percent) of the 3.2 million eligible troubled loans had been modified by
the end of October 2009, even on a trial basis.[36] Not all of the troubled
loans were eligible for government assistance, and not all of the restructured loans would avoid foreclosure. Even the Obama administration's
optimistic numbers for loan modifications fell short of what housing
experts believe is necessary to avoid severe stress to the residential
housing market.

There are a number of ways to deal with the foreclosure problem—
such as bailing out the lenders at the same time as writing down the
loans. In the absence of budget constraints and worries about future
moral hazard, a program like that would make everyone (other than the
ordinary taxpayer) happy. Individuals could stay in their homes, and
lenders would avoid taking a hit to their balance sheets. Knowing that
the government is taking the risk off of the banks' balance sheets would
help alleviate the credit crunch. The real challenge is how to save the
homes of the hundreds of thousands of people who would otherwise
lose them *without* bailing out the banks, which should be made to bear
the consequences of their failure to assess risk.

To stem the flood of defaults we have to increase the ability and willingness of families to meet their mortgage payments. The key to doing that is reducing their payments, and there are four ways of doing this: stretching out the period over which payments are made—making the families more indebted in the future; giving them assistance to help make the payments; lowering their interest rates; or lowering the amounts they owe.

The banks like the first option—restructuring the mortgages, stretching payments over a longer period, and charging an extra fee for the restructuring. They don't have to give up anything, and in fact, they get more fees and interest. But for the country, it's the worst option. It just postpones the day of reckoning. It's what the banks repeatedly tried with developing countries that owed more than they could pay back. The result was another debt crisis a few years later. Of course, for the banks, and especially for their current officers, a postponement is enough. They are in a struggle for life and death, and even a short reprieve is worth a great deal.

A homeowners' Chapter 11

The best option for the country is lowering the principal. This changes the incentives to default and means that fewer home mortgages are underwater. For the banks, it means coming to terms with reality, with the fact that they lent money on the basis of prices that were inflated by a bubble. It ends the fiction that they will get repaid the full amount lent. From a societal perspective, it makes sense.

The banks are engaged in a gamble. If they don't restructure the mortgages, there is a small probability that real estate markets will recover—very small. If the markets recover, then the banks will be in good shape—or at least in better shape than appears to be the case now. Even if they can hold on just a little longer, the increased profits from the reduced competition (with many banks having met an untimely death) might make up for the losses. But the costs to society are large. Far, far more likely than a recovery of prices is a decline, with an increasing chance of foreclosure. Foreclosures are costly for everyone

—for the banks in legal and other costs, for families, and for the community. Standard practice involves the house being stripped of anything removable: those who lose their homes are typically angry, especially when they feel that they were preyed upon. Vacant homes quickly deteriorate and trigger a downward spiral in the community: sometimes the vacant house is occupied by squatters; sometimes it becomes a locus for illicit activity. In any case, house prices in the neighborhood fall, and with more home mortgages underwater, there are more foreclosures. Typically, the house is eventually put up to auction, which recovers a fraction of the value of even the diminished market price.

It is understandable why the banks have resisted any form of a writedown of principal—any government program, any voluntary program, and most emphatically, any court program using bankruptcy—using all the political muscle they could muster. Strangely, the design of some of the bank rescues made certain banks even more reluctant to restructure their bad mortgages. The government has become an implicit (in the case of Citibank, explicit) insurer of large losses. This means taxpayers pick up the losses, while the bankers reap all the gains. If the banks don't restructure the mortgages and by some miracle the real estate market recovers, they get the gains; but if the market doesn't recover, and as a result the losses are all the larger, the taxpayers bear them. The Obama administration essentially had given the banks more reason to gamble on resurrection.

Accounting changes made in March 2009 made matters still worse.[37] These changes allowed the banks to continue to hold "impaired" mortgages (loans in which borrowers are "delinquent" in making payments) without banks writing them down, even when the market believed that there was a high probability that they would not be paid off, on the fiction that they would be held to maturity and that if borrowers got over this troubled period the banks would be fully repaid.[38]

Given that banks are reluctant to write down the principal of mortgages, they might have to be induced to do so through a "homeowners' Chapter 11"—a speedy restructuring of liabilities of poorer homeowners, modeled on the kind of relief that is provided for corporations that cannot meet their debt obligations. Chapter 11 is premised on the idea that keeping a firm going is critical for the firm's workers and other stakeholders. The firm's management can propose a corporate reorganization, which the courts review. If the courts find the reorganization to be acceptable, there is a quick discharge of all or part of the debt—the corporation is given a fresh start. Homeowners' Chapter 11 is premised on the idea that giving a fresh start to an American family is just as important as giving one to a corporation. No one gains from forcing homeowners out of their homes.

The United States changed its bankruptcy laws in April 2005 to make it more difficult for homeowners to discharge their debt, indeed more difficult to discharge a debt on a home than other debts, such as on a yacht. As with so many acts passed by the Bush administration, the title of the law signaled what it was not: it was called the Bankruptcy Abuse Prevention and Consumer Protection Act. Up to a quarter of wages could be garnished, and so with wages as low as they are for so many Americans—and especially the poor Americans upon whom the banks preyed—it meant many could be pushed into poverty.[39]

The Obama administration wanted to reverse the harsh 2005 law— but, of course, the banks opposed it, and successfully.[40] The bankers argued that softer bankruptcy laws would lead to more defaults and higher interest rates, little noting that defaults soared after the passage of the new law and that most defaults are not voluntary.[41] Most are a result of a family being hit by a tragedy—an illness or a loss of a job.[42] Another argument that the banks used against reform is that it would be a windfall gain to those who purchased a home on speculation of an increase in house prices. The criticism is a little odd, since everyone in the market was speculating on an increase in real estate prices. The government has been willing, nonetheless, to bail out the banks.

There is an easy way around this problem, one that would make the homeowners' Chapter 11 more fully analogous to corporate Chapter 11, in which the equity owners (shareholders) lose the value of their equity, and the bondholders become the new equity owners. In the case of a home, the homeowner holds the "equity" while the bank is the bondholder. Under the homeowners' Chapter 11, the debt-for-equity swap would entail writing down the value of what the homeowner owed, but, in return, when the house is eventually sold, a large fraction of the capital gain on the house would go to the lender. Those who bought a house mainly to speculate on the capital gain would find such a deal unattractive. (Economists refer to such a provision as a self-selection device.)

With the homeowners' Chapter 11, people wouldn't have to go through the rigamarole of bankruptcy, discharging *all* of their debts. The home would be treated as if it were a separate corporation. This relief should be available for households with income below a critical threshold (say, $150,000) and with non-household, non-retirement wealth below some critical threshold (perhaps dependent on age).[43] The house would be appraised, and the individual's debt would be written down to, say, 90 percent of the level of that appraisal (reflecting the fact that were the lender to proceed with foreclosure, there would be substantial transaction costs).[44]

Low-interest loans

With the 100 percent, variable-rate, teaser-rate, balloon, negative-amortization, and liar loans—all the gimmicks I described earlier in the chapter—many Americans have wound up paying 40 or 50 percent or more of their income every month to the bank.[45] If interest on credit cards is included, the numbers are even higher. Many families struggle to make these payments, sacrificing everything else. But so often, another tragedy—a small one, like a car breaking down, or a big one, like a family illness—puts them over the brink.

The government (through the Federal Reserve) has been lending money to the banks at very low interest rates. Why not use the government's ability to borrow at a low interest rate to provide less-expensive credit to homeowners under stress? Take someone who has a $300,000 mortgage with a 6 percent interest rate. That's $18,000 a year in interest ($0.06 \times \$30,000$), or $1,500 a month, even with no payback of principal. The government can now borrow money at essentially a zero interest rate. If it lends it to the homeowner at 2 percent, payments are cut by two-thirds to $6,000. For someone struggling to get along at twice the poverty rate, around $30,000 a year, that cuts house payments from 60 percent of the *before-tax* income to 20 percent. Where 60 percent is not manageable, 20 percent is. And, apart from the cost of sending out the notices, the government makes a nice $6,000 profit per year on the deal. At $6,000 the homeowner will make the repayment; at $18,000, he or she would not.

Moreover, because the house isn't being forced into foreclosure, real estate prices remain stronger, and the neighborhood is better off. There are advantages all around—except for the banks. The government has an advantage, both in raising funds (because of the almost zero probability of default) and in collecting interest. These factors have provided part of the rationale for government student loan programs and government mortgages; yet conservatives have insisted that the government not engage in these types of financial activities—except in giving money to the bankers. They argue that the government is not good at credit assessment. This line of reasoning should have little weight now: the banks have done so poorly at credit assessment and mortgage design that they've put the entire economy at risk. They did excel at predatory practices, but this is hardly a basis for commendation.

Banks have resisted this initiative too, again for an obvious reason: they don't want competition from the government. But that raises another important advantage: if the banks can't make the "easy" money by exploiting poor Americans, they might go back to the hard business, what they were supposed to be doing all along—lending money to help set up new enterprises and expand old ones.

Expanded homeownership initiatives

Advocates of the reckless subprime mortgages argued that these financial innovations would enable large numbers of Americans to become homeowners for the first time. They did become homeowners—but for a very short time, and at a very high cost. The fraction of Americans who will be homeowners at the end of this episode will be lower than at the beginning.[46] The objective of expanding homeownership is,

I believe, a worthy one, but clearly the market route has not worked well—except for the mortgage brokers and originators and investment bankers who profited from them.

At the current time, there is an argument for helping lower- and middle-income Americans *temporarily* with their housing costs. Over the longer run, there is a question about whether the current allocation of resources to housing, which is distorted to benefit upper-income homeowners, is appropriate. The United States allows mortgage interest and property taxes to be tax-deductible, and in doing so, the government pays a large fraction of the costs of homeownership. In New York, for instance, almost half of the cost of mortgage interest and real estate taxes of upper-income taxpayers is borne by the government. But, ironically, this does not help those who need the help the most.

A simple remedy would convert the current mortgage and property tax deduction into a flat-rate, cashable tax credit. (Even better would be a progressive tax credit, with a higher rate for the poor than the rich.) A uniform tax credit helps everyone the same. Assume the government gave a 25 percent tax credit for mortgage interest payments. That means the family described above, paying $6,000 in mortgage interest payments a year, would have their taxes reduced by $1,500. Currently, the family is likely to get a tax deduction worth about $900. By contrast, a higher-income family would have been given a tax deduction on their $1 million mansion worth $30,000—a gift from the government equal to the poor family's entire income. With a tax credit, the mansion owner's gift from the government would still be large ($15,000), but at least it would be cut in half. The reduction in the subsidy to upper-income Americans could help pay for the subsidy for poorer Americans. A 25 percent tax credit would increase the affordability of housing for many Americans.

Of course, such an initiative would be opposed by upper-income families and construction companies that make their money from building million-dollar homes. So far, these groups have prevailed. But the current system is neither fair nor efficient. It means that the effective price of housing for poor people is actually higher than that for the rich.

New mortgages

The financial sector, for all of its claims at innovation, has not innovated in ways that shift risk from poor Americans to those who are more able to bear the risk. For instance, with variable-rate mortgages, poor Americans struggling to make ends meet don't know what their payments are going to be from month to month. However, even variable-rate mortgages can have fixed payments, if the maturity of the mortgage (the number of years over which it is repaid) is allowed to be variable.

Danish mortgage markets provide an alternative that has worked well for that country for more than two centuries. Default rates are low, and the standardized products ensure strong competition—with low interest rates and low transaction costs. One of the reasons for the low default rate in Denmark is strict regulations—borrowers can borrow at most 80 percent of the value of the house—and the originator has to bear the first losses. America's system gives rise to the risk of negative equity and encourages speculative gambling. The Danish system is designed to prevent negative equity and discourage speculation.[47] There is a high degree of transparency, so those who buy the mortgage bonds have an accurate assessment of the quality of credit assessment by each of the mortgage originators.

The U.S. government has repeatedly had to take the initiative in innovating financial products that meet the needs of ordinary citizens. When they are proven, the private sector often steps in. The current crisis may present another instance where government will have to take the initiative because of the failure of the private sector to do what it should.

Given the private sector's massive lending mistakes, there is little that government can do now to prevent large numbers of mortgages from going underwater, but not all properties with underwater mortgages will go into foreclosure. While there are incentives for default for such properties, individuals care about their reputation. That is why the kinds of programs described in this chapter section may help: if people can stay in their homes and meet their mortgage payments, they will try to do so.

There are other proposals that affect incentives to default. One proposal pushed by the former chairman of President Reagan's Council of Economic Advisers, Martin Feldstein, would exchange, say, 20 percent of the individual's current mortgage for a lower-interest-rate government loan.[48] But the government loan would *not* be a nonrecourse loan; the borrower would still be obliged to repay what he had borrowed from the government. But because he wouldn't (couldn't) walk away on his loan from the government, he also wouldn't walk away on his nonrecourse loan from the bank. This would make defaults less likely. Lenders would be better off—this proposal would, in effect, be giving a large gift to lenders, partly at the expense of homeowners, who have been induced to trade in their nonrecourse loan for a recourse loan. As I noted earlier, having a nonrecourse loan is like having an option—a one-way bet that pays off when house prices rise, without bearing the full risk of a price decline. Converting from a nonrecourse loan to a recourse loan amounts to giving up that option. Most likely, financially unsophisticated borrowers would not understand the market value of the option that they had and would only see the reduced payments. In a sense, the government would be aiding and abetting the bankers in duplicity, unless it informed homeowners of the value of the option.

A slight modification of this proposal would, however, reduce the likelihood of foreclosure and at the same time avoid another unwarranted gift to lenders. The government could encourage lenders to buy back the option at a fair market value (thereby reducing the uncertainty they and the markets face) and encourage households to use (most of) the proceeds to buy down the value of the outstanding mortgage.[49] Take a $300,000 home with a $300,000 mortgage at grave risk of going underwater. The bank would convert $60,000 into a recourse mortgage. Assume the value of the "option" is, say, $10,000. The homeowner would use that to pay off a little of his mortgage. This would make the house more affordable—his interest payments would be reduced by $50 a month. To make the deal still sweeter (for both the bank and the borrower), the government, recognizing the benefits to all from a lower default rate, could take on the $60,000 recourse mortgage, charging 2 percent interest. Combining this with a 25 percent tax credit means

walked away with billions of dollars—even more, as it turned out, through the largesse of Washington. As a system, capitalism can tolerate a high level of inequality, and there is an argument for why the inequality exists: it is the way to motivate people. Giving rewards commensurate with one's contributions to society produces a more efficient economy. But those who were rewarded so well during the housing bubble didn't make society more efficient. For a while, they may have increased bank profits, but those profits were a mirage. Ultimately, they imposed huge costs on people all over the world. Capitalism can't work if private rewards are unrelated to social returns. But that is what happened in late-twentieth-century and early-twenty-first-century American-style financial capitalism.

In this chapter, I detail how two administrations dealt with the financial crisis, what they should have done, and the likely consequences. The full consequences are not yet known. But almost surely, the failures of the Obama and Bush administrations will rank among the most costly mistakes of any modern democratic government at any time.[1] In the United States, the magnitude of guarantees and bailouts approached 80 percent of U.S. GDP, some $12 trillion.[2] Not all of these guarantees will be called upon, so the total cost to the taxpayer will be less. But in addition to the announced sums, hundreds of billions of dollars were in hidden giveaways. The Federal Reserve, for instance, was taking on lower-quality collateral and buying mortgages, financial transactions that would almost surely be very costly to taxpayers, but at the very least exposing taxpayers to high risk. The bailouts have taken on other forms, for instance, lending money to banks at close to zero interest rates, which then can use the money either to gamble or to lend to other firms at much higher interest rates. Many other firms (or individuals) would be grateful for a zero interest rate loan—and could generate profits at least as hefty as those being earned by the "successful" banks. It is a huge gift, but one hidden from the taxpayers.[3]

As the financial crisis broke, the Bush administration decided to bail out the bankers and their shareholders, not just the banks. It provided that money in non-transparent ways—perhaps because it didn't want the public to be fully aware of the gifts that were being given, perhaps because many of those responsible were ex-bankers and non-transparency was their way of doing business.[4] The administration decided against exercising any control over the recipients of massive amounts of taxpayer money, claiming that to do so would interfere with the workings of a free market economy—as if the expensive TARP bailout was consistent with those principles. Those decisions had predictable consequences that would unfold over the ensuing months. Bank executives acted as they are supposed to act in a capitalist system—in their own self-interest—which meant getting as much money for themselves and their shareholders as they could. The Bush and Obama administrations had made a simple mistake—inexcusable given what had occurred in the years prior to the crisis—that the banks' pursuit of their own self-interest was necessarily coincident with what was in the national interest. Public outrage at the abuses of taxpayer money made further help for the banks increasingly difficult—and induced increasingly less transparent and less efficient ways of addressing the problems.

Not surprisingly, the Obama administration didn't bring a really fresh approach. That may have been part of the whole strategy: providing confidence to the market through calmness and continuity. But there was a cost to this strategy. From the start, the administration didn't ask the right questions about the kind of financial system the country wanted and needed, because such questions were uncomfortable, both politically and economically. The bankers didn't want to admit that there was anything *fundamentally* wrong; they hardly wanted to admit failure at all. Nor did the deregulators and the politicians who stood behind them want to admit the failure of the economic doctrines that they had advocated. They wanted to return to the world as it was before 2007, before the crisis, with a little tweaking here and there—they could hardly claim that everything was perfect. But more than that was required. The financial system couldn't, and shouldn't, go back to the way it was before. Real reforms were and are needed—not just cosmetic ones. For instance, the financial system had grown out of proportion. It had to be downsized, but some parts needed downsizing more than others.

The Obama administration may eventually come to the right answer;

it may even be there as this book is published. But the uncertain course followed to date has imposed high costs. The legacy of debt will compromise economic and social programs for years to come. Indeed, within months of the bailouts, the size of the deficit was being used as an excuse for reducing the scale of health care reform. The deficit hawks from the banks went on vacation beginning in the late summer of 2008—when the banks said they needed hundreds of billions of dollars, all worries about the size of the deficit were shunted aside. But as I and others predicted, they returned from their vacation as soon as it became clear that there was no more money to be had; then they went back to their usual stance of opposing spending, no matter how high the returns. (Curiously, when the bailouts were first rolled out, the bankers claimed that the government would make a large return on its "investments," a kind of argument that they had dismissed when it had been made for other forms of social, technology, and infrastructure investments before the crisis. But by now, it is clear that there is little chance that the taxpayers will recover what has been given to the banks and no chance that they will be adequately compensated for the risk borne, in the way that the bankers would have demanded had they given anyone else money.)

How the U.S. Financial System Falls Short

The success of the financial sector is ultimately measured in the well-being that it delivers for ordinary citizens, because either capital is allocated better or risk is managed better. In spite of all the pride about innovation in the bloated financial sector, it is not clear that most of the innovations actually contributed very much to the success of the U.S. economy or the living standards of the vast majority of Americans. In the last chapter, for instance, I discussed the simple task of providing money to people to help them buy homes. The financial sector should have used its ingenuity to devise products that help people manage the risk of homeownership, such as that arising from the variability of interest rates. The denizens of finance were supposed to understand risk—it was one of the reasons why they were so amply rewarded. Remarkably, neither they nor their regulators, who prided themselves in understanding markets and the meaning of risk and efficiency, really did so. They were supposed to transfer risk from those less able to bear it (poor homeowners) to others. Instead, the "innovations" imposed more risk on these homeowners.

This book is replete with examples of what can only be described as "intellectual incoherence": if markets were efficient, *on average*, there would be little gain to a homeowner in moving from a fixed-rate mortgage to a variable-rate one; the only difference would be who bore the risk of the variability. And yet, as we saw, Federal Reserve Chairman Alan Greenspan encouraged people to take out variable-rate mortgages. He simultaneously believed that they were efficient (part of the rationale for why regulation was not needed) and also believed that homeowners could, on average, save money by taking out a variable-rate mortgage. That poor homeowners who didn't understand risk might follow his ill-conceived advice is understandable; that the so-called experts in finance would do so is harder to fathom.

Judging by performance—not the artificial measures of profits and fees, but more relevant measures, ones that assess the contributions of the sector to the economy and the well-being of households—the financial sector failed. (Indeed, even looking at it from the perspective of profitability *in the longer term*—taking into account the huge losses that piled up as the housing bubble broke—it failed.) It wasn't a stroke of genius that led to the liar loans, 100 percent mortgages, or the spread of variable-rate products. These were bad ideas, and ones that many countries banned. They were the result of *not understanding* the fundamentals of markets (including the risks of imperfect and asymmetric information and the nature of market risk itself). They were the result of *forgetting* or *ignoring* the lessons of economic theory and historical experience.

More generally, while it is exceedingly easy to draw a clear link between these innovations and the economic failures, it is hard to point to any clear link, for instance, between "financial-sector innovations" and increased productivity. A small part of the financial system, the venture capital firms—many of which were on the West Coast, not in New York—did play a key role in the country's economic growth by giving capital (and managerial assistance) to many new entrepreneurial companies. Other parts of the financial system—community banks, credit unions, and local banks that supply consumers and small and medium-sized enterprises with the finance they need—have also done a good job.

The big banks that prided themselves in having gone out of the storage (read: lending) business into the moving (read: packaging complex securities and selling them to unwary customers) business were peripheral to the actual job creation. They were interested in the mega-multibillion-dollar deals putting companies together, and when that failed, stripping them apart. While they may not have played a big role in job and enterprise creation, they excelled at job destruction (for others) in the "cost-cutting" efforts that were their signature.

The inadequacies of the financial system go beyond the failures in risk management and capital allocation that led to this crisis. The banks didn't provide services that the poor needed, who had to turn to exploitive pay-day loans and check-cashing services; and they didn't provide the kind of low-cost electronic payment system that the United States should have, given the advances in technology.

There are multiple reasons why the financial system has performed so badly, and we have to understand them if we are to fix things. Previous chapters have called attention to five failings.

First, incentives matter, but there is a systemic mismatch between social and private returns. Unless these are closely aligned, the market system cannot work well. This helps explain why so many of the "innovations" that were the pride of the financial system were steps in the wrong direction.

Second, certain institutions became too big to fail—and very expensive to save. Some of them demonstrated that they are also too large to be managed. As Edward Liddy, who took over the management of AIG after the government bailout, put it, "When I answered the call for help and joined AIG in September 2008, one thing quickly became apparent:

the company's overall structure is too complex, too unwieldy, and too opaque for its component businesses to be well managed as one entity."[5]

Third, the big banks moved away from plain-vanilla banking to securitization. Securitization has some virtues, but it has to be carefully managed—something both those in the financial system and the deregulators didn't understand.[6]

Fourth, commercial banks sought to imitate the high risk–high returns of high finance, but commercial banking should be boring. Those who want to gamble can go to the racetrack or Las Vegas or Atlantic City. There, you know there is a chance you won't get back the money you've put in. When you put your money in the bank, you don't want any risk that it won't be there when you need it. Too many of the commercial bankers seem to have suffered from "hedge fund envy." But hedge funds don't have a government guarantee; the commercial banks do. They are different businesses, and too many of the commercial bankers forgot this.

Fifth, too many bankers forgot that they should be responsible citizens. They shouldn't prey on the poorest and the most vulnerable. Americans trusted that these pillars of the community had a moral conscience. In the greed that gripped the nation, there were no holds barred—including exploiting the weakest in our society.

THE RESCUE THAT WASN'T

As we saw in earlier chapters, bankruptcy is a key feature of capitalism. Firms sometimes are unable to repay what they owe creditors. Financial reorganization has become a fact of life in many industries. The United States is lucky in having a particularly effective way of giving firms a fresh start—Chapter 11 of the bankruptcy code, which has been used repeatedly, for example, by the airlines. Airplanes keep flying; jobs and assets are preserved. Shareholders typically lose everything, and bondholders become the new shareholders. Under new management, and without the burden of debt, the airline can go on. The government plays a limited role in these restructurings: bankruptcy courts make sure that all creditors are treated fairly and that management doesn't steal the assets of the firm for its own benefits.

Banks differ in one respect: the government has a stake because it insures deposits. As we saw in the last chapter, the reason the government insures deposits is to preserve the stability of the financial system, which is important to preserving the stability of the economy. But if a bank gets into trouble, the basic procedure should be the same: shareholders lose everything; bondholders become the new shareholders.[7] Often, the value of the bonds is sufficiently great that that is all that needs to be done. For instance, at the time of the bailout, Citibank, the largest American bank, with assets of $2 trillion, had some $350 billion of long-term bonds. Because there are no obligatory payments with equity, if there had been a debt-to-equity conversion, the bank wouldn't have had to pay the billions and billions of dollars of interest on these bonds. Not having to pay out the billions of dollars of interest puts the bank in much better stead. In such an instance, the role of the government is little different from the oversight role the government plays in the bankruptcy of an ordinary firm.

Sometimes, though, the bank has been so badly managed that what is owed to depositors is greater than the assets of the bank. (This was the case for many of the banks in the savings and loan debacle in the late 1980s and in the current crisis.) Then the government has to come in to honor its commitments to depositors. The government becomes, in effect, the (possibly partial) owner, though typically it tries to sell the bank as soon as it can or find someone to take it over. Because the bankrupt bank has liabilities greater than its assets, the government typically has to pay the acquiring bank to do this, in effect filling the hole in the balance sheet. This process is called conservatorship.[8] Usually the switch in ownership is so seamless that depositors and other customers wouldn't even know that something had happened unless they read about it in the press. Occasionally, when an appropriate suitor can't be found quickly, the government runs the bank for a while. (The opponents of conservatorship tried to tarnish this traditional approach by calling it nationalization. Obama suggested that this wasn't the American way.[9] But he was wrong: conservatorship, including the possibility of temporary government ownership when all else failed, was the traditional approach; the massive government gifts to banks were what was unprecedented.[10] Since even the banks that were taken over by the government were always eventually sold, some suggested that the process be called preprivatization.)

Long experience has taught that when banks are at risk of failure, their managers engage in behaviors that risk taxpayers losing even more money. The banks may, for instance, undertake big bets: if they win, they keep the proceeds; if they lose, so what? They would have died anyway. That's why there are laws saying that when a bank's capital is low, it should be shut down or put under conservatorship. Bank regulators don't wait until all of the money is gone. They want to be sure that when a depositor puts his debit card into the ATM and it says, "insufficient funds," it's because there are insufficient funds in the account, not insufficient funds in the bank. When the regulators see that a bank has too little money, they put the bank on notice to get more capital, and if it can't, they take further action of the kind just described.[11]

As the crisis of 2008 gained momentum, the government should have played by the rules of capitalism and forced a financial reorganization. *Financial reorganizations—giving a fresh start—are not the end of the world.*[12] Indeed, they might represent the beginning of a new world, one in which incentives are better aligned and in which lending is rekindled. Had the government forced a financial restructuring of the banks in the way just described, there would have been little need for taxpayer money, or even further government involvement. Such a conversion *increases* the overall value of the firm because it reduces the likelihood of bankruptcy, thereby not only saving the high transaction costs of going through bankruptcy but also preserving the value of the ongoing concern. That means that if the shareholders are wiped out and the bondholders become the new "owners," the bondholders' long-term prospects are better than they were while the bank remained in limbo, when they were not sure whether it would survive and not sure of either the size or the terms of any government handout.[13]

The bondholders involved in a restructuring would have gotten another gift, at least according to the banks' own logic. The bankers claimed that the market was underestimating the true value of the mortgages on their books (and other bank assets). That may have been the case—or it may not have been. If it is not, it is totally unreasonable to make taxpayers bear the cost of the banks' mistake, but if the assets were really worth as much as the bankers said, then the bondholders would get the upside.

The Obama administration has argued that the big banks are not only too big to fail but also too big to be financially restructured (or, as I refer to it later, "too big to be resolved"), too big to play by the ordinary rules of capitalism. Being too big to be financially restructured means that if the bank is on the brink of failure, there is but one source of money: the taxpayer. And under this novel and unproven doctrine, hundreds of billions have been poured into the financial system. If it is true that America's biggest banks are too big to be "resolved," this has profound implications for our banking system going forward—implications the administration so far has refused to own up to. If, for instance, bondholders are in effect guaranteed because these institutions are too big to be financially restructured, then the market economy can exert no effective discipline on the banks. They get access to cheaper capital than they should, because those providing the capital know that the taxpayers will pick up any losses. If the government is providing a guarantee, whether explicit or implicit, the banks aren't bearing all the risks associated with each decision they make—the risks borne by markets (shareholders, bondholders) are less than those borne by society as a whole, and so resources will go in the wrong place. Because too-big-to-be-restructured banks have access to funds at lower interest rates than they should, the whole capital market is distorted. They grow at the expense of their smaller rivals, who do not have this guarantee. They can easily come to dominate the financial system, not through greater prowess and ingenuity but because of the tacit government support. It should be clear: these too-big-to-be-restructured banks cannot operate as ordinary market-based banks.

I actually think that all of this discussion about too-big-to-be-restructured banks was just a ruse. It was a ploy that worked, based on fear-mongering. Just as Bush used 9/11 and the fears of terrorism to justify so much of what he did, the Treasury under both Bush and Obama used 9/15—the day that Lehman collapsed—and the fears of another meltdown as a tool to extract as much as possible for the banks and the bankers that had brought the world to the brink of economic ruin.

The argument is that, if only the Fed and Treasury had rescued Lehman Brothers, the whole crisis would have been avoided. The implication—seemingly taken on board by the Obama administration—is, when in doubt, bail out, and massively so. To skimp is to be penny wise and pound foolish.

But that is the wrong lesson to learn from the Lehman episode.[14] The notion that if only Lehman Brothers had been rescued all would have been fine is sheer nonsense. Lehman Brothers was a consequence, not a cause: it was the consequence of flawed lending practices and inadequate oversight by regulators. Whether Lehman Brothers had or had not been bailed out, the global economy was headed for difficulties. Prior to the crisis, as I have noted, the global economy had been supported by the bubble and excessive borrowing. That game is over—and was already over well before Lehman's collapse. The collapse almost surely accelerated the whole process of deleveraging; it brought out into the open the long-festering problems, the fact that the banks didn't know their net worth and knew that accordingly they couldn't know that of any other firm to whom they might lend.[15] A more orderly process would have imposed fewer costs in the short run, but "counterfactual history" is always problematic. There are those who believe that it is better to take one's medicine and be done with it, that a slow unwinding of the excesses would last years longer, with even greater costs. Perhaps, on the other hand, the slow recapitalization of the banks would have occurred faster than the losses would have become apparent. In this view, papering over the losses with dishonest accounting (as in this crisis, as well as in the savings and loan debacle of the 1980s) would be doing more than just providing symptomatic relief. Lowering the fever may actually help in the recovery. A third view holds that Lehman's collapse actually saved the entire financial system: without it, it would have been difficult to galvanize the political support required to bail out the banks. (It was hard enough to do so after its collapse.)

Even if one agrees that letting Lehman Brothers fail was a mistake, there are many choices between the blank-check approach to saving the banks pursued by the Bush and Obama administrations after September 15 and the approach of Hank Paulson, Ben Bernanke, and Tim Geithner of simply shutting down Lehman Brothers and praying that everything will work out in the end.

The government was obligated to save depositors, but that didn't mean it had to provide taxpayer money to also save bondholders and shareholders. As noted earlier, standard procedures would have meant that the institution be saved and the shareholders wiped out, with the bondholders becoming the new shareholders. Lehman had no insured depositors; it was an investment bank. But it had something almost equivalent—it borrowed short-term money from the "market" through commercial paper held by money market funds, which acted much like banks. (One can even write checks on these accounts.) That's why the part of the financial system involving money markets and investment banks is often called the shadow banking system. It arose, in part, to circumvent the regulations imposed on the real banking system—to ensure its safety and stability. Lehman's collapse induced a run on the shadow banking system, much as there used to be runs on the real banking system before deposit insurance was provided; to stop the run, the government provided insurance to the shadow banking system.

Those opposed to financial restructuring (conservatorship) for the banks that are in trouble say that if the bondholders are not *fully* protected, a bank's remaining creditors—those providing short-term funds without a government guarantee—will flee if a restructuring appears imminent. But such a conclusion defies economic logic. If these creditors are rational, they would realize that they benefit enormously from the greater stability of the firm provided by conservatorship and the debt-to-equity conversion. If they were willing to keep their funds in the bank before, they should be even more willing to do so now. And if the government has no confidence in the rationality of these supposedly smart financiers, it could provide them a guarantee, though it should charge a premium for the guarantee. In the end, the Bush and Obama administrations not only bailed out the shareholders but also provided guarantees. The guarantees effectively eviscerated the argument for the generous treatment of shareholders and long-term bondholders.

Under financial restructuring, there are two big losers. The executives of the banks will almost surely go, and they will be unhappy. The shareholders too will be unhappy, because they will have lost everything. But that is the nature of risk-taking in capitalism—the only justification for the above-normal returns that they enjoyed during the boom is the risk of a loss.[16]

THE INITIAL EFFORTS OF RESCUING A FAILING FINANCIAL SYSTEM

The U.S. government should have played by the rules and "restructured" the banks that needed rescuing, rather than providing them with unwarranted handouts. This is so, whether or not in the end some of the banks manage to pay back the money that was given to them. But both the Bush and the Obama administrations decided otherwise.

As the crisis broke out in late 2007 and early 2008, the Bush administration and the Fed first veered from bailout to bailout with no discernible plan or principles. This added political uncertainty to the economic uncertainty. In some of the bailouts (Bear Stearns), shareholders got something, and bondholders were fully protected. In others (Fannie Mae), shareholders lost everything, and bondholders were fully protected. In still others (Washington Mutual), shareholders and bondholders lost nearly everything. In the case of Fannie Mae, political considerations (worrying about earning the disfavor of China—as a significant owner of Fannie Mae bonds) seemed to predominate; no other good economic rationale was ever presented.[17] Though there was often some reference to "systemic risk" in explaining why some institutions got bailed out and others didn't, it was clear that the Fed and the Treasury had insufficient appreciation of what systemic risk meant before the crisis, and their understanding remained limited even as the crisis evolved.

Some of the early bailouts were done through the Federal Reserve, leading that body to take actions that were totally unimaginable just a few months before. The Fed's responsibility is mainly to commercial banks. It regulates them, and the government provides deposit insurance. Before the crisis, it was argued that investment banks didn't need either access to funds from the Fed or the same kind of tight regulation, since they didn't pose any systemic risk. They handled rich people's money, and they could protect themselves. But all of a sudden, in the most munificent act in the history of corporate welfare, the government's safety net was extended to investment banks. Then, it was extended even farther, to AIG, an insurance firm.

Eventually, by late September 2008, it became clear that more than these "hidden" bailouts through the Fed would be required, and President Bush had to go to Congress. Treasury Secretary Paulson's original idea for getting money into the banks was referred to by its critics as "cash for trash." The government would buy the toxic assets, under the Troubled Asset Relief Program (TARP), injecting liquidity and cleaning up the banks' balance sheets at the same time. Of course, the bankers didn't really believe that the government had a comparative advantage in garbage disposal. The reason they wanted to dump the toxic assets on the government was that they hoped the government would overpay—a hidden recapitalization of the banks.

The real tip-off that something was awry came when Paulson went to Congress and presented a three-page TARP bill giving him a blank check for $700 billion, with no congressional oversight or judicial review. As chief economist of the World Bank, I had seen gambits of this kind. If this had happened in a Third World banana republic, we would know what was about to happen—a massive redistribution from the taxpayers to the banks and their friends. The World Bank would have threatened cutting off all assistance. We could not condone public money being used in this way, without the normal checks and balances. Indeed, many conservative commentators argued that what Paulson was proposing was unconstitutional. Congress, they believed, could not walk away so easily from its responsibilities in allocating these funds.

Some Wall Streeters complained that the media was souring the mood by calling it a bailout. They preferred more upbeat euphemisms, a "recovery program" rather than a "bailout." Paulson transformed the toxic assets into the gentler-sounding "troubled assets." His successor, Tim Geithner, would later convert them into "legacy assets."

On the initial vote, on September 29, 2008, the TARP bill was defeated by twenty-three votes in the House of Representatives. After the defeat, the Bush administration held an auction. It asked, in effect, each of the opposing congressmen how much they needed in gifts to their districts and constituents to change their vote. Thirty-two Democrats and twenty-six Republicans who voted no on the original bill switched sides to support TARP in the revised bill, passed on October 3, 2008. The congressmen's change of vote was prompted in part by fears of a global economic meltdown and by provisions ensuring better oversight, but, for at least many of the congressmen who had changed their votes, there was a clear quid pro quo: the revised bill contained $150 billion in special tax provisions for their constituents.[18] No one said that members of Congress could be bought cheaply.[19]

Naturally, Wall Street was delighted with the program to buy the bad assets. Who wouldn't want to offload their junk to the government at inflated prices? The banks could have sold many of these assets on the open market at the time but not at prices they would have liked. There were, of course, other assets that the private sector wouldn't touch. Some of the so-called assets were actually liabilities that could explode, eating up government funds like Pacman. For example, on September 15, 2008, AIG said that it was short $20 billion. The next day, its losses had grown to some $89 billion. A little later, when no one was looking, there was a further handout, bringing the total to $150 billion. Still later, the handout was increased to $180 billion. When the government took over AIG (it took just short of an 80 percent share), it may have gotten some assets, but amidst these assets were even bigger liabilities.

Ultimately, Paulson's original proposal was thoroughly discredited, as the difficulties of pricing and buying thousands of individual assets became apparent. Pressure from those not wanting to overpay the banks was, moreover, brought to bear to set prices for the toxic assets through a transparent auction mechanism. It soon became apparent, however, that auctioning off thousands of separate categories of assets would be a nightmare. Time was of the essence, and it couldn't be done quickly. Besides, if the auction was fair, the prices might not be so high, leaving the banks with a big hole in their balance sheet. After vigorously defending the proposal as the best way forward for weeks, Paulson suddenly dropped it in mid-October 2008 and moved on to his next plan.

The next proposal was an "equity injection." There were several reasons why it was thought to be important to give more equity to banks, to recapitalize them. One was the hope that by doing so they would lend more. The other was a lesson from the 1980s: undercapitalized banks are a risk to the economy.

Three decades ago, savings and loan associations faced a problem similar to that confronting the banks today. When interest rates were suddenly raised to fight inflation in the late 1970s and early 1980s, the value of the mortgages held by the savings and loan banks plummeted. But the banks had financed these mortgages with deposits. With what they owed depositors remaining the same and the value of their assets much diminished, the savings and loans were, in any real sense, bankrupt.

Accounting rules, however, allowed them to forestall the day of reckoning. They didn't have to write down the value of the mortgages to reflect the new realities. They did, however, have to pay higher interest rates to their depositors than they were getting from their mortgages, so many had a serious cash-flow problem. Some tried to solve the cash-flow problem by continuing to grow—a kind of Ponzi scheme in which new deposits helped pay what was owed on old deposits. So long as no one blew the whistle, everything was fine. President Reagan helped them along by softening accounting standards even more, allowing them to count as an asset their "goodwill," the mere prospect of their future profits, and by loosening regulations.

The savings and loans were zombies—dead banks that remained among the living. They had an incentive to engage in what Boston College professor Ed Kane called "gambling on resurrection."[20] If they behaved prudently, there was no way they could crawl out of the hole they had dug, but if they took big risks and the gambles paid off, they might finally become solvent. If the gambles didn't work out, it didn't matter. They couldn't be *more* dead than they already were.[21] Allowing the zombie banks to continue to operate and loosening regulations so they could take bigger risks increased the eventual cost of cleaning up the mess.[22]

(There is a fine line between "gambling," or excessive risk-taking, and fraud, so it is no accident that the 1980s was marked by one banking scandal after another. It is, perhaps, no surprise that in the current crisis we have again seen so much of both.)

The advocates of the proposal for equity injections (including myself) had wrongly assumed that it would be done right—taxpayers would receive fair value for the equity, and appropriate controls would be placed on the banks. Cash *was* poured in to protect them, and when they needed more money, more cash was poured in. In return taxpayers got preferred shares and a few warrants (rights to purchase the shares), but they were cheated in the deal. If we contrast the terms that the American taxpayers got with what Warren Buffett got, at almost the same time, in a deal with Goldman Sachs,[23] or if we compare it with the terms that the British government got when it provided funds to its banks, it was clear that U.S. taxpayers got shortchanged. If those negotiating supposedly on behalf of Americans had been working on a similar deal on Wall Street, they would have demanded far better terms.

Worse still, even as taxpayers became the principal "owner" of some banks, the Bush (and later Obama) Treasuries refused to exercise any control.[24] The U.S. taxpayer put out hundreds of billions of dollars and didn't even get the right to know what the money was being spent on, let alone have any say in what the banks did with it. This too was markedly different from the contemporaneous U.K. bank bailouts, where there was at least a semblance of accountability: old management was thrown out, restrictions on dividends and compensation were imposed, and systems designed to encourage lending were put into place.[25]

In contrast, U.S. banks carried on paying out dividends and bonuses and didn't even pretend to resume lending. "Make more loans?" John C. Hope III, the chairman of Whitney National Bank in New Orleans, told a room full of Wall Street analysts in early 2009. "We're not going to change our business model or our credit policies to accommodate the needs of the public sector as they see it to have us make more loans."[26]

Wall Street kept pushing for better and better terms—making it less and less likely that taxpayers would be adequately compensated for the risk they were bearing, even if some of the banks did manage to pay back what they received. One of the benefits to come out of Paulson's initial brazen demand that there be no oversight or judicial review of his $700 billion blank check to Wall Street was that Congress established an independent oversight panel, and it showed how bad the bailout deals were for the American taxpayers. In the first set of bailouts, *at the time*, taxpayers got back only sixty-six cents in securities for every dollar they gave the banks. But in the later deals, and especially the deals with Citibank and AIG, the terms were even worse, with forty-one cents for every dollar given.[27] In March 2009, the Congressional Budget Office (CBO), the nonpartisan office that is supposed to give independent cost evaluations of government programs, estimated that the net cost of using the TARP's full $700 billion will total $356 billion.[28] The government would get paid back about 50 cents on the dollar. There was no hope for being compensated for the risk borne. In June 2009, in a closer look at the initial $369 billion of TARP spending, the CBO put the estimated loss at over $159 billion.[29]

There was a high level of disingenuousness in the whole bank bailout gambit. The banks (and the regulators who had allowed the whole problem to arise) wanted to pretend that the crisis was just a matter of confidence and a lack of liquidity. A lack of liquidity meant that no one was willing to lend to them. The banks wanted to believe that they had not made bad decisions, that they were really *solvent*, and that the "true" value of their assets exceeded the value of what they owed (their liabilities). But while each believed that about themselves, they didn't believe it about the other banks, as can be seen from their reluctance to lend to each other.

The problem with America's banks was not just a lack of liquidity.[30] Years of reckless behavior, including bad lending and gambling with derivatives, had left some, perhaps many, effectively bankrupt. Years of non-transparent accounting and complex products designed to deceive regulators and investors had taken their toll: now not even the banks knew their own balance sheet. If they didn't know whether they were really solvent, how could they know the solvency of anybody to whom they might lend?

Unfortunately, confidence can't be restored just by giving speeches expressing confidence in the American economy. Repeated pronouncements, for instance, by the Bush administration and the banks that the economy was on solid ground, with strong fundamentals, were belied by recurrent bad news. What they said was simply not credible. Actions are what matters, and the actions of the Fed and Treasury undermined confidence.

By October 2009, the International Monetary Fund (IMF) reported that global losses in the banking sector were $3.6 trillion.[31] The banks had admitted to losses of a much smaller amount. The rest was a kind of dark matter. Everyone knew it was in the system, but no one knew where it was.

When Paulson's plan failed either to rekindle lending or to restore confidence in the banks, the Obama administration floundered over what to replace it with. After flailing around for weeks, in March 2009 the Obama administration announced a new program, the Public-Private Investment Program (PPIP), which would use $75 to $100 billion in TARP capital, plus capital from private investors, to buy toxic assets from banks.[32] The words used were deceptive: it was described as a partnership, but it was not a normal partnership. The government would put in up to 92 percent of the money but get only half the profits and bear almost all of the losses. The government would lend the private sector (hedge funds, investment funds, or even, ironically, banks— which might buy up the assets from each other)[33] most of the money it had to put up, with nonrecourse loans, secured only by what was purchased. If the security or mortgage turns out to be worth less than the amount borrowed, the borrower defaults, leaving the government, not the private investors, to absorb the brunt of any losses.

In effect, the Obama team had finally settled on a slight variation of the original cash-for-trash idea. It was as if it had decided to use a private garbage-hauling service, which would buy the garbage in bulk, sort through it, pick out anything of value, and dump the remaining junk on the taxpayer. And the program was designed to give the garbage collectors hefty profits—only certain members of the Wall Street club would be allowed to "compete," after having been carefully selected by the Treasury. One could be sure that these financiers who had been so successful in squeezing money out of the economy would not be performing these duties out of civic-mindedness, *gratis.*

The administration tried to claim that the PPIP was necessary to provide liquidity to the market. Lack of liquidity, it argued, was depressing prices and artificially hurting banks' balance sheets. The main problem, however, was not a lack of liquidity. If it were, then a far simpler program would work: just provide the funds without loan guarantees. The real issue is that the banks made bad loans in a bubble and were highly leveraged. They had lost their capital, and this capital had to be replaced.

The administration tried to pretend that its plan was based on letting the market determine the prices of the banks' "toxic assets"—including outstanding house loans and securities based on those loans—as the "Partnership" bought up the assets. The magic of the market was being used to accomplish "price discovery." The reality, though, was that the market was not pricing the toxic assets themselves, but options on those assets, basically a one-sided bet. The two have little to do with each other. The private partnerships gained a great deal on the "good" mortgages, but essentially handed the losses on the bad mortgages over to the government.

Consider an asset that has a 50-50 chance of being worth either zero or $200 in a year's time. The average "value" of the asset is $100. Without interest, this is what the asset would sell for in a competitive market. It is what the asset is "worth." Assume that one of the public-private partnerships the Treasury has promised to create is willing to pay $150 for the asset. That's 50 percent more than its true value, and the bank is more than happy to sell. So the private partner puts up $12, and the government supplies the remaining 92 percent of the cost— $12 in "equity" plus $126 in the form of a guaranteed loan.

If, in a year's time, it turns out that the true value of the asset is zero, the private partner loses the $12, and the government loses $138. If the true value is $200, the government and the private partner split the $74 that's left over after paying back the $126 loan. In that rosy scenario, the private partner more than triples his $12 investment. But the taxpayer, having risked $138, gains a mere $37.

Making matters worse, there is ample opportunity for "gaming." Assume the bank buys its own asset for $300 (the administration didn't preclude the partnerships from including the banks), putting up $24. In the bad state, the bank "loses" $24 on its "partnership" investment, but still keeps the $300. In the good state, the asset is still worth only $200, so again the government swallows the loss, except for the $24. The bank has miraculously parlayed a risky asset whose true value is $100 into a safe asset—to it—worth a net $276. The government losses make up the difference—a whopping $176 on average. With so much money being thrown around, there is plenty of room for a deal; one can give a share to the hedge funds. One doesn't have to be greedy.

But Americans may lose even more than these calculations suggest because of an effect called adverse selection. The banks get to choose the loans and securities that they want to sell. They will want to sell the worst assets and especially the assets that they think the market overestimates (and thus is willing to pay too much for). But the market is likely to recognize this, which will drive down the price that it is willing to pay. Only the government's picking up enough of the losses overcomes this "adverse selection" effect. With the government absorbing the losses, the market doesn't care if the banks are "cheating" them by selling their lousiest assets.

At first, the bankers and the potential partners (hedge funds and other financial companies) loved this idea. The banks only sell the assets that they want to sell—they can't lose. The private partners would make a wad of money, especially if the government charged little enough for the guarantees. Politicians loved the idea too: there was a chance they would be out of Washington before all the bills came due. But that's precisely the problem with this approach: no one will know for years what it will do to the government's balance sheet.

Eventually, many of the banks and private partners became disillusioned. They worried that if they made too much money, the bureaucrats and the public wouldn't let them get away with it and would find some way of recouping the profits. At the very least, the participants knew they would be subject to intense congressional scrutiny—in the way that those that received TARP money had been. When accounting regulations were changed to allow banks not to write down their impaired assets—to pretend that the toxic mortgages were as good as gold—the attractiveness diminished still further: even if they got more than the asset was worth, they would have to recognize a loss, which would require finding more capital. They would prefer to postpone the day of reckoning.

The proposal was described by some in the financial markets as a win-win-win proposal. Actually, it was a win-win-lose proposal: the banks win, investors win—and, if the program works for the banks, taxpayers lose. As one hedge fund manager wrote to me, "This is a terrible deal for the taxpayer, but I'm going to make sure that my clients get the full benefit."

So, given all these flaws, what was the appeal of the administration's strategy? The PPIP was the kind of Rube Goldberg device that Wall Street loves—clever, complex, and non-transparent, allowing huge transfers of wealth to the financial markets. It might allow the administration to avoid going back to Congress to ask for more money to fix the banks, and it provided a way to avoid conservatorship.

In the many months since the proposal was rolled out, it has not worked as the administration had hoped. Within a few months, this program for taking over "legacy" loans, like so many of the other programs, was abandoned, and the program for legacy securities was vastly downsized. The most likely outcome was that whatever limited benefits the remaining PPIP for securities would bring would come with a high price. Money that might better have gone to the banks would go to the private "partners"—a high price to pay for a private garbage-removal service.[34]

Why the rescue plans were doomed to fail

The unbelievably expensive bailout failed in one of its main objectives—restarting lending.[35] Underlying this and the other failures of the program were a few elementary economic principles.

The first is *conservation of matter*. When the government buys a toxic asset, the losses don't disappear. Nor do they disappear when the government insures the losses of, say, Citibank. They simply move from Citibank's balance sheet to the government's balance sheet. This means the real battle is about *distribution*: who bears the losses? Will it be shifted away from the financial sector onto the public? In a zero-sum world—where the gains of one party are at the expense of another—a better deal for the banks' shareholders or bondholders means a worse deal for the taxpayers. This was the key problem with programs that involved buying the banks' toxic assets, whether singly or in bulk: pay too much and the government will suffer huge losses; pay too little and the hole left in banks' balance sheet will appear enormous.

The discussion of toxic assets was further confused by the metaphors used to describe it. The government had to "clean up" the banks' balance sheets, by helping them rid themselves of the toxic assets, suggesting that a toxic mortgage was akin to a rotten apple—it would contaminate everything else around it. But a toxic asset was just an asset on which the bank had made a loss—it wasn't infected with a contagious disease.

A principle borrowed from environmental economics, called *polluter pays*, offers guidance on who should pay: it is not just a matter of equity but also a matter of efficiency. American banks have polluted the global economy with toxic waste, and it is a matter of equity and efficiency—and of playing by the rules—that they must be forced, now or later, to pay the price of the cleanup, perhaps in the form of taxes. This is not the first time that American banks have been bailed out. It has happened repeatedly. The implication is that, in effect, the rest of the economy is heavily subsidizing this sector.

Imposing taxes on the banks (like taxing any "bad" externality) can generate revenues at the same time that it improves economic efficiency; it makes much more sense to impose such taxes than to tax good things like savings and work. And it is reasonably easy to design such taxes. The banks argue that imposing these costs on them will inhibit their ability to attract private capital and the restoration of the financial system to health. They have again used the fear tactic: even discussions of doing so would be harmful. The point is that not imposing such costs on them distorts the economy. Moreover, if the government has to provide temporarily additional financing because of a reluctance of the private sector to do so, it is not the worst thing in the world, provided it gets adequate claims (bonds or shares) on the banks' future value: private-sector investors have not done an exemplary job of "exercising discipline." Furthermore, eventually the economy will recover, and with the recovery, these assets will likely yield good returns.

While moving losses around the economy can be close to a zero-sum game, if it isn't done well it can be a very negative-sum game, with the losses to the taxpayers greater than the benefits to the banks' shareholders. Incentives, as I have repeatedly noted, matter. Bailouts inevitably distort incentives. Lenders, knowing that they may be saved from bearing the full consequences of their mistakes, do a poorer job at credit assessment and undertake riskier loans. This is the problem of moral hazard to which I have referred repeatedly. The fear that each bailout would increase the likelihood of another seems to have been borne out—and we have now had the "mother of all bailouts." But the way the government did the bailouts also increased the distortions—and in ways that may have made the downturn worse. For instance, a bank (like Citibank) that has losses insured by the government has little incentive to renegotiate mortgages. If it postpones dealing with the problem, there is a chance—admittedly slim—that the value of the mortgages will recover, and it will keep all the profits. If, as a result of delay, the losses are all the greater, the government bears the costs.

Failure to pay attention to incentives was costly in another way. The banks and their officers had incentives to take the government money and pay out as much as they could as dividends and bonuses. Of course, they knew that the intent of the money was to recapitalize the banks to enable them to lend; they were not being bailed out because of taxpayers' love of bankers. They knew too that using this money in this way would make the banks weaker and incur the public's wrath. But, as the old saw has it, a bird in the hand is worth two in the bush; they knew that there was more than a little chance that their banks wouldn't survive. Their interests deviated not only from that of the economy as a whole but also from that of an increasingly important "funder," the U.S.

taxpayer. But the Bush and Obama administrations decided to ignore this conflict of interest and imposed little control over how the money was used.

There is another key principle of economics: *be forward looking; let bygones be bygones*. Instead of trying to save the existing banks, which had thoroughly demonstrated their incompetence, the government could have given the $700 billion to the few healthy and well-managed banks or even used it to establish a set of new banks. At a modest 12-to-1 leverage, that would have generated $8.4 trillion of new credit—more than enough for the economy's needs. Even if the administrations had not done something so dramatic, they might have used some of the money for creating new lending facilities and some to absorb some of the uncertainty of new loans by providing partial guarantees. It would have made a great deal of sense to tailor the partial guarantees to the economic conditions—providing more help if the economy stays in recession, something for which no firm can be blamed.[36] A forward-looking more innovative strategy would have led to more lending at lower cost to the public than the U.S. strategy of either buying existing bad assets or giving more money to banks that had proved their incompetence in risk and credit assessment—and hoping that they would start lending, and praying that they would do a better job after the crisis than they had done before.

Another principle is analogous to one I discussed in chapter 3 on the design of the stimulus: money should be *targeted*, going to where it will most stimulate the economy. *If the government had no budget constraints, it could have thrown money at the banks recklessly.* In that case, the task of recapitalizing the banks would have been easy. With limited funds, one wants to make sure that every dollar that is spent is spent well. One of the reasons why TARP may not have resulted in the increased lending that was hoped for was that the government was giving much of the money to the big banks, and to a large extent, these banks years ago had shifted much of their focus away from lending to small and medium-sized businesses. If the goal was to encourage job creation—or even job preservation—we would have wanted more credit to be available to these firms, because they are the source of most job creation; if we had wanted more credit to go to small and medium-sized enterprises, we would have channeled the money to small banks and community banks.

Instead, the government lavished money on the big financial institutions that had made the biggest mistakes—some of whom didn't do much or any lending. The AIG bailout was particularly foolish. There was a worry that if one didn't bail out AIG, there would be problems with some of the firms to which it had sold credit default swaps, which were like insurance policies written on the demise of particular corporations. But throwing money at AIG was a poor way of getting money to where it made a difference. Both administrations were using a variant of trickle-down economics: throw enough money at AIG, and some of it will trickle down to where it's needed. Perhaps, but it's a very costly way of doing business. When the data on where the AIG money went finally became available, it was clear that little of it went to systemically significant institutions—though that was the argument put forward in its defense.[37]

Similarly, there was worry, for instance, that if the government does not bail out all creditors, some insurance and pension funds would experience significant losses.[38] They were being put forward as "socially worthy" claimants. The funds that might trickle down to these private claimants are funds that would be better used to strengthen the Social Security system, avoiding deeper cutbacks there. To which should we give greater weight, those with whom we have made a social contract, or those who have made bad investment decisions? If we need to rescue pension funds and insurance companies, then we should do so directly, where every dollar of government money goes directly to the group that needs it. There is no justification for spending twenty dollars to bail out investors so that one dollar can go to a pension fund that might otherwise be in trouble.

A final principle that should have guided the bailouts is again similar to that for a well-designed stimulus: *the bailout should help restructure the financial system to make it better serve the functions that it is supposed to serve.* I have repeatedly noted that the bailout has failed to do this;

the money went disproportionately not to those parts of the financial system that were promoting, say, new enterprises or expanding small and medium-sized businesses. I have noted too that the bailout was conducted in such a way as to lead to a more concentrated financial sector, worsening the problems of too-big-to-fail and too-big-to-be-resolved.

This bailout and the repeated bailouts of the 1980s, 1990s, and the early years of this decade have sent a strong signal to the banks not to worry about bad lending, as the government will pick up the pieces. The bailouts do exactly the opposite of what should be done: enforcing appropriate discipline on the banks, rewarding those that had been prudent, and letting fail those that had taken extraordinary risk. The banks that did the worst in risk management got the biggest gifts from the government.

In the name of maintaining free market economics, what the government was creating was far from a true market. While the Obama administration had avoided the conservatorship route, what it did was far worse than nationalization: it is ersatz capitalism, the privatizing of gains and the socializing of losses. The perception, and reality, that the rescue packages were "unfair"—unfairly generous to the bankers, unfairly costly to ordinary citizens—has made dealing with the crisis all the more difficult. It has become commonplace to say that underlying the crisis is the loss of confidence in the financial system. But the failure of government to undertake a fair rescue contributed to a loss of confidence in government.

The government response has set the economy on a path to recovery that will be slower and more difficult than need be. Of course, things are far better than if the opposite tactic—do nothing—had been taken. That course might have pushed the nation over the precipice into depression.

If nothing untoward happens—and there are many problems looming on the horizon, such as in commercial real estate—the banks will recapitalize themselves gradually. With the Fed keeping interest rates near zero, and with competition in banking so limited, the banks can make hefty profits by charging high interest rates even on limited lending. But this will discourage firms from expanding and from hiring new workers. The optimistic scenario is that this recapitalization proceeds faster than the troubles mount. We will have muddled through.

THE FEDERAL RESERVE

No discussion of the financial bailout would be complete without mention of the Federal Reserve. It was a partner in most of the bailouts I have just described. To save the bankers and their shareholders, as well as to stimulate the economy, not only had the United States engaged in massive spending, but also the Fed more than doubled its balance sheet (a measure of its lending) in the span of a few months, from $942 billion in early September 2008 to over $2.2 trillion in early December 2008.[39]

As the crisis unfolded, Alan Greenspan went from being the hero who had brought on the "Great Moderation," the long period of almost stable growth during the eighteen years of his reign, to villain. Public opinion has been gentler with his successor, Ben Bernanke. In August 2009, when President Obama announced that he would reappoint Bernanke for a second term as chairman of the Fed, he triumphed Bernanke's role in saving the financial system from brink of ruin. Not surprisingly, he did not note Bernanke's role in bringing it to that brink. As I noted in chapter 1, Bernanke kept the bubble going. The "Greenspan put"—assuring the market that if anything went wrong, the Fed would bail it out—was replaced by the "Bernanke put." This assurance had contributed to the bubble and the excessive risk-taking. And when the bubble broke, Bernanke honored his pledge.

At the first signs of problems, in the summer of 2007, the Fed and the European Central Bank provided massive liquidity to the market: in the first two weeks of August, the European Central Bank made injections of around $274 billion, and the Fed injected $38 billion in early August 2007.[40] The Fed, then, was also an active participant in the subsequent bailouts. It extended the "lender of last resort" facility to the investment banks.[41] It had, in effect, done nothing to stop them from undertaking risks to prevent the conflagration, suggesting they didn't represent any systemic effect, but when the fire started, the Fed hardly hesitated in putting billions of dollars of taxpayer money at risk.[42] (If the Fed thought that it didn't have authority to regulate the investment banks, if they were systemically important, it should have gone to Congress and asked for this authority. But its failure to ask for such regulatory authority was hardly surprising: the Fed had bought into the deregulatory philosophy.)

Traditionally, the Fed buys and sells T-bills, short-term government bonds. When it buys the bonds, it injects money into the economy, and that normally leads to lower interest rates. When it sells the bonds, just the opposite happens. There is no risk that the bonds will go bad—they are as safe as the U.S. government. The Fed also lends directly to banks, and by giving them money, it allows them to lend to others. But when the Fed lends to a bank, it normally demands collateral—T-bills. The Fed is thus not a bank in the usual sense—it does not assess creditworthiness, though as a bank regulator, it is supposed to shut down banks that are at risk of not repaying depositors or force them to come up with the requisite capital. The Fed is called the lender of last resort because sometimes banks that are "solvent" lack liquidity; they may not be able to get cash when they need it. The Fed provides that liquidity.

As the crisis unfolded, the Fed flooded the market with liquidity. In doing so, it pushed interest rates down to zero. Its intention was to prevent matters from getting worse, to ensure that the financial system didn't collapse. But, not surprisingly, the lower interest rates did not reignite the economy. Companies weren't going to start investing just because they could get money more cheaply. But another problem emerged: giving the banks all this money didn't result in their lending more. They simply held on to their money. They needed the liquidity, and this was no time to go out making loans.[43]

With lending frozen, the Fed took on a new role—it went from being a lender of last resort to being a lender of first resort. Large companies often get much of their funds not from banks but by borrowing "from the market," in the form of what is called commercial paper. When that market also froze, venerable giants like GE couldn't borrow. In some cases, like GE, it was partly because the company had a division that had gotten involved in making bad loans. When the market wouldn't buy this commercial paper, the Fed did. But in doing so, the Fed had gone from being a bankers' banker to being the nation's banker. There was no evidence that it knew anything about risk assessment—it was a totally different business from what it had done over its ninety-four-year history.

Some of what the Fed did to help resuscitate the banks may have been counterproductive to what should have been the main thrust of monetary policy—getting lending going again. It started paying interest on bank reserves held in deposit at the Federal Reserve—a nice way to give a big gift to the banks without almost anyone noticing, except in doing so it in effect encouraged them to keep the money there rather than lend it out (a fact the Fed itself recognized, when later it said it would increase the interest paid on reserves if it had to dampen lending in the event of an inflationary threat).

Not surprisingly, the Fed (with Treasury support) has tried to get the security market to work again through a variety of programs of guarantees and purchases of securities, such as the Term Asset-Backed Securities Loan Facility (or TALF). It has done so, however, without paying adequate attention to the underlying problem: the securities market failed in part because the models on which securitization was based were so badly flawed. With so little done to fix the models, we should be nervous about restarting the whole machine over again.[44]

The risk of inflation

Today, all over the world, as U.S. debt has soared and as the Fed's balance sheet has ballooned, there is worry about inflation in the future. China's premier openly expressed his concerns about the value of the $1.5 trillion or so his country has lent to the United States. He, and his citizens, do not want to see these hard-earned assets become worth less. There is an obvious incentive to let inflation decrease the real value of what is owed, perhaps not in a dramatic episode of very high inflation but more gradually, over ten years, with moderate inflation of, say, 6 percent a year. That would erode two-thirds of the value of the debt.[45] The United States says that it would never do such a thing, and central bankers do seem to have an extra gene that makes most of them avid inflation fighters. The Fed says it will deftly manage the economy, taking out liquidity as needed to prevent inflation. Anyone looking at the actions of the Fed in recent decades won't feel so confident.

So long as the unemployment rate remains high, the threat is as much deflation as inflation. Deflation is a serious risk, because when wages and prices fall, households and businesses are unable to repay what they owe. Defaults result, and they weaken the banks, triggering a new downward spiral. The Fed is caught in a dilemma. If it takes out liquidity too rapidly, before the recovery is firmly established, the economy could go into a deeper downturn. If it does so too slowly, there is a real risk of inflation—especially given the magnitude of excess liquidity in the system.

This balancing act is especially difficult because the full effects of monetary policy take months to be realized, which is why policymakers normally say they have to act *before* inflation becomes apparent. But that means that the Fed has to forecast what the economy will look like months ahead of time. The Fed's forecasting record in this crisis has been dismal.[46] But even if it had a more credible record, no one knows for sure what the pattern of *this* recovery will look like, since this downturn is so different, in so many ways, from any in recent memory. The Fed has, for instance, loaded its balance sheet with assets of lower quality than in the past. The reason why the Fed normally deals in T-bills is that there is a very thick market. It can buy and sell billions of dollars' worth easily, pumping money into and out of the economy. The markets for the other assets that the Fed has taken on board are much thinner. It can sell these assets (absorbing money)—but if it does this too quickly it will lower the prices, and that means big losses for the battered taxpayer. (By mid-2009, the Fed was, for instance, financing the vast majority of mortgages. It was successful in keeping down interest rates, some 0.7 percent lower than they otherwise would have been by some calculations. This was important in sustaining the housing market. But in September 2009 the Fed had announced that it would be discontinuing the program by the end of April 2010. That meant that interest rates on mortgages would likely rise, and anyone issuing a fixed-rate mortgage at the old, lower rates would experience a large capital loss. Knowing this, the private sector shied away from giving mortgages—it didn't want to bear the losses; in effect, Federal Reserve funding was "crowding out" the private sector. Even if the Fed didn't try to sell its mortgages, the market value of these assets would decline as the long-term interest rate increased with the discontinuation of these extraordinary measures and a return of short-term interest rates to more normal levels.[47]

There are, however, some ways the Fed might discourage lending without selling its mortgages and avoiding recognizing these losses (if it wanted to do so). The Fed has, for instance, proposed paying higher interest on deposits at the Fed, to encourage banks not to lend—if the recovery looks like it is getting overheated. But that's a relatively untried instrument—there is no way of knowing the precise effects of, say, a 2 percent increase in interest paid on reserves. Besides, it is costly to the government—and with the ballooning of the deficit, these costs can't be ignored.

If the Fed gets it *just* right, it may be able to manage the economy with neither inflation nor a downturn. But I wouldn't count on it. I suspect there is a greater risk of a downturn than of an episode of inflation: in the run-up to the crisis, the Fed showed itself more attuned to the thinking of Wall Street than to the concerns of Main Street, and so too for the bailouts. It's likely that this pattern will continue.[48]

Markets may help with the adjustment—but not necessarily in a way that promotes stability. If the markets worry about inflation, longer-term interest rates will rise, and this will dampen the economy, both directly, because it will reduce demand for longer-term investments, and indirectly, because banks will be induced to hold long-term government bonds rather than make loans.[49] But, as we have seen, there is little reason to believe that the market can correctly calibrate its response. Indeed, this makes the Fed's response all the more difficult, for it has to anticipate not only future rates of inflation and market responses to these inflationary expectations but also how the market will react to any actions the Fed takes.[50] Making inferences on the basis of past behavior may not give reliable predictions. The problems are of an unprecedented scale, and since market participants know this, their reactions to what the government may do may be different. In a sense, some of the problem of excess leverage has shifted from the private sector to the government (to the Fed and to Treasury). As a short-term measure, in response to the crisis, it may have made sense. The problem, however, of reducing the overall leverage (indebtedness) of the economy remains.

The Fed: its actions and governance

The Fed played a central role in every part of this drama, from the creation of the crisis through lax regulation and loose monetary policies through the failure to deal effectively with the aftermath of the bursting of the bubble.[51] There were failures in forecasting and policy. Much of this chapter has been devoted to the consequences of the ill-designed rescues that followed the Lehman bankruptcy.

It is natural to ask, how do we explain these persistent failures? Part of the answer involves a set of peculiar ideas, including but going beyond simply the belief that markets always work—and because they always work, there is little need for regulation and little to fear from bubbles. And part of the answer to why such peculiar ideas had such sway has to do with the governance of the Fed.

Soaring asset prices meant there was a party going on on Wall Street. Standard wisdom is that the Fed should rein in such parties—especially because, inevitably, others have to pay the cost for the cleanup the next morning. But Fed Chairmen Greenspan and Bernanke didn't want to be party poopers, so they had to devise a series of fallacious arguments for why they should sit idly by: there were no such things as bubbles, one couldn't tell a bubble even if there were one, the Fed didn't have the instruments to deflate a bubble, the Fed was, in any case, better to clean up the mess after the bubble broke. (In chapter 9, I will explain what's wrong with each of these contentions.)

One of the reasons why the Fed was able to get away with what it did was that it was not directly accountable to Congress or the administration. It didn't have to get congressional permission for putting at risk hundreds of billions of taxpayer dollars. Indeed, that was one of the reasons why both administrations turned to the Fed: they were trying to circumvent democratic processes, knowing that many of the actions had little public support.

Central bankers around the world have promulgated the doctrine that central banks should be independent from the political process. Many newly independent developing countries have found this particularly hard to take: they are told how important democracy is, but when it comes to the conduct of macroeconomic and monetary policy, a set of decisions that have the most effect on the lives of their people, they are told that it is too important to be left to ordinary democratic processes. The argument for independence is that it increases "credibility"—that the central bank won't give in to populist expansionary demands—and this means that there will be less inflation and greater stability.

In this recent episode, some of the independent central bankers did not do as well as those who were more directly politically accountable, perhaps because they fell less under the sway of financial markets. Brazil and India, neither of which have fully independent central banks, are among the good performers; the European Central Bank and the Fed are among the poor performers.

Economic policy involves trade-offs—winners and losers—and such trade-offs can't be left to the technocrats alone. Technocrats can decide issues like what kind of computer programs to run, but monetary policy involves trade-offs between inflation and unemployment. Bondholders worry about inflation; workers, about jobs. For a while, some economists argued that in the long run there was no such thing as a trade-off—too low a rate of unemployment gives rise to ever-increasing inflation—even if there were no trade-off in the long run, there is in the short run; and there is uncertainty about the precise critical rate below which inflation is set off (technically called the non-accelerating rate of unemployment), and that in turn means that policy affects who bears the risks.

Regardless of one's views on the long-standing issue of central bank independence, there can be little disagreement about one thing. When a country's central bank engages in a massive bailout, risking the public's money, it is engaged in actions that need to be directly politically accountable, and these actions need to be done in a transparent way. I described earlier the non-transparent (and unnecessary) gifts that had been given to the banks as part of TARP. Even less transparent have been the gifts given through the Fed, including the $13 billion that flowed to Goldman Sachs and foreign banks through the Fed bailout of AIG—information that the Fed disclosed only under congressional pressure. Other Federal Reserve bailouts (such as that of Bear Stearns) were equally non-transparent, with taxpayers still uncertain about the extent of the risks they face.[52]

Unfortunately, most central bankers naturally come out of the banking tradition, which is based on the premise of secrecy. Those with a more academic background—such as the United Kingdom's Mervyn King—have been pushing for more openness. There is even an argument that better information improves the efficiency of markets—there are fewer surprises. Ben Bernanke rightly advocated more transparency when he assumed office, but just as the need for transparency increased, the scope of transparency was reduced—and for reasons that quickly became understandable. Over time, it increasingly appears that the role of secrecy has been to hide bad decisions. With secrecy, there can be no effective democratic accountability.[53]

As bad as these governance problems are, those in the Federal Reserve Bank of New York, which assumed a particularly large role in this bailout, are even worse. The officers of the Fed are elected by its board, which in turn consists of banks and businesses in the area. Six of the nine directors are elected by the banks themselves. For instance, one director of the New York Fed was the president, chairman, and CEO of JPMorgan Chase, which was one of the beneficiaries of the Fed's generous help. The CEO of Citibank, another recipient, was a director when Geithner was elected.[54] As discussed in chapter 2, the New York Fed's attempts at self-regulation have been dubious at best, but when it came to play a central role in designing bailouts—the programs that are putting taxpayer money at risk—the questions about its ability to police itself grew deeper.

While the Federal Reserve Board in Washington benefits from better oversight and accountability, the role that it played in the bailouts should be deeply disturbing. It was the non-transparent instrument of choice used by both the Bush and Obama administrations as the bailouts became increasingly costly and as the bad behavior of the banks became increasingly clear. The full eventual costs of the bailouts and lending programs through the Fed—and the recipients of the munificent gifts—remain unknown.

CONCLUDING COMMENTS

The entire series of efforts to rescue the banking system were so flawed, partly because those who were somewhat responsible for the mess—as advocates of deregulation, as failed regulators, or as investment bankers—were put in charge of the repair. Perhaps not surprisingly, they all employed the same logic that had gotten the financial sector into trouble to get it out of it. The financial sector had engaged in highly leveraged, non-transparent transactions, many off balance sheet; it had believed that one could create value by moving assets around and repackaging them. The approach to getting the country out of the mess was based on the same "principles." Toxic assets were shifted from banks to the government—but that didn't make them any less toxic. Off-balance sheet and non-transparent guarantees became a regular feature of the Treasury, Federal Deposit Insurance Corporation, and Federal Reserve. High leverage (open and hidden) became a feature of public institutions as well as private.

Worse still were the implications for governance. The Constitution gives Congress the power to control spending. But the Federal Reserve was undertaking actions knowing full well that if the collateral that it was taking on proved bad, the taxpayer would bail it out. Whether the actions were legal or not is not the issue: they were a deliberate attempt to circumvent Congress, because they knew that the American people would be reluctant to approve more largesse for those who had caused so much harm and behaved so badly.

The U.S. government did something worse than trying to re-create the financial system of the past: It strengthened the too-big-to-fail banks; it introduced a new concept—too-big-to-be-financially-resolved; it worsened the problems of moral hazard; it burdened future generations with a legacy of debt; it cast a pallor of the risk of inflation over the U.S. dollar; and it strengthened many Americans' doubts about the fundamental fairness of the system.

Central bankers, like all humans, are fallible. Some observers argue for simple, rule-based approaches to policy (like monetarism and inflation targeting)[55] because they reduce the potential for human fallibility. The belief that markets can take care of themselves and therefore government should not intrude has resulted in the largest intervention in the market by government in history; the result of following excessively simple rules was that the Fed had to take discretionary actions beyond those taken by any central bank in history. It had to make life and death decisions for each bank without even the guidance of a clear set of principles.

✦　✦　✦

SEVERAL COMMENTATORS[56] have referred to the massive bailouts and government interventions in the economy as socialism with American characteristics, something akin to China's march to what it calls "a market economy with Chinese characteristics." But, as one Chinese friend pointed out, the description is inaccurate: socialism is supposed to *care* about people. Socialism American-style didn't do that. Had the money been spent on helping those who were losing their homes, it might have been a correct characterization. As it was, it was just an expanded version of Corporate Welfarism American-style.

The current crisis has seen the government assume a new role—the "bearer of risk of last resort." When the private markets were at the point of meltdown, all risk was shifted to the government. The safety net should focus on protecting individuals; but the safety net was extended to corporations, in the belief that the consequences of not doing so would be too horrific. Once extended, it will be difficult to withdraw: firms will know that if they are sufficiently big and their failure represents a sufficient threat to the economy—or if they are sufficiently politically influential—the government will bear the risk of failure. That is why it will be critical to prevent banks from growing so big.

There is, still, a chance for the American political system to restore a modicum of confidence in itself. Yes, Wall Street has used its power and money to buy deregulation, followed swiftly by the most generous bailout in the history of mankind. Yes, the government has failed to restructure the financial system in ways which would reduce the likelihood of a similar crisis, and which strengthened those parts of the financial system that were actually doing what they were supposed to be doing—managing risk and allocating capital. But, still, there is the chance to re-regulate, to correct the mistakes of the past. It is imperative that that be done quickly: for while one side in the struggle, ordinary taxpayers who had to bear the brunt of the cost of the financial sector's failure, might lose interest as the economy recovers, the other side, the banks, have every incentive to continue to fight to ensure that they have as much freedom to make profits as they can get. But because both the structure of the financial system has been made worse and the way the bailouts have been conducted has worsened the problem of moral hazard, the need for re-regulation is all the greater.

In the next chapter, I describe the next battle in the war to reform the financial system—the battle over regulation.

CHAPTER SIX

AVARICE TRIUMPHS OVER PRUDENCE

EXCESSIVE RISK-TAKING BY BANKS, A RASH OF CONFLICTS of interest, and pervasive fraudulent behavior—these ugly phenomena have repeatedly come to the surface when booms turn bust, and the current crisis is no exception. In the aftermath of the last big boom, which led to the Great Depression, the architects of the New Deal strove to address these insidious problems by instituting a new regulatory structure.[1] Memories are short, however, and a half century is a long time. By the time Ronald Reagan assumed the presidency, too few veterans of the Great Depression were still around to share their cautionary tales, and its lessons were not absorbed from the history books. The world had changed, or so the new financial whiz kids had convinced themselves. They thought they were so much smarter, so much savvier technologically. Advances in "science" had led to a better understanding of risk, and this enabled the invention of new risk management products.

Just as there was no one big mistake in mortgage origination and securitization, but instead a multitude of problems, so too were there a multitude of problems in American banks. Any one of the problems might have been enough to cause serious damage, but when combined, the mixture was explosive. At the same time, no one blew the whistle—not investors (who were supposed to be overseeing their own money), not money managers (who were supposed to be overseeing the money that was entrusted to them), and not even regulators (whom we trust to oversee the financial system as a whole).

The free market mantra meant not just stripping away old regulations but also doing nothing to address the new challenges of twenty-first-century markets, including those posed by derivatives. And not only didn't the U.S. Treasury and the Federal Reserve propose regulations; they forcefully—sometimes almost brutally—resisted any initiatives to do so. In the 1990s, the head of the Commodity Futures Trading Commission, Brooksley Born, had called for such regulation—a concern that took on urgency after the New York Federal Reserve Bank engineered the 1998 bailout of Long-Term Capital Management, a hedge fund whose trillion-dollar-plus failure threatened to bring down the entire global financial market. But Secretary of Treasury Robert Rubin, his deputy, Larry Summers, and Alan Greenspan were adamant—and successful—in their opposition.[2] And just to ensure that regulators in the future don't come to their senses, those in financial markets lobbied hard, and successfully, for legislation to make sure that derivatives remained unregulated (the Commodity Futures Modernization Act of 2000).

In their fight, they used the same tactics that we saw the banks use to get their mega-bailouts, the tactic that had been used in part to ensure Greenspan's reappointment a few years earlier,[3] the tactic of fear: if derivatives were regulated, capitalism as we knew it would fall apart. There would be market turmoil of untold magnitude, and risk wouldn't be managed efficiently. Evidently, believers in the strength of capital markets also believed that they were very fragile—they couldn't survive even a whisper about a change of the rules.[4]

As this book goes to press, almost two years after the beginning of the recession, too little has been done to reform financial regulation. Something will be done—but it almost surely will be less than what is needed: perhaps enough to help us muddle through, but not enough to prevent another crisis. Even more remarkable, efforts to deregulate continue: the Sarbanes-Oxley law,[5] which was passed in the aftermath of the Enron scandal to ensure better corporate governance and investor protections, has been critically weakened. The industry is clever—

whatever regulations are imposed, it will figure out ways to circumvent them. That is why regulation has to be comprehensive and dynamic. The devil is in the details. And with complex regulations and regulatory authorities "captured" by those they are supposed to regulate, there is a risk that the details will be such as to give the banks the ability to carry on much as they did before. That is why the regulations have to be simple and transparent, and the regulatory structure has to be designed to prevent excessive influence from the financial markets.

The Need for Regulation

The crisis has made it clear that self-regulation—which the financial industry promoted and which I view as an oxymoron—doesn't work. We've already seen that the banks failed to assess their own risk. When Greenspan finally admitted that there was a flaw to his approach to regulation, he said it was because the banks had done such a bad job looking after their own interests.[6] He couldn't believe that they would undertake risks that would put their very existence in jeopardy, and he evidently did not understand the importance of incentives—which encouraged excessive risk-taking.

But even if a given bank was managing its *own* risks well, that doesn't address *systemic* risk. Systemic risk can exist without there being a single systemically important bank if all of the banks behave similarly—as they did, given their herd mentality. This is an especially important point, since much of the current discussion focuses on regulating large, systemically important institutions. That is necessary, but not sufficient.

If all banks use similar models, then a flaw in the model would, for instance, lead all of them to make bad loans—and then try to sell those loans at the same time. And that is precisely what happened. All of the banks bet that there was no real estate bubble, that real estate prices would not fall. They all bet that interest rates would not rise, and if they did rise, borrowers would still be able to repay their loans. These were foolish bets, and when the world turned out differently from what they hoped, *all* of them were in trouble, not to mention the *system* itself.

If one bank has a problem and needs to liquidate its assets, that's an easy matter. When many banks have a problem, and they all need to liquidate similar assets, asset prices fall. Banks get less for the asset than they thought they would, and their problems are compounded exponentially. This kind of "correlation"—of interdependence among the actions of various banks—was not picked up by the models of the banks themselves. It is not the kind of thing that self-regulation exposes. But it *is* the kind of thing that a good regulator would have picked up on.

Normally, most markets work reasonably well on their own. But this is not true when there are externalities, when actions of one party adversely affect others. Financial markets are rife with externalities. Their failures have cost society and the economy an enormous amount. The existence of deposit insurance puts taxpayers in jeopardy if banks undertake excessive risk, and so the government needs to make sure that the banks it insures act prudently. Professor Gerald Caprio of Williams College, who worked with me at the World Bank, used to say there were two kinds of countries—those that had deposit insurance and knew it, and those that had it but didn't know it. In a time of crisis, governments bail out banks, whether there is deposit insurance or not—a truism made evident in the current crisis. But if the government is going to come in and pick up the pieces, it has to do what it can to prevent the accidents.

Throughout this book, I have emphasized the importance of "peeling back the onion," figuring out what lies behind each of the mistakes. The markets failed, and the presence of large externalities is one of the reasons. But there are others. I have repeatedly noted the misalignment of incentives—bank officers' incentives were not consistent with the objectives of other stakeholders and society more generally. Buyers of assets also have imperfect information: while one of the social functions of financial markets is to collect, assess, and disseminate information, they also have the power to exploit the uninformed, and they did so ruthlessly.

Prior to the crisis, Greenspan and others who advocated minimal regulation thought that beyond financial institutions regulating themselves, government should focus on protecting only small investors, and even then there was an increasing belief in caveat emptor.[7] Even as instances of outrageous predatory lending became evident, the common view was that individuals should fend for themselves. The tide has turned: the costs of these flawed deregulatory theories have been great and have extended to the entire global economy. The alleged benefits, an era of innovation, were an illusion. In this chapter, I discuss why the financial system has not functioned as well as it should and some of the essential reforms for the financial sector—improved incentives and transparency, restrictions on excessive risk-taking, reducing the threat of too-big-to-fail banks, and doing something about some of the most problematic financial products, including derivatives.

FLAWED INCENTIVES

Bankers are (for the most part) not born any greedier than other people. It is just that they may have more opportunity and stronger incentives to do mischief at others' expense. When private rewards are well aligned with social objectives, things work well; when they are not, matters can get ugly. Normally, in market economies, incentives are well aligned. For example, in a competitive market, the extra return for a firm producing one more ton of steel is the price of steel, and the value of an extra ton of steel to its users is reflected in the price; so too the extra cost of producing an extra ton of steel is the value of the additional inputs (iron ore, coal, etc.) used in the production, which is reflected in the costs of these inputs. That is why when firms maximize profits, they also, ideally, maximize societal well-being—the difference between the value to society of what is produced and the value of the resources used in production. In the financial markets, on the other hand, incentives are distorted, and often grossly so.

An important example of an incentive distortion is how many executives are paid: with stock options. In the financial sector, a large fraction of compensation is paid on the basis of bonuses, related to income (fees) generated. Proponents of these compensation systems argue that they provided strong incentives for executives to work hard. This argument is disingenuous because the executives found ways to get paid well even when the firm floundered. There is, it turns out, little relationship between pay and performance, a fact that was highlighted when executives at companies with record losses got multimillion-dollar bonuses. Some firms even went as far as to change the name of the pay from *performance bonuses* to *retention bonuses*. The long and the short of it, however, is that pay is high when performance is good and when it is poor.[8]

In many of the sectors where "performance pay" had been tried, it was abandoned long ago. If workers are paid on the basis of a piece rate and they have any discretion—which they almost always do—they produce the shoddiest products they can get away with. After all, they are paid on the basis of quantity, not quality. This phenomenon occurred throughout the financial chain, most notably in this crisis when real estate brokers produced as many loans as they could—never mind whether the loans could be paid back. The investment banks produced as many complex products based on the toxic mortgages as they could because, simply, that was what they were paid to do.

Executives who were paid by stock options had an incentive to do everything they could to get their firms' stock price up—including creative accounting. The higher the share price, the better they did. They knew that the higher the *reported* profits were, the higher the share prices would be, and they knew that it was easy to deceive markets. And one of the easiest ways of increasing reported profits was to manipulate the balance sheet, moving potential losses off balance sheet with one hand while recording profitable fees with the other. Investors and regulators had been forewarned, but evidently had not learned the lesson: creative accounting was behind many of the scandals related to the dot-com (tech) bubble of the late 1990s.[9]

In the "high-powered" incentive schemes in finance, bankers shared in the gains but not in the losses. Bonuses were based on short-term performance—not long-term.

Indeed, the financial sector had incentives to take risks that combined a large probability of an above-normal return with a small probability of a disaster. If things could be designed to make it likely that the disaster would occur sometime in the distant future, then all the better. The net return could even be negative, but no one would know until it was too late. Modern financial engineering provided the tools to create products that perfectly fit this description.

An example may illustrate. Assume that one could invest in a safe asset with a return of 5 percent. The finance wizards designed a product that yielded 6 percent almost always—say, 90 percent of the time. Magically, they seemed to have beaten the market, and by an amazing 20 percent. But in the remaining 10 percent of the time—everything was lost. The expected (average) return was negative—4.5 percent—far below the 5 percent of the safe asset. The innovative product had more risk and a lower average return than the safe asset. But, on average, with the bad returns occurring only one year out of ten, it will be a decade before the disastrous outcome occurs—a long period during which the financial wizards can reap ample rewards from their amazing ability to beat the market.

The disaster that grew from these flawed financial incentives can be, to us economists, somewhat comforting: our models predicted that there would be excessive risk-taking and shortsighted behavior, and what has happened has confirmed these predictions. It was hard, however, to find any substantially above-normal performance of the "real economy" related to these financial market innovations. In the end, economic theory was vindicated. The misalignment between social and private returns was clear: financial marketeers were amply rewarded but had engaged in such egregious risk-taking that, for the economy as a whole, they had created risk *without reward*.

Corporate governance

The incentive schemes that produced misaligned incentives did not serve shareholders well, and did not serve the world well. The net profits of many of the major banks over the five-year period 2004–2008 were negative.[10] A shareholder who had invested $100 in Citibank in 2005 would have shares worth $13.90 by the end of 2008.

The incentive schemes did, however, serve the banks' executives well; and, though some of them may have been foolish enough to keep much of their wealth in bank shares—even after taking account of the "losses" on their paper profits, many are now wealthy, in some cases, very wealthy.

The executives got away with this because of poor corporate governance. American corporations (and those of many other countries) are only nominally run by the shareholders. In practice, to a very large extent, they are run by and for the benefit of the management.[11] In many corporations where ownership is widely diversified among disparate shareholders, management effectively appoints most of the board, and it naturally appoints people who are likely to serve their interests most effectively. The board decides on the pay of management, and the "company" provides good rewards for its board members. It's a cozy relationship.

In the aftermath of the Enron scandal, in order to improve corporate governance, Congress passed a supposedly tough new law, the much-maligned Sarbanes-Oxley Act, enacted in July 2002. Champions of the corporate sector claimed it created undue burdens that would stifle firms. I criticized it for not having gone far enough.[12] It did not deal adequately with the perverse incentives that gave rise to all the bad behavior described earlier. It did not require companies to show in a clear and transparent way what they are giving out in stock options.[13] The accounting rules in effect encourage the use of stock options because it is a way for companies to give high pay without shareholders knowing the full cost. The law of conservation of matter says that increasing pay to executives will always come at somebody else's expense—in the case of stock options, the dilution of the ownership claims of other shareholders.

That the executives had an incentive—and the tools—to design compensation packages that benefited them at the expense of others seems abundantly clear. What is still a mystery is why shareholders didn't recognize this. Flaws in corporate governance may have made it difficult to directly change the behavior of management, but investors still should have "punished" firms that had bad incentive structures by driving down the price of their shares. They could have sent a warning, which might have changed behavior, but they didn't.[14]

What is to be done?

Reducing the scope for conflicts of interest and for shortsighted and excessively risky behavior is one of the most important sets of reforms for a simple reason: if bankers have the wrong incentives, they will go to great lengths to circumvent any other regulations. A simple reform—basing pay on long-term performance, and making sure that bankers share in the losses and not just in the gains—might make a big difference. If firms use "incentive pay" it has to be *really* incentive pay—the firm should have to demonstrate that there is a relationship between pay and long-term performance.[15]

To address effectively the problems of abusive and distorted incentive structures, however, there need to be reforms in corporate governance—to make managers more accountable to people who own the companies.[16] Shareholders should have more say in determining compensation (called "say in pay"), and the corporate accounts should at least make it clear how much is being paid out in stock options and other forms of hidden compensation. The sordid state of affairs in corporate governance is best reflected in the fact that companies mounted a campaign against laws that would simply require shareholders to have a nonbinding vote on executive compensation.[17] The shareholders may nominally own the company, but they can't even have a say in the pay of those who are supposed to be working for them.

A LACK OF TRANSPARENCY

Criticisms of financial markets always begin with their lack of transparency. *Transparency* is, of course, another word for "information." It always becomes obvious in the aftermath of a crisis that there was a lack of information: no one would have put their money into Wall Street if they knew that it was making such poor investments. There is a big difference, however, between information that one would have liked to have had in hindsight and true lack of transparency. No one can ever have all the information they would like before they make a decision. The job of financial markets is to ferret out the relevant information and, on the basis of that limited information, make judgments about the risks and returns.

To me, the issue of transparency is really about deception. American banks were engaged actively in deception: they moved risk off the balance sheet so no one could appropriately assess it. The magnitudes of the deceptions that had been achieved were mind-boggling: Lehman Brothers could report that it had a net worth of some $26 billion shortly before its demise and yet have a hole in its balance sheet approaching $200 billion.[18]

If markets worked well, banks (and countries) that were more transparent would be able to get capital at lower cost. There *should* be market incentives for this kind of transparency—a balancing out of costs and benefits of gathering, analyzing, and disclosing additional information. But markets on their own seem not able to provide the proper amount of transparency, which is why government has to step in and *require* the disclosure of information.[19]

Without good information markets can't work well, and an important part of providing good information is having good accounting systems so that market participants can interpret—in a meaningful way—the data that is being provided. No accounting system is perfect, which is why accounting has given rise to such controversy in this crisis.[20] Today, the major controversy is over "marking to market": reporting the value of a firm's assets on its balance sheet at its current market value (when there is a market).

Some in the financial sector blame all of their problems on mark-to-market accounting. If only they didn't have to report the fact that the mortgages they were holding were unlikely to be repaid, then their accounts would look better and no one would be the wiser for it. Suddenly, advocates of market fundamentalism, who talked about the virtues of "price discovery"—the miracles of the market pricing system—lost their faith. As the prices of mortgages and the complex instruments based on them plummeted, they argued that those were not "true prices"; they didn't reflect the true value. Of course, they never raised such concerns during the bubble, but then, the high prices meant high bonuses and allowed more lending. And, of course, they did not offer to give back their bonuses when the "profits" that justified them turned out to be bogus.

In reality, commercial banks didn't have to mark to market most of the assets that they held for the longer term. Prior to March 2009, they only had to mark down those mortgages that were "impaired"—that is, those with a serious likelihood of nonpayment. Then, in another move to increase non-transparency, banks were even given discretion not to write down many of *these* mortgages.[21] They went from marking to market to "marking to hope." This allowed some of the banks to report much higher profits than they otherwise would have, but it also decreased confidence in the numbers that they were producing and merely postponed banks' putting their balance sheets in order.

(This was not the only manifestation of "blaming" the messenger for bringing the bad news about the sorry state of banks' balance sheets. As the crisis unfolded, the other demand of the banks—besides moving away from mark-to-market accounting—was banning short sales. With a short sale, investors bet that a company's stock is going to decrease in value. When many investors believe that a company is going to do badly and sell shares short, obviously the price of shares falls. Short selling provides important incentives for market participants to discover fraud and reckless lending—some believe they have played a more important role in curbing such bad behavior than government regulators. But in this crisis, as I noted, the banks—usually believers in the virtues of the market—lost their faith; they wanted those who were optimistic about the banks' prospects to be able to cast their "votes" in support of the banks by buying shares, but didn't want their critics to be able to do likewise by selling short.)

Inevitably, the banks were excessively optimistic, and they had strong incentives to be so. As the crisis unfolded they hoped that the only problem was a bout of "irrational pessimism." If people felt confident, market prices would go up. Regrettably, economics gives little support to this view. Confidence is important, but underlying beliefs, feelings, desires, and aversions are important elements of reality. The reality of this particular crisis is fairly straightforward: bad loans were made, on the basis of a bubble, to people who couldn't afford to pay them back. Market prices are imperfect, but by and large they still represent the best information that is available about the value of assets. Certainly, it makes little sense to leave the valuation to the bankers. They have every incentive to distort the information that is provided, and especially so when the information might suggest that the bank is out of money.

Still, with inappropriately designed regulations, mark-to-market accounting can contribute to the magnitude of cyclical fluctuations. This crisis, as I have noted, for all the new fangled products, is very much like many that have occurred in the past: an excessive expansion of credit, based on real estate collateral. In good times, asset values are too high, bloated by a bubble. Because the borrowers look wealthier, the bank can lend them more. In the boom, defaults are low and bank profits are high, so the bank also has the capacity to lend more. When markets "correct" themselves, prices come down, defaults rise, and the bank no longer is able or willing to lend as much as before. When the banks cut back on lending, the economy suffers. The result is more bad loans, and asset values fall even more. Mark-to-market accounting puts greater discipline on the banks: when the value of the loan portfolio falls because default rates rise, the bank has to recognize that it is not as wealthy as it was before, and that means that it has to either cut back more on lending or raise more capital. But in a recession, the latter is often not an option. Thus, seemingly, mark-to-market accounting may lead to greater fluctuations in lending.

The problem isn't, though, with mark-to-market accounting, but with the way it is used. The regulators should have allowed less lending against the value of banks' capital in good times, to dampen the euphoria and the bubble, but more in bad times.[22]

There are also other, easily correctable problems with mark-to-market accounting. One is that its zealots have pushed it too far and have not recognized its limitations—including the different uses to which

accounting information is put. For instance, in mark-to-market accounting, banks also mark to market their liabilities. When the market thinks
that a bank is going to go bankrupt, its bonds decrease in value, and the
bank gets to record a capital gain. This is absurd—a bank gets to look
like it was making a profit simply because everyone thinks it's about to
go bust. For banks with demand deposits—where those who have lent
their money to the bank can demand it back at any time—one wants
a conservative value of the bank's assets. One wants to know whether
the bank can meet its obligations. If it sold off its assets (which it could
only do at market prices), would it have enough money?[23]

In the last chapter, we saw how bad accounting had allowed the
problems of savings and loan banks to fester, increasing the eventual
cost of the bailout. In the crisis of 2008, by softening the accounting
standards, the government is taking us down the same road. The hope
was that this time gambling on resurrection would pay off. Maybe yes,
but more likely not.[24]

In the current crisis, moving away from mark-to-market accounting
has had a particular adverse effect: it discourages banks from restructuring mortgages, delaying the financial restructuring the economy needs
so badly.[25] If they delay restructuring, *maybe* prices will recover and the
mortgage will be repaid. Probably not. But perhaps in the meanwhile,
they can recoup enough in fees[26] and the huge spread between lending
rates and what they have to pay for money to enable them to manage
the loss when they finally have to face it.[27]

What is to be done?

The loosening of the accounting standards in April 2009 was a move in
the wrong direction: there needs to be a reaffirmation of the commitment to mark-to-market accounting, but with greater care in the rules
and how it's used. If the bank wants to explain that it is more optimistic
than the market, it is free to do so, and if investors are convinced, so
be it.

Cooking the books to hide from investors what is going on—exaggerating income—should be as illegal as doing so from tax authorities

(understating income). None of the "off-balance sheet" magic tricks of the past should be allowed. If paying executives by stock option is not outright forbidden, then banks that do so should be required to have more capital and pay higher deposit insurance rates. At the very minimum, there should be full disclosure of stock options—none of the fiction that executive compensation falls like manna from the heaven, without coming out of shareholders' pockets.

Finally, transparency, if it is to be meaningful, has to be comprehensive. If some channels are allowed to remain in the dark, that's where all the nefarious activities will go. Vast portions of global capital flow through secrecy havens like the Cayman Islands—it hasn't become a two-trillion-dollar banking center because the weather there is particularly conducive to banking.[28] These are deliberately created "loopholes" in the global regulatory system to facilitate money laundering, tax evasion, regulatory evasion, and other illicit activities. After 9/11 the government managed to shut them down for providing a safe haven for terrorist funds, but it has done too little to curtail their use for other unsavory reasons.[29]

Complexity—going beyond transparency

Sheer complexity played as significant a role in this crisis as the lack of transparency did. The financial markets had created products so complex that even if all the details of them were known, no one could fully understand the risk implications. The banks had at their disposal all the relevant information and data, yet they couldn't figure out their own financial position.

Valuation of the complex products wasn't done by markets. It was done by computers running models that, no matter how complex, couldn't possibly embrace all of the relevant information.[30] As it turned out, some very important ingredients were not included in the models; inevitably, the "results" of models depend on the assumptions and data put into the models (see chapter 4); for example, models where little attention was paid to the risk of falling prices and the correlated risk of default could generate valuations widely off the mark—with marked changes in valuations as the probabilities of default soared.

It's not even clear that these new instruments were necessary. The financial system always had products that distributed and managed risk. Someone who wanted a very safe asset would buy a Treasury bill. Someone who wanted to absorb a little more risk could buy a corporate bond. Equities (stocks) have still more risk. Certain risks could be insured against—the death of key personnel or a fire—through insurance companies. One could even protect oneself against the risk of an increase in the price of oil. The new array of risk products was touted as "fine-tuning risk management." In principle, these new instruments could improve risk management and even lower transaction costs. In practice, however, they allowed people to take larger, riskier gambles with less and less capital.

Part of the agenda of the computer models was to maximize the fraction of, say, a lousy subprime mortgage that could get an AAA rating, and then an AA rating, and so forth, to maximize the amount of money that could be made by slicing and dicing the mortgages that, without such alchemy, would have gotten a straight F. This was called rating at the margin, and the solution was still more complexity.

As we saw earlier, banks don't like transparency. A fully transparent market would be highly competitive, and with intense competition, fees and profits would be driven down. The financial markets deliberately created complex products as a way to reduce effective transparency within the rules. The complexity thus allowed for higher fees, with the banks living off increased transaction costs. With tailor-made products, price comparisons became more difficult and competition was reduced. It worked for a while, if only to generate higher profits for the banks. But the complexity was also the financial sector's undoing. No one has ever shown that the increased efficiency in risk-bearing that resulted would ever come close to compensating the economy, and the taxpayer, for the damage that resulted.

UNBRIDLED RISK-TAKING

On November 12, 1999, Congress passed the Gramm-Leach-Bliley Act (or the Financial Services Modernization Act)—the culmination of a years-long, massive lobbying effort by the banking and financial-services industries to reduce regulation in their sector. Spearheaded in Congress by Senator Phil Gramm, the bill achieved a long-sought-after goal of the big banks—the repeal of the Glass-Steagall Act.

In the aftermath of the Great Depression, the government addressed the questions, what had caused the depression, and how can it prevent a recurrence? The regulatory structure that it adopted served the country and the world well, presiding over an unprecedented period of stability and growth. The Glass-Steagall Act of 1933 was a cornerstone of that regulatory edifice. It separated commercial banks (which lend money) and investment banks (which organize the sale of bonds and equities) to avoid the clear conflicts of interest that arise when the same bank issues shares *and* lends money.

Glass-Steagall had a second purpose: to ensure that those entrusted with caring for ordinary people's money in commercial banks didn't engage in the same kind of risk-taking as investment banks—which aim primarily to maximize the returns of the wealthy. Moreover, preserving confidence in the payment mechanism was so important that in the same Act, the government provided deposit insurance to those who put their money in commercial banks. With the public Treasury on the line, the government wanted commercial banks to be conservative. That was not the culture of the investment banks.

Depression-era regulations may not have been appropriate for the twenty-first century, but what was required was adapting, not dismantling, the existing regulatory system to new realities, including the enhanced risk posed by derivatives and securitization. To the critics who worried about the problems that had surfaced in earlier years, which had led to the passage of the Act, the proponents said, in effect, "trust us." They would create Chinese walls—insurmountable divisions between the two arms—to make sure that the problems associated with conflicts of interest did not recur. The accounting scandals a few years later demonstrated that the Chinese walls they had constructed were so low that they could be easily stepped across.[31]

The most important consequence of the repeal of Glass-Steagall was indirect. When the repeal brought investment and commercial banks together, the investment banking culture came out on top. There was a demand for the kind of high returns that could be obtained only through high leverage and big risk-taking. There was another consequence: a less competitive and more concentrated banking system dominated by ever larger banks. In the years after the passage of the Gramm bill, the market share of the five largest banks grew from 8 percent in 1995 to 30 percent today.[32] One of the hallmarks of America's banking system had been the high level of competition, with a myriad of banks serving different communities and different niches in the market. This strength was being lost while new problems were emerging. By 2002, big investment banks had a leverage as high as 29 to 1, meaning that a 3 percent fall in asset values would wipe them out. The Securities and Exchange Commission (SEC), by doing nothing, was arguing for the virtues of self-regulation: the peculiar notion that banks can effectively police themselves. Then, in a controversial decision in April 2004, it seems to have given them even more latitude, as some investment banks increased their leverage to 40 to 1. The regulators, like the investment banks, seem to have bought into the idea that with better computer models, risk could be better managed.[33]

What is to be done?

It's easy to curtail excessive risk-taking: restrict it and incentivize banks against it. Not allowing banks to use incentive structures that encourage excessive risk-taking, and forcing more transparency will go a long way. So too will requiring banks that engage in high-risk activities to put up much more capital and to pay high deposit insurance fees. But further reforms are needed: leverage needs to be much more limited (and adjusted with the business cycle), and restrictions need to be placed on particularly risky products (such as credit default swaps, discussed below).

Given what the economy has been through, it is clear that the federal government should reinstitute some revised version of the Glass-Steagall Act. There is no choice: any institution that has the benefits of a commercial bank—including the government's safety nets—has to be severely restricted in its ability to take on risk.[34] There are simply too many conflicts of interest and too many problems to allow commingling of the activities of commercial and investment banks. The promised benefits of the repeal of Glass-Steagall proved illusory and the costs proved greater than even critics of the repeal imagined. The problems are especially acute with the too-big-to-fail banks. The imperative of reinstating the Glass-Steagall Act quickly is suggested by recent behavior of some investment banks, for whom trading has once again proved to be a major source of profits. The alacrity with which all the major investment banks decided to become "commercial banks" in the fall of 2008 was alarming—they saw the gifts coming from the federal government, and evidently, they believed that their risk-taking behavior would not be much circumscribed. They now had access to the Fed window, so they could borrow at almost a zero interest rate; they knew that they were protected by a new safety net; but they could continue their high-stakes trading unabated. This should be viewed as totally unacceptable.

TOO BIG TO FAIL

As we have seen, all of America's major banks became too big to fail; furthermore, they *knew* they were too big to fail, and consequently, they undertook risk just as economic theory predicted they would. As I argued in chapter 5, the Bush and Obama administrations introduced a new concept: they contended that some banks are too big to be resolved (or financially restructured)—that is, too big to use the normal procedures of forcing shareholders to bear the losses and converting bondholders to shareholders. Instead, the government stepped in, in effect providing insurance (at no premium) to bondholders and shareholders, and undermining all market discipline.

There is an obvious solution to the too-big-to-fail banks: break them

up. If they are too big to fail, they are too big to exist. The only justification for allowing these huge institutions to continue is if there were significant economies of scale or scope that otherwise would be lost—that
is, if these institutions were so much more efficient than smaller institutions that restricting their size would come with a high cost. I have
seen no evidence to that effect. Indeed, the evidence is to the contrary,
that these too-big-to-fail, too-big-to-be-financially-resolved institutions
are also too big to be managed. Their competitive advantage arises from
their monopoly power and their implicit government subsidies.

This is *not* a radical idea. Mervyn King, the governor of the Bank
of England, has used almost exactly these words: "If some banks are
thought to be too big to fail . . . then they are too big."[35] Paul Volcker,
former chairman of the Federal Reserve, coauthored a report released
in January 2009 that also put it well:

> Almost inevitably, the complexity of much proprietary capital market
> activity, and the perceived need for confidentiality of such activities,
> limits transparency for investors and creditors alike. . . . In practice,
> any approach must recognize that the extent of such risks, potential
> volatility, and the conflicts of interests will be difficult to measure
> and control. Experience demonstrates that under stress, capital and
> credit resources will be diverted to cover losses, weakening protec-
> tion of client interests. Complex and unavoidable conflicts of interest
> among clients and investors can be acute. Moreover, to the extent
> that these proprietary activities are carried out by firms supervised
> by government and protected from the full force of potential failure,
> there is a strong element of unfair competition with "free-standing"
> institutions. . . . [And] is it really possible, with all the complexities,
> risks, and potential conflicts, that even the most dedicated board of
> directors and top management can understand and maintain control
> over such a diverse and complex mix of activities?[36]

Volcker highlights one of the key reforms for the large, government-
insured banks: restricting "proprietary" trading—gambling on their
own account, knowing that there is a backstop from the government if

things go bad. There is no reason for these risks to be commingled. But now that the big banks have gotten bigger, there are other problems: a few have, in effect, "insider information" from which they can profit. They know, in particular, what many other participants in the market are doing, and they can use that information to gain for themselves at the expense of others. In creating an "unlevel playing field," they are simultaneously distorting the market and undermining confidence in it. Moreover, they have an unfair advantage in writing credit default swaps and other similar "insurance"-like products. AIG's failure has heightened an awareness of the importance of "counterparty risk," the chance that those writing the insurance will go into default. But that gives a big advantage to the big banks, since everyone knows that they are effectively underwritten by the government. It may be no accident that the share of credit default swaps written by big banks is so large.

The result is an unhealthy dynamic: the big banks have a competitive advantage over others, not based on real economic strength but because of the distortions that arise from the implicit government guarantee. Over time, there is a risk of an increasingly distorted financial sector.

The big banks are not responsible for whatever dynamism there is in the U.S. economy. The much-vaunted synergies of bringing together various parts of the financial industry have been a phantasm; more apparent are the managerial failures and the conflicts of interest. In short, there is little to lose, and much to gain, by breaking up these behemoths. Their commingled activities—insurance companies, investment banking, anything that is not absolutely essential to the core function of commercial banking—need to be spun off.

The process of breaking them up may be slow, and there may be political resistance. Even if there were an agreement about limiting their size, there may be lapses in enforcement. That is why a three-pronged attack is needed: breaking up the too-big-to-fail institutions, strongly restricting the activities in which any remaining large institution can be engaged, and calibrating deposit insurance and capital adequacy restrictions to "level the playing field." Because these institutions impose greater risks on society, they should be required to have more capital and to pay higher deposit insurance premiums.[37] All the regulations discussed earlier must be applied to these institutions with greater stringency. They especially should not be allowed to have employee (and especially managerial) incentive structures that encourage excessive risk-taking and shortsighted behavior.[38] The restrictions on their activities may result in low returns for the big banks—but that is as it should be. The high returns that they earned in the past were the result of risk-taking at the expense of American taxpayers.

Too-big-to-fail banks should be forced to return to the boring business of doing conventional banking. There are plenty of other institutions— smaller, more aggressive companies, non-depository institutions that are not so big that their failure would bring the entire economy down—that are able to perform the other risky roles that these banks have assumed.

Teddy Roosevelt, when he first called for antitrust legislation in December 1901, was motivated as much by concerns of political power as he was by market distortions. Indeed, there is little evidence that he understood the standard economists' analysis of how monopoly power distorts resource allocation. Even if the too-big-to-fail banks had no power to raise prices (the critical condition in modern antitrust analysis), they should be broken up. The evident ability of the big banks to stop so much of the regulatory reforms that are needed is itself proof of the power that they wield, and highlights the importance of taking action.

One of the ex post excuses that the Federal Reserve and Secretary of Treasury Henry Paulson gave for allowing Lehman Brothers to fail was that they did not have the legal authority to do anything else. At the time, they claimed that because it had been so clear for so long that Lehman Brothers was at such risk of failure, they believed the markets had had ample time to protect themselves. But, by the same token, if they didn't have the legal authority required, they had had ample opportunity to go to Congress and ask for it. The unprecedented actions they took in the case of AIG, just two days later, suggest that this "lack of legal authority" was just the best defense they could come up with when the first line of defense—that Lehman's demise didn't represent any systemic threat—failed. While rumors of Lehman's demise had been swirling for months, the system evidently hadn't inoculated itself against that possibility; but, more remarkably, neither the Fed nor the Treasury seem to have realized it.

Still, one of the reforms that is needed is granting the Fed and Treasury clearer authority to "resolve" financial institutions whose failure might put the economy at risk. But while it is a reform that is needed, it does nothing about the underlying problem—the existence of these too-big-to-be-resolved institutions—and giving the Fed and the Treasury legal authority to do something doesn't answer the question, *what should be done?* If these financial institutions are too big to be resolved, or if they are in a position to persuade a gullible administration that they are too big, whatever the government's legal authority is, they have the government over a barrel. The only "solution" will be to pour out taxpayer money to keep them going.

The problems are deeper, though. It is not just size that matters, but the interlinking of the institutions. The failure of even a relatively small institution (like Bear Stearns), it was feared, could generate a cascade of effects because the financial system is so intertwined. Institutions that are too intertwined to be resolved have the same competitive advantage as too-big-to-be-resolved institutions. (One of the innovations of the financial system that led to the institutions becoming too intertwined were derivatives. See below.)

What is needed is not just "resolution" authority, but preventive action. The government needs to be able to stop the too-big-to-fail, too-big-to-be-resolved, and too-intertwined-to-be-resolved situations from arising. Government needs to have a meaningful choice—so that it doesn't "have" to do what it claims it had to do in this case, give the banks unlimited money, protecting shareholders and bondholders alike.[39]

RISKY INNOVATIONS: DERIVATIVES

The financial markets were innovative, but not always in ways that led to a more stable and productive economy. They had incentives to create complex and non-transparent products, such as collateralized debt instruments (CDOs), slicing and dicing the mortgages into securities, and then slicing and dicing the securities into ever more complicated products.[40] When gambling—speculating—on corn, gold, oil, or pork bellies didn't provide enough opportunities for risk-taking, they invented "synthetic" products, derivatives based on these commodities. Then, in a flurry of metaphysical ingenuity, they invented synthetic products based on the synthetic products. It was rarely clear whether these new products were helping the economy to manage meaningful risks well, but it was clear that they provided new opportunities for risk-taking and for earning hefty fees.

These derivatives are among the innovations that those in financial markets are most proud of. The name says much about their essence: their value is *derived* from some other asset. A bet that the price of a stock will be greater than ten dollars next Monday is a derivative. A bet that the market value of a bet that a stock will be greater than ten dollars next Monday is a derivative based on a derivative. There are an infinite number of such products that one could invent. Derivatives are a double-edged sword. On the one hand, they can be used to manage risk. If Southwest Airlines worried about the rising price of fuel, it could insure against that risk by buying oil on the futures market, locking in a price today for oil to be delivered in six months. Using derivatives, Southwest can similarly take out an "insurance policy" against the risk that the price will rise. The transaction costs may be slightly lower than in the old way of hedging, say, buying or selling oil in futures markets.

On the other hand, as Warren Buffett pointed out, derivatives can also be financial weapons of mass destruction, which is what they turned out to be for AIG, as they destroyed it and much of the economy at the same time. AIG sold "insurance" against the collapse of other banks, a particular kind of derivative called a credit default swap. Insurance can be a very profitable business, so long as the insurer doesn't have to pay out too often. It can be especially profitable in the short run: the insurer rakes in premiums, and so long as the insured event doesn't occur, everything looks rosy. AIG thought it was rolling in money. What was the chance that a large firm like Bear Stearns or Lehman Brothers would ever go bankrupt? Even if there was the potential for them to mismanage their risks, surely the government would bail them out.

Life insurance companies know how to estimate their risk accurately. They might not know how long a particular person is going to live, but on average, Americans live, say, seventy-seven years (current life expectancy at birth). If an insurance company insures a large cross-section of Americans, it can be fairly certain that the average age of death will be close to that number. Additionally, companies can get data on life expectancy by occupation, sex, income, and so forth, and make an even better prediction of the life expectancy of the person seeking insurance.[41] Moreover, with few exceptions (like wars and epidemics), the risks are "independent," the likelihood of one person dying is unrelated to that of another.

Estimating the risk of a particular firm going bankrupt, however, is not like estimating life expectancy. It doesn't happen every day, and as we've seen, the risk of one firm may be highly correlated with that of another.[42] AIG thought that it understood risk management. It did not. It wrote credit default swaps that required it to make huge payments all at the same time—more money than even the world's largest insurance company possessed. Because those who bought the "insurance" wanted to be sure that the other side could pay, they required the insurance company to pony up money (collateral) if, say, the price of the insured bond fell—suggesting that the market thought there was a higher risk of bankruptcy. It was these collateral payments, which AIG couldn't meet, that eventually did it in.

Credit default swaps played a nefarious role in the current crisis for several reasons. Without properly assessing whether the seller of the insurance could honor his promise, people weren't just buying insurance—they were gambling. Some of the gambles were most peculiar and gave rise to perverse incentives. In the United States and most other countries, one person can't buy insurance on the life of another person unless he has some economic interest (called an insurable interest). A wife can buy insurance against the death of her husband; a company, against the death of key personnel. But if Bob takes out an insurance policy against Jim, with whom he has no connection, it creates the most perverse incentive: Bob has an interest in insuring Jim's early demise.

If one financial institution were to take out an insurance policy against Lehman Brothers dying, it would, by the same token, have an incentive to see Lehman's early demise.[43] And there were ample weapons available to any player or group of players large enough to manipulate the market, an armory that only increased as financial markets grew more complex. The credit default swap markets were thin, and so it was easy to drive down the price—suggesting that there was a high probability of bankruptcy. That could trigger a whole chain of consequences. The price of the stock would likely fall. Someone holding a "short" position in the stock—a bet that the price of the stock would fall—would make a profit; the party on the other side, a loss. There might be a variety of contracts (similar to AIG's) requiring Lehman to post more collateral. It might trigger a run on the bank by those who had uninsured deposits (and in the case of Lehman, they were all uninsured). The bank might then face a liquidity crisis. Its probability of bankruptcy *had* gone up: the attack on the company through credit default swaps was, in a sense, a self-fulfilling prophecy.

Derivatives have played an important role in amplifying the crisis in another important way. The big banks failed to net out derivative positions. Bank A might have bet Bank B $1,000 that the price of oil was going up $15 next year. The next week, Bank A decides it wants to cancel the bet. The straightforward way to do this would be simply to pay a fee for ending the obligation. But that would have been far too simple. So instead they arrange another deal, where Bank B agrees to pay Bank A $1,000 if the price of oil goes up $15 next year. If the price of oil does go up, nothing happens. It is as if the deal was called off, *provided neither party goes bankrupt*. The players failed to recognize the importance of counterparty risk—the risk that one of the two banks might go bankrupt. If Bank A goes bankrupt, Bank B still owes A

$1,000 if the price of oil goes up $15. But Bank A doesn't owe B anything—or more accurately, it owes that money but may not pay it. The deals do not necessarily net out.

When asked why they didn't cancel the deals directly rather than engage in these offsetting transactions—leading to exposures to risk in the trillions of dollars—the answer was, "We couldn't imagine a default." Yet they were trading credit default swaps on the big banks, which were premised on the notion that there were risks of default. This is yet another example of the kind of intellectual incoherence that permeated these markets.

The banks were supposed to be good risk managers, and among the risks that they were supposed to manage was counterparty risk. But at least some of them did not. That was why the bankruptcy of AIG risked bringing down the entire financial system. Many banks thought that they had bought insurance—*from* AIG—against a variety of market risks, which in turn allowed them to take on more risk than they otherwise would have. AIG's demise would have left them highly exposed. Regulators had allowed them to take on more risk because they (mistakenly) thought their overall risk profile was manageable; the purchase of "insurance" put them in good stead to take on more risk. Without AIG's insurance (and similar "insurance" provided by other financial institutions), the regulators would have required the bank to show that it had enough capital to meet the risks it faced. If it couldn't find the capital it would have to pull back in lending, exacerbating the economic downturn.

When you buy life insurance, you want to make sure the company you buy insurance from is going to be around when you die. The United States has very strong regulation of life insurance, but there was no regulation of the kind of insurance that financial institutions were buying to manage their risk. In fact, America's financial markets had resisted such regulations, as we have seen.[44]

Now, *after* the crisis, there are some attempts to net out some of the trillions of dollars of risk exposure, but there are problems in doing so. Many of the derivatives are "tailor-made," each one being different from the last. In some cases, there was a good reason for this—one party wanted insurance against a very particular risk. In many cases, it seems that the real reason for relying on these tailor-made products was to increase fees. Competition in standardized products can be intense—meaning that the profits are small. If banks could persuade their customers that a tailor-made product was just what they needed, there was an opportunity for enhanced revenues. Little thought was given to the difficulties of "unwinding" these complex products.

There is still a debate about what was driving the trillions of dollars in derivatives. The ostensible argument was "improved risk management." For instance, those buying corporate bonds wanted to off-load the risk of the firm going bankrupt. This argument is not as convincing as it seems. If you want to buy a bond *without credit risk*, then you should buy a government bond of comparable maturity. It's that simple. Anyone buying a ten-year bond in a company is, by assumption, engaged in making a credit assessment, judging whether the interest rate paid in excess of the ten-year government rate suffices to compensate for the extra risk of default.[45]

There are a few possible answers to what was probably going on— none very reassuring about the contribution of derivatives to the overall performance of the economy. One, as I have mentioned, is fees. A second is regulatory arbitrage: by allegedly laying off risk onto others, the bank was able to absorb other risks. The benefits of laying off the risk (and especially the regulatory benefits) were greater than the apparent costs. Were the banks so stupid that they did not understand counterparty risk? Perhaps they did understand the risk, but they understood that the regulators underestimated them, and the short-run profit opportunities from regulatory arbitrage were simply too big to resist, even though the bets put the firm's future at risk.

There is a third explanation: Wall Street has been described as a casino for rich men. Implicit in the premium paid on a corporate bond is a judgment about the probability of default. If I think that I am smarter than the market, I would like to make a bet on the value of that judgment. Everybody on Wall Street believed that they were brighter than others—or at least brighter than the average. The credit default swaps opened up a new high-stakes table at the gambling casino. Consenting adults should be allowed to gamble—even if it is on the irrational basis that they all believe they are brighter than everybody else. But they should not be allowed to gamble at the expense of the rest of us—and that's what happens when the gambling occurs inside the financial institutions, especially within the too-big-to-fail institutions.

What is to be done?

Because derivatives *can* be a useful tool for risk management, they shouldn't be banned, but they should be regulated to make sure that they are used appropriately. There should be full transparency, effective competition, and enough "margin" to ensure that those betting can fulfill their side of the deal, and, most importantly, derivatives should not be allowed to put the entire financial system at risk. To accomplish these objectives several things have to be done: Credit default swaps and certain other derivatives should be limited to exchange-traded transactions and to situations where there is an "insurable risk." Unless there is full transparency—not just information about, say, gross exposures, but data about each position, so the market can assess counterparty risk—disasters like AIG's may not be a thing of the past. But insisting that standardized derivatives be traded in exchanges (or clearinghouses) is not enough. The exchanges have to be adequately capitalized; otherwise, when an untoward event—like the bursting of a real estate bubble—occurs, the government will again have to pick up the pieces. However, some of the products are so complex and so risky that it will be hard for even a well-intentioned regulator to be sure that there is sufficient capital—and there is a real risk that the regulators of the future will be like the regulators of the past, more focused on the well-being of financial markets than on that of the economy or the taxpayer. There is a simple remedy: requiring joint and several liability of all market participants on the exchanges, such that all of those who use the exchange would have to pony up all that they have before taxpayers shell out a dime. (I suspect that such a provision might lead to the end of the market—proving that the market only exists because of the ability to draw upon public money to support it.)

One contentious debate concerns whether tailor-made "over-the-counter" products should be allowed. The current conventional wisdom holds that while banks should be encouraged to engage in standardized products traded on exchanges, tailor-made products still have an important role to play; when over-the-counter products are used, however, they need to be backed with sufficiently high levels of capital and there should be adequate transparency. The worry is that the regulators will be "captured." They will succumb to pressure for less-than-full transparency ("business secrets" is a standard line). Given a choice between writing transparent exchange-traded derivatives and less transparent over-the-counter derivatives, banks will choose the latter, unless the extra capital required to back them is high enough. And the regulators will succumb to pressure to make sure that it is not too high. In short, if both exchange-traded and over-the-counter derivatives are allowed, we risk ending up in a situation not too different from that which got us into the current mess.

PREDATORY LENDING

The financial system has shown that it cannot be trusted to sell products that are appropriate to the needs of those who buy them. Risks are complicated. Even the bankers couldn't manage them well. How then can we expect ordinary individuals to do so? In many areas, we have come to recognize that the presumption of caveat emptor does not suffice. The reason is simple—buyers are poorly informed, and there are important information asymmetries. That's why we have, for instance, government food safety regulation and government regulation of drugs.[46] Banks and other financial institutions took advantage especially of less educated Americans; they preyed upon them in a variety of ways, some of which I have already described, some of which I will discuss shortly. It was clear that they were doing so, and consumer advocates tried repeatedly to get legislation passed to stop these practices. But, so far, the predatory financial institutions have been successful in pushing back.

What is needed is a Financial Products Safety Commission.[47] One of the tasks of such a commission would be to identify which financial products are safe enough to be held by ordinary individuals and in what circumstances.

INADEQUATE COMPETITION: SUPPRESSING INNOVATION

While banks spent much of the last two decades trying to make a buck in the derivatives markets, they also spent a fair amount of energy encouraging America's addiction to debt. We have seen how bankers enticed the unwary with mortgages that were beyond their ability to pay, but deceptive credit card practices, which grew rapidly in the years after 1980, were perhaps even more sinister.[48] Banks invented myriad new ways to increase their profits. If someone was late in making payments, not only was there a late fee, but often the interest rate rose and the bank started charging the credit card holder on balances before they were due.

The cleverest fees, however, were the "interchange" fees imposed on merchants that accepted their cards. As the cards came into wider use as cardholders were offered various reward enticements to put charges on the cards, store owners felt they had to accept them; they would otherwise lose too many sales to competitors that did. Visa and Master-Card knew this—and knew that that meant that they could exploit the merchant. If the banks charged 2 or 3 percent of the cost of a product, most merchants would still accept the cards rather than lose sales. The fact that modern computers rendered the actual costs negligible was irrelevant. There simply wasn't any effective competition, and so the banks could get away with it. To make sure that markets *didn't* work, they insisted that the merchant neither inform customers of the true cost of using the card nor impose a charge for use of the card. Visa and MasterCard also required merchants not to "discriminate" between cards. If a merchant accepted one card from Visa, he had to accept all, even if the charges to the merchant were different.[49] In short, their monopoly power was so great that *they could ensure that the price system would not work.* If merchants had been able to pass on the charges, those using the more costly cards would have seen the relative cost, and customers would choose the best card—where the benefits given by the card best reflected the charges imposed.[50] But Visa and Master-Card made sure that the price mechanism was short-circuited.

None of this would have been possible if there had been effective enforcement of competition regulations. Financial deregulation made these anticompetitive credit card practices more attractive. There used to be laws limiting interest rates—they were called usury laws. Such restrictions go back to the Bible, and have a long history in most religions—arising out of the even longer history of moneylenders (often described as the second-oldest profession) exploiting poor borrowers. But modern America threw the lessons of the dangers of usury aside. With interest rates so high, lending was highly profitable even if some percentage of cardholders didn't repay was what owed. It was easier just to hand out credit cards to anyone who breathed than to do the hard work of credit assessment and judge who was creditworthy and who was not.

Because the banks essentially own the two major credit/debit card systems, Visa and MasterCard, and enjoy the extra profits that the costly system generates, they have had every incentive to stifle the development of an efficient electronic payment mechanism, and stifle it they do. One can imagine what an efficient system would look like. At the point of purchase, there would be an instantaneous verification (as there is today) that the card was not stolen, and that there are sufficient funds in the "account" of the cardholder to pay the amount. The funds would then be instantaneously transferred from the cardholder's account to the merchant's. All of this would be accomplished for a few pennies. Some cardholders might have arranged to have a credit line with their bank, allowing them to overdraw seamlessly up to a point, at competitive interest rates. Others might have preferred to have their hands tied; they don't want an "overdraft" facility—knowing the exploitive fees that the banks would extract. The payment mechanism would work smoothly, whether there was a credit line attached or not. This efficient payment mechanism linked to a credit system would serve everybody well— except the bankers, who would see lower fees.[51]

The U.S. financial system was clever in figuring out how to exploit poor Americans, but it was unable to figure out how to serve them well. In Botswana, one of the more successful countries of Africa, I have seen how banks reach out to poor villages to provide basic financial services to people whose incomes are but a fraction of those of even the poorest Americans. (Botswana's *average* per capita income is still only $13,604.)[52] But in poor parts of America, individuals turn to check-cashing services to cash their checks, paying a fee as high as 20 percent of the value of the checks.[53] It is a major industry—another way that the poor are exploited.[54]

The blatant greed of America's financial markets is nowhere more evident than in the political pressure they have brought to bear to maintain the college student loan program. This is another example of a public-private partnership where government bears the risk, and the private sector reaps the rewards. The government insures the student loans so there is no risk, but those originating the student loans can charge interest rates as if there *were* a risk of nonpayment. Indeed, the cost to the government of using the private sector as a partner compared to the government doing the lending itself over a ten-year period is estimated at $80 billion—a munificent gift to the financial industry.[55] Giving away amounts of this size is an invitation to corruption—and that is exactly what happened. A lender would go to the school admissions officers and bribe them to feature their lending program. Even prestigious universities like Columbia University did not escape the corruption.[56] But the corruption really began in the political process that created the program and still allows it to continue.

MAKING REGULATION WORK

The financial sector needs regulation, but effective regulation requires regulators who believe in it. They should be chosen from among those who might be hurt by a failure of regulation, not from those who would benefit.[57] Fortunately, there are large numbers of financial experts in unions, nongovernmental organizations (NGOs), and universities. One doesn't have to go to Wall Street to get the so-called expertise.

We saw in the discussion of derivatives how the bankers, even as they were winning the battles of the day, wanted to make sure that the likes of Brooksley Born would never have sway: they took away the authority to regulate. We need to realize the pressure that regulators are under not to regulate—and realize the risk of the appointment of another Greenspan, someone who doesn't believe in regulation. We have to "hardwire" the system, with transparent regulations that give little leeway for nonenforcement. Some degree of duplication may even be desirable, as in the area of competition:[58] the costs of a mistake are thousands of times greater than the extra costs of enforcement. It is also clear that to have a regulatory system that works, we will need a multiplicity of regulators: those with expertise in each of the markets (insurance markets, securities markets, banks), a regulator who monitors the overall stability of the financial system, and a regulator who looks at the safety of the products the system sells.

Designing a regulatory structure for the future is obviously contentious, though the debate has been dominated by turf wars. The oddest proposal coming from the Obama administration involved giving the Federal Reserve—which failed so miserably in the run-up to the crisis—more power. It was another whitewash based on the premise of rewarding failure: the banks had a "little" problem, so give them more money to do with as they pleased, even though they had failed to use what money they had had well; the Fed had a little problem, so give it more power, even though it had failed to use what power it had had well.

BEYOND FINANCE AND
FINANCIAL REGULATION

In this and the previous chapter I described the myriad of ways that the financial system misbehaved, and how it got away with it. I have recounted the litany of the problems in the financial system in part because it is so intriguingly all-encompassing. But the problems in the economy go beyond the financial sector, as do the failures of the regulatory system.

I have already mentioned failures in the design and enforcement of competition policy and corporate governance, but there were other failures as well. In 2005, Congress passed the Bankruptcy Abuse Prevention and Consumer Protection Act. The banks had fought hard for the law because it gave them new powers to extract money from borrowers. While the banks argued for public bailouts for themselves, they argued against any reprieve for the poor. While they put aside worries about moral hazard for themselves, they argued that any forgiveness for ordinary individuals who had been misled into taking debt would have adverse incentives. It did, but the effect surfaced in the quality of the banks' assessment of creditworthiness.

Covered by the new bankruptcy laws, the banks felt confident that they could lend to anyone. One prominent bank now on government life support advertised, "Qualified at birth." Every teenager was inundated with credit card offers. Many families took on enormous debt, and in a cycle that resembled indentured servitude, they worked to pay the bank. Larger and larger fractions of their income went to pay penalty fees and exorbitant interest charges, the interest on the interest charges and fees, with little chance for a fresh start. The financiers might have liked to have gone back to the days of Oliver Twist and debtor prisons, but the 2005 bill was the best they could do under the circumstances. A quarter of a person's wages could be garnished. The new law also emboldened lenders to approve even worse mortgages, which may partially account for why so many toxic mortgages were given out *after* the passage of the bill.

A new bankruptcy law, one more commensurate with American

values, would not only provide a reprieve for hard-pressed families but also improve the efficiency of the market and induce the banks to do a better job of credit assessment. The banks complain that repealing the 2005 law might lead to higher interest rates. If so, so be it: Americans have overborrowed, at great cost to society and the whole world. An incentive for saving would be all for the better.

The tax system also played a part in the current situation. It is said that tax systems reflect the values of society. One of the strange aspects of the U.S. tax system is that it treats speculators who gamble better than those who work hard for a living. Capital gains are taxed at a far lower rate than wages. There is no good economic justification. It is true that society may want to encourage some kinds of risky investments because of their broad benefits. For instance, it might want to encourage path-breaking innovations, especially in areas of public interest, like climate change or health. In that case, government should tax the returns on these investments (whatever the form, whether capital gains or profits) at a lower rate. But real estate speculation is surely not one of the categories of investment society wants to favor with preferential treatment. The land will be there whether the purchases of it are subsidized or not.

INNOVATION

Critics of a new tough regulatory regime say that it will stifle innovation. But as we've seen, much of the innovation of the financial system has been designed to circumvent accounting standards designed to ensure the transparency of the financial system, regulations designed to ensure the stability and fairness of the financial system, and laws that try to make sure that all citizens pay their fair share of taxes. Meanwhile, the financial system not only has failed to innovate in ways that improve the ability of ordinary citizens to manage the risks they face, but also has actually resisted welfare-enhancing innovations.

When I was a member of the Council of Economic Advisors in President Clinton's cabinet, I pushed, for instance, for inflation-indexed bonds. People who are saving to retire thirty or forty years from now worry about inflation, and rightfully so. Right now, inflation is low, but there have been periods of high inflation, and many are expecting another period of high inflation. People would like to get insurance against this risk, but the market doesn't provide it. The Council proposed that the government sell inflation-indexed bonds and thereby actually provide long-term insurance against inflation. The government has a responsibility to maintain price stability at a reasonable level. If it fails to maintain price stability, it ought to pay the consequences.

Some Wall Streeters opposed this initiative because they thought that people who bought these inflation-indexed bonds would hold them until their retirement. I thought that was a good thing—why waste money on transaction costs associated with buying and selling? But it was not good for Wall Street, which was concerned with maximizing its revenue, which the firms achieved by maximizing transaction costs.

In another example, Argentina, after its financial crisis, did not know how much it could repay its creditors, so it proposed an interesting innovation. Rather than trying to pay more than it could, which would lead to another debt crisis a few years down the line, it proposed a GDP-indexed bond. This bond would pay more if and when Argentina's income went up and the country could afford to pay more. That way, creditors' interests would be aligned with Argentina's interests, and they would work to try to help Argentina grow. Again, Wall Street resisted this GDP-indexed bond.[59]

A better-regulated financial system would actually be more innovative in ways that mattered—with the creative energy of financial markets directed at competing to produce products that enhance the well-being of most citizens. It might develop the efficient electronic payment system I described earlier in the chapter, or the better mortgage system I described in chapter 4. Creating a financial system that actually fulfills the functions that a financial system is supposed to perform is an important step in restructuring the economy. This crisis can be a turning point—not only for the financial sector, but for the rest of the economy as well.

We have not done as good a job as we should restructuring the financial system and redesigning the regulatory structure under which the financial system operates. Our country won't prosper if it goes back to the financial system that existed prior to the crisis. But this is only one of the many challenges facing the country in the post-crisis world. The next chapter discusses what needs to be done—and how the crisis has many lessons that can help us do what needs to be done better.

CHAPTER SEVEN

A NEW
CAPITALIST ORDER

IN THE FALL OF 2008, THE GLOBAL ECONOMY, OR AT least its sophisticated financial markets, was at the brink of a complete meltdown. It was in freefall. Having seen so many other crises, I was sure that this sense of freefall would soon come to an end. It happens with every crisis. But what then? We neither can nor should return to the world as it was before. Many of the jobs that were being lost would not return. America's middle class had been having a hard time before the crisis. What would happen to it in the aftermath?

The crisis has distracted the United States and much of the world from longer-run problems that will have to be addressed. The list is familiar: health care, energy and the environment, and especially climate change, education, the aging population, the decline in manufacturing, a dysfunctional financial sector, global imbalances, the U.S. trade and fiscal deficits. As the nation has struggled to deal with the immediate crisis, these problems have not gone away. Some have become worse. But the resources that are available to deal with them may have been substantially reduced because of the way the government mismanaged the crisis—in particular, by the money it squandered on bailing out the financial system. The U.S. federal debt-to-GDP ratio soared from 35 percent in 2000 to nearly 60 percent in

2009—and with even the optimistic projections of the Obama administration suggesting $9 trillion more debt in the next decade, that ratio will go up further to 70 percent by 2019.[1]

The restructuring of the economy will not happen on its own. The government will have to play a central role. And that's the second major set of changes ahead: the financial crisis showed that financial markets do not automatically work well, and that markets are not self-correcting. But the lesson is more general, going beyond financial markets. There is an important role for government. The Reagan-Thatcher "revolution" denigrated that role. The misguided attempt to reduce the role of the state has resulted in government taking on a larger role than anyone would have anticipated even in the New Deal. We will now have to reconstruct a society with a better balance between the role of government and the role of market. More balance can lead to a more efficient and a more stable economy.

In this chapter, I lay out these twin and related agendas: what needs to be done to restore the balance between government and the market and to restructure the economy—including the role of the government in that restructuring. If we are to succeed in transforming America, we have to have a clearer vision of where we should be going, and we need to have a clearer vision of the role of the state.

The problems facing the United States are similar to those facing many, if not most, of the advanced industrial countries. While many did a somewhat better job of bailing out their banks, they still face a marked increase in the debt-to-GDP ratio from their (mostly successful) attempts to stimulate the economy. For some, the problems associated with the aging of the population are worse. For most, the problems in the health care sector are less acute. None will have an easy time addressing the challenges of climate change. Almost all face major challenges in restructuring their economies.

THE NEED TO RESTRUCTURE
THE ECONOMY

An honest appraisal of the prospects ahead

While America will likely remain the world's largest economy for years to come, it is not inevitable that the standard of living of most Americans will continue to increase as it did, for instance, in the years following World War II.[2] Many Americans have been living in a fantasy world of easy credit, and that world is over. It won't, and it shouldn't, return. They, and the country as a whole, will face a drop in living standards. Not only was the country living beyond its means, but so were many families.

The bubble hid the fact that the economic state of the nation was not as good as it could or should have been. The focus on GDP has been misleading—as I explain at greater length in chapter 10. For many groups, future economic prospects are already weak: the median income of males in their thirties today is lower than it was three decades ago.[3] Most Americans have seen income stagnate for a decade. In the early years of this decade, as many saw their incomes stagnate or decline, they, nonetheless, consumed as if they were part of the American dream. With the housing bubble, they could increase their consumption today and pretend that they could look forward to a comfortable retirement and provide the education to their children that would enable them to see even greater prosperity. But with the breaking of the bubble, those dreams were dashed, and at the same time, Americans faced greater economic and health insecurity—some 15 percent have no health insurance at all.[4] There were other indicators that something might be amiss: in 2007 the fraction of the United States population in prison was one of the largest—ten times that of many European countries.[5]

A host of other problems persist. Global warming necessitates a retrofitting of the economy that will require enormous investments. Now, the nation needs to make up for time lost during the Bush years. The infrastructure has decayed—evidenced so well by the collapse of New Orleans's levees and Minnesota's bridge. And while the United

States has a first-rate university system—the best in the world—the average performance of students in the elementary and secondary education system is below par. Students perform more poorly in science and mathematics than the average of most industrialized countries.[6] The result is that many workers are not well prepared to meet the challenges of twenty-first-century global competition.

The U.S. economy needs to be restructured in directions that are not yet clear. What is clear is that it will take resources, and it will take public spending. Resources will have to move from some sectors that are too large (like finance and real estate) and some sectors that are too weak (like manufacturing) to others that have better prospects for sustainable growth.

Something amiss: more than a financial crisis

As I have shown in other chapters, Americans had lived off one bubble after another for years. Further, there were massive global imbalances—the U.S. government was borrowing as much as 6 percent of GDP from other countries at the very time that it should have been setting aside money for the surge of retiring baby boomers expected in the next few years.[7]

The rest of the world was striving to emulate America, but if it did succeed in fully emulating America, the world could not survive. The consumption style was not environmentally sustainable, yet Americans continued to buy bigger and bigger gas-guzzling cars—and the entire automobile industry's profitability rested on the assumption that Americans would do so forever.

Much of the rest of the economy, including some of the most successful sectors, also rested on unsustainable foundations. One of the most profitable sectors in the economy was energy, coal, and oil, which poured greenhouse gases into the atmosphere, even with incontrovertible evidence that it was leading to massive climate change.[8]

A central part of restructuring the economy entails going from manufacturing to a service-sector economy. In the early 1990s, there was a debate about the quality of the new service-sector jobs being created.

Was the country creating hamburger flippers to replace its skilled manufacturing workers? A careful look at the data showed that a large fraction of the service-sector jobs were good jobs, paying high wages, and many of the high-paying service-sector jobs were located in the financial sector—it was to be the new basis of the American economy. But that raises the question of how could something that was a means to an end become the center of a New Economy? We should have recognized that the outsized proportions of the financial sector—in the years before the crisis, some 40 percent of corporate profits were in that sector—indicated that something was wrong.[9]

America within a global context

Any vision for America going forward must be articulated as part of a global vision. As this global recession has so forcefully reminded us, we are all intertwined. The world today faces at least six key economic challenges, some of which are interrelated. Their persistence and depth is testimony to the difficulties that our economic and political system has in addressing problems at the global scale. We simply don't have effective institutions to help identify the problems and formulate a vision of how they might be resolved, let alone to take appropriate concrete actions.

The most dramatic problem is the gap between global demand and global supply. The world's productive capacity is being underutilized, in a world in which there are huge unmet needs. The most serious underutilization is of human resources—beyond the immediate problem of up to 240 million unemployed throughout the world because of the recession, billions of people do not have the education to use their human potential fully, and even when they do, they do not work to their full capability.[10] Decent work is an important aspect of an individual's self-esteem, and the societal loss is far greater than the shortfall in output.

The biggest environmental challenge is, of course, that posed by climate change. Scarce environmental resources are treated as if they are free. All prices are distorted as a result, in some cases badly so. In earlier chapters, we have seen how distorted housing prices distorted the economy; the crisis showed the traumatic effect of the "correction" of housing prices—which was more traumatic because of the long delay before the correction occurred. The distortion in environmental prices is of equal magnitude; it has led to the using up of key resources in an unsustainable way; the correction is imperative; and a delay likely to be even more costly.

What have come to be called global imbalances also pose a problem for global stability. One part of the world is living well beyond its means; the other part produces in excess of its consumption. The two are in a tango. There may be nothing particularly worrisome about some countries consuming more than their income, and others less: that's just part of market economics. What is worrisome, as I noted in chapter 1, is that with the amount America has been borrowing from the rest of the world, more than $800 billion in 2006 alone, its borrowing would not be sustainable. There could be a disorderly unwinding of these imbalances, with possibly large disruptive changes in exchange rates.[11] What has happened in this crisis has been clearly disorderly, but imbalances persist. Especially problematic is the fact noted earlier, that the United States should be saving for the baby boomers, not borrowing.

The G-20 has proposed a coordinated macroeconomics response—the United States increase its savings and Chinese reduce its—so that the imbalances will be reduced in a way that maintains a strong global economy. The aspiration is noble, but each country's policies are likely to be driven by its own domestic agenda.

The United States is more likely to cut back on consumption faster than China expands its consumption. That in fact seems to be what is happening, though in 2009 the rapid rise in household saving was offset by an even more rapid rise in public borrowing.[12] That would weaken global aggregate demand—making a robust global recovery all the more difficult.

Over the longer run, with so many countries having borrowed so much to finance their recovery programs, there is the risk of a substantial increase in interest rates. Some highly indebted countries with limited ability to raise taxes may face a financial crisis. Countries not facing a crisis will still face difficult choices: Consider the U.S., with a national debt that soon will be approaching some 70 percent of GDP, at even a moderate 5 percent interest rate, servicing the debt will take 3.5 percent of GDP, some 20 percent of the government's tax receipts. Taxes will have to be raised and/or other spending cut. What typically gives in these situations is investment—which leads to less output in the future.

On the other hand, higher interest rates will put countries with high savings in good stead. Consider China, sitting on total reserves that are now more than $2 trillion, some three-quarters ($1.5 trillion) held in dollars. At a 1 percent interest rate, the United States has to send a mere $15 billion check to China every year, but if and when interest rates return to a more normal 5 percent, the check rises to $75 billion.

With the collapse of investments due to the crisis, it is natural to think that there is a surfeit of savings. Traditionally, saving was a virtue, and I believe it still is. That's why the G-20's focus on encouraging consumption may be misguided.[13] Of course, one hopes that citizens in the developing countries will be able to raise their standards of living, and that will entail more consumption, more health services, more education, and so forth. But the world faces huge economic needs: as I commented earlier, it has to be retrofitted to meet the challenges posed by global warming; some 40 percent of the world's population still lives on less than $2 a day, and there is a massive need for investments to improve their opportunities. The problem is one of finance: of recycling the savings to those places where it is so badly needed.

The fourth challenge I call the manufacturing conundrum. Manufacturing has long represented the pinnacle of a particular stage of development, the way for developing countries to leave traditional agrarian societies. Jobs in the sector traditionally have been well paid and provided the backbone of the twentieth-century middle-class societies of Europe and North America. Over recent decades, successes in increasing productivity have meant that even as the sector grows, employment has decreased, and this pattern is likely to continue.

The fifth challenge is that of inequality. Globalization has had complex effects on the distribution of income and wealth around the world. China and India have been closing the gap with the advanced industrial countries. For a quarter century, the gap with Africa was increasing—but then China's demand for commodities helped Africa (as well as Latin America) grow at record levels, of 7 percent. This crisis has brought an end to this short-lived era of mild prosperity. And even in this period of mild prosperity, extreme poverty remained a problem: the fortunes of the poorest in the world are markedly different from those of the richest in almost every way imaginable. There are still nearly a billion people living on less than a dollar a day.

There is growing inequality in most countries of the world, and globalization is one of the factors that has contributed to this global pattern.[14] This is not just a humanitarian concern. It has played some role in the current economic downturn: the growing inequality contributes to the problem of lack of global aggregate demand—money is going from those who would spend it to those who had more than they needed.

The final challenge is stability. Growing financial instability has become an increasing problem. In spite of the alleged improvements in global financial institutions and increased knowledge about economic management, economic crises have been more frequent and worse.

There are strong interactions among these varied elements—some problems exacerbate others, while strategies designed to address one may simultaneously reduce the impact of programs designed to remedy others. For instance, the increased unemployment that results from the financial crisis will put downward pressure on wages throughout the world, and the least skilled are most likely to lose their jobs. In the United States, the wealth of the bottom half is mostly in housing—and that wealth has been devastated. One of the reasons for the global imbalances is the high demand for reserves by many developing countries in the aftermath of the East Asian crisis. The way this crisis has impacted developing countries is such that they are likely to want to hold even more reserves, exacerbating the problem of global imbalances. The two together—the growing inequality and the growing demand for reserves—may increase the problem of the insufficiency of global aggregate demand, weakening the global economy.

A broader, longer-term vision—focusing on the plight of the poor and the challenge of global warming—will ensure that there is more than enough demand to absorb all of the world's production capacity.[15] More consumption by the poor, including by those in China, and less consumption by the rich (especially in the United States) will reduce the scale of global imbalances.

Achieving the new vision will require a *new economic model*—sustainability will require less emphasis on material goods for those who are overconsuming and a shift in the direction of innovative activity. At a global level, too much of the world's innovation has been directed at saving labor and too little at saving natural resources and protecting the environment—hardly surprising given that prices do not reflect the scarcity of these natural resources. There has been so much success at saving labor that in much of the world there is a problem of persistent unemployment. But there has been so little success at saving natural resources that we are risking environmental collapse.

The long-run challenges facing America

The problems the world faces also confront America, but in America some of them are particularly acute: the country has not just the general "manufacturing conundrum," the employment problem posed by the successes in productivity increases, but also the more specific problem of offshoring, the shift of production from here to China and elsewhere, reflecting shifting comparative advantage. Adjusting to this shift in the structure of the economy will not be easy: it is often easier to lose jobs in areas where competitiveness has been lost than to create new jobs in new areas, as I have seen in so many developing countries confronting globalization. It is especially difficult without a robust financial sector focusing on lending to small and medium-sized enterprises and new firms—the source of most job creation. And today, the United States faces an additional difficulty: restructuring will require people to move. But many Americans have lost a large fraction of their home equity—a significant fraction have lost all of it. If they sell their current home, they won't have the money to make a down payment on a new one anywhere near of comparable size. Mobility, one of the hallmarks of America's past success, will be reduced.

America, like much of the rest of the world, faces growing income inequality, but in America, it has reached levels not seen for three-quarters of a century.[16] The country also needs to adapt to global warming, but until recently it has long been the largest emitter of greenhouse gases, in total and per capita, and thus bringing emissions down will require greater adjustment.[17]

America has, in addition, two further challenges. The first is that posed by the aging of the population, which means Americans should have been saving for retirement at a time when they were living beyond their means.

America also faces a series of sectoral problems: large swaths of manufacturing are in shambles. One of the seemingly most successful sectors, finance, was overblown and based on false premises; much of another, energy, is not environmentally sustainable. Even when the sector went into the renewables market—ethanol—it was so distorted by corporate lobbying that it couldn't compete with the research of emerging market countries like Brazil. To compete, the U.S. government combined subsidies that have at times amounted to more than a dollar a gallon, with tariffs on Brazil's sugar-based ethanol of more than fifty cents a gallon![18] The energy industry should have focused on conservation; instead it lobbied for off-shore drilling rights.

America's inefficient health care sector costs more to deliver, on average, poorer health outcomes than the health care systems of other advanced industrial countries. In some cases, the quality of care in the United States is even rivaled by Third World countries—though at the top America provides health care that is unsurpassed.[19]

America has an inefficient education sector, with performance that is again rivaled by many of the emerging market countries—though again at the top, America's universities are unrivaled.[20]

As we think about a long-term vision for America, it is natural for an economist to begin by thinking about what is America's long-term competitive advantage, and how can it be achieved? To me, the long-run competitive advantage lies in America's higher-education institutions and the advances in technology that derive from the advantages that those institutions provide. No other sector in the economy has had a greater market share of global leaders; U.S. universities have attracted the best talent from around the world, many of whom stay to make America their home. None of America's leading universities—those that give it a competitive advantage—are for-profit institutions—suggesting that faith in for-profit institutions may be misplaced.

But higher education alone doesn't fully flesh out America's economic strategy—we have to figure out a way to create the high-paying, middle-class jobs that were the backbone of the country and that have been disappearing with the weakening of its industrial base. Other countries, like Germany, have created a competitive high-tech industrial and manufacturing sector, based on strong apprenticeship training. Perhaps that is a direction that Americans should be thinking about.

Reasonable people may differ in their answers to these questions, but in the panic of responding to the crisis, the United States made a mistake. Before it devoted more money to "industrial policies" (government policies that shape the structure of the economy) than any country has ever devoted before—as it did with the auto and financial-sector bailouts—these are the kinds of questions that should have been asked. The magnitude of the task ahead is enormous: the sectors that are ailing—or causing Americans to suffer—and badly need restructuring (finance, manufacturing, energy, education, health, transportation) represent more than half the economy. The rest of the country cannot simply rest on the laurels of the high-tech sector, or even the achievements of the higher-education and research establishments.

False starts

Most of these challenges have been on the United States', and the world's, agenda. Some of the attempts—including during this recession—to deal with them have, however, been moves in the wrong

direction. I've discussed one already—the failure to downsize the financial sector in a way that would enhance its ability to meet societal
needs; instead the government gave money to those who had caused
the problems.

Financial markets also tried to persuade the government to follow
a false solution to the problem of the aged: privatize Social Security.
As they skimmed 1 percent or more per year from the money that
they managed, they saw privatization as a new source of fees, new
opportunities to enrich themselves at the expense of the aged. In the
United Kingdom, a study on the impact of the partial privatization of
public pensions there showed that pensions would be reduced by 40
percent as a result of these transaction costs.[21] The financial sector
wants to maximize these transaction costs, while the well-being of retirees requires that they be minimized. Today, most Americans are truly
thankful that they rejected President Bush's initiative to partially privatize Social Security; if they hadn't, the plight of older Americans would
be even bleaker.

America had preached the gospel of globalization and global competition. Elementary economics told what that meant: the United
States had to specialize in its comparative advantage, in those areas
that reflected its relative strength. In many areas, China has been outcompeting the United States, not just because of the low wages of its
unskilled workers—there are many countries where unskilled workers
receive even lower wages. China combines high savings, an increasingly
educated labor force (the number of graduates at all levels of higher
education in China approximately quadrupled from 2002 to 2008,
while total student enrollment quintupled),[22] and large investments in
infrastructure with low-cost production and modern logistics to ensure
delivery of the massive amount of material goods that American consumers want. As hard as it is for most Americans to admit, in many
areas, including key areas of the "old" economy like steel and autos, the
country is no longer the technological leader; it is no longer the most
efficient producer; and it no longer makes the best products. America
no longer has a comparative advantage in many areas of manufacturing. A country's comparative advantage can change; what matters is

dynamic comparative advantage. The East Asian countries realized this. Forty years ago, Korea's comparative advantage was not in producing chips or cars, but in rice. Its government decided to invest in education and technology to transform its comparative advantage and to increase the standard of living of its people. It succeeded, and in doing so, transformed its society and its economy. The experience of Korea and other successful countries suggests lessons and questions for the United States: what should be our long-run dynamic comparative advantage and how do we get there?

THE ROLE OF THE STATE

The big question in the twenty-first-century global economy is, what should be the role of the state? Achieving the restructuring described earlier in this chapter will require government taking on a greater role. These changes haven't been happening on their own, and they aren't likely to do so in the future. But market mechanisms can play the central role in *delivery*, for instance, in constructing a new green economy. Indeed, a simple change—making sure that prices correctly reflect long-term environmental scarcity—would go a long way.

Unfortunately, especially in the United States, many shibboleths have inhibited figuring out the right role of the state. One common aphorism, a crib from Thomas Paine, asserts, "The government that governs best is the government that governs least." Conventional wisdom on the Republican campaign trail is that tax cuts can cure any economic ill—the lower the tax rate, the higher the growth rate. Yet Sweden has one of the highest per capita incomes, and in broader measures of well-being (such as the United Nations Development Programme's index) it outranks the United States by a considerable margin.[23] Life expectancy is 80.5 years, compared to 77 years in the United States. Its former finance minister explained to me the basis of its success: "We had high tax rates."

It wasn't, of course, the high tax rates themselves that directly led to high growth and high living standards. But Sweden understood that a country has to live within its means. If it wants to have good health, education, roads, and social protection, these public services have to be paid for, and that requires high taxes. It's obvious that a country needs to spend its money reasonably well, and that's true whether we're talking about the private sector or the public. Sweden's public sector has managed to spend its money well; America's private financial sector has done a dismal job. A country has to be attentive to incentives and at one time Sweden's tax rates may have been a little too high and its support systems a little too generous, and so it adjusted both. But Sweden discovered that a good social support system can help individuals adjust to change—and thus make them more willing to accept change and those forces that give rise to it, such as globalization. The Swedes managed to have social protection without protectionism, and they benefited from the resulting openness of their economy and their society. Better social protection combined with good education and job retraining meant that their economy could be more flexible and adjust to shocks more quickly, maintaining higher levels of employment. The combination of higher employment and better social protection meant that individuals were more willing to take risks. The well-designed "welfare state" supported an "innovative society."

It is not inevitable that this should be the case. A "nanny state" can undermine incentives, including incentives to take risks and to innovate. Getting the balance right may not be easy. One of the reasons for the success of the Scandinavian countries is that they have not been bogged down by certain ideological presumptions, such as that markets are always efficient or government is always inefficient. This financial debacle, with the massive *private sector*–led misallocation of resources, should cure anyone of such prejudices. Yet, as we saw in chapter 5, fear of "nationalization" of bankrupt banks impeded timely and effective government interventions, both in the United States and in the United Kingdom, costing taxpayers billions of dollars *unnecessarily*. In America, words like *socialism*, *privatization*, and *nationalization* carry with them emotional baggage that makes clear thinking difficult.

Herbert Simon, who won the Nobel Prize in 1978 for his path-breaking work studying how modern firms actually function, pointed

cessful is higher education, and, as I have noted, all of its first-rate universities are either state owned or not for profit.[26]

The current crisis has seen the U.S. government take on unprecedented roles in the economy. Many of those who would traditionally have been the greatest critics of government activism—and especially government borrowing massively—remained silent. But to others, Bush's massive bank bailout was a betrayal of the principles of Republican conservatism. To me, it seemed just another (albeit large) expansion of what had been happening for more than a quarter century: the establishment of a corporate welfare state, including the extension and strengthening of the corporate safety net, even as social protections for ordinary individuals were, at least in some areas, being weakened.

While tariffs (taxes on imported goods) have been reduced in recent decades, a wide range of nontariff barriers protected U.S. firms. After the United States promised to reduce its subsidies to agriculture, President Bush doubled them in 2002: agriculture was subsidized to the tune of billions of dollars every year. In 2006, twenty-seven thousand well-off cotton farmers shared $2.4 billion a year, in a program that violated international trade law and hurt millions of poor farmers in Africa, South America, and India.[27]

Other industries were subsidized, some only to a limited extent, some massively, some openly, some in a more hidden way through the tax system. While we in the United States argued that developing countries should not be allowed to subsidize their infant industries, we justified our own massive subsidies to the corn-based ethanol industry, which were introduced in 1978, on the "infant industry" argument— just help it for a while until it can compete on its own. However, it was an infant that refused to grow up.

One might have thought that the oil industry, with its seemingly unbounded profits, would not turn to the government for assistance; but greed has no bounds, and money buys political influence: it has received large tax subsidies. John McCain, the 2008 Republican presidential candidate, referred to Bush's first energy bill as the one that left no lobbyist behind.[28] The mining industry too receives billions in hidden subsidies; they take minerals from government-owned land virtually for free. In 2008 and 2009, America's automobile and finance industries joined the long list of the subsidized.

Many of the most successful U.S. industries also feel the government's presence. The Internet, on which so much recent prosperity has been based, was created through government funding—even the prototype browser Mosaic was funded by the government. It was brought to market by Netscape, but Microsoft used its monopoly power to squelch Netscape in what courts all over the world have judged to be a blatant abuse of monopoly power.

While the subsidies given over the years to U.S. corporations are in the hundreds of billions of dollars, the amounts pale in comparison to those recently given to the financial industry.[29] In previous chapters, I discussed the repeated and large bailouts to banks, of which the current bailout is only the most massive. As I anticipated when the bailouts began, *this has turned out to be one of the largest redistributions of wealth in such a short period of time in history.* (Russia's privatization of state assets was almost surely larger.)

Adam Smith may not have been quite correct when he said that markets lead, as if by an invisible hand, to the well-being of society. But no defender of Adam Smith would argue that the system of ersatz capitalism to which the United States has evolved is either efficient or fair, or is leading to the well-being of society.

SO WHAT SHOULD GOVERNMENT BE DOING?

Over the past thirty-five years, economists have developed a better understanding of when markets do and do not work well. Much of it comes down to incentives: When do markets provide the right incentives? When are private rewards aligned with social returns? And how can government help align the two? The first six chapters of this book told the story of how those incentives were not aligned in financial markets.

Economists have developed a short list of instances where markets fail—where social and private incentives are not well aligned—that account for a large fraction of the important failures. The list includes monopolies, externalities, and information imperfections. It is an irony of the current political debate that the "Left" has had to take an active role in trying to get markets to work in the way that they should, for instance, through passage and enforcement of antitrust laws to ensure competition; through passage and enforcement of disclosure laws, to ensure that market participants are at least *better* informed; and through passage and enforcement of laws on pollution, and financial-sector regulation (of the kind discussed in chapter 6), to limit the consequences of externalities.

The "Right" claims that all that needs to be done is to ensure property rights and enforce contracts. Both are necessary but not sufficient—and raise some key issues, for instance, about the appropriate definition and scope of property rights. Ownership does not give unfettered rights to do as one pleases. Owning a piece of land doesn't give me the right to pollute the groundwater below the land, or even to burn leaves that might pollute the air.

Maintain full employment and a stable economy

Making markets work is thus one of the responsibilities of the state, and the most obvious manifestations of the failure of markets to work in the way that they are supposed to are the periodic episodes of unemployment and capacity underutilization, the recessions and depressions that have marked capitalism. The Employment Act of 1946 recognized that maintaining the economy at full employment was a national goal, and one for which government had to take responsibility.

How this should best be accomplished is a matter of some controversy. Conservatives have tried their best to minimize the role of the government. Having begrudgingly admitted that markets by themselves may not ensure full employment, they have tried to narrow the scope for government intervention. Milton Friedman's monetarism tried to constrain central banks to a mechanical rule—increasing the money supply at a fixed rate. When that failed, conservatives looked for another simple rule—targeting inflation.

The current crisis has shown, however, that market failures can be complex and pervasive and are not so easily corrected, and indeed, following mechanical rules may make matters worse. Among the problems contributing to this crisis was an underpricing of risk. It may be impossible for government to force markets to price risk correctly, but, as I explained in chapter 6, it can design regulations that limit the damage resulting from market mispricing.[30]

Promote innovation

There are some goods that the market on its own will undersupply. These include public goods, the benefits of which can be enjoyed by all members of society—and among these are certain key innovations. America's third president, Thomas Jefferson, pointed out that knowledge was like a candle: as one candle lights another, its own light is not diminished. It follows that it is inefficient to restrict the use of knowledge.[31] The costs of such restrictions are particularly strong in the case of basic science. But if knowledge is to be freely disseminated, government must assume responsibility for financing its production. That is why the government takes on a critical role in the promotion of knowledge and innovation.

Some of the United States' greatest successes were derived from government-supported research, typically in either state or not-for-profit universities—from the Internet to modern biotechnology. In the nineteenth century, government had a large role in the remarkable advances in agriculture—as well as in telecommunications, laying the first telegraph line between Baltimore and Washington. Government has even played an important role in social innovations—its programs extended homeownership, without the exploitive practices that marred the recent private efforts to do so.

It is possible to induce private sector innovation by restricting the use of knowledge through the patent system, though in thus enhancing private returns, social returns are diminished. A well-designed patent system tries to get the right balance, providing incentives for innovation without unduly restricting the use of knowledge. As I explain later in the chapter, there remains ample room for improvement in the existing intellectual property regime.

In the case of financial markets, however, the problem is the *absence* of effective ways of protecting intellectual property. Anyone who makes a successful new product can be quickly imitated. Hence, it's a heads-I-lose-tails-you-win proposition: if a new product is unsuccessful, it won't be imitated, but then the firm loses money; if it is successful, it will be imitated, and profits will quickly be eroded.

The consequence is a search, not for innovations that improve the well-being of customers or the efficiency of the economy, but for innovations that can't be easily imitated or, even if they are, will still generate profits. Thus, the liar loans and usurious credit card fees were "innovations" that were quickly imitated, but nonetheless garnered huge profits. Derivatives and other complex financial products, on the other hand, were not easily imitated—the more complex, the harder to imitate. A relatively few institutions issue a large fraction of the complex, over-the-counter derivatives. Less competition meant higher profits. Market forces, in other words, played a key part in driving the complexity that did so much to undermine the functioning of the market.

Provide social protection and insurance

Government has played an important role in social protection—in providing insurance against many key risks that individuals face, such as unemployment and disability. In some cases, such as annuities, the private sector eventually followed the lead of government, but in doing so has expended large resources attempting to find those who are less risky—expenditures that may not be viewed as socially productive. Society may feel that a person who is unlucky enough to be born with a heart condition ought to be helped ("there but for the grace of God go I"), including through paying for open-heart surgery. But a private insurance company wants to be sure that it is not stuck paying the bills and so will do everything it can to find out who is at risk.[32] That's one of the reasons why government will continue to play a key role in these insurance markets.

Prevent exploitation

Efficient markets can still produce socially unacceptable outcomes. Some individuals may get so little income that they cannot survive. In competitive markets, wages are determined by the intersection of demand and supply, and there is nothing that says that the "equilibrium" wage is a living wage. Governments routinely try to "correct" the market distribution of income.

Furthermore, there is nothing about markets to ensure that they are humane, in any sense of the term. Market participants may not hesitate to take advantage of their current strength—or other market participants' current weaknesses—in any way that they can. During a hurricane, someone who has a car can help others escape the flood, but they may charge "what the market will bear" for the service. Workers desperate for a job will accept employment at companies with substandard safety and health conditions. The government can't prevent every form of exploitation, but it can reduce the scope: that is the reason why most governments of advanced industrial countries around the world have adopted and enforce usury laws (laws limiting the interest that can be paid) and laws setting minimum wages and maximum hours, setting basic health and safety conditions for work, and striving to limit predatory lending.

Private firms, when they can, try to restrict competition and are also good at exploiting systematic patterns of irrationality and consumer "weakness." Cigarette companies sold products that they knew were addictive and caused cancer and a host of other ailments—even as they denied that there was any scientific evidence that that was the case. They knew that smokers would be receptive to their message that there was scientific doubt.

Mortgage designers and credit card companies exploited the fact that many individuals would be late in their payments, at least once. They could attract them with very low initial rates; if the rate greatly increased following a late payment, it could more than compensate for the low initial rate. Banks encourage customers to sign on to overdraft facilities, with high fees, knowing that they won't check whether they have drawn down their bank balances.[33]

The Changing Role of Government

The appropriate role of the state differs from country to country and from era to era. Twenty-first-century capitalism is different from nineteenth-century capitalism. The lesson learned from the financial sector is true in other sectors: while the New Deal regulations may not work today, what is needed is not a wholesale deregulation but more in some areas, less in others. Globalization and new technologies have opened up the possibility of new global monopolies with a wealth and power beyond anything that the barons of the late nineteenth century could have dreamed.[34] As I noted in chapter 1, the agency problems created by the separation of ownership and control and by the fact that the wealth of most ordinary individuals is managed by others, supposedly on their behalf, has heightened the need for better regulations on corporate governance.

Other changes in the U.S. economy too may require a larger role for government. The fact that many of the advanced industrial economies have become innovation economies has profound implications for the nature of the market. Consider, for instance, the issue of competition, vital to the dynamism of any economy. It can easily be ascertained whether there is competition in the market for steel, for example, and if there is not, there are well-established ways to deal with the problem.

But producing ideas is different from producing steel. Even when private and social returns in the production of conventional commodities are well aligned, social and private returns to innovation may differ markedly. There are even innovations that have *negative* social returns—such as cigarettes that were more addictive.

The private sector worries about how much of the value of the idea it can appropriate for itself, not about the overall returns to society. The result is that the market may spend too much money on some areas of research—developing a me-too drug that imitates a highly successful patented drug—and too little on others. Without government support, there would be little basic research, too little on the diseases of the poor.

Under the patent system, the private return is related to being first; the social return is related to the innovation being available earlier than it otherwise would have been. A dramatic illustration of the difference is provided by research on the genes related to breast cancer. There was a systematic global effort under way to decode the entire human genome, but there was a race to beat this effort in the case of those genes that might have market value. Myriad, an American firm, got the patent on the breast cancer genes; the information was available a little earlier than it otherwise would have been—but because the firm insists on charging a high price for the tests to detect the gene, in those jurisdictions where the patent is recognized, thousands of women may die unnecessarily.[35]

In short, in the innovative economy of the twenty-first century, government may need to take a more central role—in providing the basic research on which the whole edifice rests; in shaping the direction of research, for instance, through grants and prizes to incentivize research directed at national needs; and in achieving a better balance in the intellectual property regime so that society can get more of the benefits of the incentives that it can provide without the associated costs, including that of monopolization.[36]

At the end of the last century, there was a (false) hope that the need for government action in one area was diminishing: some thought that in the new, innovative economy, business cycles were a thing of the past. As is the case with so many ideas, there was a grain of truth in the notion of a New Economy without downturns. New information technologies meant companies could control inventories better. Many of the past cycles were related to inventory fluctuations. Besides, the structure of the economy had changed, away from manufacturing—where inventories are important—to services, where they are not. As

I noted earlier, manufacturing constitutes today only 11.5 percent of GDP in the United States.[37] The 2001 recession showed, however, that the nation could still overspend on fiber optics and other investments, and this recession showed that it can still overspend on housing. Bubbles and their consequences are here in the twenty-first century, just as they were in the eighteenth, nineteenth, and twentieth.

Markets are imperfect, but so is government. To some, the inevitable conclusion is to give up on government. Markets fail, but government failures (some argue) are worse. Markets may generate inequality, but government-generated inequality may be worse. Markets may be inefficient, but governments are even more inefficient. This line of argumentation is specious and poses false choices. There is no choice but to have some forms of collective action. The last time a country tried unregulated (free) banking was Chile under the dictator Pinochet, and it was a disaster. Like America, Chile's credit bubble broke. About 30 percent of all loans became nonperforming, and it took the country a quarter century to pay off the debts from the failed experiment.

The United States will have regulation, just as government will spend money on research and technology and infrastructure and some forms of social protection. Governments will conduct monetary policy and will provide for national defense, police and fire protection, and other essential public services. When markets fail, government will come in to pick up the pieces. Knowing this, the government has to do what it can to prevent calamities.

The questions then are, What should the government do? How much should it do? and How should it do it?

Every game has rules and referees, and so does the economic game. One of the key roles of the government is to write the rules and provide the referees. The rules are the laws that govern the market economy. The referees include the regulators and the judges who help enforce and interpret the laws. The old rules, whether they worked well in the past, are not the right rules for the twenty-first century.

Society has to have confidence that the rules are set fairly and that the referees are fair. In America, too many of the rules were set by and for those from finance, and the referees were one-sided. That the outcomes have been one-sided should not come as a surprise. There were alternative responses that held open at least an equal chance of success but which put taxpayers less at risk: if only the government had just played by the rules, rather than switching midcourse to a strategy that involved unprecedented gifts to the financial sector.

In the end, the only check on these abuses is through democratic processes. But the chances that democratic processes will prevail will depend on reforms in campaign contributions and electoral processes.[38] Some clichés are still true: he who pays the piper calls the tune. The financial sector has paid the pipers in both parties and has called the tune. Can we citizens expect to have regulations passed breaking up the too-big-to-fail, too-big-to-resolve, or too-big-to-manage banks if the banks continue to be the too-big-to-ignore campaign contributors? Can we expect even to restrict the banks from engaging in excessively risky behavior?[39]

Dealing with this crisis—and preventing future crises—is as much a matter of politics as it is economics. If we as a country don't make these reforms, we risk political paralysis, given the inconsistent demands of special interests and the country at large. And if we do avoid political paralysis, it may well be at the expense of our future: borrowing from the future to finance today's bailouts, and/or creating minimal reforms today, passing on the larger problems to a later date.

Today the challenge is to create a New Capitalism. We have seen the failures of the old. But to create this New Capitalism will require trust—including trust between Wall Street and the rest of society. Our financial markets have failed us, but we cannot function without them. Our government failed us, but we cannot do without it. The Reagan-Bush agenda of deregulation was based on mistrust of government; the Bush-Obama attempt to rescue us from the failure of deregulation was based on fear. The inequities that have become manifest as wages fall, unemployment rises, but bank bonuses soar, or as corporate welfare is strengthened and the corporate safety net is expanded as that for ordinary citizens is cut back, generate bitterness and anger. An environment of bitterness and anger, of fear and mistrust, is hardly the best one in which to begin the long and hard task of reconstruction. But we have no choice: if we are to restore sustained prosperity, we need a new set of social contracts based on trust between all the elements of our society, between citizens and government, between this generation and the future.

CHAPTER EIGHT

FROM GLOBAL RECOVERY TO GLOBAL PROSPERITY

A S THE ECONOMIC CRISIS SPREAD QUICKLY FROM THE U.S. to the rest of world, the need for a coordinated global response and plan for recovery became clear, yet each country thought primarily about its own well-being. The international institutions in charge of maintaining the stability of the global economic system had failed to prevent the crisis. Now they were to fail again: they did not have the capacity to engineer the necessary coordinated response. Economic globalization had made the world more interdependent, increasing the need to act together and work cooperatively. As yet there was no effective means of doing so.

The inadequacies in globalization played out in the size of the economic stimulus, in the conduct of monetary policy, in the design of the bailouts and guarantees, in the growth of protectionism, and in the assistance given to developing countries. The problems will continue to play out, too, in the difficulties the world faces in establishing a global regulatory regime.

The current crisis provides both risks and opportunities. One risk is that if no action is taken to manage the global financial and global economic system better, there will be more, and possibly worse, crises in the future. And as countries seek to protect themselves from unbridled and unfettered globalization, they will take actions to reduce their openness. The resulting fragmentation of global financial markets may undermine the advantages to be obtained from global integration. For many countries, the way globalization has been managed—particularly financial market globalization—poses huge risks with limited rewards.

A second, related risk concerns the ongoing battle of ideas within the economics profession about the efficiency of markets (discussed more fully in the next chapter). In many parts of the world, this battle is not merely academic but a question of survival: there is an active debate about what kind of economic system will work best for them. Certainly, American-style capitalism has demonstrated that it can encounter huge problems, but America can afford the hundreds of billions of dollars to pick up the pieces. Poor countries cannot. What has happened will shape debates for years to come.

The United States will still remain the largest economy, but the way the world views America has changed, and China's influence will grow. Even before the crisis the dollar was no longer viewed as a good store of value; its value was volatile and declining. Now, with the ballooning of America's debt and deficit and the unremitting printing of money by the Fed, confidence has eroded further. This will have a long-term impact on America and its standing, but it has already generated a demand for a new global financial order. If a new global reserve system, and, more broadly, new frameworks for governing the global economic system, can be created, that would be one of the few silver linings to this otherwise dismal cloud.

From early on in the crisis, the advanced industrial countries recognized they could not address this problem alone. The G-8, a group of advanced industrial countries that met annually to solve the world's problems, always seemed remarkable to me. These so-called leaders of the world thought they could solve large-scale problems like global warming and global imbalances without inviting the leaders of other countries—representing almost half of global GDP and 80 percent of the world's population—to actively participate in the discussions. At the G-8 meeting in Germany in 2007, the leaders of the other countries were invited—for lunch—after the communiqué summarizing the views of the advanced industrial countries had been issued. It was as if other countries' views were an afterthought, something that had to be dealt with politely but not actually incorporated into any important decisions. As the economic crisis erupted, it was clear that the old club could not solve it alone. With the meeting of the G-20 in Washington—including newly emerging countries like China, India, and Brazil—in November 2008, it was apparent that the old institutions were dying.[1] What the new system of global economic governance will look like may not be clear for years to come. But, especially spurred by U.K. Prime Minister Gordon Brown, who hosted the second meeting of the G-20 in London in April 2009, it was clear that the newly emerging markets would be assured of a seat at the table in which all important global economic decisions are made. This, in itself, was a major change.

A FAILED GLOBAL RESPONSE

Developing countries had been the engine of global growth at least since the early 1990s—they accounted for more than two-thirds of the increase in GDP.[2] But developing countries were hit particularly hard by the crisis. With the notable exception of China, most didn't have the resources to engage in massive bailouts or concoct huge stimulus packages. The global community realized that the whole world was "in it" together: America had brought down other countries, but weaknesses in the rest of the world threatened America's ability to recover.

Even in a world of globalization, policy making happens at the national level. Each country weighs the benefits and costs of its actions independently of the effects on the rest of world. In the case of stimulus spending, the benefits are increased jobs or expanded GDP, while the costs are increased debt and deficit. For small economies, much of the increased spending resulting from increased income (say, as a result of some government program) occurs outside their borders, on imported goods, but even for large countries there are substantial spill-overs to others.[3] To put it another way, the "global multiplier"—the extent to which the global economy's output is increased for each dollar of spending—is much larger than the "national multiplier." Because the global benefits exceed the national benefits, unless countries coordinate their response to a crisis, the size of each country's stimulus, and hence the global stimulus, will be too small. Smaller countries, like Ireland, especially will have little incentive to spend any money on a stimulus package. Instead, they would prefer to be "free riders" on other countries' stimulus spending.[4]

Worse still, each country has an incentive to design its stimulus to capture the maximum benefit for *itself*. Countries will seek the kinds of spending that will have the smallest "leakage" abroad, spending on locally produced goods and services. The result is that not only will the global stimulus be smaller than desirable, but the effectiveness will be less—there will be less bang for the buck—and so the recovery will be more muted than it would be with a better globally coordinated stimulus.

On top of that, many countries will put in protectionist measures in order to encourage spending at home. The United States, for instance, imposed a "Buy American" provision in its stimulus bill that required spending on goods made in the United States, but then qualified it—in a way that seemed reasonable—to say that it would not apply if there were international agreements preventing such discrimination. But America has such agreements on government purchases mostly with developed countries. That meant, in effect, that the stimulus money could be used to buy goods from rich countries but not from the poor countries, which were the innocent victims of this "Made in America" crisis.[5]

One of the reasons why beggar-thy-neighbor policies don't work is that they invite retaliation, and that is already happening, as, for instance, Canadian cities adopt "Don't Buy American" provisions. Others are encouraged to imitate, with the result that today America is not alone in engaging in such protectionism. In the months after the G-20 leaders committed their countries not to engage in protectionism, seventeen of them went ahead and did it anyway.[6] In today's world, such provisions are counterproductive for another reason—it is hard to find a product that is strictly made in America and even harder to prove it. Thus, many American firms can't bid on projects if they can't certify that their steel and other products are all made in America, and with less competition, costs rise.

The design of stimulus plans was not the only area in which there was an inadequate global response. I mentioned earlier that most of the developing countries do not have the resources to finance their own stimulus. The G-20, at the meeting in London in February 2009, provided additional funds to the International Monetary Fund (IMF), the institution that traditionally has been responsible for helping countries respond to crises. The G-20 found several other ways to enhance the ability of the IMF to provide funds, such as through gold sales and a new issuance of special drawing rights (SDRs), a special kind of global money that I discuss later in the chapter. The advertised headline, some $1 trillion, was impressive.

Unfortunately, there were problems with these initiatives, well intentioned as they were. First, little of the money given to the IMF was likely to get to the poorest countries. Indeed, one of the impetuses for the Western European governments providing funds was that they hoped that the IMF would help Eastern Europe, which was having massive problems. Western Europe couldn't agree about the best way to help their neighbors, so they shifted responsibility to the IMF. Second, many of the poor countries had just emerged from a huge overhang of debt, and they were predictably reluctant to take on more. The rich countries should have provided the money in grants, money that didn't have to be repaid, rather than the short-term IMF loans. A few countries, like Germany, made an explicit gesture in this direction, devoting some of their stimulus package to helping poor countries. But that was the exception, not the rule.

The choice of the IMF as the institution to deliver the money was itself problematic. Not only had the IMF done very little to prevent the crisis, but also it had pushed deregulatory policies, including capital and financial market liberalization, that contributed to the creation of the crisis and to its rapid spread around the world.[7] Moreover, these and other policies that the IMF pushed—and indeed, its style of operation—were an anathema both to many of the poor countries that needed the funds and to the countries in Asia and the Middle East that had large pools of liquid funds that might be deployed to help the poorest countries needing the money. The central banker of one developing country shared with me a view that was not uncommon: the country would have to be on its deathbed before turning to the IMF.

Having watched the IMF firsthand, I understood some countries' reluctance to go to the IMF for money. In the past, the IMF had provided money but only with harsh conditionalities that had actually made the downturns in the afflicted countries worse.[8] These conditions were designed more to help Western creditors recoup more of their money than they otherwise would have been able to, than to help the afflicted country maintain its economic strength. The strict conditionalities the IMF frequently imposed induced riots around the world—those in Indonesia during the East Asian crisis being the most famous.[9]

The good news was that, with the appointment of Dominique Strauss-Kahn as managing director and the advent of the crisis, the IMF began reforms of its macro and lending policies. For instance, when Iceland turned to the IMF for assistance, it was allowed to impose capital controls and to maintain a budget deficit—at least for the first year of its program. The IMF finally recognized the need for Keynesian macro-stimulus policies. Its managing director explicitly talked about the risks of premature removal of stimulus, and spoke of the need to focus on employment. Good countries would be able to borrow without conditions. They could effectively "prequalify." Questions remained: Who would get the good marks? Would any country in sub-Saharan Africa qualify? Though in many countries the IMF programs were markedly different from those of the past, it appeared that strong conditionalities were still being imposed on some countries—including budget cuts and high interest rates, polar opposites of what Keynesian economics recommended.[10]

The IMF was an old boys' club of the rich industrial states, the creditor countries, run by their finance ministers and central bank governors. Its views of good economic policies were shaped by those in finance—views that were, as I have explained and as the crisis has amply demonstrated, often misguided. The United States alone had the power to veto any major decision, and it always appointed the number two in command; Europe always appointed the head. While the IMF pontificated about good governance, it didn't practice what it preached. It did not have the kind of transparency that we now expect of public institutions. At the G-20 meeting in London in February 2009, there was a consensus in favor of reform. But the glacial speed of that reform suggested to some that the world might well be knee-deep in the next crisis before any substantive change could be achieved. Still, there was at least one major advance, which had been a long time coming: there was an agreement that the head of the IMF should be chosen in an open and transparent way and that member nations should look for the most qualified person, regardless of nationality.[11]

America's lack of generosity in helping the developing countries is both noteworthy and potentially costly. Even before the crisis, America was among the stingiest of the advanced industrial countries in the assistance it provided—as a percentage of national income, it provides less than a fourth the amount of the leaders in Europe.[12] But here was a global crisis originating in the USA. America had lectured others incessantly about taking responsibility for their actions; in this case, however, it seemed to assume little responsibility for foisting on them the rules that made contagion from the United States so easy; for its protectionist policies; or for having created the global mess in the first place.[13]

Global regulation

Deregulation played a central role in the crisis, and a new set of regulations will be needed to prevent another crisis and restore trust in the banks. In some circles, in the run-up to the second meeting of the G-20 in early 2009, there was a debate as to whether a globally coordinated stimulus or a globally coordinated regulatory regime was more important. The answer is obvious: both are necessary. Without comprehensive regulation, there will be regulatory evasion—finance will go to the least regulated country. Others will then have to take action in order to prevent poorly regulated institutions from generating contagion effects.

In short, the failure of one country to regulate adequately has negative externalities on others. Without a globally coordinated regulatory system, there is a risk of fragmentation and segmentation of the global financial system, as each country tries to protect itself from the mistakes of others. Each country has to be satisfied that others are taking adequate measures to curtail abuse.

Not surprisingly, the *seemingly* strongest actions taken by the G-20 were against the countries that were not in the meeting—the so-called uncooperative states, places like the Cayman Islands, which have been centers of tax and regulatory evasion for years. Their existence is not an accidental loophole. Wealthy Americans and Europeans—and the banks that represent them—wanted a safe haven, free from the kind of scrutiny that their activities would get at home, and the regulators and legislators allowed them what they wanted. The demands that the G-20 put on these tax havens, while a move in the right direction, were sufficiently light that almost instantly the Organisation for Economic Co-operation and Development (OECD) removed all of those tax havens from the "black list."[14]

Without a regular and full exchange of information, tax authorities in a given country don't know what or who is escaping their net. For developing countries, there is an even more important issue—corruption. Corrupt dictators abscond with billions and park the money not just in offshore banks but also in some of the world's largest financial centers, including London. The developing countries are rightly condemned for not doing more about corruption, but they also rightly criticize the advanced industrial countries for facilitating corruption by providing safe haven for corrupt officials and secret bank accounts for their money. If, somehow, the money is located, it is often difficult to get it returned. These, however, were problems for the developing countries that were not at the meeting, so not surprisingly the G-20 at its initial meeting did nothing to change any of this.[15]

In earlier chapters, I outlined an agenda for a new regulatory regime. But while the G-20 paid at least lip service to some of the key issues (leverage, transparency), in its initial meetings it steered clear of some of the most critical: what to do about the politically influential too-big-to-fail institutions that were at the center of the crisis, or financial and capital market liberalization, which had helped it spread—and which some of the key countries had done all they could to promote. France among others forcefully raised some topics—the excessive compensation schemes that had encouraged shortsighted behavior and excessive risk-taking. The G-20 response in regulation was disappointing in another sense: for guidance forward, it turned to the very institutions that had failed.

The Financial Stability Forum brought together financial authorities from about a dozen of the most important advanced industrial countries to facilitate discussions and cooperation in regulation, supervision, and surveillance of financial institutions. It was created in the aftermath of the East Asian crisis as an outgrowth of meetings of G-7 finance ministers and central bankers to ensure that another such crisis did not occur. It obviously did not succeed, but its failure should hardly come as a surprise. It was imbued with the same deregulatory philosophy that had led to the earlier crises and now has led to this crisis. The G-20, however, did not ask why the Stability Forum failed. Instead, the G-20 changed the forum's name to the Financial Stability Board and expanded its membership slightly. Perhaps with a new name it would have a fresh start; perhaps it had learned the lessons. I suspect that views about economics do not change so easily or quickly.

A LOSS OF FAITH IN AMERICAN-STYLE CAPITALISM

In the United States, calling someone a socialist may be nothing more than a cheap shot. Fanatics of the Right have tried to tar Obama with the label, even as the Left criticizes him for his excessive moderation. In much of the world, however, the battle between capitalism and socialism—or at least something that many Americans would label as socialism—still rages. In most of the world, there is a consensus that government should play a larger role than it does in the United States. While there may be no winners in the current economic crisis, there are losers, and among the big losers is American-style capitalism, which has lost a great deal of support. The consequences in shaping global economic and political debates may be felt for a long time to come.

The fall of the Berlin Wall in 1989 marked the end of communism as a viable idea. The problems with communism had been manifest for decades, but after 1989 it was hard for anyone to say a word in its defense. For a while, it seemed that the defeat of communism meant the sure victory of capitalism, particularly in its American form. Francis Fukuyama in the early 1990s went so far as to proclaim "the end of history," defining democratic market capitalism to be the final stage of societal development and declaring that all humanity was now heading inevitably in this direction.[16] In truth, historians will mark the twenty years since 1989 as the short period of American triumphalism.

September 15, 2008, the date that Lehman Brothers collapsed, may be to market fundamentalism (the notion that unfettered markets, all by themselves, can ensure economic prosperity and growth) what the fall of the Berlin Wall was to communism. The problems with the ideology were known before that date, but afterward no one could really defend it. With the collapse of great banks and financial houses and the ensuing economic turmoil and chaotic attempts at rescue, the period of American triumphalism is over. So too is the debate over "market fundamentalism." Today only the deluded (which include many American conservatives, but far fewer in the developing world) would argue that markets are self-correcting and that society can rely on the self-interested behavior of market participants to ensure that everything works honestly and properly—let alone works in a way that benefits all.

The economic debate takes on particular potency in the developing world. Although we in the West tend to forget, 190 years ago almost 60 percent of the world's GDP was in Asia. But then, rather suddenly, colonial exploitation and unfair trade agreements, combined with a technological revolution in Europe and America, left the developing countries far behind, to the point where, by 1950, Asian economies constituted less than 18 percent of the world's GDP.[17] In the mid-nineteenth century the United Kingdom and France actually waged a war to ensure that China remained "open" to global trade. This was the Opium War, so named because it was fought to ensure that China didn't close its doors to the West's opium: the West had little of value to sell to China other than drugs, which it wanted to be able to dump into Chinese markets, with the collateral effect of causing widespread addiction. It was an early attempt by the West to correct a balance of payments problem.

Colonialism left a mixed legacy in the developing world, but one clear result was the view among the people there that they had been cruelly exploited. Among many emerging leaders, Marxist theory provided an interpretation of their experience; it suggested that exploitation was in fact the underpinning of the capitalist system. The political independence that came to scores of colonies after World War II did not put an end to economic colonialism. In some regions, such as Africa, the exploitation—the extraction of natural resources and the rape of the environment, all in return for a pittance—was obvious. Elsewhere it was more subtle. In many parts of the world, global institutions such as the IMF and the World Bank came to be seen as instruments of post-colonial control. These institutions pushed market fundamentalism ("neo-liberalism," it was often called), a notion Americans idealized as "free and unfettered markets." They pressed for financial-sector deregulation, privatization, and trade liberalization.

The World Bank and the IMF said they were doing all this for the benefit of the developing world. They were backed up by teams of free market economists, many from that cathedral of free market economics, the University of Chicago. In the end, the programs of the "Chicago boys" didn't bring the promised results. Incomes stagnated. Where there was growth, the wealth went to those at the top. Economic crises in individual countries became ever more frequent—there have been more than a hundred in the past thirty years alone.[18]

Not surprisingly, people in developing countries became less and less convinced that Western help was motivated by altruism. They suspected that the free market rhetoric—the "Washington consensus," as it is known in shorthand—was just a cover for the old commercial interests. The West's own hypocrisy reinforced the suspicions. Europe and America didn't open up their own markets to the agricultural produce of the Third World, which was often all these poor countries had to offer; instead, they forced developing countries to eliminate subsidies aimed at creating new industries, even as they provided massive subsidies to their own farmers.[19]

Free market ideology turned out to be an excuse for new forms of exploitation. "Privatization" meant that foreigners could buy mines and oil fields in developing countries at low prices. It also meant they could reap large profits from monopolies and quasi-monopolies, such as in telecommunications. "Financial and capital market liberalization" meant that foreign banks could get high returns on their loans, and when loans went bad, the IMF forced the socialization of the losses, meaning that the screws were put on entire populations to pay the foreign banks back. Then, at least in East Asia after the 1997 crisis, some of the same foreign banks made further profits in the fire sales that the IMF forced on the countries that needed their money. Trade liberalization meant, too, that foreign firms could wipe out nascent industries, suppressing the development of entrepreneurial talent. While capital flowed freely, labor did not—except in the case of the most talented individuals, many of whom found good jobs in a global marketplace.[20]

Of course, there were exceptions. There were always those in Asia who resisted the Washington consensus. They put restrictions on capital flows. The large giants in Asia—China and India—managed their economies their own way, producing unprecedented growth. But elsewhere, and especially in the countries where the World Bank and IMF held sway, things did not go well.

And everywhere, the debate over ideas continued. Even in countries that have done very well, there is a conviction, not just among the general populace but even among the educated and influential, that the rules of the game have not been fair. They believe that they have done well despite the unfair rules, and they sympathize with their weaker friends in the developing world who have not done well at all.

For the critics of American-style capitalism in the Third World, the way that America has responded to the current economic crisis has smacked of a double standard. During the East Asian crisis, just a decade ago, America and the IMF demanded that the affected countries reduce their government's deficits by cutting back expenditures—even if, as in Thailand, this resulted in a resurgence of the AIDS epidemic, or even if, as in Indonesia, this meant curtailing food subsidies for the starving, or even if, as in Pakistan, the shortage of public schools led parents to send their children to the madrassas, where they would become indoctrinated in Islamic fundamentalism. America and the IMF forced countries to raise interest rates, in some cases (such as Indonesia) to more than 50 percent. They lectured Indonesia about being tough on its banks and demanded that the government not bail them out. What a terrible precedent this would set, they said, and what a terrible intervention into the smooth-running mechanisms of the free market.

The contrast between the handling of the East Asian crisis and the American crisis is stark and has not gone unnoticed. To pull America out of the hole, the country engaged in massive increases in spending and massive deficits, even as interest rates were brought down to zero. Banks were bailed out left and right. Some of the same officials in Washington who dealt with the East Asian crisis are managing the response to the American implosion. Why, people in the Third World ask, is the United States administering different medicine to itself?

It is not just a matter of a double standard. Because the developed countries consistently follow countercyclical monetary and fiscal policies (as they did in this crisis), but developing countries are forced to follow pro-cyclical policies (cutting expenditures, raising taxes and interest rates), fluctuations in developing countries are larger than they otherwise would be, while those in developed countries are smaller. This raises the cost of capital to the developing countries relative to that facing developed countries, increasing the latter's advantage over the former.[21]

Many in the developing world still smart from the hectoring they received for so many years: adopt American institutions, follow American policies, engage in deregulation, open up markets to American banks so they could learn "good" banking practices, and—not coincidentally—sell their firms and banks to Americans, especially at fire sale prices during crises. They were told that it would be painful, but in the end, they were promised, they would be better for it. America sent its Treasury Secretaries (from both parties) around the planet to spread the gospel. In the eyes of many throughout the developing world, the revolving door, which allows American financial leaders to move seamlessly from Wall Street to Washington and back to Wall Street, gave them even more credibility, for these men seemed to be able to combine the power of money and the power of politics. American financial leaders were correct in believing that what was good for America or the world was good for financial markets; but they were incorrect in thinking the converse, that what was good for Wall Street was good for America and the world.

It is not so much schadenfreude that motivates the intense scrutiny by developing countries of America's economic system. Instead, it is a real need to understand what kind of an economic system can work for them in the future failure. Indeed, these countries have every interest in seeing a quick American recovery. They know firsthand that the global fallout from America's downturn is enormous. And many are increasingly convinced that the free and unfettered market ideals America seems to hold are ideals to run from rather than embrace.

Even advocates of free market economics now realize that some regulation is desirable. But the role of government goes beyond regulation—as a few countries are beginning to realize. For example, Trinidad has taken to heart the lesson that risk must be managed and that the government has to take a more active role in education—they know they can't reshape the global economy, but they can help their citizens deal with the risks it presents. Even primary-school children are being taught the principles of risk, the elements of homeownership, the dangers of predatory lending, and the details of mortgages. In Brazil, homeownership is being promoted through a public agency, which ensures that individuals take out mortgages that are well within their ability to manage.

In the end, why should we Americans care that the world has become disillusioned with the American model of capitalism? The ideology that we promoted has been tarnished, sure, but perhaps it is a good thing that it may be tarnished beyond repair. Can't we survive—even thrive—if not everyone adheres to the American way?

Inevitably, our influence will be diminished, but that, in many ways, was already happening. We used to play a pivotal role in managing global capital because others believed that we had a special talent for managing risk and allocating financial resources. No one thinks that now, and Asia—where much of the world's savings occurs today—is already developing its own financial centers. We are no longer the world's chief source of capital. The world's top three banks are now Chinese; America's largest bank is down at the number-five spot.

Meanwhile, the cost of dealing with the crisis is crowding out other needs, not only those at home, as discussed earlier, but also those abroad. In recent years, China's infrastructure investment in Africa has been greater than that of the World Bank and the African Development Bank combined, and it dwarfs America's. Anyone visiting Ethiopia or a host of other countries in the continent can already see the transformation, as new highways join together what had been isolated cities and towns, creating a new economic geography. It is not just in infrastructure that China's impact is being felt, but in many other aspects of development—for instance, in trade, resource development, enterprise creation, and even agriculture. African countries are running to Beijing for assistance in this crisis, not to Washington. And it is not just in Africa that China's presence is being felt: in Latin America, in Asia, in Australia—anywhere where there are commodities or resources—China's rapid growth provides an insatiable appetite. Before the crisis, it had contributed to growth in exports and export prices, which had led to unprecedented growth in Africa and many other countries. After the crisis, it is likely to do so once again—indeed, many were already reaping the benefits of China's strong growth in 2009.

I worry that as many in the developing world see more clearly the flaws in America's economic and social system, they will draw the wrong conclusions about what kind of system will serve them best. A few will learn the right lessons. They will realize that what is required for success is a regime where the roles of market and government are in balance, and where a strong state administers effective regulations. They will realize, too, that the power of special interests must be curbed.

For many other countries, however, the political consequences will be more convoluted, and possibly profoundly tragic. The former communist countries generally turned, after the dismal failure of their postwar system, to capitalism, but some turned to a distorted version of a market economy; they replaced Karl Marx with Milton Friedman as their god. The new religion has not served them well. Many countries may conclude not simply that unfettered capitalism, American-style, has failed, but that the very concept of a market economy itself has failed and is indeed unworkable under any circumstances. Old-style communism won't be back, but a variety of forms of excessive market intervention will return. And these will fail.

The poor suffered under market fundamentalism. Trickle-down economics didn't work. But the poor may suffer again if new regimes again get the balance wrong, with *excessive* intervention in the markets. Such a strategy will not deliver growth, and without growth there cannot be sustainable poverty reduction. There has been no successful economy that has not relied heavily on markets. The consequences for global stability and American security are obvious.

There used to be a sense of shared values between the U.S. and the American-educated elites around the world, but the economic crisis has now undermined the credibility of these elites, who advocated American-style capitalism. Those who opposed America's licentious form of capitalism now have ample ammunition to preach a broader anti-market philosophy.

Faith in democracy is another victim. In the developing world people look at Washington and see a system of government that allowed Wall Street to write self-serving rules, which put at risk the entire global economy, and then when the day of reckoning came, Washington turned to those from Wall Street and their cronies to manage the recovery—in ways that gave Wall Street amounts of money that would be beyond the wildest dreams of the most corrupt in the developing world. They see corruption American-style as perhaps more sophisticated—bags of money don't change hands in dark corners—but just as nefarious. They see continued redistributions of wealth to the top of the pyramid, transparently at the expense of ordinary citizens. They see the institutions that oversaw the growth of the bubble, like the Federal Reserve, being given more power as a reward for its failures of the past. They see, in short, a fundamental problem of political accountability in the American system of democracy. Seeing all this, they take but a short step to conclude that something is very wrong, and perhaps inevitably so, with democracy itself.

The U.S. economy will eventually recover, and so too, up to a point, will America's standing abroad. Like it or not, America's actions are subject to minute examination. Its successes are emulated. But its failures—especially failures of the kind that led up to this crisis and are so easily mocked as hypocrisy—are looked upon with scorn. Democracy and market forces are essential to a just and prosperous world. But the "victory" of liberal democracy and a balanced market economy are not inevitable. The economic crisis, created largely by America's (mis)behavior, has been a major blow in the fight for these fundamental values, more damaging than anything a totalitarian regime ever could have done or said.

A NEW GLOBAL ECONOMIC ORDER: CHINA AND AMERICA

The current crisis is so deep and so disturbing that things will change, whether leaders strive to make it happen or not. The most profound changes may concern the sometimes difficult relationship between the United States and China. China has a long way to go before it surpasses the United States in GDP—in "purchasing power parity," reflecting differences in costs of living, it is still about one-half that of the United States—and even further before it approaches the U.S. income per capita—it is about one-eighth.[22] But still, China has been achieving some impressive records. The year 2009 saw it likely becoming the world's largest merchandise exporter, car producer, and manufacturer more generally.[23] It also earned the dubious distinction of outpacing the United States in carbon emissions to become the leader in the world.[24] Its growth, while slower than it was before the crisis, remains markedly higher than that of the United States, by 7 percentage points a year (in 2009, the difference was more like 11 percent), and at that rate the gap in GDP is cut in half every ten years. Moreover, well within the next quarter century, China is likely to become the dominant economy in Asia, and Asia's economy is likely to be larger than that of the United States.

Though China's economy is still so much smaller than the United States', the U.S. imports far more from China than it exports, and these large trade imbalances have generated growing tensions as U.S. unemployment mounts. The relationship may be symbiotic—China helps finance America's massive fiscal deficits, without China's inexpensive goods the standard of living of many Americans might be markedly lower, and America provides the markets for China's ever-growing supply—but in the Great Recession, the focus is on jobs. Most Americans don't understand the principles of comparative advantage—that each country produces the goods that it is *relatively* good at; and they find it difficult to grasp that the United States may have lost its comparative advantage in many areas of manufacturing. If China (or any other country) is outcompeting the United States, they believe it *has to be* because they are doing something unfairly: manipulating exchange rates or subsidizing their products or selling products below costs (which is called "dumping").

The crisis has, in fact, turned everything topsy-turvy. America is being accused of massive and unfair subsidies (to its banks and auto companies). A loan from the Fed at close to zero interest rate to a large corporation that would have to pay a very high interest rate on the open market—if it could get financing at all—too can be viewed as a massive subsidy. Maintaining low interest rates is one of the critical ways that countries "manage" their exchange rate (when interest rates are low, capital flows out of the country to places where it can get a higher return), and many in Europe believe that the United States is using the low exchange rate to get a competitive advantage.

While both the United States and China have imposed protectionist actions (the United States, partly in response to union pressure, China, partly as a matter of retaliation and partly as an element of its development strategy), as this book goes to press, the extent is limited. But as I noted earlier, there is a recognition that *something* needs to be done about global imbalances, of which the U.S.-China trade imbalance is the most important component.

In the short run, America may find it easier to adjust than China. China needs to consume more, but it is hard to induce households to consume more when they face high levels of uncertainty. China's problems arise less, however, from a high household savings rate than from the fact that household income is a smaller fraction of GDP than in most other countries. Low wages ensure high profits, and there is little pressure to distribute the profits. The result is that enterprises (both public and private) retain a large fraction of their income. But changing the distribution of income in any country is difficult.

China's growth model has been driven by supply: profits are reinvested, increasing production far faster than consumption, and the difference is exported. The model has worked well—creating jobs in China and keeping prices low in the rest of the world—but the crisis has highlighted a flaw in the model. In this downturn, it has been hard for China to export the surplus; over the longer run, as its share of many manufactured goods has increased, it will be difficult for it to maintain its growth rate. This would be true even if there were no protectionist responses in many of its trading partners—there are only so many television sets and other consumption goods that those in the West can buy—but not surprisingly, as China has demonstrated its prowess not just in low-skill manufactured goods but across a wide range of products, protectionist stridency has increased.

Many in China realize that they will have to change their growth strategy—providing more support for small and medium-sized enterprises, for instance, through creating more local and regional banks. Such enterprises are, in most countries, the basis of job growth. Job growth will lead to higher wages, and this will shift the distribution of income in ways that will support more domestic consumption. Some of the apparent corporate profits arise from China's failure to charge appropriately for natural resources (including land). In effect, the corporations were given these assets, which really belong to the people; if, for instance, they auctioned off those resources, the revenues would generate a hefty income. If China captured the return on these assets for all of its people, it would have more revenues to finance health, education, and retirement benefits, and this would reduce some of the need for high household savings.

While this new growth strategy may seem sensible, there are powerful political forces arrayed against it: the large enterprises and their officials, for instance, enjoy the current system, and they hope that it can somehow be made sustainable. Those same political forces will also oppose allowing China's exchange rate to appreciate, which would both decrease the competitiveness of China's exports and increase the real wages of its workers. Those in the West who argue for the need for large banks and other large enterprises provide succor to these New Industrialists. China, they contend, needs equally large firms (sometimes called "national champions") to compete globally. It is too soon to know how this struggle will play out.

China's stimulus package—one of the largest in the world (relative to the size of the country)[25]—reflected these tensions in economic policy. Much of the money went to infrastructure and to help "green" the economy. A new high-speed railroad system may have an impact on China analogous to that of the construction of the intercontinental railroad in the post–Civil War United States. It may help forge a stronger national economy, as economic geography changes almost overnight. The stimulus package also provided explicit encouragement for consumption, especially in the rural sector, and especially to buy products that face marked declines in sales abroad. It also provided for rapid increases in expenditure on rural health and education. At the same time, there were efforts to strengthen certain key sectors, like automotive and steel. The government argued that it is simply trying to "rationalize" production—increasing efficiency—but critics worry that these efforts might exacerbate the problems of excess supply and/or might reduce effective competition. This would increase corporate profits and lower real wages, exacerbating the problem of underconsumption.

There are equal uncertainties concerning America's longer-term responses to the crisis. As I made clear in earlier chapters, America needs to consume less over the long run, and with households less willing and able to borrow and with wealth so diminished, America's adjustment has been relatively rapid. But as I noted in chapter 7, while households have been saving more, the government has been borrowing more. The need for outside finance remains strong. Global imbalances—especially as defined by America's huge trade deficit and China's smaller but still persistent trade surpluses—will remain. This will cause tensions, but these may remain muted, as America knows that it is dependent on financing from China.[26]

But inside China, there is growing reluctance to increase its lending to the U.S. government, where returns remain low and risk high. There are alternatives—China can invest in real assets in America. But when China has tried to do so, it has sometimes met resistance (as when it tried to buy Unocal, a relatively small American oil company, most of whose assets were actually in Asia). The United States allowed China to buy its highest-polluting car, the Hummer, as well as IBM's laptop division, which became Lenovo. While America is seemingly open to investments in many areas, it has had a broad notion of sectors that are critical for national security and are to be protected from such invest-ments, and this risks undermining the fundamental principles of global-ization: America told developing countries that they must open up their markets to foreign ownership as part of the basic rules of the game.

If China sells significant amounts of the dollars it holds in reserves, it will lead to a further appreciation of its currency (the RMB) against the dollar, which will, in turn, improve America's bilateral trade balance with China. It is likely to do less, however, than one might hope for the U.S. overall trade deficit—America will just buy its textiles from some other developing country. However, it will mean that China will take a big loss on its remaining massive holdings of U.S. T-bills and other dollar-denominated assets.

To some, it appears that China is caught between a rock and a hard place. If it moves out of the dollar, it takes massive losses on its reserves and exports. If it stays in the dollar, it postpones the losses on the reserves, but adjustment may eventually have to come in any case. The worry about the loss of sales is perhaps exaggerated: China is currently providing "vendor" finance—that is, it provides the money to those who buy its goods. Instead of lending to America to buy its goods, it can lend to those in other parts of the world—as it is increasingly doing—or even to its own citizens.

A NEW GLOBAL RESERVE SYSTEM

Concerned about its holdings of dollars, in March 2009 the head of China's central bank lent support to a long-standing idea: creation of a global reserve currency.[27] Keynes pushed the idea some seventy-five years ago, and it was part of his original conception for the IMF.[28] Additionally, support for this idea has come from another quarter—a UN commission of experts on the restructuring of the global financial and economic system, which I chaired.[29]

Developing countries, *China foremost*, today hold trillions of dollars in reserves—money they can draw upon in the event of a crisis, such as the Great Recession. In chapter 1, I emphasized that this crisis exposed the problem of a global insufficiency of aggregate demand. Sadly, *so far*, neither the U.S. administration nor the G-20 has even begun to discuss this underlying problem—let alone take action. Annual emissions of a new global reserve currency would mean that countries would no longer have to set aside part of their current income as protection against global volatility—instead, they could set aside the newly issued "money." This would thereby increase global aggregate demand and strengthen the global economy.

There are two other important reasons for this initiative. The first is that the present system is unstable. Currently, countries hold dollars to provide confidence to their currency and country as a kind of insurance against the vicissitudes of the global marketplace. As more and more dollars are held by foreigners in their reserves, there is greater and greater anxiety about America's increasing indebtedness abroad.

There is another reason why the current system contributes to instability. If some countries insist on having a trade surplus (exporting more than they import) in order to build up reserves, other countries have to have trade deficits; the sum of the surpluses must equal the sum of the deficits. But trade deficits can be a problem—countries with persistent trade deficits are more likely to face an economic crisis—and countries have worked hard to get rid of them. If one country gets rid of its trade deficit, then some other country's deficit must rise (if the surplus countries don't change their behavior), so trade deficits are like a hot potato. In recent years, most countries have learned how to avoid deficits, with the result that the United States has become the "deficit of last resort." In the long run, America's position is clearly untenable. Creating a global reserve currency with annual emissions would provide a buffer. A country could run a small trade deficit and still build up its reserves, because of the allocation of new global reserve currency that it receives. As investors see reserves build up, they would gain confidence.

Poor countries are lending to the United States hundreds of billions, indeed trillions, of dollars at a low (in 2009, near zero) interest rate. That they do it even when there are so many high-return investment projects within their own countries is testament to the importance of reserves and the magnitude of global instability. While the costs of maintaining reserves are very high, the benefits still exceed the costs. The value of the implicit foreign aid that the United States receives, in being able to borrow at a lower interest rate than it otherwise would be able to, exceeds by some calculations the total value of the foreign aid that the country gives.[30]

A good reserve currency needs to be a good store of value—a stable currency—but the dollar has been highly volatile and is likely to remain so. Already, many smaller countries have moved much of their reserves out of dollars, and even China is reported to have a quarter or more of its reserves in other currencies. The question is not whether the world will move away from the dollar reserve system altogether, but whether it does it thoughtfully and carefully. Without a clear plan the global financial system would become even more unstable.

Some within the United States will resist the move to create a global reserve system. They see the benefit in being able to borrow at a low

cost, but they don't see the costs, which are huge. Producing and exporting T-bills to be held in foreign reserves creates no jobs, whereas exporting goods most certainly would. The flip side of the demand for U.S.
T-bills and money to hold in reserves is the U.S. trade deficit, and the
trade deficit weakens America's aggregate demand. To offset this, government runs a fiscal deficit.[31] It is all part of an "equilibrium": to finance
the deficit the government sells T-bills abroad (another way of saying it
borrows money), and many of these T-bills are then put into reserves.

With the new global reserve currency, countries wouldn't need to buy
U.S. T-bills to hold in their reserves. Of course, that would mean that
the value of the dollar would decrease, U.S. exports would increase,
U.S. imports would decrease, aggregate demand would be stronger, and
there would be less need for the government to run a big deficit to
maintain the economy at full employment. Knowing that it would be
more difficult to borrow might curb America's profligacy, which would
enhance global stability. America, and the world, would benefit from
this new system.

Already, there are initiatives to create regional reserve arrangements.
The Chiang Mai Initiative in East Asia allows countries to exchange their
reserves; in response to the crisis, they increased the size of the program
by 50 percent.[32] The world may move to a two- (or three-) currency
system, with both the dollar and euro in use. But such a system could be
even more unstable than the current one. For the world, it might mean
that if the euro is expected to gain relative to the dollar, countries would
start to shift their holdings into euros. As they do this, the euro strength-
ens, reinforcing their beliefs—until some event, a political[33] or economic
disturbance, starts the reverse process. For Europe, it would pose a special problem, since countries in the European Union have constraints on
their ability to run fiscal deficits to offset weak demand.

The dollar-based global reserve system is fraying, but efforts to create
an alternative are only just beginning. Central bankers have at last
learned the basic lesson of wealth management—diversification—and
for years many have been moving reserves out of the dollar. In 2009,
the G-20 agreed to a large ($250 billion) issuance of special drawing
rights (SDRs), which are a kind of global reserve currency created by

the IMF. But the SDRs have strong limitations. They are allocated to countries on the basis of their IMF "quotas" (their effective share holdings)—with the United States getting the largest piece. But the United States obviously has no need to hold reserves, since it can simply print dollar bills. The system would work far better if the reserve emissions were allocated to countries that otherwise would be expanding their reserves; alternatively, new global reserve emissions could go to poor countries needing assistance.[34]

It would be even better if the new system was designed to discourage trade surpluses. The United States hectors China about its surplus, but in current arrangements there are strong incentives for countries to maintain reserves, and to run surpluses to add to reserves. Those countries that had large reserves fared far better in this crisis than those without adequate reserves. In a well-designed global reserve system, countries with persistent surpluses would have their reserve currency allocation diminished, and this, in turn, would encourage them to maintain a better balance. A well-designed global reserve system could go further in stabilizing the global economy, for if more of the global reserve currency were issued when global growth was weak, it would encourage spending—with a concomitant increase in growth and employment.[35]

With support from the United States, a new global reserve system can be quickly achieved. The question is whether and when the Obama administration will realize how much the United States, and the world, have to gain. The risk is that America will bury its head in the sand. The world will be moving away from the dollar-based reserve system. Without an agreement on the creation of a new global reserve system, the world is likely to move out of the dollar and into a multiple-currency reserve system, producing global financial instability in the short term and a regime more unstable than the current system in the long term.

The crisis will almost surely mark a change in the global economic and political order. America's power and influence will be diminished; China's increased. Even before the crisis, a global reserve system depending on one country's currency seemed out of synch with twenty-first-century globalization—but it seems especially so given the vagaries of the dollar and the U.S. economics and politics.

Toward a New Multilateralism

Out of the disaster of the Great Depression and the Second World War, a new global order emerged and a new set of institutions were created. That framework worked for many years but increasingly became unsuited for managing the evolving global economic system. The current crisis has brought into full view its limitations. But just as the United States tried to muddle through in the domestic arena, attempting largely to re-create the world as it was before the crisis, so too in the international arena. In the aftermath of the last global crisis ten years ago, there was much discussion of reforms in the "global financial architecture." There was a suspicion that those who wished to maintain the status quo (including those from the U.S. and other Western financial markets who benefited from the way things were working, and their allies in government) used grandiose language to cover up their true agenda: people would talk and talk and talk, until the crisis was over, and with the end of the crisis would come the end of the resolve to do anything. In the years following the 1997–1998 crisis, little was done—obviously, much too little to prevent an even grander crisis. Will this happen once again?

The United States should, in particular, do what it can to strengthen multilateralism—which means democratizing, reforming, and funding the IMF and the World Bank so that developing countries find less need to turn to bilateral support in times of need (whether from China, Russia, or Europe). It must turn away from protectionism and the bilateral trade agreements of the Bush era. These undermine the multilateral trading system that so many have worked so hard to create over the past sixty years. The United States should help design a new coordinated global financial regulatory system, without which these markets are at risk of fragmentation, and support the new global reserve system described earlier. Without these efforts global financial markets risk a new era of instability and the world a continued era of economic weakness. More broadly, the United States needs to support and strengthen the international rule of law—without which none of this is possible.

During the years of American triumphalism, between the fall of the Berlin Wall and the fall of Lehman Brothers, the United States did not use its power and influence to shape globalization in a way that was fair, especially to developing countries. Its economic policy was based less on principles than on its own self-interest—or more accurately, the desires and aversions of the special interest groups that have played, and will continue to play, such a key role in shaping economic policy. Not only has Europe been more vocal in articulating the concerns of the poor in developing countries, but many of the European countries have actually put their money where their mouth is. During the Bush years, America often did what it could to undermine multilateralism.

America's economic hegemony will no longer be taken for granted in the way that it was. If America wishes to have the respect of others, if it wishes to exercise the influence that it once did, it will have to earn it not just by its words but by its actions, both by the examples that it sets at home—including the way it treats those who are disadvantaged—and by what it does abroad.

The global economic system has not worked as many had hoped. Globalization has led to unprecedented prosperity for many, but in 2008 it helped transmit the U.S. recession to countries around the world—to those that had managed well their financial systems (far better than the United States) and to those that had not, to those that had gained enormously by globalization and to those that had benefited less. Not surprisingly, those countries that were most open, most globalized, were hit the worst. Free market ideology underlay many of the institutions and agreements that provided the framework for globalization; just as these ideas had been the basis for the deregulation that played such a big role in the creation of the current crisis, they underpinned the capital and financial market liberalization that played such a big role in the rapid spread of the crisis around the world.

This chapter has shown how the crisis is likely to change the global economic order, including the global balance of economic power—and how certain key reforms, including the creation of a new global reserve system, can help restore global prosperity and stability. But over the long term, success in maintaining global prosperity depends on understanding better how the economy functions. And this will require reforming not just the economy, but *economics*. This is the subject of the next chapter.

CHAPTER NINE

REFORMING ECONOMICS

THERE IS PLENTY OF BLAME TO BE SHARED IN THIS crisis—we have seen the role that regulators and legislators, the Federal Reserve and the financiers, have all played. As each of them went about their business, they argued that what they were doing was right, and more often than not, the arguments were based on economic analysis. As we peel back the layers of "what went wrong," we cannot escape looking at the economics profession. Of course, not all economists joined in the jubilation of free market economics; not all were disciples of Milton Friedman. A surprisingly large fraction, though, leaned in that direction. Not only was their advice flawed; they failed in their basic tasks of prediction and forecasting. Relatively few saw the coming disaster. It was not an accident that those who advocated the rules that led to the calamity were so blinded by their faith in free markets that they couldn't see the problems it was creating. Economics had moved—more than economists would like to think—from being a scientific discipline into becoming free market capitalism's biggest cheerleader. If the United States is going to succeed in reforming its economy, it may have to begin by reforming economics.

THE WAR OF IDEAS

During the Great Depression, the economics profession, especially in America, was having a hard time. The reigning paradigm then, as now, held that markets were efficient and self-correcting. As the economy plunged into recession and then depression, many gave some simple advice: do nothing. Just wait and the economy will quickly recover. Many also supported Andrew Mellon, President Herbert Hoover's Secretary of Treasury, in his attempt to restore fiscal balance: the recession had lowered tax revenues faster than expenditures. To restore "confidence," Wall Street fiscal conservatives believed, one had to lower expenditures in tandem.

Franklin Roosevelt, who became president in 1933, argued for another course and got support from across the Atlantic: John Maynard Keynes said to increase expenditures to stimulate the economy—and this meant *increasing* the deficit. To those who were skeptical of government in the first place, this was an anathema. Some called it outright socialism, and others saw it as a precursor to socialism. In fact, Keynes was trying to save capitalism from itself; he knew that unless a market economy could create jobs, it could not survive. American disciples of Keynes, like my teacher Paul Samuelson, argued that once the economy was restored to full employment, one could return to the marvels of the free market.

In the Great Recession of 2008, many voices argued that Roosevelt's New Deal had in fact failed and even made matters worse.[1] In this view, it was World War II that finally got America out of the Great Depression. That was partly true—but largely because President Roosevelt failed to have a consistent, national expansionary spending policy. Just as now, as he increased federal spending, the states were contracting spending.[2] By 1937, worries about the size of the deficit had induced a cutback in government spending.[3] But even war spending is spending—it just doesn't happen to be spending that improves the future productivity of the economy or (directly) the well-being of citizens. Even the critics of Roosevelt agree that if New Deal spending didn't get the economy out of the depression, war spending did. Regardless, the Great Depression showed that the market economy was not self-correcting—at least in a relevant time frame.[4]

By 1970 there was a new problem, inflation, and a new generation of economists. The problem in the 1930s was *deflation*, the fall in prices. To the young economists who were making their mark, that was ancient history. Another deep recession seemed unimaginable. The fact that most of the postwar recessions were associated with the Fed tightening credit excessively confirmed conservatives' prejudices that it was government failures, not market failures, that were responsible for any aberration from perfection.

There were, however, other perspectives. According to the late distinguished economic historian Charles Kindleberger, financial crises have occurred at roughly ten-year intervals for the last four hundred years.[5] The quarter century from 1945 to 1971 was exceptional in that, though there were fluctuations, there were no banking crises anywhere in the world except in Brazil, in 1962. Both before and after this period they were a regular feature of economic life. Professor Franklin Allen of the Wharton School of the University of Pennsylvania and Douglas Gale of New York University provide a convincing interpretation for why the quarter century after World War II was free from crises: the global recognition of the need for strong regulation.[6] The greater stability may have been one of the factors contributing to the high rate of growth during this period. Government intervention had resulted in a more stable economy—and may have even contributed to the rapid growth and greater equality of that era.

Astoundingly, by the 1980s the view that the market was self-correcting and efficient came to predominate again, not only in conservative political circles but also among American academic economists. This free market view was in accord with neither reality nor modern advances in economic theory, which had also shown that even when the economy was near full employment and markets were competitive, resources likely still were not efficiently allocated.

The general equilibrium approach

The mainstream of theoretical economics for more than a hundred years has been dominated by what is called the Walrasian or general equilibrium model, named after the French mathematician and economist Léon Walras, who first articulated that model in 1874.[7] He described the economy as an equilibrium—like Newtonian equilibrium in physics—with prices and quantities determined by balancing supply and demand. One of the great achievements of modern economics was to use that model to assess the efficiency of the market economy. In the same year that America declared its independence, Adam Smith published his famous treatise, *The Wealth of Nations*, in which he argued that the pursuit of self-interest would lead to the general well-being of society. A hundred and seventy-five years later, Kenneth Arrow and Gerard Debreu, using the Walrasian model, explained what was required for Smith's insight to be correct.[8] The economy was efficient, in the sense that no one could be made better off without making someone else worse off, only under very restrictive conditions.[9] Markets had to be more than just competitive: there had to be a full set of insurance markets (you could buy insurance against every conceivable risk), capital markets had to be perfect (you could borrow as much as you wanted for as long as you wanted at competitive, risk-adjusted, interest rates), there could be no externalities or public goods. The circumstances under which markets failed to produce efficient outcomes were referred to, quite naturally, as *market failures*.

As often happens in science, their work inspired vast amounts of research. The conditions under which they had shown that the economy was efficient were so restrictive as to question the relevance of the view that markets were efficient at all. Some failures, though important, required only limited government intervention. Yes, the market by itself would lead to an externality like too much pollution, but the government could restrict pollution or charge the firms for emitting pollution. Markets could still solve most of society's economic problems.

Other market failures, such as imperfect risk markets—individuals can't buy insurance against many of the most important risks that they face—presented a more difficult problem. Economists asked whether, even with imperfect risk markets, markets were still efficient in some sense.

Quite often in science certain assumptions are so strongly held or are so ingrained in the thinking that no one realizes they are only assumptions. When Debreu listed the assumptions under which he had proved the efficiency of the market, he didn't mention the implicit assumption that everyone had perfect information. Moreover, he assumed that commodities or goods were uniform, whether houses or cars, a kind of Platonic ideal.[10] As we know, the real world is messier. One house or one car is different from another in ways that can be quite complex. Similarly, Debreu treated labor just like any other commodity. All unskilled workers were identical, for example.

Economists assumed that information was perfect even though they understood that it was not so. Theorists *hoped* that a world with imperfect information was very much like a world with perfect information— at least so long as the information imperfections were not too large. But this was just a hope. And besides, what did it mean that information imperfections were large? Economists had no rigorous way to think about the size of information imperfections. It was obvious that the world was rife with information imperfections. One worker was different from another and one product from another; large amounts of resources were spent figuring out which workers or products were better than others. Insurance companies hesitated in insuring some who wanted insurance because they were unsure of the risks, and so too, lenders hesitated in lending money to those who wanted loans because they were uncertain about being repaid.

One of the popular arguments *for* a market economy was the spur it provided to innovation. Yet Arrow and Debreu had assumed that there was no innovation; if there was technological progress, its pace was unaffected by any decision made within the economy. Of course, these economists knew that innovation was important. But just as their technical apparatus had trouble dealing with imperfect information, so too with innovation. Market advocates could only hope that the conclusions they reached about market efficiencies remained valid in a world with innovation. But the very assumptions of the model meant that it could not address such key questions as whether the market allocated enough resources to innovation or whether it directed innovation expenditures in the right way.

The answers to the question about the generality of the results of the Walrasian model—whether they were sensitive to the assumptions of perfect information, imperfect risk markets, no innovation, and so forth—were made plain in a series of papers that I wrote with several coauthors, most notably my Columbia University colleague Bruce Greenwald.[11] We showed, in effect, that Arrow and Debreu had established the singular set of conditions under which markets were efficient. When these conditions were not satisfied, there were always some government interventions that could make everyone better off. Our work also showed that even small information imperfections (and especially information asymmetries—where one person knew information that others didn't) dramatically changed the nature of the market equilibrium. With perfect markets (including perfect information), there was always full employment; with imperfect information, there could be unemployment. It simply wasn't true that a world with almost perfect information was very similar to one in which there was perfect information.[12] By the same token, while it was true that competition could provide a spur for innovation, it was not true that the markets were efficient in determining the ideal amount of spending or the best direction of research.

The response

These new results showed that there was no scientific basis for the presumption that markets were efficient. Markets did provide incentives, but market failures were pervasive, and there were persistent differences between social and private returns. In some sectors—such as health care, insurance, and finance—the problems were larger than in others, and quite naturally, government focused its attention on these sectors.

Government, of course, faced imperfections of information. Sometimes it had access to information that the market did not, but more importantly, it had objectives and instruments that were different. The government could, for instance, discourage smoking *even if the cigarette industry by itself was profitable*, because it realized that there were other social costs (such as increased health care costs) that were not borne by the cigarette companies. And it could do so both by regulating advertising and by imposing taxes.

Academic economists on the right did not receive these new results with enthusiasm. At first, they attempted to look for hidden assumptions, mistakes in the mathematics, or alternative formulations. It is easy for these kinds of "errors in analysis" to happen—as demonstrated by earlier work analyzing the efficiency of the market economy. These attempts at refutation have all failed; a quarter century after the publication of our work, the results still stand.

Conservative economists were left with two choices. They could argue that the issues we had raised, such as those associated with information imperfections, were theoretical niceties. They reverted to the old argument that with perfect information (and all the other assumptions), markets are efficient, and they simply asserted that a world with only a limited degree of information imperfection was accordingly almost perfectly efficient. They ignored analyses that showed that even small information asymmetries could have a very big effect. They also simply ignored the many aspects of the real economy—including the repeated episodes of massive unemployment—that could not be explained by models with perfect information. Instead, they focused on a few facts that were consistent with their models. Yet they had no way of proving that the market was *almost* efficient. It was a theological position, and it soon became clear that no piece of evidence or theoretical research would budge them from it.

The second approach conceded on the economics but moved on to politics: yes, markets are inefficient, but government is worse. It was a curious line of thinking; suddenly economists had become political scientists. Their economic models and analyses were flawed, and their political models and analyses proved no better. In all successful countries, the United States included, government has played a key role in that success. In the preceding chapters I described some of those roles—in regulating banks, in controlling pollution, in providing education, and even in research.

Government has played an especially large role in the highly successful economies of East Asia. The increases in per capita incomes there during the past three to four decades have been historically unprecedented. In almost all of these countries, government took an active role in promoting development through market mechanisms. China has grown at an average rate of 9.7 percent per year for more than thirty years and has succeeded in bringing hundreds of millions out of poverty. Japan's government-led growth spurt was earlier, but Singapore, Korea, Malaysia, and a host of other countries followed and adapted Japan's strategy and saw per capita incomes increase eightfold in a quarter century.

Of course governments, like markets and humans, are fallible. But in East Asia, and elsewhere, the success far outweighed the failures. Enhancing economic performance requires improving both markets and government. There is no basis to the argument that because governments *sometimes* fail, they should not intervene in markets when the markets fail—just as there is no basis to the converse argument, that because markets sometimes fail they should be abandoned.

The failure of the neoclassical model

The model of perfect markets is sometimes called the neoclassical model.[13] Economics is supposed to be a predictive science, yet many of the key predictions of neoclassical economics can easily be rejected. The most obvious is that *there is no unemployment.*[14] Just as market equilibrium entails the demand for apples equaling the supply, so too (in this theory) the demand for labor equals the supply. In the neoclassical model, any deviations from equilibrium are short-lived— so short-lived that it would not be worth the government's resources to do anything about them. Believe it or not, there are mainstream economists—including at least one recent winner of the Nobel Prize in Economics—who believe that this current crisis is no big deal. A few people are simply enjoying a little more leisure than they would normally enjoy.

This is not the only odd conclusion of neoclassical economics. Its acolytes also argue that there is no such thing as credit rationing—anybody can borrow as much as they want, of course at an interest rate that reflects appropriately the risk of default. To these economists, the liquidity crunch that happened on September 15 was just a phantasm, a figment of somebody's imagination.[15]

A third example of mainstream economics' divorce from reality concerns corporate financial structure: whether a firm finances itself with debt or equity doesn't matter. This was one of the main contributions of Franco Modigliani and Merton Miller, who received the Nobel Prize in Economics in 1985 and 1990, respectively.[16] As with so many neoclassical ideas, there is a grain of truth—and one can learn a great deal by following through the logic. They argue that the value of the firm depends solely on the value of the returns it delivers, and it doesn't matter much whether one delivers those returns mostly as debt (giving a fixed payment regardless of the level of profits) with the residual going to equity, or mostly as equity. It's just like the value of a quart of whole milk can be thought of as simply the value of the skim milk plus the value of the cream. Modigliani and Miller ignored the possibility of bankruptcy and the costs associated with it—and the fact that the more the firm borrows, the higher the probability of bankruptcy. They also ignored the information that might be conveyed by an owner's decision to sell shares: an owner's eagerness to sell his shares at a very low price almost surely says something to the market about his views of the firm's future prospects.

A fourth, critical aspect of neoclassical economics that has been belied by the current crisis is its explanation of what determines incomes and inequality. How do we explain the relative wages of skilled or unskilled workers or the pay of corporate executives? Neoclassical theory provided a justification of inequality by saying that each worker gets paid according to his *marginal* contribution to society. Resources are scarce, and scarcer resources need to have a higher price to ensure that they are used well. To interfere with the payment of executives would, in this view, interfere with the efficiency of the market. Over the past quarter century, there have been increasing doubts about the ability of this theory to explain soaring executive compensation, as senior executives' pay went from around forty times that of average workers thirty years ago to hundreds or thousands times that.[17] High-level executives hadn't suddenly become more productive, nor had they suddenly become scarcer. And there was no evidence that the number-one person was that much more skilled than the number-two person. Neoclassical theory couldn't explain either why, in a globalized world, with similar technologies available in different countries, these compensation disparities were so much greater in the United States than elsewhere. Doubts about the theory have increased as executive bonuses in finance remained strong even as there was evidence of strong negative contributions both to the firms they served and to society more broadly. Earlier, I suggested an alternative explanation: problems in corporate governance meant there was no close relationship between pay and "marginal" social contribution. If true, this has profound implications for policies attempting to achieve a better distribution of income.

A final example is that under neoclassical theory, there is no such thing as discrimination.[18] The theoretical argument was simple: if there were discrimination, and anybody in society was not discriminatory, they would hire members of the discriminated-against group since their wages would be lower. This would drive up wages to the point that any differences among racial groups would be eliminated.

I'm from Gary, Indiana, a steel town on the southern shores of Lake Michigan. As I grew up, I saw persistent unemployment, which grew much larger as the economy faced one downturn after another. I knew that when people in my town faced hard times, they couldn't go to the bank and get money to tide them over. I saw racial discrimination. As I began to study economics, none of these conclusions of neoclassical theory made sense to me. It helped motivate me to look for alternatives. As graduate students, my classmates and I argued about which of the assumptions of (neo)classical economics was critical—which was responsible for the "absurd" conclusions of the theory.[19]

It was, for instance, obvious that markets were far from perfectly competitive.[20] In a perfectly competitive market, a firm that lowered its prices even by a little bit could grab the entire market. A small country would never face unemployment; simply by lowering its exchange rate, it could sell as much of the goods it produced as it wanted. The assumption of perfect competition was crucial, but it seemed to me that its main impact in a large economy such as the United States was on the distribution of income. Those who had monopoly power could garner for themselves more of the nation's income—and as a result of their exercise of market power, the nation's income might be smaller. But there was no reason to believe that an economy rife with monopolies would be marked by unemployment, racial discrimination, or credit rationing.

As I embarked on my research as a young graduate student, it seemed to me that there were two critical assumptions, those concerning information and those concerning the nature of man himself. Economics is a social science. It is concerned with how individuals interact to produce goods and services. To answer the question of how they interact, one has to describe more broadly their behavior. Were they "rational"? The belief in rationality is deeply ingrained in economics. Introspection—and even more so, a look at my peers— convinced me that it was nonsense. I soon realized that my colleagues were irrationally committed to the assumption of rationality, and shaking their faith in it would not be easy. So I took the easier course: I stuck with the assumption of rationality but showed that even slight changes in information assumptions totally changed every result. One could easily derive theories that seemed so much more in accord with reality—including new theories of unemployment, credit rationing, and discrimination—and it was easy to understand why corporate financial structure (whether firms chose to finance themselves by borrowing or issuing shares) mattered a great deal.

Homo economicus

Most of us would not like to think that we conform to the view of man that underlies prevailing economic models, which is of a calculating, rational, self-serving, and self-interested individual. There is no room for human empathy, public spiritedness, or altruism. One interesting aspect of economics is that the model provides a better description of economists than it does of others, and the longer students study economics, the more like the model they become.[21]

What economists mean by rationality is not exactly what most people mean. What economists mean is better described as *consistency*. If an individual prefers chocolate ice cream to vanilla, whenever he is given a choice at the same price he makes the same decision. Rationality also involves consistency in more complex choices: if an individual prefers chocolate to vanilla and vanilla to strawberry, then given a choice between chocolate and strawberry, he will always choose chocolate.

There are other aspects of this "rationality." One is the basic principle I mentioned in chapter 5, to let bygones be bygones. Individuals should always be forward looking. A standard example illustrates that most individuals are not rational in this sense. Assume you like watching football games, but you hate getting wet even more. If someone gave you a free ticket to go to a football game in the rain, you would decline the offer. But now, assume you paid $100 for the ticket. Like most individuals, you would find it difficult to throw away the $100. You will go to the game, even if getting wet makes you miserable. The economist would say you are irrational.

Unfortunately, economists have pushed their model of rationality beyond its appropriate domain. You learn what you like—what gives you pleasure—by repeated experiences. You try different kinds of ice cream or different kinds of lettuce. But economists have tried to use that same model to explain decisions over time, such as savings for retirement. It should be obvious: there is no way you can find out whether you should have saved more or less until it is too late, at which point there is no way that you can learn from your experience. At the end of your life you might say, I wish I had saved more—the last few years have been really painful, and I would willingly have given up one of my earlier beach vacations to have had some more spending today. Or you might say, I wish I had saved less. I could have enjoyed the money so much more when I was younger. Either way, you can't go back to relive your life. Unless reincarnation is real, what you have learned is of no value. It's not even of much value to your children and grandchildren, because the economic and social context that will prevail in future years is so different from that of today. Accordingly, it's not clear what economists really mean when they try to extend the model of rationality that applies to choices among flavors of ice cream to life's really big decisions, such as how much you save or how you invest that savings for your retirement.

Moreover, rationality to an economist does not mean that individuals necessarily act in ways that are more broadly consistent with what makes them happy. Americans talk about working hard for their families—but some work so hard that they have no time to spend with them. Psychologists have studied happiness and many of the choices individuals make, and many of the changes in the structure of our economy may not enhance happiness.[22] Connectedness with other people is important for a sense of well-being, and yet many of the changes in our society have undermined that sense of connectedness—reflected so well in Robert Putnam's classic book, *Bowling Alone*.[23]

Economists traditionally have had little to say about the links between what individuals do and what gives rise to happiness or a sense of well-being, so they focus on the much narrower issue of consistency.[24] Research over the last quarter century has shown that individuals do act consistently—but in ways that are markedly different from those predicted by the standard model of rationality. They are, in this sense, predictably irrational.[25] Standard theories, for instance, argue that "rational" individuals should look only at *real wages and incomes*, adjusted for inflation. If wages fall by 5 percent but prices also fall by 5 percent, they are unaffected. However, there is overwhelming evidence that workers don't like seeing their wages fall. An employer who cut pay in tandem with falling prices would be viewed far more negatively than an employer who gave 1 percent wage increases when prices were going up 5 percent—even though the real wage cut for the former is smaller.

Many homeowners trying to sell their houses display a similar irrationality. They won't sell their home unless they can get back what they put into it. Assume that they bought the house for $100,000, and today's market price is $90,000. Inflation, though, is increasing *all* prices at the rate of 5 percent a year. Many homeowners will wait two years—inconveniencing themselves greatly in the interim—until the house price is up to $100,000—even though *in real terms* they are no better off for waiting.

In earlier chapters, I noted examples of almost schizophrenic behavior in financial markets. Bank officers claimed that they didn't net out positions on credit default swaps because there was no risk that the counterparty would go into bankruptcy—and yet the swaps themselves were bets on various counterparties going into bankruptcy. Borrowers, lenders, and securitizers alike believed that housing prices would rise without end, despite the fact that real wages were declining and the estimates of future default rates were based on historical data that showed low default rates, *as if recently lowered underwriting standards made no difference.*[26]

The prevailing models in economics fancifully assumed that individuals were not only rational but super-rational—they could use sophisticated statistics, employing all past data, to make the best possible predictions of the future. The irony is that not even the economists who believed that others could make such predictions did a very good job. They failed to see the bubble as it was forming, and indeed, even after the bubble broke, they failed to see what was in store for the economy. They irrationally ignored key data and were irrationally committed to the idea that markets were rational, that there were no such things as bubbles, and that markets were efficient and self-correcting.

Bubbles themselves provide considerable insight into economic theory and behavior. The standard model assumes that not only do there exist futures markets (markets in which one can buy and sell, say, corn today for delivery tomorrow), but such markets exist for everything: one can buy and sell not only for delivery tomorrow but also for the day after, and the day after that, all the way to eternity. The standard model also assumes that one can buy insurance against every conceivable risk. These unrealistic assumptions have profound implications. If there were markets for all goods and all risks extending infinitely far into the future and covering all risks, it is unlikely that bubbles could occur. Homeowners would have bought insurance against the risk of a price collapse. In all likelihood, the high insurance premium they would have had to pay—if they and the markets were rational—would have told them that the market was *not* confident that prices would continue to rise, no matter what the real estate agent said.[27]

Bubbles are, however, usually more than just an economic phenomenon. They are a social phenomenon. Economists begin with the assumption that preferences (what individuals like or dislike) are simply given. But we know that that is not true. There is no genetic difference between the French and the Americans that would explain their different preferences for food; no genetic difference that can explain why those in Europe enjoy spending more of their time in leisure while Americans spend more time working; no genetic difference between those in the 1960s who enjoyed the hula hoop and those today who don't.

Our beliefs about the world are equally affected by the beliefs of others around us. The beliefs of union members and those of Wall Street magnates on many topics are markedly different. Some of these beliefs arise from differences in interests: generally we each have beliefs that lead to policies that support our own well-being. But mindsets differ also because we live in different communities, and those in each come to have some shared views. Most Americans were outraged that Wall Street took taxpayer money and paid out supersize bonuses in spite of record losses. However, the standard view on Wall Street was that it was an outrage for President Obama to have criticized these bonuses—it smacked of populism, riling up the masses against Wall Street.

Biologists study herding behavior—the way that groups of animals move in one direction or another, sometimes seemingly oblivious even to individual self-interest. Lemmings will follow each other over a cliff. Humans sometimes behave in ways that seem equally foolish.[28] Jared Diamond, in his book *Collapse*, describes how Easter Islanders may have followed each other in cutting down trees—even though it eventually led to the collapse of their civilization.[29]

Bubbles have similar characteristics. Some people are foolish enough to believe that the price of housing will go up forever. Some may have some degree of skepticism—but believe that they are smarter than others and so will be able to get out of the bubble before it collapses. It is a perfectly human fault; like most of my students, they all believe that they are in the top half of the class. As people talk to each other, their beliefs—for instance, that the bubble won't break any time soon—get reaffirmed. The authorities are affected too and energize the whole process: there is no bubble, just a little froth; besides, you can't tell a bubble before it breaks. This cycle of affirmation makes it hard for the naysayers to break in.

When the bubble breaks, everyone says, "Who could have predicted it?" I was at a meeting in Davos in January 2008; the bubble had broken the preceding August, though the optimists were still of the view that it would have little consequence. As I and a couple of other colleagues explained how the bubble had developed and what its breaking meant, a chorus of central bankers in the front row chimed in: "No one predicted it," they claimed. That claim was immediately challenged by the same small band that had been talking about the bubble for several years. But the central bankers were, in a sense, right: no one *with credibility in their circle* challenged the prevailing view, but there was a tautology: no one challenging the prevailing view would be treated as credible. Sharing similar views was part of being socially and intellectually acceptable.

Consequences

There are several implications of the fact that individuals act systematically in an irrational way. Smart firms can find profitable opportunities in exploiting irrationalities. The financial sector understood that most individuals don't read or can't understand the fine print in their credit card application. Once individuals have the credit card, they will use it, and that use will generate huge fees. In spite of the huge fees, most borrowers won't search for a better card—partly because they believe they will be cheated in a similar way by any other card and perhaps worse. In that sense, they may be rational. People in the real estate sector knew that most individuals wouldn't understand the array of fees and transaction costs and that the real estate brokers, and even more, the mortgage brokers, would be "trusted." They knew too that the deception would not be found out until long after the loans were made. Even if they were found out, there would be few consequences, and, in any case, the money was good while things were going well.

These systemic irrationalities also can give rise to macroeconomic fluctuations. Irrational exuberance leads to bubbles and booms; irrational pessimism to downturns. In the period of irrational exuberance, individuals underestimate risks. They have done so in the past, and almost surely, when memories of this crisis have passed, they will do so in the future. When asset prices start to rise, people will borrow against the collateral, so long as banks allow them to do so, and that can fuel a credit bubble. Because the problems are predictable, government—through monetary, fiscal, and regulatory policy—can take actions to help stabilize the economy.[30]

Government has an important role to play: it should not only prevent the exploitation of individual irrationalities but also help individuals make better decisions. Consider the situation described earlier of deciding how much to save for retirement. One of the discoveries of modern "behavioral economics," the branch of economics that has explored these systematic irrationalities, is that how questions get posed and framed may affect the choices individuals make. Thus, if an employer gives a worker a choice of three different rates of contribution to retirement, say, 5 percent, 10 percent, or 15 percent, it matters a great deal how it presents those choices. If the employer says, for instance, "We will deduct 10 percent for your retirement, unless you instruct us otherwise. Please check if you wish 5 percent or 15 percent," individuals will go along with the suggestion of the employer. These are called defaults, and by thinking through what defaults make the most sense for individuals in different circumstances and setting the defaults accordingly, individuals may be led to make on average better decisions.[31]

Obviously, it is important that those shepherding the individuals in this way do not have an axe to grind: an employer running his own pension fund might have an incentive to garner more fees from a higher contribution rate. As firms have learned about how individuals make choices, not surprisingly, they have tried to take advantage of these insights.

While the U.S. government has not begun to use knowledge of human psychology to prevent abuses, it did make a concerted effort in the spring of 2008 to use that knowledge to help the country emerge from its recession. Keynes had argued that investors were best described as if they were motivated by animal spirits—"a spontaneous urge to action rather than inaction, and not as the outcome of a weighted average of quantitative benefits multiplied by quantitative probabilities."[32] If so, and if one could change the spirits of the time, one might be able to move the economy out of a mental state of depression into a mood of hope—and perhaps even a sense of exhilaration that the worst was behind us. Perhaps motivated by this,[33] a couple of months after Barack Obama's inauguration, his administration launched its "green shoots" campaign—that there were signs of recovery. And there were real bases for hope: in many areas, there was an end to the sense of freefall; the rate of decline had slowed—as the more mathematically inclined put it, the second derivative had turned positive.

Economists had long emphasized the important role that expectations had on actions: beliefs could affect reality. Indeed, in many areas, economists had constructed models where there were multiple equilibria, each with self-fulfilling expectations. If market participants believed that there would be many bankruptcies, they would charge high interest rates to compensate for the losses; with the high interest rates, there would in fact be many bankruptcies. But if they believed that there would be few bankruptcies, they would charge low inter-est rates, and with the low interest rates, there would in fact be few bankruptcies.[34]

Here, the administration and the Federal Reserve were hoping that optimistic beliefs would become contagious. If people believed things were getting better, they would start consuming and investing—and if enough people believed this, then things would in fact get better. But expectations have to be grounded in reality. Would they get better enough to satisfy their hopes and beliefs? If not, there would be disap-pointment ahead. And with the disappointment, there could be further contractions, a reinforcement of the original belief that the nation was in for a long downturn. In the case at hand, there were good reasons for concern. Even if the banks were repaired, even if Americans felt *more* optimistic about the future, the reality was that the bubble—and the irrational optimism that had sustained consumption prior to 2008—were gone.[35] With the bursting of the bubble, many households and banks had sustained large losses. Even when the period of freefall stopped, even when growth turned (slightly) positive, unemployment would remain high, and even grow, for a considerable length of time. Economists might engage in a semantic quibble—claiming that once growth turned positive, the recession was over. But for most Ameri-cans, as I noted earlier, the recession is only over when full employ-ment is restored and wages start growing again; optimism based simply on the end of freefall and a *technical* end to a recession would not be sustainable—even if Americans were told repeatedly things were better. The disparity between their hopes and reality might then make them even more depressed. Talking up animal spirits can only take you so far. It can temporarily raise stock prices. It can even temporarily induce more spending. But one can't talk one's way out of a recession of the depth of the Great Recession of 2008.

THE MACROECONOMIC BATTLES

Within the cathedral of mainstream economics, there are many chapels devoted to specialized problems. Each has its own priests and even its own catechism. The war of ideas that I have described is reflected in a myriad of battles and skirmishes within each of these subdisciplines. In this and the next three sections, I describe four, related to four themes of this debacle: macroeconomics, monetary policy, finance, and the economics of innovation.

Macroeconomics studies the movements of output and employment and seeks to understand why economies are marked by fluctuations, with intermittent episodes of high unemployment and underutilization of capacity. Battles in the arena of economic ideas are typically affected by a curious interplay between the evolution of thinking within the discipline and events. As we saw earlier, in the aftermath of the Great Depression there was a consensus that markets were not self-correcting—or weren't at least in a relevant time frame. (It is irrelevant that markets might eventually—in ten or twenty years—return to full employment, if just left on their own.) To most economists, the fact that unemployment could soar to nearly 25 percent (in 1933) was evidence enough that markets were not efficient. While for the past quarter century macroeconomists have focused on models in which markets are stable and efficient, hopefully this crisis will induce them to rethink the underlying assumptions.

I described earlier how economists abandoned Keynesian economics as attention shifted away from unemployment to inflation and growth. But there was another, more conceptual basis for the shift. Microeconomics, focusing on the behavior of firms, and macroeconomics, focusing on the behavior of the overall economy, had developed in the years after Keynes into two separate subdisciplines. The two used different models and came to different conclusions. The "micro" models said that there could be no such thing as unemployment—but unemployment was the centerpiece of Keynesian macroeconomics. Microeconomics emphasized the efficiency of markets; macroeconomics, the massive waste of resources in recessions and depressions. By the mid-

1960s, both microeconomists and macroeconomists realized that this dichotomy in economics was an unsatisfactory state of affairs.[36] Both wanted to provide a unified approach.

One school of thought—influential in shaping the deregulatory policies that played a role in the current crisis—argued that the competitive equilibrium approach of microeconomics provided the correct foundations for macroeconomics. This school, based on the neoclassical model, was sometimes referred to as the "New Classical" school, or the "Chicago School," because some of its high priests taught at the University of Chicago.[37] Because they believed that markets are always efficient, they contended that one should not be worried about economic fluctuations, such as the current recession—it was simply the efficient adjustment of the economy to shocks (such as changes in technology) coming from the outside. It was an approach that had strong policy prescriptions—a minimal role for government.

Though they based their analyses on the neoclassical (Walrasian) models, they made a further simplification that all individuals were identical. This was called the "representative agent" model. But if all individuals are identical, there can be no borrowing and lending—that would simply be moving money from the left pocket to the right pocket. There can then be no bankruptcy. While I argued earlier that problems of imperfect information are central to an understanding of modern economics, in their models there can be no information asymmetries, where one person knows something that someone else doesn't. Any information asymmetry would reflect intense schizophrenia, hardly consistent with their other assumptions of full rationality. Their models have nothing to say about the critical issues that are at play in the current crisis: so what if one gives the bankers an extra trillion dollars or two? In the model, the bankers and the workers are the same people. Key policy debates were simply assumed away. For instance, the representative agent model precludes any discussion of distribution. In a sense, views of values (including the view that the distribution of income is not important) are embedded in the very formulation of their analyses.

Many of the (what seem to be absurd) conclusions of this school's analyses come from these and other extreme simplifications in their models. I noted one in chapter 3, that government deficit spending does not stimulate the economy. The conclusion is the result of assumptions that are even more unrealistic than the one that markets are perfect.[38] (a) It is assumed that the "representative agent" knows that there will be taxes in the future to pay for the expenditure and so sets aside today money to pay for those taxes. This means that decreased consumer spending fully offsets the increased government spending. (b) In addition, it is assumed that the spending has no direct positive benefit. On the contrary, though, spending has both direct and indirect benefits: the construction of a road generates income today but also might induce some firm to expand because of the lower costs of getting its goods to market.[39] As another example, they argue that unemployment benefits are unnecessary, since individuals are never unemployed (they are just enjoying leisure), and in any case, they can always borrow to smooth out consumption if they wish to do so. Worse, unemployment benefits are harmful, because the problem is not a shortage of jobs— there are always jobs for anyone who wants them—but lack of effort in looking for them, and unemployment insurance just exacerbates this "moral hazard."

The other school of thought, championed by the New Keynesians (of which there were many subschools), took a different tack in trying to reconcile macroeconomics with microeconomics. The problem, in their view, was with the simplistic microeconomic models and with the myriad of unrealistic assumptions that I described earlier in this chapter.[40] Research over the past three decades showed that the neoclassical model—on which the Chicago School's analyses rested—was simply not robust.

In this view, the Great Depression—and this Great Recession—were evidence of an inefficiency so large that one couldn't miss or ignore it. But at other times, there were many market failures, harder to detect but nonetheless real. Recessions were like the tip of an iceberg—signs of much deeper problems hidden beneath the surface. There was ample evidence that this was in fact the case. Because the true weakness in modern economics was not Keynesian macroeconomics but standard microeconomics, the challenge for the economics profession was to develop a microeconomics consistent with the behavior of the macroeconomy.

Economics, as I have noted earlier, is supposed to be a predictive science. If so, the Chicago School approach has to be given a failing grade: it did not predict the crisis (how could it, when there are no such things as bubbles or unemployment), and it had little to say about what to do when it occurred, except nay-saying about the risks of government deficits. Their prescription is an easy one: just keep government out of the way.

This economic downturn has not only discredited the "perfect markets" macro-school but also reinvigorated the debates within the New Keynesian approaches. There are, for instance, two major strands of New Keynesian economics. One shared most of the neoclassical assumptions—with one important exception. It assumed that wages and prices were rigid—that is, for instance, they failed to fall when there was an excess supply of labor (unemployment). The implication was clear: *if* only wages and prices were more flexible, the economy would be efficient and behave according to the standard neoclassical model.[41] This strand shared some of the Chicago School's concerns about inflation, and paid little attention to financial structure.

The other strand, arguably more in line with Keynes's own thinking, sees far deeper problems in the market. A fall in wages would actually exacerbate the downturn, as consumers cut back on spending. Deflation—or even a slowing of the rate of inflation from what was expected—can cause firms to go into bankruptcy, as the revenues fall short of debt payments. In this view, part of the problem originates in financial markets, for instance, in the fact that debt contracts are not indexed to the price level. Part of the problem arises too from the fact that when the economy goes through a period of stability, firms and households are induced to take on more risk, especially through more debt, and as they do this, the economy becomes more fragile—more vulnerable to being hit by an adverse shock. As we have seen, with high leverage, even a slight decrease in asset values can result in wholesale collapse.[42]

The policy prescriptions offered by different New Keynesian schools vary markedly. One argues that policies intended to maintain wage stability are part of the problem; the other, that they help stabilize the economy. One worries about deflation; the other encourages it. One focuses attention on financial fragility—such as the leverage of banks—while the other ignores it.

In the run-up to this crisis the Chicago School and the wage-price rigidity Keynesian schools had a predominant role in many policy circles. The Chicago School adherents said that there was no need for government to do anything, that if it did anything it was likely to be ineffective—the private sector would just undo what the government did; and if it had any effect, it was likely to be the wrong effect. Of course, they could point to examples where the government had done the wrong thing and to instances where the private sector partially offset what the government did, as an increase in savings partially offset an increase in government spending. But their strong conclusions that government was *always* ineffective were based on flawed models of only limited relevance to the real world and out of touch with the statistical evidence and historical experiences. In the Keynesian wage-price rigidity school, there was a more active role for government—though in support of a conservative agenda. What was required was more wage flexibility, weakening unions, and other measures to soften worker protections. It was another example of "blame the victim": workers were blamed for any unemployment they faced. While in some countries, job protections may have gone too far, their role in causing unemployment was at most minimal—and in this crisis, but for them, matters could have been far worse.

THE BATTLE OVER MONETARY POLICY

Perhaps the worst outcomes arose when the Chicago School and the wage-price rigidity school got together to shape monetary policy, in their fight against inflation.[43] The result was that central banks focused on the inefficiencies that arise when prices get slightly out of line during even moderate inflation—and they totally ignored the problems that arise when financial markets become excessively fragile. The losses from the failures in the financial markets were a thousand times larger than those that arise even from inflation, so long as it remains low or moderate.

Central bankers are a club prone to fads and fashions. They tend to be conservative and, by and large, do not believe in government intervention in the market. There is something strange in this: their central task is setting one of the most important prices in the economy, the interest rate. So the question is not whether government will intervene, but how and when. Chicago School adherents saw government polices as *causing* inflation. The monetarist disciples of Milton Friedman used simplistic models to support an ideological thrust to limit the role of government. A simple prescription (called monetarism, which became fashionable in the 1970s and early 1980s) provided the guide: tie government hands by having it increase the money supply at a fixed rate each year. With government thus tamed, markets could perform their wonders.

Monetarism was based on the notion that the best way to keep prices stable (inflation low) was to increase the money supply at a fixed rate, at the rate of expansion of real output. Unfortunately, just as that idea became fashionable, evidence against it mounted. The underlying empirical hypothesis of monetarism was that the ratio of money to GDP (called the velocity of circulation) was constant. In fact, over the past thirty years, it has varied greatly, at least in some countries. Monetarism failed, and today, almost no governments rely on it.

Inflation targeting came into vogue in the late 1990s and this decade. With inflation targeting, government chose an inflation rate, say, 2 percent. If the inflation rate exceeded 2 percent, the central bank raised interest rates. The more inflation exceeded the target, the higher interest rates went. Inflation was the supreme evil, and the main job of the central bank was to slay this dragon. Underlying inflation targeting was the belief that if the economy realized that the central bank would take strong measures against inflation that exceeded, say, 2 percent, there would be less incentive for unions or anyone else to ask for wage increases that would result in inflation exceeding that level.

The focus on inflation was predicated on four propositions, none of which had much empirical or theoretical support. First, central bankers argued that inflation had a significant adverse effect on growth. On the contrary, so long as inflation remained low to moderate,[44] there seemed to be no discernable negative effect—though excessively harsh attempts to suppress inflation did slow growth.[45] Second, they claimed that inflation is particularly hard on the poor. One should be suspicious when one hears bankers take up the cause of the poor. The fact of the matter is that the people who lose the most are bondholders, who see the real value of their bonds eroded. In the United States and most other countries, Social Security (old-age pensions) increases with inflation. When inflation becomes persistent, even wage contracts have automatic cost-of-living adjustments. This is not to say that there aren't many poor who do suffer—Social Security isn't enough to maintain the living standards of many retirees, and many, perhaps most, don't avail themselves of inflation-indexed bonds (TIPS), designed to provide complete protection against inflation. And it is true that there have been periods of high inflation in which the poor have suffered—but that was not so much because of inflation. The rapid increase in the price of oil in the late 1970s meant that Americans were poorer—consumers had to pay more for the oil they bought. Not surprisingly, workers suffered. The oil price shock also led to higher inflation. Some see the decline in living standards and mistakenly blame it on the inflation, but they both have common cause. What matters most to workers are jobs, and if high interest rates lead to more unemployment, workers suffer twice—both from lack of work and from the downward pressure on wages.

The third fallacy was that the economy was on a precipice—a slight deviation in the direction of inflation would send one quickly and perilously down a slippery slope of inflation at an ever-increasing rate. Or to use another metaphor: fighting inflation has to be approached like fighting alcoholism. Former alcoholics are told not to let any alcohol pass their lips, lest they return to their wayward ways. It is called falling off the wagon. So too, the bankers argued, once a country has tasted the elixir of inflation, it will demand more and more of it. What starts out as low inflation quickly accelerates. Again, the evidence is quite the

seems to have won the day. Today, fortunately, most central bankers realize that they must pay attention to financial markets and asset price bubbles as well as commodity inflation, and they have the tools to do that.[47]

THE BATTLE IN FINANCE

The belief in the rationality of markets suffused financial market theory more than perhaps any other branch of economics. I suspect that this was a result of contagion from the conservative market participants themselves. The belief that markets were efficient and self-regulating was convenient for many special interests. The fact that they were not was inconvenient. Many, including those in the financial market, saw real profit opportunities if only markets were deregulated. After all, regulations are *restrictions*. Almost of necessity, profits where firms are restricted in what they can do will *appear* to be less than they would be if they were not restricted.

I say that profits *appear* to be less because in thinking this way, each firm fails to take into account the full consequences of removing the restrictions. The behavior of others will change as well. Indeed, we know what standard economic theory would say *if it were correct that markets were efficient and competitive*: in the end, profits would once again be driven down to zero. Removing the restrictions might allow the first firm to seize the new opportunity and make a higher profit, but any such profits would quickly be dissipated. Some firms realize that the only way to make sustained profits is either to be more efficient than one's competitors *or* to figure out how to make markets work imperfectly.

The intellectual battle over the efficiency of financial markets has numerous strands: Do prices in financial markets reflect all available information? What role do they play in determining investment activities? As we have seen, well-functioning financial markets are at the center of a successful market economy because they direct the allocation of scarce capital, one of the key scarce resources. The price mechanism is at the core of the market process of gathering, processing, and transmitting information. The extreme "efficient markets hypothesis" held that prices accurately reflect all available information in the market, providing all the information that is relevant for firms to make decisions, for instance, concerning investment. In this view then it is critical to enhance the "price discovery" role of markets.

Prices reflect some of what is going on in the economy, but there is a lot of extraneous noise, so much so that few businessmen would rely on *just* information provided by prices in these markets. Of course, stock prices affect decisions—because the market affects firms' cost of capital. But what steel firm would decide to invest in a new steel mill simply because some investment club of dentists and doctors in Peoria, Illinois, decides steel is the metal of the future, and it and other investors drive up the price of steel stocks today? What oil firm would base its exploration decisions just on today's price of oil, affected as it may be by short-term speculation?

If the efficient markets hypothesis had been right and market participants were fully rational, they all would know that they could not beat the market. They all would then just "buy the market"—that is, someone with .01 percent of the country's wealth would buy .01 percent of each of the assets. This is effectively what stock index funds do, but while index funds have grown enormously over the past three decades, there is a large industry out there trying to beat the market. The very fact that market participants spend billions and billions trying to beat the market itself refutes the twin hypotheses that markets are efficient and that most market participants are rational. What gave credence to the theory was that it was, in fact, difficult to "beat the market." Market prices typically exhibited a certain consistency: the price of soybeans was systematically related to the price of soy meal and soy oil. It is easy to test the "efficiency" of the market, in this sense, at any point of time.[48] But assessing the "efficiency" of markets in more complex situations is difficult. If markets were efficient, there would never be bubbles. But they have occurred repeatedly. It was, of course, not easy to tell that we were in a real estate bubble—most investors missed it, though there were some telltale signs. But a few didn't (such as John Paulson, who made billions for his hedge fund).

It may be difficult to beat the market, however, for two different reasons. The market could be fully efficient, with prices reflecting all available information, or the market could be nothing more than a rich man's gambling casino, with prices randomly affected by shifts in moods and expectations. In both cases, futures prices are "unpredictable." Over the years, there has been strong evidence against the "efficient markets" interpretation. The current crisis has reinforced a conclusion based on innumerable prior episodes. For instance, on October 19, 1987, stock markets around the world crashed, falling some 20 percent or more. No news, no event, could explain a decline of this magnitude in the value of the world's capital—a devastation greater than anything that could be brought on by even the worst of wars. One couldn't predict such an event, but neither could one say that this volatility in the market reflected the market's all-wise processing of relevant information.[49]

There was a curious inconsistency in the views of many of the efficient markets advocates. They believed that markets were *already* fully efficient. Yet they boasted of the virtues of new innovations in financial markets, and they claimed their huge bonuses and profits were their just rewards for the social benefits brought by these innovations. In these fully efficient markets, the advantage of these innovations, however, was very limited: it was only that they were lowering transaction costs—enabling rational individuals to manage at lower costs risks that they could have managed otherwise.

A few people (hedge funds) do seem to consistently beat the market. There is one way to do that that is consistent with the efficient markets hypothesis: have inside information. Trading on insider information is illegal—if market participants believe that others are informationally advantaged, they will be less willing to trade. One of the concerns raised earlier (chapter 6) was that a few big banks, almost by virtue of their size and the reach of their transactions, have an informational advantage. They may not be violating any laws, but it is not a level playing field.[50] A rash of cases in the fall of 2009 suggested that large numbers in the hedge fund industry based their success on inside information.[51]

Efficient markets and markets for information

The Chicago School and its disciples wanted to believe that the market for information was like any other market. There was a demand and supply for information. Just as markets were efficient in the production of steel, they would be efficient in the production and transmission of information. Unfortunately, like the notion that markets with imperfect information would behave very much like markets with perfect information, this view was not based on any deep analysis, and when economists considered these questions both theoretically and empirically, the notions turned out to be false.

The theoretical arguments are complex, but the following may give a flavor of some aspects of the critique. Consider, for instance, the argument that market prices convey all relevant information. Then someone who simply looked at the market price would be as fully informed as someone who spent a lot of money buying research and analyzing data. In that case there would be no incentive to gather information, which would then mean that the prices conveyed by the market would not be very informative. There was, in a sense, a logical inconsistency between the belief that markets conveyed all information and that market prices were very informative.[52]

The standard argument took no account of the differences between the social and private value of information. Knowing a short time before anyone else that a large new field of oil has been discovered can have enormous private returns. I can sell oil futures (betting that the price will go down) and make a lot of money. I can sell my shares in oil companies. I can make even more money by selling stock in oil companies short. In these cases, my gain is at the expense of someone else's loss. It is a matter of redistribution of wealth, not a creation of wealth. Having this knowledge a few minutes before everyone else probably won't affect any real decision, and so this knowledge has little or no social benefit.[53] So too, some of the most successful investment banks have made much of their money from trading. But in each trade, there is another side: the gains of one side are at the expense of the other side.

From this perspective, much of the expenditures on information are a waste—it is a race to be first, to discover something before someone else, to gain at their expense. In the end, everyone has to spend more money not to be left behind.

I explain the problem to my students in another way. Assume that while you're listening to my lecture, a $100 note falls by each of you. You can go on listening to the lecture, learning the important principles of economics. At the end of the lecture, each of you bends down to pick up the $100 bill next to you. That's the efficient solution. But it's not a market equilibrium. One of you, noticing that your neighbors are not bending down, will quickly do so, not only to pick up the $100 that's by you but also to get the $100 that's by your neighbor. As each of you realizes what your neighbor is going to do, you too will instantaneously bend down. Each wants to get there before the others. In the end, you each get the $100 bill that you would have had you waited, but the lecture has been interrupted and your education shortchanged.

The efficient markets hypothesis and failed monetary policy

The widespread belief in the efficient markets hypothesis played a role in the Federal Reserve's failure. If that hypothesis were true, then there were no such things as bubbles. While the Fed didn't go quite that far, it argued that one could not tell a bubble until after it broke—bubbles were, in a sense, unpredictable. The Fed was correct that one can't be *sure* there is a bubble until after it breaks, but one can make strong probabilistic statements. All policy is made in the context of uncertainty and it was very clear, especially as the economy moved into 2006, that what was going on was very likely a bubble. The longer prices continued to soar, the more unaffordable housing became, the more likely it was that there was a bubble.

The Fed focused on the prices of goods and services, not the prices of assets—and worried that raising interest rates could have led to an economic downturn. In this, the Fed was right. But the Fed had other instruments at its disposal, which it chose not to use. It had made exactly the same flawed arguments during the tech bubble. Then, it could have raised margin requirements (how much cash individuals have to put up to buy stock). In 1994, Congress had given the Fed additional authority to regulate the mortgage market, but Chairman Alan Greenspan refused to use it. But even if the Fed didn't have the regulatory authority, it could and should have gone to Congress to get the powers needed (just as I argued earlier that if it didn't have appropriate authority over investment banks, it could, and should, have gone to Congress). In the run-up to this crisis, the Fed should have reduced maximum loan-to-value ratios as the likelihood of a bubble increased—rather than allowing them to increase. It should have lowered the maximum house payment-to-income ratios allowed, rather than allowing them to increase. It could have restricted variable-rate mortgages. Instead, Greenspan promoted them. It could have restricted negative-amortization and low-docu-mentation (liar) loans. There were ample instruments at its disposal.[54] They might not have worked perfectly, but there is little doubt that they would have taken some air out of the bubble.

One of the reasons why the Fed was so blasé about the bubble was that it subscribed to another flawed idea: if a problem arose, it could be easily dealt with. One of the reasons why it believed that the problems could be easily dealt with was that it believed in the new securitization model: risks had been spread around the world to such an extent that the global economic system could easily absorb them. So what if the housing market in Florida collapsed? That asset was a miniscule part of global wealth. Here, the Fed made two mistakes: First, it (like the investment bankers and rating agencies) underestimated the extent of correlation—real estate markets within the United States (and, indeed, in much of the world) might go down together, and for obvious reasons. Second, it overestimated the extent of diversification. It didn't realize the extent to which the big banks had kept these risks on their own books. It had underestimated the incentives for excessive risk-taking and overestimated the competence of bankers at risk management.[55]

When Greenspan said that government could easily "fix" the economy, he didn't explain that dealing with the problems would cost the taxpayers hundreds of billions of dollars and cost the economy even more. It was a strange notion, the idea that it was easier to repair the car after the wreck than to prevent the wreck. The economy had recovered from previous recessions. The crises in East Asia and Latin America had not spread to the United States. But each had exerted its toll: think of the suffering of those who lose their jobs, their homes, a retirement in comfort. From a macroeconomic perspective, the cost of even a mild recession is great, but the real and budgetary costs of this Great Recession will be in the trillions. Greenspan and the Fed were just wrong. The Fed was created, in part, to prevent accidents of this sort. It was not created just to help clean up. It had forgotten its original mission.

BATTLE OVER INNOVATION ECONOMICS

Standard economic theory (the neoclassical model discussed earlier in this chapter) has had little to say about innovation, even though most of the increases in U.S. standards of living in the past hundred years have come from technical progress.[56] As I noted earlier, just as "information" was outside the old models, so too was innovation.

As mainstream economists grasped the importance of innovation, they began to try to develop theories that explained its level and direction.[57] As they did so, they reexamined some ideas that had been put forth by two great economists of the first half of the twentieth century, Joseph Schumpeter and Friedrich Hayek, that somehow had been left out by the mainstream.

Schumpeter, an Austrian who did some of his most influential work at Harvard, argued against the standard competitive model.[58] His focus was on competition for innovation. He saw each market as being dominated temporarily by a monopolist but soon displaced by another innovator, who becomes the new monopolist. There was competition *for* markets, rather than competition *in* markets, and this competition was *through* innovation.

There was, obviously, more than a little truth in Schumpeter's analysis. His focus on innovation was a big improvement over standard economic analysis (the Walrasian general equilibrium theories discussed earlier in this chapter, which ignored innovation). But Schumpeter hadn't asked the critical questions: Wouldn't monopolists take actions to deter the entry of new rivals? Would innovators direct their attention at trying to capture the market share of an incumbent, rather than developing a really new idea? Was there any sense in which one could argue that this innovative process was efficient?

Recent experiences show that matters may not be as rosy as market advocates claim. For instance, Microsoft had leveraged its monopoly power in the PC operating system to have a dominant role in applications like word processing, spreadsheets, and browsers. Its squelching potential competitors had a chilling effect on innovation by potential rivals. Indeed, an incumbent monopolist can take numerous actions to discourage entry and to maintain a monopoly position. Some of these actions may have a positive social value—such as simply innovating faster than one's rival. But some of these actions have no socially redeeming value. Of course, in a dynamic economy, every dominant firm eventually gets challenged. Toyota usurped GM; Google is challenging Microsoft in many spheres. But the fact that competition *eventually* works says nothing about the overall efficiency of market processes, or the desirability of a hands-off, laissez-faire attitude.

Hayek, like Schumpeter, moved away from the equilibrium approach that has dominated mainstream economics. He wrote in the midst of the controversies posed by communism, where government took a dominant role in managing the economy. In these systems, decision making was "centralized" in a planning bureau. Some of those who had experienced the Great Depression and had seen the massive misallocation of resources—and the enormous human suffering—believed that government should take the central role in determining how resources should be allocated. Hayek challenged these views, arguing not only for the informational advantage of a decentralized price system, but also more broadly for the decentralized evolution of institutions themselves. While he was correct that no planner could possibly gather and process all the relevant information, as we have seen, that does not mean that the unfettered price system itself is efficient.

Hayek was influenced by the biological metaphor of evolution (in contrast to Walras, who was inspired by notions in physics of "equilibrium"). Darwin had talked about the survival of the fittest, and Social Darwinism similarly contended that ruthless competition with the survival of the fittest firms would imply ever-increasing efficiency of the economy. Hayek simply took this as an article of faith, but the fact of the matter is that unguided evolutionary processes may, or may not, lead to economic efficiency. Unfortunately, natural selection does not necessarily choose the firms (or institutions) that are best for the long run.[59] One of the main criticisms of financial markets is that they have become *increasingly* shortsighted. Some of the institutional changes (such as investors' focus on quarterly returns) have made it more difficult for firms to take longer-run perspectives. In this crisis, some firms complained that they didn't want to take on as much leverage as they did—they realized the risk—but if they hadn't, they wouldn't have survived. Their return on equity would have been low, market participants would have misinterpreted the low return as a result of lack of innovativeness and enterprise, and their stock price would have been beaten down. They felt that they had no choice but to follow the herd—with disastrous effects over the long run, both to their shareholders and to the economy.

Interestingly, while Hayek has become a god among conservatives, he (like Smith) understood that government has an important role to play. As he put it, "Probably nothing has done so much harm" to the market advocates' cause as the "wooden insistence . . . on certain rules of thumb, above all of the principle of *laissez-faire* capitalism."[60] Hayek argued that government had a role to play in diverse areas, from work-hours regulation, monetary policy, and institutions to the flow of proper information.[61]

Economic theories of the past quarter century have provided enormous insights into why markets often fail and what can be done to make them work better. The ideologues of the Right and the economists who gave them succor—supported by the financial interests who were doing very well by the deregulation movement—chose to ignore these advances in knowledge. They chose to pretend that Adam Smith and Friedrich Hayek had had the last word to say on market efficiency—perhaps updated by some fancy mathematical models corroborating the results—but ignored these scholars' warnings about the need for government intervention.

The marketplace for ideas is no more perfect than the marketplace for products, capital, and labor. The best ideas do not always prevail, at least in the short run. But the good news is that while the nonsense of perfect markets may have predominated in certain parts of the economics profession, some scholars were trying to understand how markets actually worked. Their ideas are there, now, to be used by those who wish to construct a more stable, prosperous, and equitable economy.

CHAPTER TEN

TOWARD A
NEW SOCIETY

I T IS SAID THAT A NEAR-DEATH EXPERIENCE FORCES ONE
to reevaluate priorities and values. The global economy has just had
a near-death experience. The crisis exposed not only flaws in the prevailing economic model but also flaws in our society. Too many people
had taken advantage of others. A sense of trust had been broken. Almost
every day has brought stories of bad behavior by those in the financial
sector—Ponzi schemes, insider trading, predatory lending, and a host
of credit card schemes to extract as much from the hapless user as possible. This book has focused, though, not on those who broke the law,
but the legions of those who, within the law, had originated, packaged
and repackaged, and sold toxic products and engaged in such reckless
behavior that they threatened to bring down the entire financial and
economic system. The system was saved, but at a cost that is still hard
to believe.

The simple thesis of this chapter is that we should take this moment
as one of reckoning and reflection, of thinking about what kind of society we would like to have, and ask ourselves, Are we creating an economy that is helping us achieve those aspirations?

We have gone far down an alternative path—creating a society in
which materialism dominates moral commitment, in which the rapid
growth that we have achieved is not sustainable environmentally or

socially, in which we do not act together as a community to address our common needs, partly because rugged individualism and market fundamentalism have eroded any sense of community and have led to rampant exploitation of unwary and unprotected individuals and to an increasing social divide. There has been an erosion of trust—and not just in our financial institutions. It is not too late to close these fissures.

HOW ECONOMICS SHAPES SOCIETY AND INDIVIDUALS

One of the lessons of this crisis is that there is need for collective action—there is a role for government, as I have repeatedly emphasized. But there are others: we allowed markets to blindly shape our economy, and in doing so, they also helped shape ourselves and our society. This is an opportunity to ask whether the way that they have been shaping us is what we want.

Misallocation of our scarcest resources: our human talent

I have described how our financial markets misallocated capital. But the real cost of our runaway financial sector may have been far greater: it led to the misallocation of our scarcest resource, our human talent. I saw too many of our best students going into finance. They couldn't resist the megabucks. When I was an undergraduate, the best students went into science, teaching, the humanities, or medicine. They wanted to change the world by using their brains. I remember clearly my parents' advice when, like all teenagers, I wondered what I would do when I grew up. They said, "Money is not important. It will never bring you happiness. [Strange advice to a future economist.] Use the brain God has given you, and be of service to others. That is what will give you satisfaction."

If only social returns were commensurate with private returns, then the megabucks the financial sector has earned would have reflected mega-increases in societal productivity. Sometimes that has been the case, but too often it has not—as in the run-up to this disaster.

How the market has altered how we think and misshaped our values

Standard economic theory assumes that we are born with fully formed preferences. But we are shaped by what happens around us, including, and perhaps most importantly, by the economy.

Too many came to believe in the theory that pay reflected social contributions, and they concluded that those who received such high pay must have been making the most important social contributions. Too many came to value what the market was valuing. The high pay of bankers said that banking was important.

How the market has altered the way we think is illustrated by attitudes toward incentive pay. What kind of society is it in which a CEO says, "If you pay me only $5 million, I will give you only a fraction of my effort. To get my full attention, you have to give me a share of the profits"? But that is exactly what CEOs are saying when they claim they need to be incentivized by pay which increases with performance.

There used to be a social contract about the reasonable division of the gains that arise from acting together within the economy. Within corporations, the pay of the head used to be forty times that of the average worker, a seemingly large number, and larger than that in Europe and Japan. (The executives in most of these firms are workers too, in the sense that they don't own the firm. But they are in the position of making decisions, including the decisions about how much of the income of the firm goes to shareholders, to the workers, and to themselves.) But something happened some quarter century ago, as the era of Margaret Thatcher and Ronald Reagan was ushered in. Any sense of fairness in compensation was replaced by how much the executives could appropriate for themselves.

What happens in markets and politics says a great deal about economic and political power. It also sends strong messages to which the youth respond, and in doing so, our society is shaped. When we tax the returns to speculation at much lower rates than the income of those who work hard for an income, not only do we encourage more young people to go into speculation, but we say, in effect, that as a society we value speculation more highly.

A Moral Crisis

Much has been written about the foolishness of the risks that the financial sector undertook, the devastation that the financial institutions have brought to the economy, and the fiscal deficits that have resulted; too little has been written about the underlying "moral deficit" that has been exposed—a deficit that may be larger and even harder to correct. The unrelenting pursuit of profits and the elevation of the pursuit of self-interest may not have created the prosperity that was hoped, but they did help create the moral deficit.

There was perhaps a fine line between creative accounting and deceptive accounting—a fine line that the financial sector has crossed time and time again, including a few short years ago, in the WorldCom and Enron scandals. It is not always possible to distinguish between incompetence and deception, but it is not likely that a firm claiming to have a net worth of more than a hundred billion dollars would suddenly find itself in negative territory without knowing that its accounting was deceptive. It is not believable that the mortgage originators and the investment bankers didn't know that the products they were creating, purchasing, and repackaging were toxic and poisonous. The investment bankers would like us to believe that they were deceived by those that sold the mortgages to them. But they were not. They encouraged the mortgage originators to go into the risky subprime market because it was only through the ample supply of mortgages and the transformation of the risky assets into new products that they earned the fees and generated the returns that, through leverage, made them look like financial wizards. If they were deceived, it was because they didn't want to know. It is possible that a few didn't know what they were doing, but they are also guilty then, of a different crime, that of misrepresentation, claiming that they knew about risk when clearly they did not.

Exaggerating the virtues of one's wares or claiming greater competency than the evidence warrants is something we might have expected from many businesses, though the extent was almost surely outsized, just as were the egos and the pay. (As the old adage puts it, caveat emptor.) But far harder to forgive is the moral depravity—the financial sector's exploitation of poor and even middle-class Americans. As I noted, financial institutions discovered that there was money at the bottom of the pyramid and did everything they could within the law (and many went beyond the law) to move it toward the top. But instead of asking why the regulators didn't stop this, we should have asked what happened to the moral compunctions of those engaging in these practices.

In chapter 6, I explained that Bernie Madoff's Ponzi scheme was not all that different from the schemes of others who undertook high leverage. The financiers knew—or should have known—that the high returns in the short run (with the concomitantly high fees) would likely be followed by large losses, which under their contracts would not affect their bonuses. These devotees of perfect markets should have known that leverage can't deliver a free lunch—outsized returns with no outsized downside risks. High leverage generated high returns in good years; but it also exposed the banks to large downside risks.

With earning money the end-all of life, there were no limits to acceptable behavior. Like the many other banking crises that preceded this, each episode is marked by moral scruples that should make us blush, with a few of the most egregious personalities marching off to jail (but often left with hundreds of millions of dollars in their accounts, even after paying staggering fines): Charles Keating and Michael Milken in the 1980s, and Kenneth Lay and Bernard Ebbers in the early years of this decade.

Madoff crossed the line between "exaggeration" and "fraudulent behavior." But every day the list of "ethically challenged" financiers grows longer. Angelo Mozilo, the head of Countrywide Financial, the country's largest originator of subprime mortgages, is another example. He has been charged by the SEC with securities fraud and insider trading: he privately described the mortgages he was originating as toxic, even saying that Countrywide was "flying blind," all while touting the strengths of his mortgage company, with its prime quality mortgages using high underwriting standards.[1] For many entrepreneurs, the big gains come from selling their company. Everyone's dream is to find some fool willing to pay a high price. He succeeded: he sold his Countrywide stock for nearly $140 million in profits.

No matter how you look at it, our banks and our bankers, both before and during the crisis, did not live up to the moral standards that we should hope for, especially in their exploitation of ordinary borrowers. The subprime mortgages are just another example of a long litany of abusive practices in a variety of venues, which include student loans, pay day loans, rent-a-centers,[2] and credit and debit cards.

Sometimes, the financial companies (and other corporations) say that it is not up to them to make the decisions about what is right and wrong. It is up to government. So long as the government hasn't banned the activity, a bank has every obligation to its shareholders to provide funds so long as its profitable to do so. In this logic, there is nothing wrong with helping the cigarette companies, as they knowingly produce increasingly addictive products that kill.[3]

Those who are suggesting that they are free to operate as they like, so long as they remain within the law, are attempting to get by too easily. After all, the business community spends large amounts of money trying to get legislation that allows it to engage in these nefarious practices. The financial industry worked hard to stop legislation to prevent predatory lending, to gut state consumer protection laws, and to ensure that the federal government—with its lax standards during the Bush years—overrode state regulators. Worse, many corporations have tried hard to get legislation to protect them from ordinary liability. The dream of the tobacco companies is to have the kind of "light" regulation that doesn't prevent them from doing anything that they otherwise would do, but allows them to say, in defense of any deaths that result from their activities, that they had assumed that everything they did was okay—because it was all legal and done with complete oversight of the government.

Taking responsibility

Economics, unintentionally, provided sustenance to this lack of moral responsibility.[4] A naive reading of Adam Smith might have suggested that he had relieved market participants from having to think about issues of morality. After all, if the pursuit of self-interest leads, as if by an invisible hand, to societal well-being, all that one has to do—all that one should do—is be sure to follow one's self-interest. And those in the financial sector seemingly did that. But clearly, the pursuit of self-interest— greed—did not lead to societal well-being, either in this episode or in the earlier scandals involving WorldCom and Enron.

The theory of market failure that I presented in earlier chapters helps to explain why things went so wrong; how it was that the bankers, in the pursuit of their private interests, led to such disastrous social consequences; and why the pursuit of self-interest by the bankers did not lead to societal well-being—or even the well-being of their shareholders. When there are market failures, such as externalities, the consequences (the marginal benefits and costs) of an action are not fully reflected in prices (received or paid). I have explained how the world is rife with externalities. The failure of one bank has potentially disastrous effects on others; the failure of the banking system—or even the potential failure—has already had huge effects on the economy, on taxpayers, workers, businesses, homeowners. The foreclosure of one mortgage decreases market values of neighboring homes, increasing the probability of their going to foreclosure.

The swash-buckling model of rugged American individualism, epitomized so strongly by President Bush with his cowboy boots and his manly swagger, pictures a world in which we are responsible for our own successes and failures—and we reap the rewards of our efforts. But like the *Homo economicus* of chapter 9 and the nineteenth-century firm managed by its owner, these are myths. "No man is an island."[5] What we do has large effects on others; and we are what we are at least partly because of the efforts of others.

The irony of the way the model of American individualism worked in practice was that people took credit for successes but showed little sense of accountability or responsibility for the failures or the costs imposed on others. When there were mega-(recorded) profits, the bankers took credit, claiming that it was due to their efforts; when there were mega-(real) losses, they were the result of forces beyond their control.

These attitudes were reflected in executive compensation schemes, which, in spite of the emphasis on incentives, often had little overall connection between pay and performance: *incentive* pay is high when performance is good, but when performance is weak, the deficiency is made up by other forms of pay, with another name, like "retention pay." Those in the industry say, We have to pay the worker highly even though performance has been poor, because others might grab him away. One might have expected the banks to want to get rid of those whose performance is poor. Those in the industry say, But profits are poor not because of inadequate performance but because of events beyond anyone's control. But the same thing was true when profits were high. This is one of many examples of cognitive dissonance, of the ability of those in the financial market to make a reasonably good argument on one side but fail to see the full implications.[6]

Much of the talk about accountability too seems just a matter of words: In Japanese society, a CEO who was responsible for destroying his firm, forcing thousands of workers to be laid off, might commit harikari. In the United Kingdom, CEOs resigned when their firms failed. In the United States, they are fighting over the size of their bonuses.

In today's financial markets, almost everyone claims innocence. They were all just doing their jobs. And so they were. But their jobs often entailed exploiting others or living off the results of such exploitation.[7] There was individualism but no individual responsibility. In the long run, society cannot function well if people do not take responsibility for the consequences of their actions. "I was just doing my job" cannot be a defense.

Externalities and other market failures are not the exception but the rule. If that is the case, it has profound implications. There is meaning to individual and corporate responsibility. Firms need to do more than just maximize their market value. And individuals within corporations need to think more about what they do and the impacts on others. They cannot get by by saying that they are "just" maximizing their incomes.

WHAT YOU MEASURE IS WHAT YOU VALUE, AND VICE VERSA[8]

In a performance-oriented society such as ours, we strive to do well—but what we do is affected by what we measure. If students are tested on reading, teachers will teach reading—but will spend less time developing broader cognitive skills. So too, politicians, policymakers, and economists all strive to understand what causes better performance *as measured by GDP*. But if GDP is a bad measure of societal well-being, then we are striving to achieve the wrong objective. Indeed, what we do may be counterproductive in terms of our true objectives.

Measuring GDP in the United States didn't really give a good picture of what was going on before the bubble burst. America thought it was doing better than it was, and so did others. Bubble prices inflated the value of investments in real estate and inflated profits. Many strived to imitate America. Economists did sophisticated studies relating success to different policies—but because their measure of success was flawed, the inferences they drew from the studies were often flawed.[9]

The crisis shows how badly distorted market prices can be—with the result that our measure of performance is itself badly distorted. Even without the crisis, the prices of *all* goods are distorted because we have treated our atmosphere (and, too often, clean water) as if it were free, when in fact it is scarce. The extent of price distortion for any particular good depends on the amount of "carbon" that is contained in its production (including in the production of all the components that go into its production).

Some of the debates that we have concerning trade-offs between the environment and economic growth are off the mark: if we correctly measured output, there would be no trade-off. Correctly measured output will be higher with good environmental policies—and the environment will be better as well. We would realize that the seeming profits from the gas-guzzlers, like the Hummer (which, in any case, turned out to be ephemeral), are false: they are at the expense of the well-being of the future.

Our economic growth has been based too on borrowing from the future: we have been living beyond our means. So too, some of the growth has been based on the depletion of natural resources and the degradation of the environment—a kind of borrowing from the future, more invidious because the debts we owe are not so obvious.[10] We are leaving future generations poorer as a result, but our GDP indicator doesn't reflect this.

There are other problems with our measure of well-being. GDP per capita (per person) measures what we spend on health care, not the output—the status of our health reflected, for instance, in life expectancy. The result is that as our health care system gets more inefficient, GDP may appear to increase, even though health outcomes become worse. America's GDP per capita appears higher than that of France and the United Kingdom partly because our health care system is less efficient. We spend far more to get far worse health outcomes.

As a final example (there are many more)[11] of the misleading nature of our standard measures, *average* GDP per capita can be going up even when most individuals in our society not only feel that they are worse off, but actually are worse off. This happens when societies become more unequal (which has been happening in most countries around the world). A larger pie doesn't mean that everyone—or even most people—gets a larger slice. As I noted in chapter 1, in the United States, by 2008, the median household income was some 4 percent lower than it was in 2000, adjusted for inflation, even though GDP per capita (a measure of what was happening on average) had increased by 10 percent.[12]

The objective of societal production is an increase in the well-being of the members of society, however that is defined. Our standard measure is not a good one. There are alternatives. No single measure can capture the complexity of what is going on in a modern society, but the GDP measure fails in critical ways. We need measures that focus on how the typical individual is doing (measures of median income do a lot better than measures of average income), on sustainability (measures that take account, for instance, of resource depletion and the worsening of the environment, as well as the increase of indebtedness), and on health and education. The United Nations Development Programme (UNDP) has devised a more comprehensive measure that includes education and health, as well as income. In these metrics, the Scandinavian countries do far better than the United States, which ranks thirteenth.[13]

But even when *economic* measures are broadened to include health and education, they leave out much that affects our sense of well-being. Robert Putnam has emphasized the importance of our connectedness with others. In America, that sense of connectedness is weakening, and the way we have organized our economy may contribute.[14]

The Himalayan Buddhist kingdom of Bhutan has attempted to carve out a different approach. It is trying to create a measure of GNH—gross national happiness. Happiness is only partly related to material goods. Some aspects, like spiritual values, can't and probably shouldn't be quantified. But there are others that can be (like social connectedness). Even without quantification, though, focusing on these values highlights some ways that we should be thinking about redirecting our economy and our society.

Security and rights

One important dimension of societal well-being is security. Most Americans' standards of living, their sense of well-being, have declined more than the national income statistics ("median household income") might suggest, partly because of the increase in insecurity. They feel less secure about their job, knowing that if they lose their job they will also lose their health insurance. With soaring tuition costs, they feel less secure that they will be able to provide their children with an education that will enable them to fulfill their aspirations. With retirement accounts diminished, they feel less secure that they will spend their old age in comfort. Today, a large fraction of Americans are also worried about whether they will be able to keep their home. The cushion of home equity, the difference between the value of the home and the mortgage, has disappeared. Some 15 million homes, representing about one-third of all mortgages nationwide, carry mortgages that exceed the value of the property.[15] In this recession, 2.4 million people have lost their health insurance because they lost their job.[16] For these Americans, life is on a precipice.

Greater security can even have an indirect effect of promoting growth: it allows individuals to undertake greater risk, knowing that if things don't work out as hoped, there is some level of social protection. Programs that assist people in moving from one job to another help ensure that one of our most important resources—our human talent—is better used. These kinds of social protection also have a political dimension: if workers feel more secure, there will be fewer demands for protectionism. Social protection without protectionism can thus contribute to a more dynamic society. And a more dynamic economy and society—with the appropriate degree of social protection—can provide greater satisfaction for both workers and consumers.

Of course, there can be excessive job protection—with no discipline for bad performance, there can be too little incentive for good performance. But again, ironically, we have worried more about these moral hazard/incentive effects among individuals than among corporations, and this has vastly distorted responses to the current crisis. It hampered the willingness of the Bush administration to respond to the millions of Americans losing their homes or jobs. The administration didn't want to seem to be "rewarding" those who had engaged in irresponsible borrowing. It didn't want to increase unemployment insurance because that would diminish incentives to look for a job. It should have worried less about these problems and more about the perverse incentives of the newly established corporate safety net.[17]

Well-off American corporations also talk about the importance of security. They emphasize the importance of security of property rights, and how without such security, they won't undertake investment.

They—like ordinary Americans—are "risk averse." Public policy, especially among the Right, has paid a great deal of attention to these concerns about security of property. But ironically, many have argued that individual security should be reduced, cutting back Social Security and job security for ordinary citizens. It is a curious contradiction, and it is paralleled by recent discussions of human rights.[18]

For decades after the beginning of the Cold War, the United States and the Soviet Union were engaged in a battle over human rights. The Universal Declaration of Human Rights listed both basic economic and political rights.[19] The United States only wanted to talk about political rights, the Soviet Union about economic rights. Many of those in the Third World, while noting the importance of political rights, gave greater weight to economic rights: What good does the right to vote mean to a person starving to death? They questioned whether someone without any education could meaningfully exercise the right to vote when there are complex issues in dispute.

Finally, under the Bush administration the United States began to recognize the importance of *economic rights*—but the recognition was lopsided: it recognized the right of capital to move freely in and out of countries, capital market liberalization. Intellectual property rights and property rights more generally are other economic rights that have been emphasized. But why should these economic rights—rights of corporations—have precedence over the more basic economic rights of individuals, such as the rights of access to health care or to housing or to education? Or the right to a certain minimal level of security?

These are basic issues that all societies have to face. A full discussion of the issues would take us beyond the scope of this short book. What should be clear, however, is that these matters of rights are not God given. They are social constructs. We can think of them as part of the social contract that governs how we live together as a community.

Leisure and sustainability

There are other values that are not captured well in our standard measure of GDP: we value leisure, whether we use it for relaxation, for time with family, for culture, or for sports. Leisure can be particularly important for the millions whose jobs provide limited immediate satisfaction, those who work to live rather than who live to work.

Seventy-five years ago, Keynes celebrated the fact that mankind was, for the first time in its history, about to be freed from the "economic problem."[20] For all human history, man had devoted most of his energies to finding food, shelter, and clothing. But advances in science and technology meant that these basic needs could be provided with only a few hours of work a week. For instance, less than 2 percent of the American labor force produces all the food that even an overconsuming and rapidly becoming obese country can eat—with enough left over for our nation to be a major exporter of wheat, corn, and soybeans. Keynes wondered what we would do with the fruits of these advances. Looking at how England's upper classes spent their time, he quite rightly had grounds for worry.

He did not anticipate fully what has happened, especially in the last third of a century. America and Europe have seemingly responded differently. Contrary to Keynes's prediction, America, as a whole, has not enjoyed more leisure. The number of hours worked per household has actually gone up (by some 26 percent over the past thirty years).[21] We have become a consumer/materialistic society: two cars in every garage, iPods in every ear, and clothes without limit. We buy and dispose.[22] Europe took a very different tack. A five-week vacation is the norm— Europeans shudder at our two-week standard. France's output per hour is higher than that in the United States, but the typical Frenchman works fewer hours a year and so has a lower income.

The differences are not genetic. They represent different evolutions of our societies. Most Frenchmen would not trade places with most Americans; and most Americans would not trade places with most Frenchmen. The evolution both in America and in Europe has come without any premeditation. We should ask ourselves if it is a course that we would have chosen. And as social scientists, we can try to explain why each chose the course it did.

We may not be able to say which lifestyle is better. But the U.S. lifestyle is not sustainable. Others may be more so. If those in the developing countries try to imitate America's lifestyle, the planet is doomed. There are not enough natural resources, and the impact on global warming would be intolerable. America will have to change—and it will have to change quickly.

Community and Trust

The model of rugged individualism combined with market fundamentalism has altered not just how individuals think of themselves and their preferences but how they relate to each other. In a world of rugged individualism, there is little need for community and no need for trust. Government is a hindrance; it is the problem, not the solution. But if externalities and market failures are pervasive, there is a need for collective action, and voluntary arrangements will typically not suffice (simply because there is no "enforcement," no way to make sure that people behave as they should).[23] But worse, rugged individualism combined with rampant materialism has led to an undermining of trust. Even in a market economy, trust is the grease that makes society function. Society can sometimes get by without trust—through resort to legal enforcement, say, of contracts—but it is a very second-best alternative. In the current crisis, bankers lost our trust, and lost trust in each other. Economic historians have emphasized the role that trust played in the development of trade and banking. The reason why certain communities developed as global merchants and financiers was that the members of the community trusted each other.[24] The big lesson of this crisis is that despite all the changes in the last few centuries, our complex financial sector was still dependent on trust. When trust broke down, our financial system froze. But we have created an economic system that encourages shortsighted behavior—behavior that is so shortsighted that the costs of the breakdown in trust are never taken into account. (This shortsighted behavior accounts, as we have seen, for other troubling aspects of financial-sector behavior—and it accounts for society's unwillingness to deal with the environmental problems that just won't go away.)

The financial crisis has brought home, and accelerated, the erosion of trust. We have taken trust for granted, and the result is that it has been weakened. Going forward, if we do not make fundamental changes, we will not be able to rely on trust again. If so, this will fundamentally alter how we treat each other, it will impede our relationships with each other, and it will change how we think about ourselves and each other. Our sense of community will be further eroded, and even the efficiency of our economy will be impaired.

Securitization, and how it was abused, epitomized this process of how markets can weaken personal relationships and community. The "friendly" relationship within a stable community between the banker and the borrower, in which the banker knew the person who was borrowing money (so if the borrower genuinely had a problem, the banker knew when and how to restructure the loan), may have been partly a myth. But, still, there was also some truth in it; it was a relationship that was based partly on trust. With securitization, trust has no role; the lender and the borrower have no personal relationship. Everything is anonymous, and all the relevant information on the characteristics of the mortgage is summarized in statistical data. With those whose lives are being destroyed described as merely data, the only issues in restructuring are what is legal—what is the mortgage servicer allowed to do—and what will maximize the expected return to the owners of the securities. Not only has trust been destroyed between borrower and lender but it also does not exist among the various other parties: for example, the holder of the securities does not trust the service provider to act in his interests. Given the lack of trust, many contracts restrict the scope for restructuring.[25] Enmeshed in legal tangles, both lenders and borrowers suffer. Only the lawyers win.

But even when restructuring is possible, the same incentives that led the lenders to take advantage of the borrowers are still at play. If bankers ever had compassion for others, this is not the time for it: they are worried about their own next paycheck. And why then shouldn't we expect that the practices they honed so finely, how to exploit ordinary homeowners to increase their profits, not be used once again? The media and government seemed surprised as story after story came out about the slow speed of restructuring, and the fact that too many of the restructurings seemed so disadvantageous to the borrowers. A restructuring that simply stretches the payments out for a longer period, increasing the fees paid in the short run (which go directly to the lenders' bottom line), is what the lenders want, and they know that many borrowers strapped to make their monthly payments and reluctant to lose their home and their sense of dignity will fall for these bad deals.

Securitization will not go away. It is part of the reality of a modern economy. But implicitly, through our bailouts, we have subsidized securitization. We should at least create a level playing field—and we may want to discourage it.

A *house divided*

This crisis has exposed fissures in our society, between Wall Street and Main Street, between America's rich and the rest of our society. I have described how while the top has been doing very well over the last three decades, incomes of most Americans have stagnated or fallen. The consequences were papered over; those at the bottom—or even the middle—were told to continue to consume *as if* their incomes were rising; they were encouraged to live beyond their means, by borrowing; and the bubble made it possible. The consequences of being brought back to reality are simple—standards of living are going to have to fall. I suspect that the realization of this lies behind the intensity of the debate over bank bonuses.

The country as a whole has been living beyond its means. There will have to be some adjustment. And someone will have to pick up the tab for the bank bailouts. Even a proportionate sharing would be disastrous for most Americans. With median household income already down some 4 percent from 2000, there is no choice: if we are to preserve any sense of fairness, the brunt of the adjustment must come from those at the top who have garnered for themselves so much over the past three decades, and from the financial sector, which has imposed such high costs on the rest of society.

But the politics of this will not be easy. The financial sector is reluctant to own up to its failings. Part of moral behavior and individual responsibility is to accept blame when it is due; all humans are fallible—including bankers. But as we have seen, they have repeatedly worked hard to shift blame to others—including to those they victimized.

We are not alone in facing hard adjustments ahead. The U.K. financial system was even more overblown than that of the United States. The Royal Bank of Scotland, before it collapsed, was the largest bank in Europe and suffered the most losses of any bank in the world in 2008. Like the United States, the United Kingdom had a real estate bubble that has now burst. Adjusting to the new reality may require a decrease in consumption by as much as 10 percent.[26]

The vision thing

American governments have not consciously engaged in thinking about structuring or restructuring the economy, with one exception—the movement into and out of a war economy. In the case of World War II, this was done quite well. But the fact that we have not done so consciously does not mean that public policy hasn't shaped our society. Eisenhower's superhighway program created modern suburbia—with all its faults, including the costs in terms of energy, emissions, and commuting time. It led to the destruction of some of our cities, with all of the social problems that has brought with it.

As I argued in chapter 7, like it or not, our modern society requires that government take on a large role: from setting the rules and enforcing them, to providing infrastructure, to financing research, providing education, health, and a variety of forms of social protection. Many of the expenditures are long term and many have long-term effects (exemplified by Eisenhower's superhighway program). If this money is to be spent well, there has to be thought about what we want and where we are going.

Throughout this book, we have seen several changes that, interacting with each other, have altered the nature of the market and our society: a move away from a more balanced perspective of the individual and the community (including the government), from a more balanced perspective of economic and noneconomic activities, from a more balanced role of the market and the state, and from individual relationships mediated through trust to market-mediated relationships relying on legal enforcement.

We have also seen an increasing short-termism, on the part of individuals, firms, and government. As we have noted, part of the reason for the recent problems in many sectors of the American economy, including the financial, is an excessive focus on the short term (itself one of the aspects of managerial capitalism). Long-run success requires long-run thinking—a vision—but we have structured markets today in ways that encourage just the opposite, and we have discouraged government from filling in the gap. The argument for the government to think long term is even greater—though the incentives for politicians to think short term are as powerful or even more so than for corporate managers.

Thinking long term means having a vision. Gilles Michel, head of France's Strategic Investment Fund, put it forcefully, "The state has the right to have a vision." "We consider it legitimate for the public authority to worry about the nature and evolution of the industrial fabric of our country."[27] Economic theory has provided part of the rationale: the presence of externalities (to return to a common theme in this book). The development of a new industry or product can have ripple effects on others—benefits that the entrepreneur may not see, and even if he can see them, he cannot capture them.

In a sense, with the government spending as much money as it does, it is hard for it not to have a vision, a vision both in the small and in the large: a country more dependent on gas-guzzling vehicles, or on public transportation, on air or railroad transportation; an economy focused more on research, innovation, and education or on manufacturing. The stimulus package passed in February 2009 exhibits examples of what can happen without a vision: the nation is building new roads at a time when communities are forced to lay off teachers and universities are forced to have major cutbacks. Tax cuts encourage consumption, when the government should be promoting investment.

Politics, economics, and society— corruption American-style

There has long been an awareness of many of the problems discussed, and yet progress in addressing them has been slow. Why can't a country with so many talented people—a country that can send a man to the moon—do better in solving these problems here on earth?

President Eisenhower warned of the dangers of the industrial-military complex.[28] But in the last half century, that complex has been extended: the special interest groups that shape American economic and social policy include finance, pharmaceuticals, oil, and coal. Their political influence makes rational policy making all but impossible. In some cases, lobbyists play an understandable role in interpreting complex social and economic phenomena—obviously with a slant. But on many of the key issues, their actions have been little more than a naked grab for money, exemplified by the pharmaceutical industry's recent demand that the government, the largest buyer of drugs, not bargain with it on drug prices. But the financial sector, both before and during the crisis, has exemplified the worst.

It will be hard for America to achieve whatever vision it sees for itself when it is so blinded by campaign contributions and lobbyists and its system of revolving doors. Perhaps we will be able to muddle through, but at what costs to us today and what costs to future generations? This crisis should be an awakening sign: the costs can be high, very high, beyond even what the richest country of the world can afford.

CONCLUDING COMMENTS

I write this book midstream. The sense of freefall has ended. Perhaps by the time the book is out, the sense of crisis will be over. Perhaps the economy will have returned to full employment—though that is unlikely.

I have argued that the problems our nation and the world face entail more than a small adjustment to the financial system. Some have argued that we had a minor problem in our plumbing. Our pipes got clogged. We called in the same plumbers who installed the plumbing—having created the mess, presumably only they knew how to straighten it out. Never mind if they overcharged us for the installation; never mind that they overcharged us for the repair. We should be grateful that the plumbing is working again, quietly pay the bills, and pray that they do a better job this time than the last.

But it is more than just a matter of "plumbing": the failures in our financial system are emblematic of broader failures in our economic system, and the failures of our economic system reflect deeper problems in our society. We began the bailouts without a clear sense of what kind of financial system we wanted at the end, and the result has been shaped by the same political forces that got us into the mess. We have not changed our political system, so we should perhaps not be surprised by any of this. And yet, there was hope that change was possible. Not only possible, but necessary.

That there will be changes as a result of the crisis is certain. There is no going back to the world before the crisis. But the questions are, How deep and fundamental will the changes be? Will they even be in the right direction? We have lost the sense of urgency, and what has happened so far does not portend well for the future.

In some areas, regulations will be improved—almost surely, the excesses of leverage will be curbed. But in other areas, as this book goes to press, there is remarkably little progress—the too-big-to-fail banks will be allowed to continue much as before, over-the-counter derivatives that cost taxpayers so much will continue almost unabated, and finance executives will continue to receive outsized bonuses. In each of these areas, something cosmetic will be done, but it will fall far short of what is needed. In still other areas, deregulation will continue apace, shocking as it may seem: unless a popular outcry prevents it, it appears that basic protections of ordinary investors will be undermined with a critical weakening of the Sarbanes-Oxley Act, passed in the aftermath of the Enron and other dot-com scandals, by a Republican Congress and signed into law by a Republican president.

In several critical areas, in the midst of the crisis, matters have already become worse. We have altered not only our institutions—encouraging ever increased concentration in finance—but the very rules of capitalism. We have announced that for favored institutions there is to be little, or no, market discipline. We have created an ersatz capitalism with unclear rules—but with a predictable outcome: future crises; undue risk-taking at the public expense, no matter what the promise of a new regulatory regime; and greater inefficiency. We have lectured about the importance of transparency, but we have given the banks greater scope for manipulating their books. In earlier crises, there was worry about moral hazard, the adverse incentives provided by bailouts; but the magnitude of this crisis has given new meaning to the concept.

The rules of the game have changed globally too. The Washington consensus policies and the underlying ideology of market fundamentalism are dead. In the past, there might have been a debate over whether there was a level playing field between developed and less developed countries; now there can be no debate. The poor countries simply can't back up their enterprises in the way that the rich do, and this alters the risks that they can undertake. They have seen the risks of globalization badly managed. But the hoped-for reforms in how globalization is managed still seem on the distant horizon.

It has become a cliché to observe that the Chinese characters for crisis reflect "danger" and "opportunity." We have seen the danger. The question is, Will we seize the opportunity to restore our sense of balance between the market and the state, between individualism and the community, between man and nature, between means and ends? We now have the opportunity to create a new financial system that will do what human beings need a financial system to do; to create a new economic system that will create meaningful jobs, decent work for all those who want it, one in which the divide between the haves and have-nots is narrowing, rather than widening; and, most importantly of all, to create a new society in which each individual is able to fulfill his aspirations and live up to his potential, in which we have created citizens who live up to shared ideals and values, in which we have created a community that treats our planet with the respect that in the long run it will surely demand. These are the opportunities. The real danger now is that we will not seize them.

AFTERWORD TO THE PAPERBACK EDITION

━━━

IN THE EIGHT MONTHS SINCE THE HARDCOVER VERSION of *Freefall* was published, events have (sadly) unfolded much as expected: growth has remained weak, sufficiently anemic that unemployment has remained stubbornly high; mortgage foreclosures have continued apace; and while bank bonuses and profits have been restored, the supply of credit has not, even though the resumption of credit was supposedly the reason for the bank bailout. And, as predicted, political fallout from these failures means it is unlikely that Congress will pass the kind of second stimulus package that is needed.

A few matters—the crisis in Europe and the extent of the banks' fraudulent and unethical practices—were worse than anticipated, and a few matters—the size of the losses on the bank bailouts—somewhat less. The reforms in financial sector regulation are stronger than I anticipated, for which we owe thanks especially to Goldman Sachs—the public outrage engendered by its behavior overcame the money and lobbying of the banks. However, the banks were able to temper the regulations enough that the prospect of another crisis down the road remains not insignificant: we have bought ourselves a little extra time before the next crisis and, perhaps, have reduced the likely cost to our economy and our treasury.

The real news of the last eight months has been the slow acceptance by government officials and economists alike of the dismal picture of the immediate future about which I had warned: a new "normal" with higher unemployment rates, lower growth, and lower levels of public services in the advanced industrial countries. Prosperity has been replaced by a Japanese-style malaise, with no end in sight. But at least in Japan's "lost decade," in spite of low growth, unemployment remained low and social cohesion remained high. In Europe and America, by contrast, some economists are talking about a persistent unemployment rate of 7.5 percent, well above the 4.2 percent we enjoyed in the 1990s. The financial crisis had indeed done long-term damage to our economy, from which we will only gradually recover.[1]

It was not just the private sector that had been living in a dream world sustained by housing and stock bubbles. Governments had been indirectly sharing in that dream, as they received some of the "phantom income" of the bubbles in the form of tax revenues. When the crisis hit, those that thought they had been fiscally prudent, like Spain, and had run a surplus before the crisis, discovered that they faced not just a temporary cyclical deficit, but also a structural deficit.[2] Even if their economies were to return to full employment, they would likely have a budgetary gap. For fiscally reckless countries like the United States under President George W. Bush and Greece under Prime Minister Kostas Karamanlis, matters were even more unpleasant. By 2009, the U.S. deficit soared to almost 9.9 percent of GDP, Greece's to 13.6 percent. Returning those deficits to zero will *not* be just a matter of waiting for recovery, because these countries had run deficits even when their economies enjoyed close to full employment and their tax receipts were enriched by taxes on the bubble profits, but will entail substantial increases in taxes or cuts in expenditures. But there's the rub: with the global recovery faltering, any cutbacks in expenditures or increases in taxes will surely lead to even slower growth, perhaps pushing many economies into a double-dip recession.

Despite these stark prospects for the world economy, cries for curbing deficits soon emanated from Wall Street and the financial markets. Their shortsightedness had created the crisis, and now they were being equally shortsighted in demanding policies that would lead to its persistence. They demanded budget cutbacks. Without them, they and the rating agencies warned, interest rates would rise, access to credit would be cut off, and countries would have no choice but to cut back. But no sooner had Spain announced budget cutbacks in May than the rating agencies and markets responded: they claimed, I believe correctly, that the cutbacks would slow growth. With slower growth, tax revenues would decrease, social expenditures (such as on unemployment benefits) would increase, and deficits would remain large. Fitch, one of the three leading rating agencies, downgraded Spain's debt, and interest rates that it had to pay continued to rise. Evidently, countries were damned if they cut back spending and damned if they didn't. The only time that the financial markets seemed to show some charity was when the money went directly into their coffers, as it had during the Great Bailout.

These outcomes prove all the more distressing when you consider that there was a moment of national and international unity at the height of the crisis, when countries stood together facing a global economic calamity. For the first time, the G-20 brought developed countries together with emerging market countries to solve the world's global problem. There was a moment when the whole world was Keynesian, and the misguided idea that unfettered and unregulated markets were stable and efficient had been discredited. There was the hope that a new, more tempered capitalism and a new, more balanced global economic order would emerge—one that might at last achieve greater stability in the short run and address the long-standing issues that I describe at length in chapter 7 (such as the large and growing inequalities between the rich and poor, adapting our economy to the threat of global warming, freeing it from its dependence on oil, and restructuring it to compete effectively with the emerging countries in Asia).

The hope that suffused those early months of the crisis is quickly fading. In its place is a new mood of despair: the road to recovery may be even slower than I suggested, and the social tensions may be even greater. Bank officials have walked home with seven-figure bonuses while ordinary citizens face not only protracted unemployment but an unemployment insurance safety net that is not up to the challenges of the Great Recession. The divides—economic and ideological—within and between countries may be growing larger. As the economic downturn continues, so too does the imperative for global action, but these divides make it increasingly difficult for the United States to respond appropriately, and hopes for the kind of concerted global action that would be desirable become increasingly dim.

In this afterword to the paperback edition, I review the major events—both the politics and the economics—that have occurred since *Freefall*'s first publication, and examine how they reinforce or modify my earlier conclusions. These events have given rise to new perceptions and questions and have put new impetus behind finding answers to old questions. Critics claim that Keynesian economics, for instance, only put off the day of reckoning. But I argue in this afterword that, to the contrary, unless we go back to the basic principles of Keynesian economics, the world is doomed to a protracted downturn.

The crisis has moved the world into uncharted territory, with great uncertainties. But there is one thing about which we can be relatively certain: if the advanced industrial countries continue along the path they seem to have embarked on today, the likelihood of a robust recovery anytime soon is bleak; the relative economic and political positions of America and Europe will, as a result, be greatly diminished; and so will our ability to address the long-term issues on which our future well-being depends.[3]

THE COURSE OF THE ECONOMY

Soon after it took office, the Obama administration began championing the recovery of the economy in the hope that good news would get Americans back into the shopping malls. The supposed green shoots that their eagle eyes saw in March 2009 had withered by early summer, but growth resumed toward the end of the year, so much so that Larry Summers, the head of Obama's National Economic Council, could announce that the recession was over. And it was—for the banks that had created the crisis: with the government giving them money at essentially a zero percent interest rate and allowing them to return to high-risk trading and other speculative activities, profits at least looked good. For the rest of the economy, things remained bleak—and nowhere is this seen more clearly than in the labor market, where each month has seen new records in the number of Americans who are unemployed (or who would be called unemployed if they hadn't given up looking for a job).[4] I had anticipated this disappointing state of affairs, as I saw nothing on the horizon that would replace the housing bubble and the boost that it had given to aggregate demand. America's output was limited by demand. The collapse of the housing bubble had brought an end to the consumption boom. These realities, combined with a problematic financial sector, meant that investment was weak. America's problems were shared by those who bought our products, so exports, too, were weak. Only the government was preventing an even worse disaster.

The labor market

By mid-2009, it was clear that the pace of job destruction that had marked early 2009—750,000 jobs were lost in January alone—would not continue. There was, in some quarters, jubilation as the tide finally seemed to turn in the first quarter of 2010. Yet, the 150,000 jobs created in that quarter constituted less than half the number that would normally have to be created for the new entrants into the labor force—the jobs deficit had, in fact, continued to increase. Behind the statistic of an unemployment rate that remained steady (well above 9 percent) were large numbers of "discouraged workers," who knew that there were no jobs to be found. Only about 1 percent of the unemployed found a job in the first quarter, and a third of those jobs were as temporary census workers. More and more workers were using up their savings or facing the bleak prospect of an end to their unemployment benefits. The fraction of the unemployed who had been jobless for six months or more—nearly half—reached levels not seen since data started being collected in 1948.[5] As the recession stretched on, each passage of extended benefits proved a temporary palliative—and each time those concerned about the plight of these long-term unemployed tried to get another extension, some congressman or other would put roadblocks in the way. This happened again in June 2010, so that Congress went into its annual Fourth of July recess without passing an extension, leaving more than 3 million people at risk of being without benefits by the end of the month.[6] Moreover, it was likely that the experiences of previous downturns would be borne out: those who had a long bout of unemployment would find it increasingly difficult to get reemployed, and when they did succeed in getting a job, it would be at a much lower wage.[7]

While the data that became available in early 2010 showed what many had anticipated, that growth had resumed in the second half of 2009, the precariousness of that growth was reflected by the refusal of the National Bureau of Economic Research—the independent group of academics responsible for dating recessions—to "call" the recession over, even by the middle of 2010. With a real risk that the economy might slide quickly into another downturn, it would be wrong to classify a subsequent decline as a separate recession; it would really be a continuation of the long Great Recession of 2008.

The mortgage crisis

There were many other reasons to worry about where the economy was going, besides the continuing weaknesses in the labor markets. One was the ongoing problem of the housing market: The housing market may have "stabilized," but at prices that were still 30 percent below the peak, and that was an average; in many parts of the country, the declines were 50 percent or more. A quarter of all mortgages remained underwater, and forecasts suggested that somewhere between 2.5 and 3.5 million Americans would lose their homes in 2010, a larger number than in each of the previous two years. To put some perspective on how bad things were, single-family housing starts in May 2010 were less than one-third the level of May 2005, and less than half the level *fifteen years earlier*, in May 1995.[8]

As I had anticipated, the administration's mortgage initiatives were simply inadequate. Other initiatives to help the housing market were just short-run Band-Aids. As some of the measures that had helped keep the market afloat ended in mid-2010, such as the tax credit for first-time home buyers, the market seemed to sink even more. When mortgages were "restructured" to lower monthly payments and make them more affordable, the lower payments often simply translated into more money owed down the line, especially when the banks added more transaction fees.

Most important, while the administration's initiatives had helped a few Americans who still had jobs and homes but couldn't make mortgage payments, little was done about the underwater mortgages, where the homeowner owed more than the value of the house. With the total gap between what American homeowners owed and the value of their homes estimated to be between $700 and $900 billion, it was understandable why the banks didn't want to write down the mortgages: they didn't want the losses to appear on their balance sheets. But without a true restructuring of mortgages, it was hard to believe that the American economy could return to "normal" any time soon. Faced with this burden of debt, Americans would not likely consume as they had when the (household) savings rate was zero—and this was even more so given the weaknesses in the labor market. Yet among those looking for an early recovery, hope remained. They scrutinized the data, searching for signs of the "return of the consumer." Of course, after so much consumption had been put off in the months immediately after the Lehman Brothers disaster, there had to be a short bounce in spending (just as the excess depletion of inventories by businesses led to restocking). But there was little prospect of that bounce being *sustained*. Indeed, as I emphasize in the book, any return to pre-crisis profligacy should be a cause for concern, not jubilation—such consumption would not and could not be sustainable, and any recovery based on it would be short-lived.

The collapse of commercial real estate

Another problem loomed in the commercial real estate sector, where prices had fallen as badly as (and in some places worse than) residential real estate. Homeowners had learned the risks of "balloon payments"—

mortgages that have to be fully repaid in, say, five or ten years, normally by taking out a new mortgage. Most of commercial real estate is financed that way, with the mortgages typically being refinanced ("rolled over") every five to ten years. This means that the mortgages taken out at the peak of the bubble will have to be rolled over in coming years. In February 2010, the Congressional Oversight Panel estimated that $1.4 trillion of commercial real estate will have to be refinanced in 2011–2014 alone, and that nearly half of the mortgages on these properties were underwater.[9] The scale of the problems confronting the commercial real estate market was hinted at by the multi-billion-dollar bankruptcy of the 11,000-unit Peter Stuyvesant project in New York in January 2010.

Apart from the magnitude of the discrepancy between what is owed and the value of the property, three factors make such rollovers particularly problematic. Normally, banks would follow the policy of pretend and extend: pretend that nothing is wrong, extend the rollover loans, and pray that in the meanwhile prices will recover and make the losses manageable. But bank supervisors, rightly criticized for having failed to do their job in the run-up to the crisis, are taking a harder line this time around.[10]

Further, a large fraction of the loans have been securitized, and the more senior creditors may want their money out now, rather than risk having it tied up for another five years.

Moreover, I noted earlier in the book the legal tangles between the holders of first and second residential mortgages.[11] These are practically child's play compared to those confronting commercial real estate, where there may be many more tranches[12] and many more conflicts of interest.

The collapse of the real estate markets is obviously painful to those who have put so much of their money there—for most Americans, their house is their most important asset. But the collapse also weakens the overall economy: families who see their most important asset lose so much value are less likely to spend money; they need to rebuild their nest egg, whether it is to finance their retirement or to pay for their children's education. Families and businesses that have borrowed using their house as collateral will find it more difficult to do so, constraining both consumption and investment. In the years prior to the crisis, real estate construction accounted for 30 to 40 percent of total investment, but with such low real estate prices, it has been cheaper to buy an old property than build a new one; the earlier overbuilding has resulted, for instance, in housing construction falling (as a percent of GDP) to the lowest levels since World War II (when the country obviously had other priorities). It will be years and years before housing construction gets back to pre-crisis levels.[13]

The banking crisis

There is one more consequence of the breaking of the housing bubble and the economic downturn: with so many Americans unable or unwilling to repay their loans, banks have had massive defaults that impair their ability to lend. This spiral brought on the financial crisis, but, unfortunately, the focus on the *banking* crisis deflected attention from the broader underlying economic problems. Again unfortunately, deficiencies in the Bush and Obama administrations' response to the banking crisis have meant that not even that problem has been resolved.

President Obama made it clear that the economy would not recover until lending resumed. The entire defense for giving money to the banks was that we were doing it, not because we love the banks, but because we wanted to restart lending. But, as I explain in the text, the way the Obama and Bush administrations went about dealing with the banking crisis was not designed to restart lending. And it did not do so. In fact, as this book goes to press, lending is continuing to decline. Outstanding credit is well below what it was before the crisis. In May 2010, business lending *in nominal terms* was almost 20 percent below what it was five years earlier.[14] Small and medium-sized firms that rely on banks for credit are finding that credit is tight. Banks can borrow from the Fed at close to a zero percent interest rate, but the country's other businesses—those that create jobs—must pay high interest rates to the same banks that caused the crisis, if they can obtain credit at all. For the big banks, it is a bonanza. For the rest of the country, it is a nightmare.

As I note in the text, the government focused on saving the too-big-to-fail banks, allowing the smaller banks to go belly up. These smaller banks are the mainstay for credit for small and medium-sized enterprises, which are the major source of job creation. The number of banks that are expected to go bankrupt in 2010 is larger than the 140 that went under in 2009. Meanwhile the FDIC (which insures banks) has run out of money and has had to turn to the Treasury to act as a backstop.[15]

The bankrupt banks, though, are just the tip of the iceberg. For every bank that goes down, there are many others flirting with the line. These banks typically constrain lending. The fake accounting, allowing bad mortgages to be kept on banks' books as if they were fine, fools no one. The banks and their supervisors know that they are at risk.

Even healthy banks have a problem in extending credit. Most small firms borrow on the basis of collateral (assets they use to guarantee to the bank that they will repay what is owed); the collateral is normally real estate, and with real estate prices having plummeted, the amount they can borrow has decreased. Not only does that mean that these small firms can't expand—they even have to contract. This problem is not likely to be resolved any time soon.

Export as America's salvation

In his State of the Union Address on January 27, 2010, President Obama raised one possible source of aggregate demand for underpinning the recovery: exports. An export-based recovery rested on three assumptions: a weak dollar, which makes American goods competitive; strength in our major trading partners, Europe and Canada; and the United States producing goods that others want. Each of these has come under question. The result is that even in the first four months of 2010, when the dollar was weak, the dollar value of exported goods, adjusted for inflation, was still some 5 percent below the level two years earlier.[16]

The deindustrialization of the United States—partly caused by the same ideology that led to deregulation—has meant that we have fewer goods to sell that others want to buy. Restrictions on high-technology exports to China have imposed barriers in a growing market where we could make sales. And onerous visa restrictions have impeded other areas of strength in tourism and education.

Moreover, growth in our trading partners has remained weak. And the crisis in Europe has even taken away America's one advantage, its low exchange rate. The prognosis going forward is no better. Europe's response to its crisis is likely to result in even weaker growth.

The declining value of the euro

In the Great Depression, countries sought to restore their own economies to health through beggar-thy-neighbor policies: imposing tariffs would shift the limited amount of demand from foreign goods toward home-produced goods; the strengthened demand would, it was hoped, lead to lower unemployment. Competitive devaluations were another popular technique: lowering exchange rates relative to one's competitors meant that one's own goods became cheaper and others' more expensive. Neither policy worked in practice because trading partners, quite naturally, retaliated. They too imposed tariffs. They too lowered the value of their currency relative to gold, and so the *relative* price (dollars for pounds, say)—which was all that really mattered—was unchanged.

Perhaps America was attempting a similar strategy in response to the Great Recession, this time though not through protectionism (but as I note in chapter 8, it did impose "Buy American" provisions in its stimulus plan), but through competitive devaluations. While the Secretary of the Treasury would continue to give speeches about the virtues of the strong dollar, the persistent low interest rates and ballooning deficits, if not designed to weaken the dollar, certainly had that effect.

Today, exchange rates are like negative beauty contests. It's not a matter of which country has the best economic prospects but which has the least bad prospects. And markets are fickle. They focus on one thing at one moment, another at another. The Great Recession has introduced new uncertainties—and new opportunities for the market to demonstrate its capriciousness, its lack of foresightedness. The problems in Greece—and the seeming opportunities that Greece's travails provided speculators—shifted attention away from the problems in America to those in Europe. I'll discuss these problems later in this afterword. For now, there is only one simple point to make: as markets focused on Europe's problems, the value of the euro sank, from a high of $1.60 in August 2009 to $1.20 in June 2010. The implication for American exports and competitiveness should be clear: with the euro's value falling 25 percent, suddenly European goods were drastically cheaper. American firms could not respond, at least in the short run, by increasing efficiency or cutting wages. In most competitive industries, much smaller cuts in prices would easily push them into bankruptcy.

The only hope, then, for American firms competing with European firms is a turnaround in the views of financial markets. America's deficit, which in 2009 stood at 9.9 percent of GDP, was much higher than that of the Eurozone,[17] which was only 6.3 percent.[18] And there are further problems in the finances of states and localities; for instance, large hidden holes exist in state and local pension funds around the country. Perhaps, in a few months, as financial markets see Washington gridlock in action—or as the United States pursues mindless deficit reductions that lead to a weakening economy—financial markets will wake up to these looming problems. The dollar will then weaken, and exports strengthen.

What seemed clear was that the future of the country's exports, and more broadly its economy, did not rest on the wisdom of farsighted markets, working in mysterious ways that helped steer this complex enterprise calmly and stably toward ever-increasing prosperity. Rather, it became clear that our future prosperity was yoked to the whimsy of shortsighted and volatile markets, trying to game each other and the political process. It increasingly appeared to be a game in which there were only a few winners—and they were the ones writing the rules of the game.

State and local spending

With the private sector so weak, only the government can provide support to the economy. But unfortunately the problems in the states and localities that I described earlier in the book have proved every bit as bad as I feared—the mistake of not providing additional support for states in the original stimulus bill became evident as states laid off teachers and other public employees. By the beginning of 2010, eighty-eight percent of communities reported that their problems in 2009 were *worse* than they were in the previous year,[19] and for an obvious reason: many depend on property taxes; property values are reassessed gradually, meaning that an increasing number of communities face a reduced tax base. Tax revenues have continued to decline as a percentage of GDP. The stimulus provided some help in filling the gap, but that assistance is coming to an end. States and localities will figure out how to make ends meet, either by cutting back expenditures or by raising taxes. But either option will lead to a reduction in aggregate demand—a negative stimulus.

The bottom line: the shape of the recovery

At the beginning of the crisis, there was much discussion about the shape of the recovery. Some hoped there would be a quick bounce back, a V-shaped recovery. No one talks about that anymore: with unemployment still high almost three years after the beginning of the recession, that notion seems pure fantasy. The only questions now are, how long will it be before a return to normal—and will the new "normal" entail persistently higher unemployment?

DASHED DREAMS

The Obama administration hoped that the problems facing the financial sector would be short-lived, that doling out money to the banking sector would quickly restore it to health (and that as it returned to profitability, the rest of the economy would start to grow), that the government would act as a substitute source of aggregate demand in the meantime, and that government support would quickly diminish as the private sector recovered. The stimulus was a short-run remedy designed from this perspective. It was a gamble: I feared that by asking for a stimulus package that was smaller and shorter than required, the administration left possible a risk that the recovery would be weak and that the stimulus would not be given the credit it deserved. (It did, in fact, work—but for the stimulus, the unemployment rate might have hit 12 percent, rather than 10 percent.) The consequence of perceptions that the stimulus had failed was that prospects of a second stimulus became bleak, especially as the magnitude of the deficits and debt became more apparent. And those fears have turned out to be true. Normally, if unemployment were even 8 percent, there would be a demand for government action. Now, with unemployment in excess of 9 percent, there are no prospects of government action other than a small $15 billion "jobs" program—passed into law in March with President Obama's signature—that is unlikely to have much impact on the unemployment rate.[20] The ending of the stimulus will weaken aggregate demand, and growth will slow.

The cost of the bank's malfeasance

Meanwhile, the Treasury Department tried to persuade Americans that its largesse toward the banks would not cost the economy much. It pointed out that it had recovered much of the money it had spent. But its partial accounting of the costs further strengthened the view of some that the Treasury was in the pocket of the financial sector, whose dishonest accounting had helped create the crisis.[21] This view was reinforced by the stances the Treasury took on financial regulation, which I describe more fully later. It repeatedly talked about the need for stronger regulation, but it vacillated on the important issues, often coming down on the side of the banks. *After* this book first came out, the Treasury finally decided to support certain restrictions on bank trading (the Volcker rule)—but then lent its support for another year's delay until the issue could be studied more, as if the years that had passed since the crisis began hadn't given Treasury officials time to study the issue. When Senator Blanche Lincoln of Arkansas, fighting for her political survival, helped push through the Senate a provision to restrict banks from trading in highly risky derivatives, the administration and the Federal Reserve, both behind the scenes and sometimes openly, opposed the reform.

Nothing symbolizes the flawed bailout—and the ambiguous role of the Fed and the administration—more than the $180 billion bailout of AIG. As more details about the AIG bailout emerged, it became increasingly clear why those in the administration and the Fed had tried to keep the whole thing secret. It turned out that the biggest recipient of the AIG bailout was Goldman Sachs (the only Wall Street chief executive in the room during the final discussion about AIG's fate was the head of Goldman Sachs).[22] Each time the Fed and Treasury tried to come up with a defense for what they did, the more suspicions grew. Earlier in the text, I noted that when the risky derivative positions were closed out, the banks were paid 100 cents on the dollar: it was as if an insurance company cancelled a fire insurance policy, but in doing so, paid you *as if the house had burned down*. The Fed and Treasury said they had no choice—they asserted that French law *required* that the French banks be paid 100 cents on the dollar, that we couldn't treat Goldman Sachs any worse than we treated the French banks, and therefore we had to give Goldman Sachs 100 cents on the dollar. But that was a sham: the French banks settled with private parties for far less. Were our government officials taken in by this attempt to get as much money from our government as possible? Were they that gullible? Or did they *want* to be taken in? Or were they thinking that we could so easily be fooled? These questions remain unanswered today.

The equivocal stance toward AIG (and the banks more generally) is nicely illustrated by an ongoing court case between AIG and the IRS involving hundreds of millions of dollars.[23] In effect, it is a suit between the U.S. Treasury (the owner of AIG) and the U.S. Treasury (responsible for the IRS), with the lawyers being the sure winners. AIG claims that its complicated tax scam (which ironically may have used complex financial products—the kinds of financial instruments that eventually proved its undoing and have been used successfully to deceive regulators, investors, and tax collectors alike) was legal.[24] If AIG wins, then one pocket of the Treasury forks over money to the other. To be sure, Secretary of Treasury Tim Geithner can then claim that the government has lost less money in the massive bailout. But the cost of this public relations gesture is enormous—and goes beyond the large legal bills that are mounting on both sides (in effect all paid by U.S. taxpayers). If AIG were to prevail, a loophole in the U.S. corporate income tax system would be opened up so large that a substantial fraction of all corporate income taxes could be avoided. Why would anyone, let alone the Secretary of the Treasury, who is supposedly concerned about the deficit, want to open up a tax loophole like that?

There is a pattern here: in bailing out the banks, both the Bush and the Obama administrations didn't want to interfere with the operations of these financial institutions—even when those running the companies had demonstrated incompetence and had engaged not only in excessive risk-taking but also in abusive lending practices and deceptive accounting. When government becomes even a part owner of a private firm, it should encourage corporate social responsibility—that means, at the very least, not trying to skirt the law either in the payment of taxes or in the treatment of customers.

If the U.S. Treasury as owner of AIG prevails, it will mean, of course, that AIG will be able to "pay back" more of the bail-out money. But this is hardly justification for the U.S. Treasury defending the use of tax schemes by a firm now owned by the American people. Even if all of the money were to be repaid, the accounts should not be viewed as cleared. The most important omission from the Treasury accounts was the costs of the crisis imposed on the entire economy—the trillions of dollars in shortfall between the economy's potential production and its actual output—costs borne by workers, homeowners, and retirees. The long-term cost on taxpayers was also omitted: the national debt is likely to be several trillions of dollars more than what it would have been without the crisis. Most of the debt increase (in the United States as well as in Europe) is *not* because of the stimulus or even the bank bailouts. Most of the increase arises from "automatic stabilizers," the fact that as the economy weakens, tax revenues decline and expenditures on unemployment and other social programs increase.[25] Indeed, in the absence of these automatic stabilizers, our economy would have risked going into depression.

But the huge increase in deficits and national debts, whether they arise from automatic stabilizers or stimulus programs, will put pressure on all manner of government spending, including social programs for the poor, Social Security retirement programs for the middle class, and investments in technology and education that are essential for the nation's long-term growth. Reduced public investments will lead to reduced future growth, with effects that will be felt for years.

The Obama administration's accounting was amiss in other ways as well. For instance, banks' access to money at close to a zero percent interest rate (a result of Fed policies) was, in effect, a redistribution of wealth from ordinary investors, including retirees, to the banks. This, like the bailouts, was intended to lead to more lending, but because of the refusal of the Fed or Treasury to put conditions on the banks, they didn't use it for that purpose. As I noted, lending continued to contract and bonuses and dividends continued apace. The bankers seem to feel that even as the rest of the country continued to suffer the consequences of their reckless lending, they had an inalienable birthright to exorbitant bonuses.

The administration's willingness to allow the banks to buy back their preferred shares and warrants opened it to further criticisms. First, it would allow the banks to return to their old ways, including their unseemly bonuses. Second, by closing out the investments early, the government reaped less than it might have had it held on to the investments longer. Third, with bank capital weakened by the buybacks, lending might be more circumscribed—and the recovery weakened. And fourth, if the economy were to hit one of the many possible bumps, the financial sector would be in a more precarious position.

There was a kind of disingenuousness in the administration's stance. The terms of the deals—and the accounting—were not the kind that the banks would have countenanced for their own activities. No oil company would claim that it had done well because some wells reaped a return. The successful wells must yield a return sufficient to compensate for the unsuccessful wells—and for the risk that all of the wells will turn up dry. So too, when Warren Buffett invested in Goldman Sachs, he demanded a return to compensate for risk and the time value of money. The banks demand the same: in defending high interest rates charged to credit card recipients, for instance, they refer constantly to those who do not repay. Surely the government cannot claim that it charged adequately if it did not receive adequate compensation for risk and the time value of money, and if those who repaid did not make up for the losses of those who didn't.

As I point out in the text, the taxpayers were cheated, and nothing that has happened since has changed that perspective—even if it now appears that the Treasury's losses may be smaller than was originally thought. The failure to get a better deal for taxpayers is important, partly because of a sense of fairness: those who benefited from the bailout had caused the problems in the first place and were among the wealthiest Americans. But it is also a matter of the long-run fiscal position of the country, which would be far better if the Treasury and the Fed had designed a better program.

Today, we are beginning to see another consequence of the poorly designed bank bailouts: a broader disillusionment with government. I had written, correctly, that the bank bailout would make it more difficult to get money for a second round of stimulus, which would almost surely be needed. What I hadn't fully anticipated was the size of the backlash: having seen their hard-earned money go to the bankers, who have continued to enjoy their bonuses while the rest of the country has remained mired in a recession that *they* had caused, Americans are increasingly displaying a mistrust of government—of which the Tea Party movement is emblematic. Ordinary citizens may not understand the subtleties of macroeconomics, they may not see how budget cutbacks will lead to a deeper recession and more job cuts, but what they do understand is that the biggest bailout in the history of the planet went to help the bankers. The money did not trickle down to them as promised, and they are angry.

NEW WORRIES, OLD REMEDIES

Nearly three years after the beginning of the recession, four years after the bursting of the bubble, it is clear that while the economy may be on the path to recovery, that path is marked with unforeseen obstacles. Changing politics and public attitudes are among the most unpredictable factors as we look forward.

Is inflation a threat?

Even before the economy's growth had been restored and even as the country seemed mired in high unemployment, attention—at least in some quarters—shifted to inflation and the national debt. Right now, inflation is not a threat, and is unlikely to be so as long as unemployment remains high. The low interest rates on long-term bonds and inflation-indexed bonds that the government issues to pay its debts suggest that the "market" itself is not too worried about inflation, even over a longer period. Indeed, with continuing unemployment, deflation remains the more imminent danger (though this could change quickly, with cost-push inflation, if China's growth continues to drive up prices of steel and other commodities).[26] Deflation can be a problem, because as wages and prices fall, households and firms are less able to pay back the money they owe. Defaults result, leading to further turmoil in the already frail and overleveraged financial system.[27]

To me, the real problems—not now, but possibly in the next few years—are not so much inflation and debt, but the *financial markets' concerns* about inflation and debt. If the market starts to anticipate inflation, then it will demand higher interest rates to compensate for the reduced value of the dollars received in repayment. Higher interest rates will lead to higher government deficits and debts, and combined with the inflation worries, these will create pressure for cutbacks in government spending *before the economy is on firm footing*.

A *Keynesian solution to a Keynesian problem*

Today, as at the time this book was first completed, the real problems remain unemployment and a lack of aggregate demand, precisely the problem John Maynard Keynes faced seventy-five years ago during the Great Depression. Monetary policy then and now had reached its limits: further declines in interest rates either are impossible or won't have much effect in stimulating the economy.

We must then rely on fiscal policy to help restore the economy to health. In chapter 3, I explain—and dismiss—the arguments that have been put forward for why fiscal policy might not work.[28] The evidence then was overwhelming that it would work in the situation the United States and the world confronted in 2008. The evidence since has supported that conclusion: China deployed one of the world's largest stimulus packages and had one of the strongest recoveries, in spite of facing significant shocks to its economy.[29] In Europe and America, the stimulus packages were too small to offset fully the "shock" from the financial sector, but had it not been for these actions, unemployment rates would have been *much* higher.

The financial markets' attack against Greece (discussed more fully in the next section) shows that deficits cannot be ignored.[30] Large deficits can lead to increases in interest rates, worsening a country's fiscal problems. Americans are used to thinking that they are immune from such "market discipline." But they are not: forty years ago, financial markets lost confidence in the dollar, and the global financial system had to be revamped as a result.

But the naive response—cut back spending and/or raise taxes—will make matters only worse, as the market response to Spain's retrenchment showed so dramatically. There is a metaphor that likens governments to households; however, this way of looking at public finances is not just wrong, but dangerous. Households that are living beyond their means—that is, their spending exceeds their income—and can't find a bank to finance their consumption spree have no choice but to cut back on their spending. A large enough cutback will bring the household accounts into order. But when governments cut spending, growth slows, unemployment increases, and income—and tax revenue—declines. The accounts may not improve or may improve only a little. Moreover, the U.S. government can usually finance its spending—right now, it can borrow at close to a zero percent interest rate, even though it is running a large deficit.

There is a way out of this seeming quandary. Worries about the size of the debt should lead to a shift in the pattern of government spending, toward spending that yields a high economic return. As I explain in the text, markets are shortsighted: before the crisis, they were shortsighted in their lending, and they are once again so. Borrowing to finance investments (such as in technology, infrastructure, and education) with returns as low as 5 or 6 percent can lead to a lower long-term national debt, as the growth—both short term and long term—generates more than enough additional tax revenue to pay the interest due—and in the past, these public investments have yielded a far higher return than that.[31]

So too, the *structure* of taxes can change, leading to higher growth *and* lower deficits. Raising corporate income taxes for corporations that don't reinvest in their businesses, and lowering them for those that do (through, say, investment tax credits), is one example. The increased investment leads to higher growth, and the higher growth leads to more tax revenues. Raising taxes on high-income individuals and lowering them on lower-income individuals is another.

Government can do still more to help the private sector grow—if the old banks won't lend, create some new banks that will. For a fraction of what was spent on dealing with the bad loans of the old banks, the government could have created a set of new financial institutions, unencumbered by past bad decisions.

The administration, meanwhile, has repeatedly tried to bolster consumer confidence, with the hope that in doing so, consumption and investment will be restored. It has failed—but not because growing deficits have eroded consumer confidence, as the conservatives claim, but because the administration has relied on trickle-down economics. It has hoped that pouring money into the banks, without restrictions, would suffice to restart lending, and that would suffice to restore growth. The banks may have been helped, and the green shoots of March 2009 may have reflected this, but jobs weren't created, and that is what matters for most Americans. Confidence in the economy has not been restored, but confidence in the administration's economic prognoses (and its remedies) has eroded.

GLOBAL PERSPECTIVES

The fact that the situation is worse elsewhere is small comfort. And the fact that the crisis wore a "Made in the USA" label hardly adds to the country's international stature. Indeed, the Treasury's efforts to fight back against Europe's attempt to rein in American hedge funds in the spring of 2010 only gave rise to resentment, and to a view of an administration that is captured by the forces that had given rise to the crisis itself.

In the beginning of this crisis, there was a hope of decoupling—that Europe and Asia would be able to grow even if America sank into a recession. That proved to be a false hope. But there was partial decoupling, at least for the moment. Growth in Asia since this book first appeared on the shelves has been truly impressive. China's growth in 2009 was 8.7 percent; India grew 5.7 percent; growth in the first quarter of 2010 was 11.9 and 8.6 percent, respectively. Their strong growth drove up commodity prices and helped commodity exporters around the world. The emerging markets had been the source of a large fraction of the global growth over the preceding decade; they now seemed to be *the* source of growth.[32] But their growth on its own seemed unlikely to revive that of Europe and America. While China markedly increased its consumption,[33] it was buying goods made in China, and educational and health services, also produced in China.

As this paperback edition goes to press, forecasts suggest that Europe's unemployment rate—now comparable to that in the United States—will remain stubbornly high. This is especially so because pressure in Europe to cut back spending is even stronger than it is in the United States. Europe's fiscal framework calls on countries to limit deficits to 3 percent of GDP and debt to 60 percent of GDP. In the crisis, none could come close to achieving the deficit target: Spain's fiscal deficit in 2009 was 11.2 percent; the United Kingdom's, 11.5 percent; Italy's, 5.3 percent; and Ireland's, 14.3 percent. (While Spain's debt was only 60 percent of GDP, Greece and Italy both had debt-to-GDP ratios of around 115 percent, and rising.)[34]

The return of Herbert Hoover and the demise of Keynes

The deficits and debts are not surprising. What is worrisome, though, is the political ramifications of the financial markets' response to them. As we saw, in the beginning of the crisis there was a short victory for Keynesian economics, when the entire world believed that government spending was not only effective, but also desirable and necessary. For a century there has been a conflict between two views, this Keynesian view and the "Hooverite" view, which says that to restore economic strength, confidence has to be restored; to restore confidence, deficits have to be reduced; and to reduce deficits, spending has to be cut and taxes increased. The IMF programs in East Asia, Latin America, and Russia a decade ago should have provided convincing evidence that normally the Hooverite approach doesn't work. Cutbacks in spending erode strength in the economy; the weaker economy erodes tax revenue, so the deficit reductions are less than hoped; confidence is not restored, nor are consumption and investment. The "confidence fairy" is more likely to make her appearance with Keynesian policies that restore growth than with austerity measures that destroy it.[35] In spite of this unfailing record of failure, the Hooverites have returned, and while in some countries—such as the United Kingdom—there is a full-fledged intellectual battle underway, in others—such as Germany—the Hooverites seem to have won the day.

But even countries that are committed to Keynesian economics, such as Greece and Spain, worry that they have no choice but to cut their deficits. If they don't cut their deficits voluntarily, they won't be able to get funds from the financial markets, and they will then be *forced* to cut their deficits.

The attack against Greece

Greece's experience in 2010, as it was attacked by financial markets, was similar to that of many developing countries. What was a surprise was that it occurred in an advanced industrial country. The financial sector, having been saved by governments throughout the world (including the Greek government), turned on those that had saved them.

In the United States, there is anger at the banks for now lecturing governments about the debt that has grown so much because of the banks' bad behavior; in Europe, they decided to bite the hand that fed them. Seeing the huge deficits, and the countries' need for funds, some in the financial sector saw a new opportunity for profits. Recognizing that when Greece came to the market to roll over its debt, or to finance its deficits, it might have trouble raising the funds without paying a high interest rate, the banks sold existing bonds short—betting that the bonds would fall in price.[36] They used the new weapons of financial mass destruction, credit default swaps, to mount their attack.[37]

Exposing long-festering flaws

When the euro was created as a common currency in Europe, I raised concerns along with many others. Countries that share a currency have a fixed exchange rate with each other and thereby give up an important tool of adjustment. Had Greece and Spain been allowed to decrease the value of their currency, their economies would have been strengthened by increasing exports. Moreover, in switching their currencies to the euro, the two countries gave up another instrument for reacting to downturns: monetary policy. Had they not done so, they could have responded to their crises by lowering interest rates to stimulate investment (though in the current severe recession, lowering interest rates would not have worked). Instead, the hands of the countries of the Eurozone were tied. So long as there were no shocks, the euro would do fine. The test would come when one or more of the countries faced a downturn. The recession of 2008 provided that test—and as this edition goes to press, it appears that Europe may be failing the test.

To make up for the losses of these vital tools for adjustment, the Eurozone should have created a fund to help those facing adverse problems. The United States is a "single currency" area, but when California has a problem, and its unemployment rate goes up, a large part of the costs are borne by the federal government. Europe has no way of helping countries facing severe problems. Spain has an unemployment rate of 20 percent, with 40 to 50 percent of young people unemployed. It had a fiscal surplus before the crisis; after the crisis, its deficit exceeded 11 percent of GDP. But under the rules of the game, Spain must now cut its spending, which will almost surely increase its unemployment rate still further. As its economy slows, the improvement in its fiscal position may be minimal. Spain may be entering the kind of death spiral that afflicted Argentina just a decade ago. It was only when Argentina broke its currency peg with the dollar that it started to grow and its deficit came down. At present, Spain has not been attacked by speculators, but it may be only a matter of time.

It was, perhaps, not a surprise that Greece was the first to be attacked. Speculators like small countries—they can mount an attack with less money. And Greece's problems were, in many ways, the most serious (though its unemployment rate of 10 percent was in line with the euro-area average, its deficit, at 13.6 percent of GDP in 2009, was the second largest in Europe, after Ireland). Its debt was 115 percent of GDP. Like the United States, it had a deficit before the crisis (5.1 percent of GDP in 2007, even worse than that of the United States, which was 2.5 percent). Like many governments and many firms in the financial sector, Greece had engaged in deceptive accounting, aided and abetted by financial firms. America's financial firms, having discovered how they could use such accounting practices and financial products (like derivatives and repos) to deceive shareholders and the government alike, marketed these techniques and products to governments wanting to hide their deficits.

In October 2009, Greece elected a new government. The new prime minister, Georges Papandreou, ran on a platform of increased transparency. Unusually, once elected, he fulfilled his promise, disclosing problems in the government's accounts, and when a further problem was discovered—the use of a Goldman Sachs derivative to create a prettier picture of its fiscal position as it strived to meet the conditions for entry into the Eurozone—that was disclosed too.[38] But the financial markets opted not to reward such honesty; instead, they punished Greece with a vengeance. At first, there was some hope that Europe would take the occasion to remedy the institutional deficiency present since the euro's birth. But Germany had insisted on there being no bailouts and it was reluctant to come to Greece's assistance.

To many observers, both in and outside of Greece, Europe's stance was peculiar: it had already come to the rescue of the big banks.[39] Saving corporations was evidently acceptable; saving a country of 11 million was taboo. And saving a country would not be, in some sense, a bailout. As with the assistance that the IMF provided a decade earlier to Brazil, if Greece were given access to funds at a reasonable interest rate, it would be able to meet its obligations. Obviously if interest rates soared, or the country went into a deep recession, it would face difficulties, but so would a country with much lower debt, such as Spain.

A series of half-offers and vague promises intended to calm the markets failed—and not surprisingly. Finally, Europe put together an assistance program with the IMF—a trillion dollars, an amount exceeding even America's bank bailout. It was a "shock and awe" program: by announcing such a large program, members of the Eurozone hoped to convince the markets that Europe would come to the rescue of any country that needed help. With the program in place, interest rates charged to countries like Greece would (it was hoped) remain low. And because of that, the countries wouldn't have to turn to Europe and the IMF for help. It was the familiar "confidence game" that the IMF had tried during the East Asia crisis a decade earlier. It hadn't worked then, and it was far from obvious that it would work now. The market responses indicated as much: interest rates for some of the "problematic" governments came down from the stratospheric levels to which they had risen, but they remained high, suggesting that the markets had not been fully convinced.

Greece is a relatively small country, with its short-term economic prospects closely linked to that of the rest of Europe. If Germany has a strong recovery, German tourists will go to Greece, and the Greek economy will be strong. Tax revenues will rise, and its deficit will come down.

Europe and the IMF put conditions on their assistance to Greece—that Greece quickly reduce its deficit through cutbacks in spending and large increases in taxes. If Greece alone engaged in austerity, Greece would suffer and that would be the end of the matter. The worry is that there is a wave of austerity building throughout Europe (and, as I noted earlier, even hitting America's shores). As so many countries cut back on spending prematurely, global aggregate demand will be lowered and growth will slow—even perhaps leading to a double-dip recession. America may have caused the global recession, but Europe is now responding in kind.

The future of the euro

There are further risks, including the future of the euro. The Icelandic debacle[40] had shown that the European conception that financial institutions should be able to operate freely anywhere in Europe, so long as they were regulated by a "good" government, made no sense. But the Greek tragedy exposed a more fundamental flaw: a single currency cannot work without more cooperation (including fiscal assistance) than what currently exists.

As I note later, the United States has complained about China's current account (trade) surpluses,[41] but as a percentage of GDP, Germany's surplus is even greater. With Europe as a whole in rough balance, the fact that Germany is in surplus means that the rest of Europe is in deficit. And the fact that countries other than Germany are importing more than they are exporting contributes to their weak economies. The United States has also expressed concern about China's refusal to allow its exchange rate to increase relative to the dollar, but the euro system means that Germany's exchange rate cannot increase relative to that of other currencies in the Eurozone. If the exchange rate did increase, Germany would find it more difficult to export, its surplus would disappear, and its economic model, based on strong exports, would face a challenge.

Some in Germany (and hardliners elsewhere) have responded: nothing was wrong with the euro's original framework. The only problem was laxity in enforcing the rules concerning fiscal discipline. If only Europe had been tougher, countries would have been forced to cut their deficits and debt. In short, they support a further embrace of Hooverite policies.

To me, such an approach is sheer nonsense. Spain had a surplus before the crisis, and if it were forced to quickly cut its deficit now, its unemployment rate would soar and its deficits may even increase. Spain's problems were not caused by the lack of enforcement of the budget rules *before the crisis*, but they would be exacerbated by the enforcement of the rules *after the crisis*. Spain's problems were caused by market fundamentalist ideologies which said that governments should sit idly by as a bubble forms, even a bubble that puts an entire economy at risk.

The Eurozone needs better economic cooperation—not just the kind that *merely* enforces budget rules, but cooperation that also ensures that Europe remains at full employment, and that when countries experience large adverse shocks, they get help from others. Europe created a solidarity fund to help new entrants into the European Union, most of whom were poorer than the others. But it failed to create a solidarity fund to help any part of the Eurozone that was facing stress. Without some such fund, the future prospects of the euro are bleak.

Will Europe accept the consequences of Germany's hard-line approach, its insistence that Greece and others cut their deficits? Germany (like China) views its high savings and its export prowess as virtues, not vices. But for every country with a surplus, there are others with a deficit, and countries with a trade deficit often must run fiscal deficits to maintain aggregate demand.[42] Without the fiscal deficits, they will have high unemployment. The social and economic consequences of that are, and should be, unacceptable.

One way out that has been proposed is for Spain and the other countries to engineer the equivalent of a devaluation—a uniform decrease in wages. This is, I believe, unachievable, and its distributive consequences unacceptable. In practice, governments can only force down the wages of public employees. In some countries, where they are overpaid, this might make sense; but in others, where pay is already low, it would further impede the government in recruiting the talent it needs for essential public services. The social tensions would be enormous. But even its economic consequences could be adverse: with declining wages and prices, the ability of households and firms to meet their debt obligations would decrease; bankruptcies would increase, as would the problems in the financial sector. The notion that cutting wages is a solution to the problems of Greece, Spain, and others within the Eurozone is a fantasy.

There is a far easier solution: the exit of Germany from the Eurozone or the division of the Eurozone into two subregions. The euro has been an interesting experiment, but like the almost forgotten ERM (Exchange Rate Mechanism) system[43] that preceded it, and that fell apart when speculators attacked the UK sterling in 1992, it lacks the institutional support required to make it work.

It would, of course, be preferable to provide that support now. If Europe cannot find a way to make these institutional reforms, then it is perhaps better to admit failure and move on than to extract a high price in unemployment and human suffering, all in the name of flawed institutional arrangements that did not live up to the ideals of their creators.

Perhaps the most likely course is a form of brinkmanship—as Europe comes to the assistance of those countries *in extremis* (the ones that have difficulty financing their deficits and rolling over their debt) at the last minute and with onerous terms. The imposed austerity will itself not only cause hardship in the afflicted countries but also weaken the European economy and undermine support for European integration. And brinkmanship carries with it a risk: in waiting too long or demanding too onerous conditions, the Eurozone may face a crisis far worse than that which it has experienced so far.

In the short run, the Eurozone may have found a partial way out:

its temporary victory in the negative beauty contest has led to a weak euro, which may help Europe's growth—though almost surely not enough to offset the austerity measures already in place. At most, the weak euro offers a temporary palliative: some day, in the not-too-distant future (perhaps even by the time this paperback edition is published), financial markets will focus once again on America's financial and economic problems, and America may once again win the negative beauty contest.

GLOBAL IMBALANCES

Greece presented the most daunting challenge to emerge from the global crisis. But Sino-American economic relations also suffered, taking a marked turn for the worse largely because of the crisis, with potential spillovers to other areas in which cooperation is necessary, such as containing the nuclear ambitions of Iran.

I describe the underlying problem earlier in this book: the United States imports from China much more than it exports. American workers see themselves as losing jobs to China. While politicians may tout the virtues of exports in creating jobs, imports are widely viewed as bad because imports destroy jobs. The problem is that imports and exports are inextricably linked in trade policy. When the economy is at full employment, those who lose jobs can get jobs elsewhere. When the economy is in a deep recession, they can't. This gives rise to pressures toward protectionism, which, so far, have been largely contained. I still worry that they may grow worse as unemployment persists and the ability to revive the economy through fiscal and monetary measures seems limited.

Popular discussions often focus around bilateral trade relations, in particular, the fact that the United States imports $226.9 billion more from China than it exports.[44] But economists argue that attention should center on multilateral trade deficits (the overall difference between exports and imports), not the trade deficits between any two countries. The United States runs a trade deficit with Saudi Arabia because it

buys more from that country (oil) than it sells to it (say, hi-tech products). But if Saudi Arabia buys goods from Europe, and Europe buys
goods from the United States, then there is no grounds for complaint: a
well-functioning global trading system is supposed to allow each country to produce according to its comparative advantage, and buy from
those countries that produce the particular goods it wants.

Running a multilateral surplus—producing more than one
consumes—can, however, present a problem in a world with insufficient global demand. These countries view their savings as a virtue,
not a vice, and in normal times, it is a virtue. But these are not normal
times. China is, of course, not alone: Japan, Germany, and Saudi Arabia
have also been running persistent surpluses. As a percentage of GDP,
Germany and Saudi Arabia's surpluses are larger than those of China.

But China's surplus has increasingly become the focus of U.S. concern. The United States has demanded that China allow its currency
to appreciate. China has argued that if the United States wanted to
redress its trade imbalance with China, it should lift its ban on exports
of high-technology products. It had desperately requested to buy heli-
copters after the Sichuan earthquake in 2008, in which nearly 70,000
lives were lost, to no avail. (Meanwhile, the United States sold helicop-
ters to Taiwan.) A revaluation of its currency, the renminbi, would help
other developing countries, but China knew it would do little for the
United States' overall trade balance. The United States would simply
import textiles and apparel from Bangladesh or Sri Lanka. China had,
in any case, been appreciating its currency—by almost 20 percent
since 2005, about two-thirds of the amount that many experts thought
was necessary for a full adjustment.[45] China made it clear that it would
resume appreciation once the global economy has stabilized, but in its
view, it was in no one's interest for China to do anything to destabilize
its own economy, which has been a pillar of stability in an otherwise
volatile global economy. As the euro weakened, China had another
argument not to appreciate its currency: relative to the euro, its currency *had* appreciated greatly.

Ironically, even China's multilateral trade policy is partly a result
of policies that the United States pushed. For the past three decades,

trade has been heralded as the best approach to development. But in the Uruguay Round trade agreement signed in 1994, which created the World Trade Organization (WTO), developing countries, including China (which is still categorized by the World Bank and IMF as a developing country, even though it is a large country), were restricted in using industrial policies (subsidies) to encourage the development of their nascent industries, even as American and European agricultural subsidies were allowed. This left developing countries one major instrument—exchange rates—to promote their development. A lower exchange rate not only encouraged exports but also helped the countries build up reserves that protected them from increasingly volatile global financial markets. And, again partly because of the policies pushed by the United States during the East Asia and other crises, turning to the IMF for assistance in a crisis became increasingly unacceptable.[46]

A new global political balance of power— and new global institutions

China's success in combating the recession and the continuing problems in Europe and the United States have given a new sense of confidence to those in Asia, and new influence in the rest of the world. Indian and Asian regulators proudly (and correctly) explain how they prevented the abuses that afflicted the United States and Europe.

Meanwhile, China's influence has grown, not only in Africa but around the world. In earlier eras, European powers used military might to secure their trade routes and access to resources. In this century China uses its economic power. It sits on $2.4 trillion in reserves from which to draw. In what economists might call "mutually beneficial exchanges," China can give some of this hard-earned cash in return for ports, mines, oil—whatever it takes to keep its modern industrial engine going. (In 2008, China's Cosco Pacific signed a $4 billion deal to run the Greek port of Piraeus for 35 years.)[47] With America so absorbed in its fruitless wars in Afghanistan and Iraq and dealing with the aftermath of its financial crisis, China has much of the globe to itself. America may have built the mightiest armed forces in the world, but the $4.7 trillion spent on defense during the past decade is money that could have been used to create a stronger economy and extend the country's economic influence.[48] Economics is the science of scarcity: the United States spent its money one way; China chose to spend it another. It is, perhaps, too soon to render judgment, but it increasingly appears that America made a strategic blunder.

While the Great Recession has done little to correct global trade imbalances, the crisis is leading to a new balance of global geopolitical/geoeconomic power. The G-8 is, for instance, dying a rapid death, being replaced by the G-20. To its critics, the G-8 was little more than a talking forum. There was hope that the G-20, better suited for addressing the world's problems simply because of its global membership, would be more than that. And for a moment that seemed the case, as there was a concerted effort at Keynesian expansionary policies. However, as the recession has continued, the split between those pushing for Hooverite austerity measures and those still believing in Keynesian economic policies could not be masked. And from the beginning there was disunity on regulatory reform—with the Obama administration seemingly attempting to fend off Europe's increasingly strident tones that stressed the importance of taming bonuses and, with the attack on Greece, curtailing speculative activities.

FINANCIAL SECTOR REFORM

When I first sent my book off to the publisher, I was pessimistic about the prospects of Congress passing reforms to the financial sector that were anything more than cosmetic. With the financial community's interests so well represented in the Obama administration, it was no surprise that what the administration put forward was mild. With money from financial firms pouring into Congress, it looked like their political investments were once again about to pay off. In the end what emerged is far stronger than what I had anticipated. But that's not good enough: it is still too weak to prevent a recurrence of a crisis or to ensure that financial markets return to performing their essential societal roles. But for what was achieved, Goldman Sachs deserves a thank-you note for delivering—by its behavior—what all the public interest groups, all the economists, and all the newspaper editorials could not. Public respect for finance—already at a low level—plummeted after revelations about the behavior of Goldman Sachs and other investment banks, and their defenses did little to restore confidence.

New abuses uncovered

With the innumerable stories of predatory lending and credit card abuses, and payments of outlandish bonuses while banks reported record losses, it seemed that the reputation of America's leading banks couldn't sink much lower. But in the months after this book was first published, there were repeated disclosures of misdeeds that further undermined confidence in America's financial system. With the head of Goldman Sachs, Lloyd Blankfein, claiming that he was simply "doing God's work,"[49] and he and others denying that there was anything wrong with what they had done, it seemed that the bankers were living on a different planet. At the very least, they had a markedly different ethical compass.

I describe in the text the marked discrepancy between, for instance, Lehman Brothers' accounts shortly before the collapse and afterward. In the aftermath of the bankruptcy, it was possible to go through Lehman Brothers' records and find out what the company had done. It had indeed engaged in creative—more accurately described as deceptive—accounting: the use of a transaction called "repo 105" whereby assets were moved off the books—in exchange for cash— *temporarily*, only when the regulators were scheduled to look at the company's books, so the regulators would think that the company had less leverage than it really did.[50]

The demand for creative accounting of this sort led to the creation of a large number of new "financial products" that did much the same thing as traditional loans and insurance policies, but were treated differently from a legal or regulatory perspective. A derivative can be like an insurance policy—but without the oversight of the regulator, so less money has to be set aside as a reserve, and the insurer can take on unreasonable risks. A repo may be little different from a collateralized loan, but on the books it may be treated as a sale—even if there is an agreement to buy the collateral back. And our brilliant financial engineers figured out how to get around most of the legal requirements. They could design a product where the other side of the party didn't *have* to buy it back, but there were incentives in place so that each party would behave as if they had to.

The transaction for which, on April 16, 2010, the SEC formally charged Goldman Sachs with committing fraud—but for which the firm seemed to feel that it had done nothing wrong—involved the creation of a "synthetic product," which was nothing more than a gamble on how well a large pool of subprime mortgages would perform. Advocates of these products claimed that they helped the economy manage risk, but it was hard to see how a transaction that ultimately entailed a hedge fund run by John Paulson winning a billion dollars, and some banks losing the comparable amount—with a large part of the tab ultimately picked up by taxpayers—improved the efficiency of the economy in any way. (Finally, in July 2010, Goldman Sachs admitted that it had made a mistake—though it did not admit to fraud—and in the largest penalty ever assessed against a Wall Street firm, paid $550 million to the Securities and Exchange Commission. It is also almost surely going to face suit from those who suffered from its "mistake.")

Betting is, of course, not illegal, but it should be clear that banks insured by the government should not engage in gambling. Betting is regulated by the states, but the big banks putting together these megagambles and making billions of dollars in transactions fees had managed to ensure that they were not regulated—either as gambling or as insurance. The charges brought against Goldman Sachs were not for running an illicit gambling house, but for fraud. Paulson had approached Goldman Sachs asking for help to put the gamble together. He would help Goldman Sachs pick out the worst of the subprime mortgages—those most likely to go down in value when the bubble broke—to create a security, dubbed Abacus 2007-AC1, that could be sold to investors. The security was, in effect, a bet on what would happen to this carefully selected—selected to lose—bundle of securities. Then, Paulson would bet against the security, so that if the security turned sour, he would stand to make hundreds of millions.[51] No one could look through to the individual mortgages that made up these complex products—there were just too many—and no one did. Not only were the mortgages chosen because they were likely to fail, but Goldman also didn't disclose to the buyers of these products how the mortgages were chosen—with the assistance of the hedge fund that wanted to bet against them. The buyers *trusted* Goldman, something that they are not likely to do in the future.[52] While Paulson would have won big on a randomly chosen portfolio of subprime mortgages, he won even bigger on a portfolio chosen to lose money. And that meant those taking the other side of the bet would lose more—which meant that the taxpayers would ultimately have to put up more money when the government decided the banks needed a bailout to save the economy.

Trying to make profits out of other big banks—or an insurance company like AIG that thinks it understands risks but doesn't—is one thing; putting an entire country at risk is another. The double dealing with Greece has deservedly earned the ire of citizens around the world. What happened as Greece's financial situation worsened was, however, not just a matter of one speculator winning at the expense of others. As banks sold short Greek bonds (that is, took a bet that the country would face higher interest rates, an expression of a lack of confidence in the government), the country's bonds went down.[53] But there are real consequences to these speculative attacks; what is at stake is not just a transfer of money from one rich gambler to another. The country has been forced to cut back expenditures, lay off workers, cut back services, and cut wages.

Financial reform begins to take shape

It is no accident that some countries have fared better than others in this crisis. Some countries (such as Canada and Australia) had better financial regulation. Sometimes these regulations prevented bubbles from forming; but even in those cases, like in Spain, where they did not prevent a real estate bubble, the financial sector fared better than expected. Given the size of Spain's housing bubble (in 2006, there were more housing starts in Spain than in France, Germany, Italy, and the United Kingdom combined), one would have expected its banking system to be bankrupt and the number of foreclosures to be even worse than in the United States.[54] But Spain's regulators did a better job of provisioning for losses and did not allow the kinds of abusive mortgages that were so prevalent in the United States.[55]

It is remarkable, though not surprising, that so long after the bubble broke, so long after the crisis began, reforming the global financial system is still a work in progress. But in the United States, the outlines of financial reform are now clear, though many of the details have been left to regulators—and, as in so many areas, the devil is in the details.[56] With so much discretion in the hands of regulators—some even the same ones who, before the crisis, did not believe in regulation—there is little assurance that the reforms are strong enough to protect us against a repeat of the calamities of recent years.[57]

The regulatory reform bill, officially called the Dodd-Frank bill after Chris Dodd and Barney Frank, the heads of the Senate and House Committees responsible for financial sector regulation (passed as H.R. 4173, the Dodd-Frank Wall Street Reform and Consumer Protection Act, and signed by President Obama on July 21, 2010), has five key provisions.[58] In a sense, each of the provisions recognized an important principle. But unfortunately, a key part of the legislative strategy of the banks was to get exemptions so that the force of any regulation passed would be greatly attenuated. The result is a Swiss cheese bill—seemingly strong, but with large holes. The bill provides for:

1. A (hopefully) strong and independent financial product safety commission (now called the Consumer Financial Protection Bureau) to protect ordinary Americans against the rampant abuses pervasive in the industry. The recognition that the financial sector had engaged in outrageous, abusive practices, and something needed to be done about it—that one could not simply say "caveat emptor" ("buyer beware")—was a major victory for the critics of the sector and a major defeat for the banks. But the financial sector managed to achieve a huge exemption for automobile loans. There is no reason why a car dealer should be allowed to exploit a poor or uninformed consumer any more than a big bank should be able to. Yet, under political pressure, auto loans—the second most important form of lending, after mortgages—were given an exemption.

The states have been active in curbing many of the abuses, and in a provision that may have been a step in the wrong direction, the federal government assumed the right to override state regulations. With federal regulators of the kind that we had prior to the crisis, they will do that—and consumers may be left less protected even than they are today.

As I note in the text, modern technology allows for an efficient electronics payment mechanism, which our uncompetitive financial sector has resisted; it imposes what is, in effect, a tax on every transaction. The regulatory reform bill instructs the Federal Reserve to issue rules to ensure that debit card fees charged to merchants are reasonable and proportional to the cost of processing those transactions. It thus delegates to the Federal Reserve—which in the past has shown little interest in consumer protection—responsibility for ensuring that banks do not continue to gouge merchants in debit card transactions, but it leaves banks free to do so in the far larger credit card market.[59] [60]

2. A systemic regulator who sees the system as a whole. This regulator is in the form of a council, but its main power is to make recommendations to the Fed, an institution that failed in the run-up to the crisis and is so closely tied to the banking system and reflective of those interests.

3. Curbs on excessive risk-taking. That the banks had engaged in excessive risk-taking is clear. The question was how best to prevent this in the future. The banks needed stronger incentives to have better incentives, for instance, for those that made risk decisions. As I point out in the text, the too-big-to-fail banks posed an especially big problem—with their "heads-I-win-tails-you-lose" situation, the excessive risk-taking of the big banks should have come as no surprise. Nothing seems to have been done about the too-big-to-fail banks and the bonus structures that provide incentives for excessive risk-taking (though under existing powers, regulators can do something about the latter).

But given the well-known problems in corporate governance, providing banks with *incentives* would not have been enough: the bonus system, the incentive structures that induced excessive risk-taking, should have been proscribed, along with the myriad of excessively risky practices. European countries put curtailing bonuses at the center of their regulatory reforms, but America's banks successfully resisted these efforts. Paul Volcker, with Obama's support, had argued for restricting trading (speculation) by commercial banks using their own capital (called proprietary trading). Some viewed this as a "mini-restoration" of the Glass-Steagall Act, which prior to 1999 had separated commercial and investment banking, and whose repeal was closely linked with the travails of our financial system. Such trading gives rise to conflicts of interest (in the run-up to the crisis, banks sometimes made profits on their own account at the expense of their customers); the inside information from handling customers' accounts gives them an unfair advantage, and, most important, losses are effectively underwritten by taxpayers.

The bill that was passed contains a greatly weakened version of the Volcker rule: while it imposed limits on proprietary trading, they aren't likely to be binding for most banks.

4. Curbs on derivatives. The $180 billion bailout of AIG (whose losses were due to its derivatives business) should have made curbing derivatives a no-brainer. There is a legitimate debate about whether certain derivatives should be viewed as insurance or as gambling instruments. But in either case, the government should be regulating them, and it should not be *encouraging* or *subsidizing* them—as it effectively does today.[61] The reform bill makes a little—but only a little—progress in dealing with the problem. The failure to do more is understandable: with a few big banks reaping $20 billion a year or more in fees, they resisted strongly.

For a moment, it looked like a strong provision restricting government-insured banks from writing derivatives would be included. In the end, banks were allowed to retain the bulk (some 70 percent) of their derivatives business, but derivatives based on equities, commodities, and certain credit default swaps will have to be placed in a separate subsidiary with higher capital requirements—hopefully lowering the risk of another bailout.[62]

There were significant advances in transparency, with most contracts standardized, cleared, and traded on electronic platforms.[63] But there is a gaping hole in enforcement: if a swap has not been properly cleared and traded on an exchange, regulators have no clear legal authority to undo an unlawful deal.

5. Resolution authority. Government was given more authority to deal with failing banks. But the legislation didn't adequately deal with the problem of too-big-to-fail institutions. We need to be realistic. In the last crisis, government "blinked," bailing out shareholders and bondholders when it didn't have to. It feared that doing otherwise would lead to economic trauma. As long as there are mega-banks that are too big to fail, more likely than not the government will "blink" again. Too-big-to-fail institutions not only have an incentive to engage in excessive risk-taking, but also have a competitive advantage—based not on greater efficiency but on the implicit subsidy from a future government bailout.

REWRITING HISTORY

Even though the crisis has not ended, its protagonists are busy rewriting history. As evidence of regulatory lapses and deficiencies—most notably at the Securities and Exchange Commission, the Federal Reserve, and other bank regulatory agencies—has mounted, many of the regulators have repeatedly claimed that they did all that they could have done. Those at the Fed and Treasury who want to take credit for the "victory" do not mention their repeated misdiagnoses (even after the bubble broke, the Fed argued that its effects were contained).[64] They do not mention that they supported a "regulatory" system that was fundamentally flawed—relying heavily, for instance, on "self-regulation," something that at last is being recognized for the oxymoron that it is. When they say they were powerless to do more, they do not mention that they did in fact have other powers to prevent the bubble from growing, and they do not mention that they refused to go to Congress before the demise of Lehman Brothers to ask for the powers that they now, finally, belatedly, recognize they needed.

They and their supporters prefer that we forget the fierce battles over regulation in the decade prior to the crisis and the failures in implementing existing regulations. They would like us, instead, to extend them congratulations for having saved capitalism, for having brought us back from the brink of disaster to which they had pushed us in the fall of 2008. Yes, they agree, it was expensive; yes, they agree, it was unpleasant to give so much money to those who had behaved so badly. But we had no choice.

WE HAD CHOICES

We did have choices. The choices that we make at one moment shape those at the next. President Bush's tax cuts of 2001 and 2003 did not lead to the sustained growth that was promised but rather to higher deficits that have made it more difficult to deal with the breaking of the housing bubble.[65] In this book, I explain how the *repeated* bailouts of the banks around the world during the preceding two decades gave rise to a moral hazard that contributed to banks' reckless lending. I explain, too, how the way that the U.S. Treasury and IMF imposed harsh and counterproductive conditions on developing countries—making them bear the brunt of the banks' bad lending decisions—contributed to soaring foreign exchange reserves, which fueled global imbalances and low global interest rates.

Already, in the many months since the Bush and Obama administrations made their choices on the bailout strategies, the economic and political consequences have become evident.

The crisis is not over. Far from it. What has been going on is akin to a slow train wreck: one can see the massive destruction that will follow as the train speeds excessively around the curve. At this juncture, when we say that the rescue *worked*, all that we can be sure of is that it avoided the immediate disaster—the global economy pulled back from the brink on which it was poised. The course of history going forward is, to put it mildly, uncertain: all we can say, nine years after the Fed undertook its policy of creating a housing bubble as a strategy for recovering from the bursting of the tech bubble, is that the recovery is *not* on firm foundations, and the global economy appears precarious.

Of course, we can never be sure that the alternatives for which I argue here would have worked better. Perhaps if we had demanded a fairer deal with the banks, they would have been slower in returning to health. Almost surely, their shareholders and executives would have fared less well. But it is hard to believe that lending would have been more constrained than it has been. To my mind, there is absolutely no doubt that we could have put conditions on the bank rescue that would have led to more lending, a stronger recovery, and a better fiscal position for the United States. We could also have rescued the banks in a way that would have led to a more competitive banking system, rather than a less competitive one. And a more competitive banking system would have resulted in firms paying lower interest rates, and that too would have meant a more robust recovery.[66]

The choices that our government made were by no means the worst possible, but they were far from the best. The events since my book was first published have done little to allay the concerns that I raised at the time the rescue packages were put together. On the contrary, just as the crisis provided ample evidence that bank-friendly regulatory "reforms" of the 1990s and the early years of this century were a mistake, today's wavering recovery suggests that the bank-friendly rescue was a mistake—or at least far from ideal. The full consequences of these choices will not be known for years, but the events that have occurred since the publication of the hardcover edition of *Freefall* have reinforced the conclusions reached there, the criticisms of the bailout and the recovery program.

FUTURE PROSPECTS AND THE WAY FORWARD

As I emphasize in chapter 7, while the world dealt with the problems the global crisis posed, the long-run problems (the aging of the population, a dysfunctional health care and public education system, a manufacturing sector in rapid decline, global warming, an excessive dependence on oil) continued to fester. At the same time, the resources available for dealing with these problems became greatly diminished. While doing something meaningful about global warming would have provided a spur to the economic recovery, the failure to reach an agreement at Copenhagen in December 2009 that would have forced firms to pay an appropriate price for their carbon emissions added new uncertainty. While most believed that *eventually* they would have to pay, when and how much were not clear. And the response to such uncertainty is normally to postpone investments until the uncertainty is resolved.

To those in the United States (and elsewhere) opposed to doing anything about global warming, the continuing recession provided an excuse. The strategy of "muddling through" has had the predicted effect of sustaining only an anemic recovery, and that means it will be all the longer before the United States begins to effectively address this and the other longer-term issues. Many of these issues, like global warming, affect the entire world. And if the United States doesn't do a better job addressing them, it will be hard for it to exercise leadership in shaping global solutions. That, in turn, means that the issues are not likely to be addressed. We can pretend that global warming will go away, or that technology will somehow get us out of the box in which we have put ourselves. But this policy of pretend and extend will work no better for global warming than it did for economic recovery.

The fears I expressed more than a year ago—that the Bush and Obama strategies for rescuing the banks would not lead to a quick rekindling of lending, or a quick recovery to the economy—have been largely realized. The strategy of recapitalization through profits earned on high-interest loans funded by banks' access to low-interest-rate funds not only did not lead to a rapid recovery, but may even have extended the duration of a weak economy. Those who never thought there was a deep problem with the economy may have been convinced that such medicine, directed at relief of symptoms, might work. But others were not so gullible.

There is a sense that the Rooseveltian moment—a New Deal, rethinking capitalism, a new social contract—has largely passed. We will not return to the exact world as it was before the crisis, but neither have we enacted the kinds of reforms that would prevent another crisis. Given the pressure that Congress has been under from financial lobbyists, we should perhaps celebrate that it produced as good a bill as it did. But, in the end, that is not the test that matters. What counts is whether our economy is protected from another crisis, whether our citizens are protected from a recurrence of the abuses, and whether there is confidence that the financial sector will perform the societal functions for which it is so amply rewarded.

The cost for the United States of these failures will be high: not only does it face the risk of another major crisis within the next fifteen years, not only have the vast array of problems barely been addressed, but the divide between Wall Street and Main Street (both businesses and workers) has become wider, and with that growing divide, the sense of community and the ability to resolve common problems has become ever weaker.

Moreover, the country has lost the opportunity for moral and intellectual global leadership. The newly emerging global balance of power means that the United States will not be able to dictate the terms of the emerging world order. If it is to lead, it must be through moral suasion, by example and by the force of its arguments. The question today is, as it was at the time of *Freefall*'s original publication, would the United States offer that kind of leadership?[67] Or would partisanship and the internecine warfare between Wall Street and the rest of the country prevent it from doing so?

If the country cannot resolve its own problems in a way that the rest of the world believes is fair; if it cannot, with all of its wealth, even provide health care for all of its citizens; if it cannot, with all of its wealth, deliver quality education for all of its young; if it cannot, with all of its wealth, afford to spend the money required for the kind of modern infrastructure, energy, and transportation systems that global warming demands—then how can it provide advice to others on how they should resolve their problems?

The first decade of the twenty-first century is already being written down as a lost decade. For most Americans, income at the end of the decade was lower than at the beginning. Europe began the decade with a bold new experiment, the euro—an experiment that may now be faltering. On both sides of the Atlantic, the optimism of the beginning of the decade has been replaced with a new gloom. As the weeks of the downturn—the New Malaise—stretch into months, and the months become years, a new gray pallor casts its shadow.

At the time the hardcover edition was published, I wrote that muddling through would not work, and that it was still not too late to set an alternative course. We have continued to muddle through—in some areas, like regulatory reform, better than I had feared but worse than I had hoped; in others, like the creation of a new vision, my fears have been fully realized. It is still not too late. But the window of opportunity may be rapidly closing.

NOTES

Preface

1. Sharon LaFraniere, "China Puts Joblessness for Migrants at 20 Million," *New York Times*, February 2, 2009, p. A10. The Department of Economic and Social Affairs of the United Nations Secretariat estimates that between 73 and 103 million more people will remain poor or fall into poverty in comparison with a situation in which pre-crisis growth would have continued. United Nations, "World Economic Situation and Prospects 2009," May 2009, available at http://www.un.org/esa/policy/wess/wesp2009files/wesp09update.pdf. The International Labour Organization (ILO) estimates that global unemployment could increase by more than 50 million by the end of 2009, with some 200 million workers pushed back into extreme poverty. See Report of the Director-General, "Tackling the Global Jobs Crisis: Recovery through Decent Work Policies," presented at the International Labour Conference, June 2009, available at http://www.ilo.org/global/What_we_do/Officialmeetings/ilc/ILCSessions/98thSession/Reportssubmittedtotheconference/lang--en/docName--WCMS_106162/index.htm.

2. Alan Schwartz, who headed Bear Stearns, the first of the big investment banks to go under—but in a way that still cost taxpayers billions—was asked by the Senate Banking Committee if he thought he had made any mistakes: "I can guarantee you it's a subject I've thought about a lot. Looking backwards and with hindsight, saying, 'If I'd have known exactly the forces that were coming, what actions could we have taken beforehand to have avoided this situation?' And I just simply have not been able to come up with anything . . . that would have made a difference to the situation that we faced." Statement before the U.S. Senate Committee on Banking, Housing, and Urban Affairs, Hearing on "Tur-

moil in U.S. Credit Markets: Examining the Recent Actions of Federal Financial Regulators," Washington, DC, April 3, 2008.

3. Luc Laeven and Fabian Valencis, "Systemic Banking Crises: A New Database," International Monetary Fund Working Paper, WP/08/224, Washington, DC, November 2008.

4. George W. Bush suggested in an interview that "the economy is down because we've built too many houses." Interview with Ann Curry on the *Today Show*, NBC, February 18, 2008.

5. Bob Woodward, *Maestro: Greenspan's Fed and the American Boom* (New York: Simon and Schuster, 2000).

6. There is another explanation for the differences in policies: the United States and Europe acted in ways that responded to the interests of their electorates—the policies that were foisted on East Asia would have been unacceptable to Americans and Europeans. By the same token, in East Asia, the International Monetary Fund (IMF) and the U.S. Treasury were, in part at least, responding to the interests of their "constituencies," the creditors in their financial markets, which were focused on getting repaid what they had lent to these countries—even if doing so entailed socializing private obligations. For a more extensive discussion of these episodes, see Joseph E. Stiglitz, *Globalization and Its Discontents* (New York: W. W. Norton, 2002).

7. U.S. Department of Labor, Bureau of Labor Statistics, Consumer Price Index, All Urban Consumers, All Items, available at ftp://ftp.bls.gov/pub/special .requests/cpi/cpiai.txt.

8. See Susan S. Silbey, "Rotten Apples or a Rotting Barrel: Unchallengeable Orthodoxies in Science," paper presented at Arizona State University Law School, March 19–20, 2009. The fraction of those who contributed to the crisis, who crossed the line and engaged in illegal behavior, is small: they were well advised by their lawyers on how to stay out of prison, and their lobbyists worked hard to make sure that the laws gave them great latitude. Still, the list of those facing conviction is increasing. Allen Stanford faces up to 375 years in jail if convicted on twenty-one charges of multibillion-dollar fraud, money laundering, and obstruction. Stanford was aided by his chief financial officer, James Davis, who pleaded guilty to three counts of mail fraud, conspiracy to commit fraud, and conspiracy to obstruct an investigation. Two Credit Suisse brokers were charged with lying to customers—leading to losses of $900 million; one was convicted by a jury and one pleaded guilty.

9. There is an obvious retort: the circumstances differ. Were these countries to pursue expansionary fiscal policies, the effects would have been counterproductive (so went the argument). It is worth noting that the East Asian countries that followed the traditional Keynesian recipe (Malaysia and China) did far better than those that were forced to follow the IMF dictates. In order to have lower interest rates, Malaysia had to impose temporary restrictions on capital flows. But Malaysia's downturn was shorter and shallower than those of other East

Asian countries, and it emerged with less of a legacy of debt. See Ethan Kaplan and Dani Rodrik, "Did the Malaysian Capital Controls Work?" in S. Edwards and J. Frankel (eds.), *Preventing Currency Crises in Emerging Markets* (Boston: NBER, 2002).

10. To the list of international bailouts, we should add the "domestic" bailouts, where governments have had to bail out their own banks without turning to the assistance of others. In this long list, one should include the savings and loan debacle in the United States in the 1980s and the bank collapses in Scandinavia in the late 1980s and early 1990s.

11. The close cooperation between government and the private sector in Malaysia led many to refer to "Malaysia, Inc." With the crisis, discussions of government–private sector cooperation were relabeled as crony capitalism.

12. See Nicholas Lardy, *China's Unfinished Economic Revolution* (Washington, DC: Brookings Institution Press, 1998), for the standard interpretation. The irony that it was U.S. banks that collapsed, not those of China, has not escaped those on both sides of the Pacific.

13. The nation's output fell by an additional 10.9 percent in 2002 (relative to 2001) on top of an accumulated fall of 8.4 percent since its previous peak year (1998), for a total 18.4 percent loss of output and a decrease in per capita income of more than 23 percent. The crisis also caused a rise in joblessness to 26 percent in the wake of the enormous contraction of consumption, investment, and output. See Hector E. Maletta, "A Catastrophe Foretold: Economic Reform, Crisis, Recovery and Employment in Argentina," September 2007, available at http://ssrn.com/abstract=903124.

14. In a study of eight North American and European economies (United Kingdom, United States, West Germany, Canada, Norway, Denmark, Sweden, and Finland), the United States had the lowest intergenerational income mobility. The intergenerational partial correlation (a measure of immobility) of the United States is twice that of the Nordic countries. Only the United Kingdom comes close to having similar immobility. The study concludes that the "idea of the US as 'the land of opportunity' persists and clearly seems misplaced." See Jo Blanden, Paul Gregg, and Stephen Machin, "Intergenerational Mobility in Europe and North America," London School of Economics Centre for Economic Performance, April 2005, available at http://www.suttontrust.com/reports/Inter generationalMobility.pdf. French mobility also exceeds that of the United States. See Arnaud Lefranc and Alain Trannoy, "Intergenerational Earnings Mobility in France: Is France More Mobile than the US?" *Annales d'Économie et de Statistique*, no. 78 (April–June 2005), pp. 57–77.

15. The Program for International Student Assessment (PISA) is a system of international assessments that measures fifteen-year-olds' performance in reading literacy, mathematics literacy, and science literacy every three years. On average, U.S. students scored lower than the OECD average (the mean of the thirty

countries in the Organisation for Economic Co-operation and Development) on the combined science literacy scale (489 vs. 500) and the mathematics literacy scale (474 vs. 498). In science, U.S. students lagged behind sixteen of the other twenty-nine OECD countries; in math, they lagged behind twenty-three OECD countries. See S. Baldi, Y. Jin, M. Skemer, P. J. Green, and D. Herget, *Highlights from PISA 2006: Performance of U.S. 15-Year-Old Students in Science and Mathematics Literacy in an International Context* (NCES 2008-016) (U.S. Department of Education, Washington, DC: National Center for Education Statistics, December 2007).

Acknowledgments

1. The list of members of the Commission is available at http://www.un.org/ga/president/63/PDFs/reportofexpters.pdf.

Chapter One THE MAKING OF A CRISIS

1. See Milton Friedman and Anna Schwartz, *A Monetary History of the United States, 1867–1960* (Princeton: Princeton University Press, 1971), and Barry Eichengreen, *Golden Fetters: The Gold Standard and the Great Depression, 1919–1939* (Oxford: Oxford University Press, 1995).

2. From 2000 to 2008, real median household income (that is, adjusting for inflation) decreased by almost 4 percent. At the end of the last expansion, in 2007, incomes were still some 0.6 percent below the level attained before the end of the previous expansion, in 2000. See U.S. Census Bureau, "Income, Poverty, and Health Insurance Coverage in the United States: 2008," *Current Population Reports*, September 2009, available at http://www.census.gov/prod/2009pubs/p60-236.pdf.

3. James Kennedy, "Estimates of Mortgage Originations Calculated from Data on Loans Outstanding and Repayments" (not seasonally adjusted), November 2008, available at http://www.wealthscribe.com/wp-content/uploads/2008/11/equity-extraction-data-2008-q2.pdf. Updated estimates from Alan Greenspan and James Kennedy, "Estimates of Home Mortgage Originations, Repayments, and Debt on One-to-Four-Family Residences," Finance and Economics Discussion Series, Division of Research and Statistics and Monetary Affairs, Federal Reserve Board, Working Paper 2005-41, September 2005.

4. The tech bubble itself is another story, told more fully in Joseph E. Stiglitz, *Roaring Nineties: A New History of the World's Most Prosperous Decade* (New York: W. W. Norton, 2003).

5. The NASDAQ Composite Index (generally used as a measure of the perfor-

mance of technology stocks) closed at a high of 5,046.86 on March 9, 2000. On October 9, 2002, the NASDAQ Composite closed at a low of 1,114.11. Google Finance, NASDAQ Composite Historical Prices, available at http://www.google .com/finance/historical?q=INDEXNASDAQ:COMPX.

6. U.S. Energy Information Administration, "Petroleum Navigator" database, U.S. Imports of Crude Oil (Thousand Barrels per Day) [accessed on August 28, 2009] and Weekly All Countries Spot Price FOB Weighted by Estimated Export Volume (Dollars per Barrel) [accessed on September 2, 2009], available at http:// tonto.eia.doe.gov/dnav/pet/pet_pri_top.asp.

7. Alan Greenspan is often given credit for the era of low inflation, but many other countries around the world had low inflation—it was not a distinctively American phenomenon. The fact that China was supplying the world with manu-factured goods at low and even declining prices was one of the common critical factors.

8. How this could have happened is a matter of extensive debate. Part of the problem was that like any trading firm, they held "inventory." Part of the prob-lem too was that, in the complicated repackagings, they may have been fooled by their own calculations; they held on to some securities and absorbed some risk. Some of these were held off-balance sheet—they could record fees from the repackaging without recording the risks associated with the parts that had not been sold. Their incentives to engage in these off-balance-sheet activities are discussed in later chapters.

9. See Bureau of Economic Analysis, National Income and Product Accounts Table, "Table 6.16D. Corporate Profits by Industry," available at http://www.bea .gov/National/nipaweb/SelectTable.asp.

10. One of the standard arguments for why the market put such a low price on risk was that with interest rates on safe assets so low, the market clamored for assets with slightly higher yields, driving up the price of the assets and driv-ing down the returns. Some in Wall Street make a parallel argument: when the spread between the long rate and the short rate was reduced when the Federal Reserve raised its interest rates, beginning in June 2004, many said they "had" to take on more risk to get the earnings that they had previously had. That's like a robber saying in his defense, when honest ways of making a living disappeared, I had to turn to a life of crime. Regardless of the interest rate, investors should have insisted on adequate compensation for the risk borne. (The Fed raised the interest rate seventeen times by 25 basis points from June 2004 to June 2006, moving the intended federal funds rate from 1.25 percent to 5.25 percent over that period. Federal Reserve, "Intended Federal Funds Rate, Change and Level, 1990 to Present," December 16, 2008, available at http://www.federalreserve .gov/fomc/fundsrate.htm. During that period, the rate on ten-year U.S. Treasury bonds fell from 4.7 percent in June 2004 to as low as 3.9 percent in June 2005 before rising to 5.1 percent in June 2006. See 10-year Treasury Note, TNX, on

finance.yahoo.com. Thus, the yield curve flattened significantly and actually
inverted by June 2006.)

11. Alan Greenspan, "Understanding Household Debt Obligations," remarks at
the Credit Union National Association 2004 Governmental Affairs Conference,
Washington, DC, February 23, 2004, available at http://www.federalreserve.gov/
boarddocs/speeches/2004/20040223/default.htm. See also the discussion in
chapter 4.

12. Alan Greenspan, "The Fed Didn't Cause the Housing Bubble," *Wall Street
Journal*, March 11, 2009, p. A15.

13. The Fed normally focuses its attention on short-term government interest
rates, allowing the market to determine long-term interest rates. But this is a self-
imposed restraint: during the crisis, the Fed showed its ability and willingness to
determine other interest rates.

14. Community Reinvestment Act (CRA) loans perform comparably to other
subprime loans. In fact, loans originated under NeighborWorks America, a
typical CRA program, had a lower delinquency rate than subprime loans. See
Glenn Canner and Neil Bhutta, "Staff Analysis of the Relationship between
the CRA and the Subprime Crisis," memorandum, Board of Governors of the
Federal Reserve System, Division of Research and Statistics, November 21,
2008, available at http://www.federalreserve.gov/newsevents/speech/20081203_
analysis.pdf, and Randall S. Kroszner, "The Community Reinvestment Act and
the Recent Mortgage Crisis," speech at Confronting Concentrated Poverty Policy
Forum, December 3, 2008, available at http://www.federalreserve.gov/newsevents/
speech/kroszner20081203a.htm.

15. Freddie Mac purchased a total of $158 billion, or 13 percent, of all sub-
prime and Alt-A securities created in 2006 and 2007, and Fannie Mae purchased
an additional 5 percent. The biggest suppliers of the securities to Fannie and
Freddie included Countrywide Financial Corp. of Calabasas, California, as well
as Irvine, California–based New Century Financial Corp. and Ameriquest Mortgage Co., lenders that either went bankrupt or were forced to sell themselves.
Fannie and Freddie were the biggest buyers of loans from Countrywide, according to the company. See Jody Shenn, "Fannie, Freddie Subprime Spree May Add
to Bailout," *Bloomberg.com*, September 22, 2009.

16. One reason why the financial sector may have failed to perform its critical
social functions is that those in the sector didn't understand what they were.
But in a well-functioning market economy, markets are supposed to provide the
incentives that lead individuals to do what is in society's interest, even if individual market participants may not understand what that is.

17. Adolf Berle and Gardiner Means emphasized the separation of ownership and
control in their classic book, *The Modern Corporation and Private Property* (New
York: Harcourt, Brace and World, 1932), seventy-eight years ago, but since then
matters have become much worse, with so much of savings generated by pension

funds. Those who manage these funds typically do not even attempt to exercise control over the behavior of the firm. John Maynard Keynes worried extensively about the shortsighted behavior of investors. He suggested that they were much like a judge in a beauty contest, trying to judge not who was the most beautiful person but who others would think was (chapter 12 of *General Theory of Employment Interest and Money* [Cambridge, UK: Macmillan Cambridge University Press, 1936]). Again, matters have almost surely become worse since he wrote. Some of my own research helped put Berle and Means's theory on sounder theoretical grounds. See J. E. Stiglitz, "Credit Markets and the Control of Capital," *Journal of Money, Banking, and Credit*, vol. 17, no. 2 (May 1985), pp. 133–152, and A. Edlin and J. E. Stiglitz, "Discouraging Rivals: Managerial Rent-Seeking and Economic Inefficiencies," *American Economic Review*, vol. 85, no. 5 (December 1995), pp. 1301–1312.

18. The seasonally adjusted rate of "Total unemployed, plus all marginally attached workers plus total employed part time for economic reasons, as a percent of all civilian labor force plus all marginally attached workers" was 17.5 percent in October 2009. Bureau of Labor Statistics, "Current Population Survey: Labor Force Statistics, Table U-6," available at http://www.bls.gov/news.release/empsit.t12.htm.

19. Statement of Ben S. Bernanke, Chairman, Board of Governors of the Federal Reserve System, before the Joint Economic Committee, U.S. Congress, Washington, DC, March 28, 2007.

20. Buyers and sellers of mortgages failed to recognize that if interest rates rose or the economy went into recession, the housing bubble might break, and most would be in trouble. That is precisely what happened. As I note below, securitization also created problems of information asymmetries, attenuating incentives for good credit assessments. See Joseph E. Stiglitz, "Banks versus Markets as Mechanisms for Allocating and Coordinating Investment," in J. Roumasset and S. Barr (eds.), *The Economics of Cooperation* (Boulder, CO: Westview Press, 1992).

21. In the years immediately preceding the crisis, as noted earlier, domestic demand had also been weakened by high oil prices. The problems of high oil prices and growing inequality—reducing domestic aggregate demand—afflicted many other countries. Income inequality increased in more than three-quarters of OECD countries from the mid-1980s to the mid-2000s, and the past five years saw growing poverty and inequality in two-thirds of OECD countries. See Organisation for Economic Co-operation and Development (OECD), *Growing Unequal? Income Distribution and Poverty in OECD Countries*, Paris, October 2008.

22. In *Globalization and Its Discontents* (op. cit.), I explain more fully the reasons for this discomfort: the IMF's policies (often based on the flawed market fundamentalism that I have discussed in this chapter) led downturns into recessions, recessions into depression, and imposed unpalatable (and often unnecessary) structural and macro-policies that impeded growth and contributed to poverty and inequality.

23. Daniel O. Beltran, Laurie Pounder, and Charles P. Thomas, "Foreign Exposure to Asset-Backed Securities of U.S. Origin," Board of Governors of the Federal Reserve System, International Finance Discussion Paper 939, August 1, 2008. At the same time, foreign purchases of U.S. mortgages and mortgage-backed products fueled the bubble.

24. As I explain later, the issue is more complex, since the supply of foreign funds may itself have fed the bubble.

25. To be fair, some other countries (such as the United Kingdom under Margaret Thatcher) had bought into the deregulatory philosophy on their own. For later U.K. governments, "light regulation" was used as a competitive instrument to attract financial firms. In the end, the country surely lost more than it gained.

26. "An Astonishing Rebound," *Economist*, August 13, 2009, p. 9.

27. In spite of its efforts, lending in the United Kingdom remained constricted. It is not easy to determine precisely what "fair value" means. But it entails receiving enough of the shares (claims on the future income of the banks) to compensate the government for the money provided and the risk borne. As I note later, a careful study of the U.S. bailout has shown that the U.S. taxpayer did not get fair value.

28. See Joseph E. Stiglitz, "Monetary and Exchange Rate Policy in Small Open Economies: The Case of Iceland," Central Bank of Iceland, Working Paper 15, November 2001, available at http://www.sedlabanki.is/uploads/files/WP-15.pdf.

29. Willem H. Buiter and Anne Sibert, "The Icelandic Banking Crisis and What to Do about It: The Lender of Last Resort Theory of Optimal Currency Areas," Centre for Economic Policy Research (CEPR) Policy Insight 26, October 2008, available at http://www.cepr.org/pubs/PolicyInsights/PolicyInsight26.pdf.

30. Britain turned to the International Monetary Fund (IMF) for help in 1976.

31. The total combined foreign liabilities of Iceland's banks were in excess of $100 billion, dwarfing the country's GDP of $14 billion. "Iceland Agrees Emergency Legislation," *Times Online (UK)*, October 6, 2008, available at http://www.timesonline.co.uk/tol/news/world/europe/article4889832.ece. Iceland's parliament passed legislation in late August 2009 to repay the United Kingdom and the Netherlands about $6 billion that those governments had given depositors who lost money in Icelandic savings accounts during the financial crisis. See Matthew Saltmarsh, "Iceland to Repay Nations for Failed Banks' Deposits," *New York Times*, August 29, 2009, p. B2. However, the United Kingdom and the Netherlands objected to terms in the law that the repayment guarantee ran out in 2024. Iceland agreed to a new deal in October 2009 which said that if the money is not repaid by 2024, the guarantee will be extended in five-year blocks. The release of IMF funds to Iceland had been held up by the disagreement on the repayment. See "Iceland Presents Amended Icesave Bill, Eyes IMF Aid," Reuters, October 20, 2009.

32. Capital market liberalization meant allowing short-term money to flow

freely into and out of the country. One can't build factories and schools with such hot money; but such hot money can wreak havoc on an economy. Financial market liberalization entails opening up an economy to foreign financial institutions. There is increasing evidence that foreign banks do less lending to small and medium-sized enterprises and, in some instances, respond more strongly to global shocks (like the current crisis), thereby generating more volatility. There is also evidence that capital market integration did not lead to reduced volatility and higher growth in the manner expected. See Eswar Prasad, Kenneth Rogoff, Shang-Jin Wei, and M. Ayhan Kose, "Effects of Financial Globalisation on Developing Countries: Some Empirical Evidence," *Economic and Political Weekly*, vol. 38, no. 41 (October 2003), pp. 4319–4330; M. Ayhan Kose, Eswar S. Prasad, and Marco E. Terrones, "Financial Integration and Macroeconomic Volatility," *IMF Staff Papers*, vol. 50 (Special Issue, 2003), pp. 119–142; Hamidur Rashid, "Evidence of Financial Disintermediation in Low Income Countries: Role of Foreign Banks," Ph.D. dissertation, Columbia University, New York, 2005; and Enrica Detragiache, Thierry Tressel, and Poonam Gupta, "Foreign Banks in Poor Countries: Theory and Evidence," International Monetary Fund Working Paper 06/18, Washington, DC, 2006.

Chapter 2 FREEFALL AND ITS AFTERMATH

1. There is an apocryphal story that John Kenneth Galbraith, one of the great economists of the twentieth century, and author of the classic book *The Great Crash* (New York: Houghton Mifflin, 1955), was once asked when the next depression would occur. His prophetic answer: fifteen years after the first president who was born after the Great Depression.

2. See Richard Wolf, "Bush Mixes Concern, Optimism on Economy," *USA Today*, March 23, 2008, p. 7A.

3. In a survey ascertaining what recipients would do with their tax rebates, only one-fifth of respondents said the rebates would lead them to increase spending; most respondents said they would either mostly save the rebate or mostly use it to repay debt. The survey estimates imply that only 30 to 40 percent of the rebate went to increased spending. See Matthew D. Shapiro and Joel Slemrod, "Did the 2008 Tax Rebates Stimulate Spending?" *American Economic Review*, vol. 99, no. 2 (May 2009), pp. 374–379.

4. At the time, Bear Stearns said its book value was more than $80 per share. In March 2007, a year earlier, Bear Stearns shares had sold for $150 each. See Robin Sidel, Dennis K. Berman, and Kate Kelly, "J.P. Morgan Buys Bear in Fire Sale, as Fed Widens Credit to Avert Crisis," *Wall Street Journal*, March 17, 2008, p. A1.

5. Citibank got a cash injection of $25 billion in October 2008 (along with eight other banks, as part of the Troubled Asset Relief Program, or TARP), was rescued

again with another $20 billion in cash plus guarantees for $306 billion in toxic assets in November 2008, and then got helped a third time, when the government converted $25 billion of its preferred shares to common stock in February 2009. AIG also received three bailouts, including a $60 billion credit line, an investment of as much as $70 billion, and $52.5 billion to buy mortgage-linked assets owned or backed by AIG.

6. The stimulus bill that was eventually passed in February 2009, the American Recovery and Reinvestment Act, included more than $60 billion in clean-energy investments: $11 billion for a bigger, better, and smarter electrical grid that will move electricity derived from renewable energy from the rural places where it is produced to the cities where it is mostly used, as well as for 40 million smart electric meters to be deployed in American homes; $5 billion for low-income home weatherization projects; $4.5 billion to make federal buildings green and cut the government's energy bill; $6.3 billion for state and local renewable energy and energy-efficiency efforts; $600 million in green job–training programs; and $2 billion in competitive grants to develop the next generation of batteries to store energy.

7. Barack Obama, "Renewing the American Economy," speech at Cooper Union, New York, March 27, 2008.

8. Trade Statistics of Japan Ministry of Finance, General Trade Statistics, Yearly and Monthly Data for Total Value of Exports and Imports, September 2009, available at http://www.customs.go.jp/toukei/srch/indexe.htm?M=27&P=0, and German Federal Statistical Office, "German Exports in June 2009: –22.3% on June 2008," Press Release No. 290, August 7, 2009, available at http://www.de statis.de/jetspeed/portal/cms/Sites/destatis/Internet/EN/press/pr/2009/08/PE09 __290__51,templateId=renderPrint.psml.

9. Home prices fell beginning in July 2006 through April 2009, but even when they stabilized, it was not clear the extent this was the result of temporary government programs—the Fed's unorthodox interventions to lower mortgage rates and the program to help first-time homebuyers. Forty-eight states faced budget shortfalls, totaling 26 percent of state budgets, forcing forty-two states to lay off workers and forty-one states to reduce services to residents. See Standard & Poor's, "The Pace of Home Price Declines Moderate in April according to the S&P/Case-Shiller Home Price Indices," press release, New York, June 30, 2009, and Elizabeth McNichol and Nicholas Johnson, "Recession Continues to Batter State Budgets; State Responses Could Slow Recovery," Center for Budget and Policy Priorities, October 20, 2009, available at http://www.cbpp.org/files/9-8-08sfp.pdf.

10. After the stress test, several banks were required to get more capital, which they succeeded in doing. Remarkably, though the stress test was not very stressful, it did seem to restore a certain degree of confidence to the market.

11. Bureau of Economic Analysis, National Income and Product Accounts,

"Table 2.1. Personal Income and Its Disposition (Seasonally adjusted at annual rates)," available at http://www.bea.gov/national/nipaweb/TableView.asp?Selected Table=58&Freq=Qtr&FirstYear=2007&LastYear=2009.

12. From Chrystia Freeland, "'First Do No Harm' Prescription Issued for Wall Street," *Financial Times*, April 29, 2009, p. 4.

13. "New Citi Chair: Bankers Aren't 'Villains,'" *CBS News.com*, April 7, 2009.

14. Anonymous, "Confessions of a TARP Wife," Conde Naste Portfolio, May 2009, available at http://www.portfolio.com/executives/2009/04/21/Confessions-of-a-Bailout-CEO-Wife/.

15. Bailouts in developing countries tend to lead to an appreciation of the exchange rate from what it otherwise would be. One of the main ways that economies recover is through increased exports, but higher exchange rates impede exports and therefore recovery. The Mexican bailout of 1994 may have had little to do with that country's recovery and may have impeded it. See D. Lederman, A. M. Menéndez, G. Perry, and J. E. Stiglitz, "Mexican Investment after the Tequila Crisis: Basic Economics, 'Confidence' Effects or Market Imperfections?" *Journal of International Money and Finance*, vol. 22 (2003), pp. 131–151.

16. Elizabeth Mcquerry, "The Banking Sector Rescue in Mexico," *Federal Reserve Bank of Atlanta Economic Review*, Third Quarter, 1999.

17. Many other factors also contributed to Mexico's poor performance over the ensuing decade. See Lederman, Menéndez, Perry, and Stiglitz, "Mexican Investment after the Tequila Crisis," op. cit., and chapter 3, "Making Trade Fair," in Joseph E. Stiglitz, *Making Globalization Work* (New York: W. W. Norton, 2006).

18. Robert Weissman and James Donahue, "Sold Out: How Wall Street and Washington Betrayed America," Consumer Education Foundation, March 2009, available at http://wallstreetwatch.org/reports/sold_out.pdf.

19. In 1953, Charlie Wilson, president of GM, famously said, "For years I thought what was good for the country was good for General Motors and vice versa." U.S. Department of Defense, bio of Charles E. Wilson, available at http://www.defenselink.mil/specials/secdef_histories/bios/wilson.htm.

20. The financial markets had done exactly that after the global financial crisis of 1997–1998. At the time, there was much talk of reforming the global financial architecture. Talk continued until the crisis was over and interests in reforms waned. Rather than putting in place new regulations, the government continued deregulating apace. It is obvious that little was done—too little to prevent another crisis.

21. Ben Bernanke took office in February 2006, and subprime lending intensity (subprime loans originated as a percentage of all loans originated) continued to rise in the ensuing months, peaking in the middle of 2006. Major Coleman IV, Michael LaCour-Little, and Kerry D. Vandell, "Subprime Lending and the Housing Bubble: Tail Wags Dog?" *Journal of Housing Economics*, vol. 17, no. 4 (December 2008), pp. 272–290.

22. "There are a few things that suggest, at a minimum, there's a little froth in this market," Greenspan said. While "we don't perceive that there is a national bubble," he said that "it's hard not to see that there are a lot of local bubbles." Edmund L. Andrews, "Greenspan Is Concerned about 'Froth' in Housing," *New York Times*, May 21, 2005, p. A1.

23. Citigroup, Quarterly Financial Data Supplement, October 16, 2008, available at http://www.citibank.com/citi/fin/data/qer083s.pdf.

24. Editorial, "Mr. Obama's Economic Advisers," *New York Times*, November 25, 2008, p. A30.

25. See Joe Hagan, "Tenacious G," *New York Magazine*, August 3, 2009, p. 28. See also Gretchen Morgenson, "Time to Unravel the Knot of Credit-Default Swaps," *New York Times*, January 24, 2009, p. A1.

26. It is noteworthy that Mervyn King, governor of the Bank of England, has supported the view that if banks are too big to fail, they are too big to exist—or at least need to be very restricted in what they can do. Speech delivered at the Lord Mayor's Banquet for Bankers and Merchants of the City of London at the Mansion House, June 17, 2009, available at http://www.bankofengland.co.uk/publications/speeches/2009/speech394.pdf, and Speech delivered to Scottish business organizations, Edinburgh, October 20, 2009, available at http://www.bankofengland.co.uk/publications/speeches/2009/speech406.pdf.

27. U.S. banks receiving $163 billion in bailout money planned to pay out more than $80 billion in dividends during the subsequent three years, with government permission. Some banks paid more in dividends than they received in assistance from the government. Binyamin Appelbaum, "Banks to Continue Paying Dividends," *Washington Post*, October 30, 2008, p. A1. Nine banks receiving government assistance paid more than $33 billion in bonuses, including more than $1 million apiece to nearly five thousand employees. Susanne Craig and Deborah Solomon, "Bank Bonus Tab: $33 Billion," *Wall Street Journal*, July 31, 2009, p. A1.

28. There was ample justification for worry about economic collapse, and because the economy was in uncharted territories, no one could be sure of the consequences of any action government might take. Not surprisingly, the banks wanted big checks from the government, and they alleged anything less risked trauma. But, as I explain at greater length later in the text, the rationale put forward for the "blank check" approach was unpersuasive, especially so because in the end the government provided guarantees to virtually anyone who could have responded adversely (e.g., suppliers of short-term funds). Long-term bondholders might be unhappy, but, by definition, they couldn't pull their money out. The Obama administration was afraid that if one didn't treat suppliers of capital to banks gingerly, finance would not be forthcoming in the future. This was a particularly absurd conclusion—capital will go to where there are returns. And if the private sector wouldn't supply it, the government had more than shown its capac-

ity to do so. The private sector had demonstrated its incompetence in managing risk and capital; government couldn't have done worse—and likely would have done better. Government would not have perverse incentives but would be constrained by accountability from engaging in predatory practices.

There were risks of litigation—risks that would be there no matter what was done. Litigation risk may have been especially important in explaining the handling of credit default swaps, though almost surely, congressional action could have limited it.

29. A U.S. district judge gave the Federal Reserve five days to turn over records that identify the companies receiving money through its emergency lending programs. Mark Pittman, "Court Orders Fed to Disclose Emergency Bank Loans," *Bloomberg.com*, August 25, 2009, at http://www.bloomberg.com/apps/news?pid=20601087&sid=a7CC61ZsieV4. On September 30, 2009, the Fed filed a notice that it would appeal the judge's order. See Mark Pittman, "Federal Reserve Appeals Court Order to Disclose Loans," *Bloomberg.com*, September 30, 2009, available at http://www.bloomberg.com/apps/news?pid=20601087&sid=aSab0xkcV8jc. The U.S. Court of Appeals in Manhattan upheld the August 2009 decision that the Fed must disclose its documents. David Glovin and Bob Van Voris, "Federal Reserve Must Disclose Bank Bailout Records," *Bloomberg.com*, 19 March 2010, http://www.bloomberg.com/apps/news?pid=20601087&sid=aUpIaeiWKF2s.

30. This was not the first attempt to circumvent Congress to help Wall Street. After Congress refused to go along with the Clinton administration's request for funding Wall Street investors in Mexican bonds (in what came to be called the Mexican bailout), Robert Rubin turned to the Exchange Stabilization Fund, created in 1934 for a quite different purpose. Congress created the fund to stabilize the value of the dollar during an unsettled period in international finance, when Great Britain had gone off the gold standard and was depreciating the pound in order to gain a competitive advantage in international trade. See J. Lawrence Broz, "Congressional Politics of International Financial Rescues," *American Journal of Political Science*, vol. 49, no. 3 (July 2005), pp. 479–496, and Anna J. Schwartz, "From Obscurity to Notoriety: A Biography of the Exchange Stabilization Fund," *Journal of Money, Credit and Banking*, vol. 29 (May 1997), pp. 135–153.

31. Parsing the 3.5 percent growth of the third quarter of 2009 that marked the end of recession points out the problems: 1.6 percent, just under half, was due to the expired "cash for clunker" program (see chapter 3); half of the remaining 1.9 percent was generated through rebuilding of inventories.

32. See *Economic Report of the President* (Washington, DC: U.S. Government Printing Office, 1996).

33. Stijn Claessens, M. Ayhan Kose, and Marco E. Terrones, "What Happens During Recessions, Crunches and Busts?," *Economic Policy*, vol. 24 (October 2009), pp. 653–700.

34. Based on a survey by pay consultant Johnson Associates. While traders' bonuses are expected to increase 60 percent, those of investment bankers are expected to rise only 15 to 20 percent. Pay at the seven companies that received extraordinary government support will, however, be limited. See Eric Dash, "Some Wall Street Year-End Bonuses Could Hit Pre-Downturn Highs," *New York Times*, November 5, 2009, p. B3.

Chapter Three A FLAWED RESPONSE

1. Some economists argue that multipliers may be even larger than these numbers suggest because the boost in spending adds to consumer confidence (a "confidence multiplier"). If stimulus spending reduces unemployment, and the reduced unemployment reduces workers' anxieties, they might be induced to spend more, and the overall effect on the economy will be even greater. This is one of the arguments for careful timing and targeting: if the stimulus proves to be less effective than promised, there can be a "negative confidence multiplier." While those in finance put a great deal of stress on "confidence," standard economic models do not; these emphasize "real variables," like unemployment and real wages. Moreover, the efficacy of fiscal stimulus is higher when the interest rate is reaching its lower bound of zero, as in the United States in the recent crisis, and the short-run fiscal multiplier may be substantially bigger than 1.6. See, e.g., L. Christiano, M. Eichenbaum, and Sergio Rebelo, "When Is the Government Spending Multiplier Large?" NBER Working Paper 15394, October 2009, available at http://www.nber.org/papers/w15394.

2. Some estimates put the multiplier of an extension of unemployment insurance benefits at 1.6. See Martin Schindler, Antonio Spilimbergo, and Steve Symansky, "Fiscal Multipliers," International Monetary Fund Staff Position Note, SPN/09/11, May 20, 2009.

3. From 1999 to 2006, the last year before the bubble broke, average income increased 4.6 percent for the top 5 percent of Americans, while median income fell by 1 percent. U.S. Census Bureau, Historical Income Tables, Tables H-3 and H-6, 2008, available at http://www.census.gov/hhes/www/income/histinc/inch htoc.html.

4. The inequities associated with the bank bailouts that protected bondholders are especially large, as the banks' bonds and shares became viewed as highly risky—too risky to be held by pension funds and others looking for safety—and many got bought up by hedge funds and other speculators.

5. Christina Romer and Jared Bernstein, "The Job Impact of the American Recovery and Reinvestment Plan," Council of Economic Advisers, January 9, 2009, available at http://otrans.3cdn.net/ee40602f9a7d8172b8_ozm6bt5oi.pdf.

6. Bureau of Labor Statistics, "Employment Level (Seasonally Adjusted),"

Labor Force Statistics, Current Population Survey, November 2009, available at http://data.bls.gov/cgi-bin/surveymost?ln. A little more than six months into the program, the administration claimed that their expenditure programs had created a modest 640,000 jobs. Elizabeth Williamson and Louise Radnofsky, "Stimulus Created 640,000 Jobs, White House Says," *Wall Street Journal*, October 31, 2009, p. A5.

7. See also Paul Krugman, "Averting the Worse," *New York Times*, August 10, 2009, p. A17. As I note below, this underestimates the scale of the problem, because of the large numbers of people who have been forced into part-time jobs because no full-time jobs are available.

8. Federal Reserve Bank of Philadelphia, "Forecasters See the Expansion Continuing," Fourth Quarter 2009 Survey of Professional Forecasters, November 16, 2009, available at http://www.phil.frb.org/research-and-data/real-time-center/survey-of-professional-forecasters/2009/survq409.cfm.

9. Officially, the broader measure of unemployment goes back to 1994, but the *New York Times*, working with the Labor Department, extended the series back to 1970. The October 2009 rate was the highest "since at least 1970 and most likely since the Great Depression." David Leonhardt, "Jobless Rate Hits 10.2%, with More Underemployed," *New York Times*, November 7, 2009, p. A1.

By October 2009, the proportion of working-age people who either have jobs or are actively looking for one was 65.5 percent, the lowest in twenty-two years. Bureau of Labor Statistics, Current Population Survey, "Table U-6. Total Unemployed, Plus All Marginally Attached Workers, Plus Total Employed Part Time for Economic Reasons, as a Percent of the Civilian Labor Force Plus All Marginally Attached Workers," September 2009, available at http://www.bls.gov/news.release/empsit.t12.htm.

10. Current Population Survey, Unemployment Statistics, Table A2, Bureau of Labor Statistics, November 6, 2009, available at http://www.bls.gov/news.release/pdf/empsit.pdf, and Table 3, Civilian Labor Force and Unemployment by State and Selected Area (seasonally adjusted). Regional and State Employment and Unemployment, Labor Force Data, Bureau of Labor Statistics, November 20, 2009, available at http://www.bls.gov/news.release/pdf/empsit.pdf.

11. See Conor Dougherty, "The Long Slog: Out of Work, Out of Hope," *Wall Street Journal*, September 23, 2009, p. A1.

12. In October 2009, 35 percent of people unemployed have been out of a job for twenty-seven weeks or longer, the highest since World War II. June 2009 was also the first month since the government began collecting data, in 1948, that more than half of unemployed people had been out of work for at least fifteen weeks. Bureau of Labor Statistics, "Table A-12. Unemployed Persons by Duration of Employment, seasonally adjusted," October 2009, available at http://www.bls.gov/web/cpseea12.pdf. See also, Floyd Norris, "In the Unemployment Line, and Stuck There," *New York Times*, July 11, 2009, p. B3.

13. Bureau of Economic Analysis, Industry Economic Accounts, GDP by Industry Accounts, "Value Added by Industry as a Percentage of GDP," April 28, 2009.

14. Adjusting for demographics, the 2009 fourth quarter unemployment rate was 11.3 percent, compared to an unadjusted rate of 10.0 percent. Marianna Kudlyak, Devin Reilly, and Stephen Slivinski, "Comparing Labor Markets Across Recession: A Focus on the Age Composition of the Population," Federal Reserve Bank of Richmond Economic Brief EB10-04, April 2010, http://www.richmond fed.org/publications/research/economic_brief/2010/pdf/eb_10-04.pdf.

15. Bureau of Labor Statistics, Job Openings and Labor Turnover Survey, available at http://data.bls.gov/cgi-bin/surveymost?jt, and Labor Force Statistics Current Population Survey, available at http://data.bls.gov/cgi-bin/surveymost?ln.

16. Bureau of Labor Statistics, Current Employment Statistics Survey, "Employment, Hours, and Earnings: Average Weekly Hours of Production Workers," available at http://data.bls.gov/cgi-bin/surveymost?ce.

17. For private workers, participation in defined contribution programs grew to 43 percent in 2009 from 36 percent in 1999, while participation in defined benefit programs remained stable at around 20 percent. Overall participation in some retirement plans increased to 51 percent in 2009 from 48 percent in 1999 (note that some workers participate in both types of retirement programs). Bureau of Labor Statistics, National Compensation Survey of Employee Benefits, "Table 2. Retirement Benefits: Access, Participation, and Take-up Rates, Private Industry Workers, National Compensation Survey," March 2009, available at http://www .bls.gov/ncs/ebs/benefits/2009/ownership/private/table02a.pdf.

18. A Pew Research survey reported that nearly 40 percent of workers over the age of sixty-two have delayed retirement because of the recession. Among workers ages fifty to sixty-one, 63 percent say they might have to push back their expected retirement date because of current economic conditions. Pew Research Center, "America's Changing Workforce: Recession Turns a Graying Office Grayer," Social and Demographic Trends Project, Washington, DC, September 3, 2009.

19. I had called for a much larger stimulus, as had, reportedly, Christina Romer, the chairman of Obama's Council of Economic Advisers (who suggested more than $1.2 trillion). The president was confronted by his economic team with only two choices: the $890 billion package or one that was somewhat smaller, around $550 billion. See Ryan Lizza, "Inside the Crisis," The New Yorker, October 12, 2009, available at http://www.newyorker.com/reporting/2009/10/12/091012fa_fact_lizza.

20. Elizabeth McNichol and Iris J. Lav, "New Fiscal Year Brings No Relief from Unprecedented State Budget Problems," Center on Budget and Policy Priorities, Washington, DC, September 3, 2009, available at http://www.cbpp.org/files/9-8-08sfp.pdf.

21. Jordan Rau and Evan Halper, "New State Budget Gap Is Forecast," Los Angeles Times, March 14, 2009, p. A1.

22. The White House, Office of the Press Secretary, "New Recipient Reports Confirm Recovery Act Has Created Saved over One Million Jobs Nationwide," press release, October 30, 2009, available at http://www.whitehouse.gov/the-press-office/new-recipient-reports-confirm-recovery-act-has-created-saved-over-one-million-jobs-.

23. Bureau of Labor Statistics, "All Employees (Sector: Government), Employment, Hours, and Earnings from the Current Employment Statistics survey (National)," November 10, 2009, available at http://data.bls.gov/PDQ/outside.jsp?survey=ce.

24. With these exceptional measures, plus the basic state-level benefits of 26 weeks, total unemployment benefits ranged from 60 to 99 weeks by the end of 2009, depending on the state-level unemployment rate. See National Employment Law Project, "Senate Extends Jobless Benefits 14–20 Weeks." Washington, DC, November 4, 2009, available at http://www.nelp.org/page/-/UI/PR.SenateExtensionVote.pdf?nocdn=1.

25. Despite the extensions by Congress, if the American Recovery and Reinvestment Act is not reauthorized in December 2009, 1 million unemployed will lose their benefits during January 2010 and 3 million will be left without federal benefits between January and March of 2010. National Employment Law Project, "NELP Analysis: 1 Million Workers Will Lose Jobless Benefits in January if Congress Fails to Reauthorize ARRA," Washington, DC, November 18, 2009, available at http://nelp.3cdn.net/596480c76efd6ef8e3_pjm6bhepv.pdf.

26. The Obama administration tried to design the tax cut in such a way as to encourage more spending. Rather than a one-time rebate, they lowered withholding rates, hoping that households, seeing a little more money in their take-home pay, would be tricked into spending more. Spending increased a little bit, but less than the advocates of the tax cut had hoped. See also John Cogan, John B. Taylor, and Volker Weiland, "The Stimulus Didn't Work," *Wall Street Journal*, September 17, 2009, available at: http://online.wsj.com/article/SB10001424052970204731 80457438523386703644.html.

27. See, for instance, Amity Shlaes, *The Forgotten Man: A New History of the Great Depression* (New York: HarperCollins, 2007), and Jim Powell, *FDR's Folly: How Roosevelt and His New Deal Prolonged the Great Depression* (New York: Crown Forum, 2003).

28. Keynesian economics had been repeatedly put to the test—and, by and large, proved correct. The most dramatic tests were those conducted by the International Monetary Fund (IMF) in East Asia and elsewhere, where, instead of responding to the crises by expansionary monetary and fiscal policies, the IMF had done just the opposite. The marked contractions in the economy were just what Keynesian economics had predicted.

29. The Federal Reserve's assets (which include holdings of mortgages, T-bills, etc.) increased from $900 billion in August 2008 to over $2.2 trillion in December 2008. The Fed normally buys just T-bills (short-term government debt). As

the Fed tried to affect long-term rates and mortgage rates, it purchased a wide spectrum of products, in what is sometimes called quantitative easing.

30. As we should realize by now, markets are not always so smart. Many in the financial markets seem to look only at the liability side of the government's balance sheet, never at the asset side.

31. See chapter 8 for a more extensive discussion of the global reserve system and how it has to be reformed.

Chapter 4 THE MORTGAGE SCAM

1. Over 4 million became homeowners during the housing rush—but by the third quarter of 2009, the percentage of those owning a home (67.6 percent) was little different from that in 2000 (67.4 percent). U.S. Census Bureau, Housing and Household Economic Statistics Division, "Housing Vacancies and Homeownership: Table 14, Third Quarter 2009," available at http://www.census.gov/hhes/www/housing/hvs/historic/index.html.

2. From 2001 to 2007, the number of severely burdened households (paying more than 50 percent of income on housing) alone surged by more than 4 million. Joint Center for Housing Studies of Harvard University, *The State of the Nation's Housing 2009*, June 22, 2009, available at http://www.jchs.harvard.edu/son/index.htm.

3. Joe Weisenthal, "Dick Parsons: Don't Just Blame the Bankers," *Business Insider*, April 7, 2009, available at http://www.businessinsider.com/dick-parsons-dont-just-blame-the-bankers-2009-4.

4. Abby Aguirre, "The Neediest Cases: After a Nightmare of Refinancing, Hope," *New York Times*, November 8, 2008, p. A47.

5. Peter J. Boyer, "Eviction; The Day They Came for Addie Polk's House," *The New Yorker*, November 24, 2008, p. 48.

6. RealtyTrac, "US Foreclosure Activity Increases 75 Percent in 2007," press release, January 29, 2008, and "Foreclosure Activity Increases 81 Percent in 2008," press release, January 15, 2009, available at http://www.realtytrac.com/contentmanagement/.

7. Sonia Garrison, Sam Rogers, and Mary L. Moore, "Continued Decay and Shaky Repairs: The State of Subprime Loans Today," Center for Responsible Lending, Washington, DC, January 2009, available at http://www.responsiblelending.org/mortgage-lending/research-analysis/continued_decay_and_shaky_repairs.pdf; Editorial, "Holding Up the Housing Recovery," *New York Times*, April 24, 2009, p. A26; and Credit Suisse, "Foreclosure Update: Over 8 Million Foreclosures Expected," Fixed Income Research, December 4, 2008, available at http://www.chapa.org/pdf/ForeclosureUpdateCreditSuisse.pdf. As of March 2009, 5.4 million American homeowners holding a mortgage, nearly 12 percent,

were at least one month behind in their payment or in foreclosure at the end of 2008, according to the Mortgage Bankers Association. FBI, *2008 Mortgage Fraud Report*, "Year in Review," available at http://www.fbi.gov/publications/fraud/mortgage_fraud08.htm, pp. 11–12.

8. Matt Apuzzo, "Banks Torpedoed Rules That Could Have Saved Them," Associated Press, December 1, 2008, available at http://www.usatoday.com/money/economy/housing/2008-12-01-ap-report-lenders_N.htm. Others also saw what was going on and could not countenance it, but they were a small minority.

9. The data became available only because of the efforts of New York Attorney General Andrew Cuomo. It was not disclosed by the U.S. Treasury, which was responsible for the bailout. Susanne Craig and Deborah Solomon, "Bank Bonus Tab: $33 Billion," *Wall Street Journal*, July 31, 2009, at http://online.wsj.com/article/SB124896891815094085.html.

10. In fact, Alan Greenspan blocked a proposal to increase scrutiny of subprime lenders under the Fed's broad authority. Greg Ip, "Did Greenspan Add to Subprime Woes?" *Wall Street Journal*, June 9, 2007, p. B1, available at http://www.online.wsj.com/article/SB118134111823129555.html.

11. This list of the purposes of regulation is not meant to be exhaustive: regulations also are designed to ensure access to finance, prevent discrimination, promote macro-stability, and enhance competition. Some of these other regulations remained in place.

12. Not all of American mortgages are nonrecourse, but in practice, the vast majority are.

13. Critics of deposit insurance are wrong, however, in the belief that without deposit insurance all would be well, since depositors have an incentive to make sure that the banks use their funds well. There have been bank failures in countries with and without deposit insurance alike. Indeed, how could depositors assess the risk of a major bank like Citibank, when even its management and the regulators gave markedly different appraisals from day to day?

14. If the borrower realized that the mortgage broker had misrepresented his income and raised concerns, he was quickly silenced—it was a mere formality.

15. U.S. Census Bureau, Current Population Survey, Historical Income Tables, Table H-6, http://www.census.gov/hhes/www/income/histinc/inchhtoc.html.

16. See also Robert J. Shiller, *Irrational Exuberance*, 2nd ed. (Princeton: Princeton University Press, 2005).

17. The Federal Housing Finance Board Monthly Interest Rate Survey, Table 36, available at http://www.fhfa.gov/Default.aspx?Page=252.

18. Alan Greenspan, speech at Credit Union National Association 2004 Governmental Affairs Conference, Washington, DC, February 23, 2004. In his usual convoluted way (sometimes called "Fedspeak") he covered himself against future criticism: "Calculations by market analysts of the 'option adjusted spread' on mortgages suggest that the cost of these benefits conferred by fixed-rate mort-

gages can range from 0.5 percent to 1.2 percent, raising homeowners' annual after-tax mortgage payments by several thousand dollars." He noted though that there would not have been these savings "had interest rates trended sharply upward."

19. See, for instance, James R. Hagerty and Michael Corkery, "How Hidden Incentives Distort Home Prices," *Wall Street Journal Online*, December 20, 2007.

20. See also Aubrey Cohen, "Rules Set to Cut Off Mortgage Originators from Appraisers This Week," *Seattle Post-Intelligencer Online*, April 29, 2009, available at http://www.seattlepi.com/local/405528_appraisal25.html. (Wells Fargo was not alone.)

21. As subprime lending increased, a survey of five hundred appraisers in forty-four states revealed that 55 percent reported being pressured to overstate property values, and 25 percent had experienced pressure in at least half of the appraisals they were commissioned to perform. David Callahan, "Home Insecurity: How Widespread Appraisal Fraud Puts Homeowners at Risk," Borrowing to Make Ends Meet Briefing Paper #4, March 2005, available at http://www.cheatingculture.com/home_insecurity_v3.pdf. The FBI monitors mortgage fraud, which includes appraisal fraud, and reported a 36 percent increase in the number of cases of such fraud in 2008, with the top states including those in which the numbers of mortgage defaults and foreclosures are largest. FBI, *2008 Mortgage Fraud Report*, op. cit. There is likely to be a flood of litigation, exemplified by the class-action lawsuit on behalf of purchasers of Bear Stearns' Asset-Backed Securities, alleging, for instance, false statements and/or omissions about the appraisals of properties underlying the mortgage loan. "Cohen Milstein and Coughlin Stoia Announce Pendency of Class Action Suits . . . ," *Market Watch*, September 11, 2009, available at http://www.marketwatch.com/story/cohen-milstein-and-coughlin-stoia-announce-pendency-of-class-action-suits-involving-mortgage-pass-through-certificates-of-structured-asset-mortgage-investments-ii-inc-and-bear-stearns-asset-backed-2009–09–11.

22. Keith Ernst, Debbie Bocian, and Wei Li, "Steered Wrong: Brokers, Borrowers, and Subprime Loans," Center for Responsible Lending, April 8, 2008, available at http://www.responsiblelending.org/mortgage-lending/research-analysis/steered-wrong-brokers-borrowers-and-subprime-loans.pdf.

23. Since an increase in interest rates would pose problems throughout the country, the risks of default would be highly correlated throughout the country. For a more complete analysis of the problems with securitization, see, for instance, Stiglitz, "Banks versus Markets as Mechanisms for Allocating and Coordinating Investment," op. cit.

24. Some have argued to the contrary, that because foreign demand for U.S. mortgages contributed to the bubble, it made matters worse. What seems clear to me is that there was sufficient domestic demand for bad mortgages and sufficient misjudgment of risk, and that America would have had a bubble without

this foreign demand. One cannot blame foreigners, as some are wont. Without the foreign demand, risk premium on the risky products would have been higher, which would have attracted more American purchases.

25. That's why one of the "reforms" advocated by some free-marketers—increase the number of rating agencies and hence competition among them—could make matters even worse, unless there were other reforms.

26. The models the investment banks and rating agencies used typically assumed what are called lognormal distributions, a variant of the familiar bell-shaped curve. In fact, they should have used what are called "fat-tailed" distributions, in which relatively rare events happen more frequently than they do in the lognormal distribution.

27. Mark Rubinstein, "Comments on the 1987 Stock Market Crash: Eleven Years Later," in *Risks in Accumulation Products* (Schaumburg, IL: Society of Actuaries, 2000).

28. These models used, for instance, probability distributions, which underestimated the occurrence of "rare" events. But not only were such technical assumptions flawed, so was the underlying economics. They ignored the possibility of the kinds of liquidity crises that have been a feature of financial markets throughout history; such crises are related to problems of imperfect and asymmetric information—which these models ignored.

29. Eric Lipton, "After the Bank Failure Comes the Debt Collector," *New York Times*, April 17, 2009, p. B1.

30. That securitization made it more difficult to renegotiate mortgages is another example of something that both market participants and regulators should have been aware of: it had been far harder to renegotiate and restructure debts in the East Asian crisis of the late 1990s than in the Latin American debt crisis of the early 1980s because of securitization. In the latter case, one could sit the principal creditors around a table; in the former, there was no room big enough for all of the claimants.

31. See the statement of Sheila C. Bair, Chairman, Federal Deposit Insurance Corporation, "Possible Responses to Rising Mortgage Foreclosures," Committee on Financial Services, U.S. House of Representatives, Washington, DC, April 17, 2007.

32. In chapter 5, I explain how the way the Obama administration designed the bank bailouts eviscerated incentives to restructure mortgages further.

33. More than 15.2 million U.S. mortgages, almost one-third of all mortgaged properties, were underwater as of June 30, 2009. First American CoreLogic, "Negative Equity Report, Q2 2009," August 13, 2009, available at http://www.facorelogic.com/uploadedFiles/Newsroom/RES_in_the_News/FACL%20Negative%20Equity_final_081309.pdf.

34. The plan provided as much money to the mortgage servicers and investors as to the borrower: For "successful modifications" in which the borrower remained

current for five years, it paid the lender 50 percent of the cost of the reduction of payments from 38 percent to 31 percent of the borrower's income, and gave $4,000 to servicers and $5,000 to the borrower. The bank would have to bear the full cost of the reduction of payments to 38 percent. (Consider, for instance, someone with a $400,000 mortgage, paying just over 38 percent of his income on an interest-only mortgage. After five years, the lender would get more than $11,000—more than the service provider and the borrower combined.) The plan provided essentially no help for the unemployed. A few states, such as Pennsylvania, stepped in to provide loans for them. Department of the Treasury, "Making Home Affordable Updated Detailed Program Description," Washington DC, March 4, 2009, available at http://www.treas.gov/press/releases/reports/housing_fact_sheet.pdf.

35. The Fed's direct actions lowered mortgage interest rates, and greatly facilitated the modifications that did take place. Payments were also lowered through the extension of mortgage terms to forty years from the date of modification, and by converting mortgages into interest-only mortgages—leading to large balloon payments down the line. Such balloon payments contributed greatly to the crisis, and meant that potential problems were being passed on to the future.

36. U.S. Department of Treasury, "Making Home Affordable Program: Servicer Performance Report through October 2009," November 2009, available at http://www.financialstability.gov/docs/MHA%20Public%20111009%20FINAL.PDF.

37. Financial Accounting Standards Board, "Determining Fair Value When the Volume and Level of Activity for the Asset or Liability Have Significantly Decreased and Identifying Transactions That Are Not Orderly," FSP FAS 157-4, April 9, 2009, available at: http://www.fasb.org/cs/BlobServer?blobcol=urldata&blobtable=MungoBlobs&blobkey=id&blobwhere=1175818748755&blobheader=application%2Fpdf.

38. The banks claimed that the impairment for many of the mortgages was only temporary, justifying the refusal to write down the value of the mortgages. But from a statistical point of view this was nonsense: the probability that any impaired mortgage, even mortgages classified as only temporarily impaired, would not be repaid was significantly greater than that for an unimpaired mortgage, and good accounting would have reflected this. This was especially the case in this deep recession, and even more so for mortgages that were underwater.

39. When wages are garnished (in payment of a debt), the employer turns over the money directly to the creditor.

40. A lobbyist for several banking trade associations told the *New York Times* that Republicans will get "professional donors and lobbyists to look at them in a different light" if they show they can affect policy. Editorial, "Holding Up the Housing Recovery," *New York Times*, April 24, 2009, p. A26.

41. The rate of charge-offs (the annualized percentage of loans and leases removed from the books of banks and charged against loss reserves, net of recov-

eries) of residential real estate loans increased from 0.08, before April 2005 when the Bankruptcy Abuse Prevention and Consumer Protection Act was passed, to 2.34 by the second quarter of 2009. See Federal Reserve, "Charge-Off Rates: All Banks, SA," Federal Reserve Statistical Release, available at http://www.federal reserve.gov/releases/chargeoff/chgallsa.htm.

42. David U. Himmelstein, Elizabeth Warren, Deborah Thorne, and Steffie Woolhandler, "Illness and Injury as Contributors to Bankruptcy," *Health Affairs*, vol. 24 (January–June 2005), p. 63.

43. There might be further criteria as to which households would be eligible for relief, e.g., restrictions on the ratio of mortgage payments to income.

44. There are other ways of providing relief to households. Any strategy has to allocate the losses among the banks, the homeowners, and the government. If the government had written down the mortgages, passed a "tax" that would have captured a large fraction of the capital gain from the written-down value, and used the proceeds to help make the banks whole, providing them financing in the interim, the outcome would have been much the same. The basic principles are: (i) it is important to allow homeowners to stay in their home, provided they can afford to do so, with a written-down value and a modicum of assistance—foreclosures are expensive both to families and to communities and exacerbate downward pressures on prices; and (ii) the brunt of the cost of bad lending should be borne by the banks and other lenders.

45. U.S. Department of the Treasury, "Homeowner Affordability and Stability Plan Fact Sheet," press release, February 18, 2009, available at http://www .ustreas.gov/press/releases/20092181117388144.htm.

46. As noted in note 1, p. 315, by the third quarter of 2009, the homeownership rate was approximately that in 2000, but with one in four borrowers underwater by mid-2009, it was likely that many would lose their homes in the ensuing months and years. (See, e.g., Ruth Simon and James R. Hagerty, "One in Four Borrowers Is Underwater," *Wall Street Journal*, November 24, 2009, p. A1.)

47. In the Danish system, whenever a mortgage is issued by the mortgage originator, a mortgage bond is created, and the homeowner can repay the loan (with a corresponding reduction in the mortgage bond). In the American system, when interest rates rise, with the concomitant risk of house prices declining, there is a big risk of negative equity (as we have seen). In the Danish system, when house prices decline, the mortgage bond goes down in value simultaneously, so the homeowner can more easily repay what is owed. This prevents negative equity. In effect, the Danish mortgage bond encourages refinancing when interest rates rise; Americans do so only when interest rates fall.

48. Martin Feldstein, "How to Stop the Mortgage Crisis," *Wall Street Journal*, March 7, 2008, p. A15.

49. Lenders participating in this buy-back program would have to waive any prepayment penalties.

Chapter 5 THE GREAT AMERICAN ROBBERY

1. Perhaps the only mistake of comparable magnitude in its economic conse-
quences was America's decision to go to war with Iraq. See Joseph E. Stiglitz, *The
Three Trillion Dollar War: The True Costs of the Iraq Conflict* (New York: W. W.
Norton, 2007).

2. Mark Pittman and Bob Ivry, "Fed's Strategy Reduces U.S. Bailout to $11.6
Trillion," Bloomberg News, September 25, 2009.

3. When one is lending at a zero interest rate, all matters of wonder can be
accomplished. A Central Bank could, for instance, engineer the recapitalization
of the banks. The Central Bank lends money to Bank A, which lends money to
Fund Alpha, which invests the money in the shares of Bank A: presto, we have
a well-capitalized bank, and we can celebrate the wonders of the market. This is
too transparent a ruse. But Bank A can lend to Fund Alpha that invests in Bank
B, and Bank B lends to Fund Beta that invests in Bank A. The effect is much the
same, without the obvious conflicts of interest. In fact, the recapitalization of
the banks (e.g., by pension funds) may simply be based on rational or irrational
exuberance, the belief that bank shares were underpriced. Still, the provision of
liquidity will show up somewhere in the system, if not in lending. It may, for
instance, fuel another set of asset bubbles.

4. Politics too played a role. As I noted, the way the bailouts were done—and
the banks' own behavior—meant that it was probably impossible to go back to
Congress to ask for more funding. Robert Johnson and Tom Ferguson argue that
hidden subsidies through a variety of government agencies were a central part of
the Bush administration's attempt to cover up the problem (and the subsidies)
in the months preceding the election, in the hope that they could prevent a real
crisis from breaking out until after the election. The attempt almost succeeded.
See Tom Ferguson and Robert Johnson, "Too Big to Bail: The 'Paulson Put,' Presidential Politics, and the Global Financial Meltdown, Part I: From Shadow Banking System to Shadow Bailout," *International Journal of Political Economy*, vol. 38,
no. 1 (2009), pp. 3–34, and Robert Johnson and Thomas Ferguson, "Too Big to
Bail: The 'Paulson Put,' Presidential Politics, and the Global Financial Meltdown,
Part II: Fatal Reversal—Single Payer and Back," *International Journal of Political Economy*, vol. 38, no. 2 (Summer 2009), pp. 5–45, available at http://www
.ony.unu.edu/FergJohn%20Too%20Big%20Part%20II%20IJPE%20%20codes%20
removed%20for%20circulation.doc.

5. Edward M. Liddy, "Our Mission at AIG: Repairs, and Repayment," *Washington Post*, March 18, 2009, p. A13.

6. As I noted earlier, almost twenty years ago, at the beginning of the era of securitization, I predicted that there was a good chance it would end in disaster, as
investors underestimated the problems posed by information asymmetries, the
risks of price declines, and the extent to which risks are correlated.

7. Banks have complex legal structures, which add to the complexity of restructuring, with some being owned by bank holding companies. Currently, the government has the authority to place into conservatorship the bank, but limited ability to deal with the holding company. Limitations in its "resolution" authority have been given as an excuse for the failure to handle better some of the problem institutions (Lehman Brothers, Bear Stearns). There is a broad consensus that one of the reforms that is needed is to strengthen the government's powers in this area.

8. Sometimes the financial assets of the bank are less than what it owes depositors, but a new bank is willing to pay for its customer base. The bank may have a value as an ongoing organization—even if the bank hasn't done a stellar job in making credit assessments.

9. In an interview with ABC News' *Nightline*, Obama argued that nationalization of banks was not a good option in the United States, though it had worked well for Sweden, in part because we "have different traditions in this country." Terry Moran interview with President Obama, *Nightline*, ABC News, transcript, February 10, 2009.

10. Banks go through this process almost every week, with hardly a ripple. By the end of November, 124 banks had gone into bankruptcy in 2009 alone. Federal Deposit Insurance Corporation, "Failed Bank List," November 20, 2009, available at http://www.fdic.gov/bank/individual/failed/banklist.html. Even large banks can go bankrupt. In 1984, the then sixth-largest bank in the United States, Continental Illinois, was placed into conservatorship ("nationalized"), in an orderly way. Several years later, it was reprivatized.

11. There is a critical question on how to value a bank's assets and liabilities. The principles are clear, but the practice is complex, because it may be especially hard to value assets in a time of crisis.

12. Because the government is on the hook for so much money, it has to take an active role in managing the restructuring; even in the case of airline bankruptcy, courts typically appoint someone to oversee the restructuring to make sure that the claimants' interests are served. Usually, the process is done smoothly.

13. There are some complications arising from taxes. And, of course, once bondholders become the new shareholders, they do bear more risk. But if they don't want to bear so much risk, they can trade their shares for a safer asset.

14. The advocates of this new notion of too-big-to-be-resolved argued that letting another large institution go down might create a similar disturbance. The problem, however, was the disorderly way in which Lehman Brothers was handled. The first excuse given for this failure was that the market had had plenty of time to take appropriate actions. After all, the collapse of Lehman Brothers had been widely anticipated at least since the spring. The old faith in markets was repeated—even as markets were clearly not functioning in the way that the government had hoped. Later, the excuse was that it didn't have legal authority

to do anything—an excuse made hollow by the strong actions taken a couple days later to effectively nationalize, and bail out, AIG, the largest insurer in the United States. This was surely a stretch—the Federal Reserve supposedly had powers over commercial banks, not insurance companies. But the more telling criticism is that *the Fed and the Treasury* had had plenty of time to figure out what legal authority they needed. If they didn't have the legal authority to protect the financial stability of the U.S. economy, and that of the world, then they had a responsibility to ask Congress for that authority. Interestingly, while the Treasury seems to have learned the wrong lesson from the Lehman Brothers experience, it seems not to have paid any attention to an earlier experience in Indonesia in which it, together with the IMF, helped bring down the Indonesian economy. After shutting down sixteen banks, it announced that more would be closed, and there would be at most limited deposit insurance. Not surprisingly, panic ensued, and funds fled from the private banks to the public. The forecast that other banks would be in trouble was self-fulfilling.

The similarities between the closing of Indonesia's banks and Lehman Brothers are striking. For instance, in both cases, there was a lack of transparency—no one could tell which firm would be saved (Bear Stearns was saved, though it was smaller than Lehman Brothers) and which one would be let go. In both cases, the economic consequences of these financial mistakes were enormous.

The financial disturbances that followed Lehman Brothers collapse were, in part, a result of the increased uncertainty about the scope of the government guarantee. The underlying problem—that so many banks were in fact in deep trouble—had been hidden by the widespread assumption that there would be government bailouts. (Some people, such as John Cochrane and Luigi Zingales, have argued that it was TARP which "scared" the market; seeing the magnitude of the government rescue, market participants assumed that the problems were deep. In support of this view, they cite the timing of increases in interest rate spreads. See John H. Cochrane and Luigi Zingales, "Lehman and the Financial Crisis," *Wall Street Journal*, September 15, 2009, p. A21.) But both TARP and the increases in spreads were a result of the underlying problem: the deterioration in bank balance sheets and the surrounding uncertainties. And a look at a wider set of credit indicators shows the extent to which the market froze as soon as it became clear that there was not an automatic government bailout. See Thomas Ferguson and Robert Johnson, "The God That Failed: Free Market Fundamentalism and the Lehman Bankruptcy," *The Economists' Voice*, vol. 7 (2010): Issue 1, Article 1, pp.1–7.

15. While the public may not have been aware of the problems (partially perhaps because of the actions to hide them by Secretary of Treasury Hank Paulson described elsewhere), there was, in effect, an ongoing crisis in the financial sector from early 2007. The first public tremors were seen in August 2007, following the collapse of a couple large funds. As investors realized the problems

with mortgage-backed securities, these markets began to have problems; and it was just a matter of time before the problems reverberated back to the banks. The economy was in recession by the end of 2007, nine months before the Lehman Brothers collapse.

16. With financial restructuring, a sweetener can even be thrown in: give existing shareholders warrants that allow them to get some of the upside potential if the bank does recover.

17. Fannie Mae began as a government-sponsored enterprise but was privatized in 1968. There never was a government guarantee for its bonds; had there been, its bonds would have earned a lower return, commensurate with U.S. Treasuries.

18. David Herszenhorn, "Bailout Plan Wins Approval; Democrats Vow Tighter Rules," *New York Times*, October 3, 2008, p. A1.

19. Among the subsidies included in the bill that was eventually passed were an exemption from a thirty-nine-cent excise tax for wooden arrows for children (introduced by Oregon senators and worth $200,000 to an arrow manufacturer in Oregon); a seven-year cost recovery period for NASCAR racetracks—less than half of what the IRS thought appropriate (worth $109 million); a change in a provision relating to rum excise taxes in Puerto Rico and the Virgin Islands (worth $192 million); incentives for films to be shot in the United States, including adult films (worth $478 million over ten years); and increased funding for the Wool Research Trust Fund, which provides grants to wool makers and sheep farmers. See "Spoonful of Pork May Help Bitter Economic Pill Go Down," *CNN.com*, October 4, 2008, and Paul Waldie, "Bill Larded with 'Goodies' for All," *Globe and Mail*, October 3, 2008, p. B1.

20. See Edward J Kane, *The S&L Insurance Mess: How Did It Happen?* (Washington, DC: Urban Institute Press, 1989), and Edward J. Kane, "Dangers of Capital Forbearance: The Case of the FSLIC and 'Zombie' S&Ls," *Contemporary Economic Policy*, Western Economic Association International, vol. 5, no. 1 (1987), pp. 77–83.

21. See George Akerlof and Paul M. Romer, "Looting: The Economic Underworld of Bankruptcy for Profit," *Brookings Papers on Economic Activity*, vol. 2 (1993), pp. 1–73.

22. At the time, the cost of the savings and loan debacle was estimated to be $160 billion (what then seemed to be an unbelievable sum, which in current dollars is approximately $313 billion). In the end, the government was able to recover a substantial amount as a result of the economic recovery of 1993, but the amounts usually reported did not adequately account for the full opportunity cost of the funds. Federal Deposit Insurance Corporation, "An Examination of the Banking Crises of the 1980s and Early 1990s," Washington, DC, 1997, available at http://www.fdic.gov/bank/historical/history/.

23. Buffett put in $5 billion, and in return got $5 billion in perpetual preferred shares yielding 10 percent, *plus* warrants to buy $5 billion of Goldman Sachs

common stock at $115 a share, 8 percent below market price. By November 2009, with Goldman Sachs shares trading at $170, Buffett had earned a high return on the money he had given the firm a little over a year earlier—incomparably higher than the return obtained by the U.S. government.

24. The financial sector used "fear" to persuade the administrations to impose no controls, just as it used fear to engineer the bondholder and shareholder protection schemes. The argument was that if these measures were taken, the banks wouldn't be able to raise private money—as if "private" high-cost money was a special kind of money that would ensure that the financial markets work well. But the government's refusal to impose these controls led to weaker banks—with so much capital being paid out in bonuses and dividends—and this made the banks more precarious and less attractive.

One of the arguments, noted earlier, for requiring that banks be adequately capitalized is that it improves incentives: with more equity, they have more to lose if they undertake excessive risk. But the Obama and Bush administrations seemed to make a basic mistake: the *private* owners of the banks might care little about imposing losses on government. It was not *their* equity that was at risk. Hence, without government having a say, it was predictable that they would act in the reckless way they did—paying out money in dividends and bonuses, even though they were in a precarious financial state.

25. Though because of the severity of the problems confronting the United Kingdom, lending in that country remained weak.

26. Mike McIntire, "Bailout Is a Windfall to Banks, if Not to Borrowers," *New York Times*, January 18, 2009, p. A1.

27. Congressional Oversight Panel, "Valuing Treasury's Acquisitions," February Oversight Report, February 6, 2009, available at http://cop.senate.gov/reports/library/report-020609-cop.cfm.

28. Congressional Budget Office, "A Preliminary Analysis of the President's Budget and an Update of CBO's Budget and Economic Outlook," March 2009, available at https://www.cbo.gov/ftpdocs/100xx/doc10014/03-20-PresidentBud get.pdf.

29. Congressional Budget Office, "The Troubled Asset Relief Program: Report on Transactions through June 17, 2009," June 2009, available at http://www.cbo.gov/ftpdocs/100xx/doc10056/06-29-TARP.pdf.

30. A bank (or any other firm) is "solvent" but "illiquid" if its assets exceed its liabilities but nonetheless it cannot get access to funds. Of course, if it were self-evident that the assets exceeded the liabilities, then the bank would normally have no problem getting access to funds. The banks believed that they were solvent because they wanted to believe that their assets (in particular, the mortgages) were worth more than the "market" said they were.

The problem with banks is that most of what they owe is in the form of "demand deposits," money that has to be returned on demand. Banks take that money and invest it in longer-term investments (like mortgages), believing that large numbers of depositors would *almost never* demand their money back at the same time. If everyone were to demand their money back at the same time, the bank would have to sell its assets quickly, and if it did so, it might not be able to get the "full value" of the asset. In that sense, a bank could be solvent if it were given time to sell, but not if it had to sell its assets overnight. The Fed is supposed to step into that breach—it is supposed to assess whether the bank really can sell the assets for what it claims if it just had a little more time. If (and only if) the Fed determines that the answer to that question is yes, then it provides the liquidity the bank needs.

31. International Monetary Fund, "Global Financial Stability Report," Washington, DC, October 2009, available at http://www.imf.org/external/pubs/ft/gfsr/2009/02/index.htm.

32. See U.S. Treasury, "Treasury Department Releases Details on Public Private Partnership Investment Program," March 23, 2009, available at http://www.treas.gov/press/releases/tg65.htm.

33. The argument for the program was to "clean up" the banks' balance sheets. But if one bank bought the asset from another, it would imply that the latter bank would become "soiled" as the first was cleansed. This suggests that the real reason for the Public-Private Investment Program (PPIP) may have been the hidden transfer of money to the banks.

34. The PPIP had a couple of other advantages: for example, it might inoculate directly the government from accusations of overpaying for some asset and simultaneously give money to banks without any government control (a curious objective, but one that seemed to be central to Obama's conception). The program, however, had other disadvantages, which were exacerbated as the administration and Federal Reserve struggled to keep the economy going. Lower mortgage interest rates, designed to stabilize the mortgage market, had an indirect effect of worsening the "adverse selection" problem: the old mortgages that remained to be purchased by the PPIP included an increasingly large proportion of toxic mortgages, those that could not be refinanced.

35. Obviously, money that went into the banks and immediately went out again in the form of dividends and bonuses didn't enable the banks to restart lending. But the remaining funds may have helped—though lending didn't expand, it might have otherwise contracted *even more*. Better-designed programs would have had a much bigger "bang for the buck."

36. It is apparent that the people structuring these rescue programs did not think deeply (or at least deeply enough) about the determinants of credit flows. In fact, these concerns should be at the center of any monetary theory. Other factors also affect lending—among them being risk, which has only grown worse as the economy's woes have deepened. This is one of the central themes of my earlier book: B. Greenwald and J. E. Stiglitz, *Towards a New Paradigm in Monetary Economics* (Cambridge, UK: Cambridge University Press, 2003).

37. See Mary Williams Marsh, "AIG Lists Firms to Which It Paid Taxpayer Money," *New York Times*, March 16, 2009, p. A1. It became clear why the government was so reluctant to reveal where the AIG money had gone. The single biggest American recipient was Goldman Sachs—which claimed (perhaps disingenuously) that it would have survived fine on its own, that there was no systemic risk, though it was quite naturally willing to receive a $13 billion gift from the government. Several of the other big recipients were foreign banks. If the failure of these banks represented a systemic problem, their governments would presumably have bailed them out. We were, in effect, giving foreign aid to other rich countries (France, Germany), rather than the poor countries that needed it so much more. And the magnitude of this aid was in fact larger than that given to all of Africa. (U.S. official development assistance to all of Africa was $6.5 billion in FY 2008, half of the amount that went to a single firm, Goldman Sachs, through the AIG bailout. See U.S. Department of State, "The US Commitment to Development," Fact Sheet, Bureau of Economic, Energy and Business Affairs, July 7, 2009, available at http://www.state.gov/e/eeb/rls/fs/2009/113995.htm.)

38. Because bank bonds and stocks are constantly being bought and sold, the real winners from the bailouts are those that happen to be holding these securities at the time the bailout is announced (or comes to be widely expected). Pension funds that sold the bonds as the stock prices collapsed because they were too risky do not benefit.

39. Federal Reserve Bank, Table H.4.1, "Factors Affecting Reserve Balances," Washington, DC, September 24, 2009, available at http://www.federalreserve.gov/releases/h41/.

40. See European Central Bank, Monthly Bulletin, September 2007, p. 33, available at http://www.ecb.int/pub/pdf/mobu/mb200709en.pdf, and Federal Reserve Bank, Table H.4.1, "Factors Affecting Reserve Balances," Washington, DC, August 16, 2007, available at: http://www.federalreserve.gov/releases/h41/20070816/.

41. The fact that the Federal Reserve extended the lender of last resort facility right after it let Bear Stearns go down has been a subject of criticism: had the facility been extended a couple of days earlier, perhaps the firm would have been saved.

42. Technically, the Fed is an independent institution. But confidence in the Fed is not derived from its own equity but from the fact that everyone understands that the U.S. government stands behind the institution. All profits of the Fed go to the Treasury, and it's clear that any losses would come out of the Treasury.

43. Seventy-five years ago, Keynes had discussed a similar phenomenon, which he called a liquidity trap. Flooding the economy with money didn't work because households would just hold on to the money. Now, money was being given to the banks, and they just held on to it.

44. The Fed has, however, managed to put much of the country's outstand-

ing mortgages onto its balance sheet. While much of the credit risk is held by the government (mortgages that were refinanced as interest rates were lowered were underwritten by the Federal Housing Administration, Fannie Mae, and Freddie Mac), the Fed picked up the interest rate risk. As I note later, in the end, all the risk is borne by the taxpayer.

45. It is actually not so easy to inflate away much of the government's debt: most of government borrowing is short term, and as inflation worries increase, so too will the interest the government has to pay. There is a risk that interest rates will rise on the basis of inflation worries and yet the inflation itself won't materialize. We will have then paid for the inflation without getting its benefits in terms of debt reduction; our debt will be all the higher as a result of the higher interest.

46. The Fed was forecasting, for instance, that the economy was on the road to recovery in the spring of 2008, just months before the collapse. A year earlier, it had said that the problems of subprime mortgages had been fully contained.

47. The Fed will, perhaps, claim that by holding the mortgages to maturity, it will have avoided bearing losses (except on the mortgages that go into default). But it will be earning a low interest rate on these assets—which is an opportunity cost. The low interest rate is why private investors will pay less for these assets. If the Fed had to use mark-to-market accounting, it would have to recognize this loss. But it doesn't, and the lost revenue associated with the opportunity cost will go largely unnoticed. But all of the Fed's profits are passed on to the Treasury. Lower Fed profits mean higher taxes and/or a higher national debt in the future.

48. There is one argument to the contrary—that the Fed, recognizing its pivotal role in creating the crisis, will not want to be seen as pushing the economy into another recession just as it is recovering.

49. Part of the reason why banks will hold long-term government bonds are flaws in accounting and banking regulations. Banking regulations treat these bonds as safe, even though there is a risk of a decrease in value, if, say, interest rates rise, which might be the case if inflationary expectations increase. Banks are allowed to record the long-term interest rate as "income," without making any provision for the risk of loss associated with the fall in the price of the bond. (If markets are well functioning, then the difference between the short-term rate and the long-term rate is the expectation of a fall in price.) See Stiglitz, *Roaring Nineties*, op. cit.

50. What matters, of course, is how firms' investment responds, which will depend both on their beliefs about real interest rates (i.e., an increase in interest rates will matter less if they believe, at the same time, that inflation is increasing) and on credit constraints. It is easy to see how the process described in the text gives rise to fluctuations. The market reacts to inflationary expectations, leading long-term interest rates to rise, and the economy goes into a slowdown. As the Fed eases, inflationary expectations get even worse. Financial market participants today have little confidence that the Fed will be able to manage the whole pro-

cess smoothly, but in the financial press and among Wall Streeters, there appears to be more fear of the Fed underreacting—a bout of inflation—than overreacting (though as this book goes to press, inflationary expectations revealed by prices of TIPS securities remain muted).

51. For an excellent detailed description and assessment of the Fed's actions, see David Wessel, *In Fed We Trust: Ben Bernanke's War on the Great Panic* (New York: Crown Business, 2009).

52. The bailout of Bear Stearns was a particularly complex one, with the Fed lending money (in a largely nonrecourse loan, with collateral of uncertain value) to JPMorgan Chase to buy Bear Stearns. It appears that the Fed will face significant losses on this collateral. By November 4, 2009, the Fed had already recorded a loss of almost 10 percent. See Federal Reserve Statistical Release H.4.1., Factors Affecting Reserve Balances, available at http://www.federal reserve.gov/releases/h41/Current/.

53. As I noted earlier, the Fed claimed that it was exempt from the Freedom of Information Act. On February 26, 2009, Ron Paul introduced a bill into Congress demanding more transparency in the operation of the Fed. See Declan McCullagh, "Bernanke Fights House Bill to Audit the Fed," *CBS News.com*, July 28, 2009. Since then, support for such an audit has been growing. On November 19, 2009, the House Financial Services Committee voted overwhelmingly for such an audit.

54. JPMorgan Chase benefited through the Bear Stearns bailout. In another instance of questionable governance, Stephen Friedman became chairman of the Federal Reserve Bank of New York in January 2008, while he was simultaneously a member of the board of Goldman Sachs and had a large holding in Goldman stock. He resigned in May 2009 after the controversy over the obvious conflicts of interest (including share purchases, which enabled him to make $3 million). See Hagan, "Tenacious G," op. cit., and Kate Kelly and Jon Hilsenrath, "New York Fed Chairman's Ties to Goldman Raise Questions," *Wall Street Journal*, May 4, 2009, p. A1.

55. Monetarism held that the money supply should be increased at a fixed rate; inflation targeting held that central banks should increase interest rates whenever the inflation rate exceeded the target.

56. See in particular Wessel, *In Fed We Trust*, op. cit.

Chapter 6 AVARICE TRIUMPHS OVER PRUDENCE

1. The Pecora Commission was established by the Senate Committee on Banking and Currency on March 4, 1932, to ascertain the causes of the stock market crash of 1929. The commission uncovered a wide range of abusive practices on the part of banks and bank affiliates, and as a result of the findings, the U.S.

Congress passed the Glass-Steagall Banking Act of 1933, the Securities Act of 1933 (which set penalties for filing false information about stock offerings), and the Security Exchange Act of 1934 (which formed the U.S. Securities and Exchange Commission, or SEC, to regulate the stock exchanges). Following this example, in May 2009 Congress established the Financial Crisis Inquiry Commission to investigate the current crisis.

2. See Manuel Roig-Franzia, "Credit Crisis Cassandra," *Washington Post*, May 26, 2009, p. C1.

3. Many were surprised that Alan Greenspan, whose economic philosophy seemed to differ so markedly from that of Bill Clinton, was reappointed as chairman of the Federal Reserve. His supporters within the Clinton administration (he was still viewed with reverence by many) used fear that market turmoil might upset a recovering economy to engender presidential support in the face of opposition within the president's economic team.

4. When I was chairman of the Council of Economic Advisers during the Clinton administration, I served on a committee with all the major federal financial regulators, a group that included Greenspan and Treasury Secretary Robert Rubin. Even then, it was clear that derivatives posed a danger. And yet, for all the risk, the deregulators in charge of the financial system—including the Fed—decided to do nothing, as they were too worried that any action might interfere with "innovation" in the financial system. They seemed to think that it was just better to clean up the mess after it occurred than to "stifle" the economy at that time—the same argument that was used against pricking the housing bubble.

5. On November 4, 2009, the House Financial Services Committee approved an amendment to the Investor Protection Act to exempt small and medium-size enterprises (those with capitalizations under $75 million) from Section 404 of the Sarbanes-Oxley Act. Section 404 required that firms report on the effectiveness of their internal financial controls, which is essential for investor confidence. Arthur Levitt, former chairman of the SEC, has called this provision the "holy grail" of investor protection. After the vote, Levitt said, "Anyone who votes for this will bear the investors' mark of Cain." See Floyd Norris, "Goodbye to Reforms of 2002," *New York Times*, November 5, 2009, p. B1.

6. Before the House Committee on Oversight and Government Reform's hearing on "The Financial Crisis and the Role of Federal Regulators," on October 23, 2008, Alan Greenspan said, "I made a mistake in presuming that the self-interest of organizations, specifically banks and others, were such as that they were best capable of protecting their own shareholders and their equity in the firms."

7. Greenspan didn't even believe that there was a need for fraud laws. Brooksley Born, former chairman of the Commodity Futures Trading Commission, relates that he argued that "there wasn't a need for a law against fraud because if a floor broker was committing fraud, the customer would figure it out and stop doing business with him." Cited in Roig-Franzia, "Credit Crisis Cassandra," op. cit.

8. This receiving high pay regardless of performance was exemplified by the bonuses banks gave in 2008, a year with record losses and almost record bonuses—some $33 billion. (Six of the nine banks paid out more in bonuses than they received in profit.) See Craig and Solomon, "Bank Bonus Tab: $33 Billion," op. cit.

9. Executives who defended their deceptive accounting practices argued that shareholders benefited as the banks booked high profits. But while some shareholders gained, others lost, particularly those who had put their faith in the doctored numbers and held onto the shares under false pretense. Eventually, the truth would come out, and when it did, share prices would fall, sometimes (as in the case of Citibank) dramatically.

10. In the case of the nine largest banks, profits from early in 2004 until the middle of 2007 were a combined $305 billion. But since July 2007, those banks have marked down their valuations on loans and other assets by just over that amount. See Louise Story and Eric Dash, "Banks Are Likely to Hold Tight to Bailout Money," *New York Times*, October 16, 2008, p. A1.

11. There are limits on the extent to which management can abuse its position—provided by proxy battles and takeovers. But there is a large economic literature explaining why these mechanisms are of limited efficacy.

12. See Stiglitz, *Roaring Nineties*, op. cit.

13. The respected former head of the SEC, Arthur Levitt, came to believe that the failure to deal with stock options (in Sarbanes-Oxley) was one of his critical mistakes. See Arthur Levitt, *Take On the Street: How to Fight for Your Financial Future* (New York: Random House, 2002).

14. Perhaps investors didn't send a warning partly because too many of them were also caught up in the same "bubble" mentality that drove Wall Street; besides, there is little reason to expect most investors to understand risk better than the so-called experts on Wall Street. They trusted Wall Street. It will be interesting to see how long it takes for trust to be restored.

15. One of the unintended consequences of a tax provision introduced in 1993, which imposed an extra tax on high pay that is not related to performance, may have been to encourage the charade of performance pay. It didn't set up adequate standards for assessing whether compensation was truly related to performance.

16. The conflict over reporting of stock options provides an example of the disparity of interests. Shareholders would like to know how the value of their shares is being diluted by the issuance of stock options. But corporations (meaning their officers) have strongly resisted improvements in reporting requirements—making the issuance more transparent—because they have realized that if shareholders understood how much their share value was being diluted, there would be resistance to the size of the awards.

17. The Shareholder Vote on Executive Compensation Act passed the House of Representatives and was introduced into the Senate in April 2007; it stalled

in the Senate and never became law. See Tomoeh Murakami Tse, " 'Say-on-Pay' Movement Loses Steam," *Washington Post*, May 6, 2008, p. D1.

18. See Jonathan Weil, "Lehman's Greatest Value Lies in Lessons Learned," *Bloomberg.com*, June 11, 2008, and Jeffrey McCracken and Alex Frangos, "Lehman Considers Spinoff of Remnants," *Wall Street Journal*, May 14, 2009, p. C1.

19. It is the banks' managers' incentives that matter, and as we have seen, these are not well aligned with shareholders' interests. There are strong managerial incentives for lack of transparency. See Edlin and Stiglitz, "Discouraging Rivals: Managerial Rent-Seeking and Economic Inefficiencies," op. cit.

20. I was disappointed some fifteen years ago, when members of both the Clinton administration (including Robert Rubin) and Congress (including Senator Joseph Lieberman) put political pressure on the supposedly independent Financial Accounting Standards Board (FASB) not to force firms to take appropriate account of their stock options. But what has happened in the current crisis is even more appalling, as members of Congress have threatened that they would overrule the FASB unless it went along with the banks' demand for worsening accounting standards.

21. The FASB voted to approve the change on April 2, 2009. See Floyd Norris, "Banks Get New Leeway in Valuing Their Assets," Financial Accounting Standards Board, Summary of Board Decisions, April 2, 2009, available at http://www.fasb.org/action/sbd040209.shtml.

22. Allowing lower lending against the value of banks' capital during good times, and more during bad times, is called countercyclical capital adequacy standards. Such regulations are sometimes referred to as macro-prudential regulations.

23. Full mark-to-market accounting might, in this instance, give some indication of the expected (average) return to shareholders, recognizing that, on average, they will be paying off to bondholders less than they promised.

24. Other accounting problems can distort behavior. After the savings and loan crisis, banks were naturally required to hold more capital (something that is happening again), but because long-term government bonds were viewed as safe, less capital was required if banks held these bonds. At the time these long-term bonds yielded a far higher return than the deposit rate or short-term government bonds, and they could book the higher returns as profits, even if the higher returns reflect an expectation of a fall in bond prices (a capital loss). This favorable accounting induced a shift in bank portfolios toward long-term government bonds, and away from loans, contributing to the economic downturn of 1991. See Stiglitz, *Roaring Nineties*, op. cit.

25. Actually, the older accounting standards (before April 2009) were not that stringent. They did not force the banks to mark to market all assets, only, as I mentioned, certain "impaired" assets, loans that were in delinquency. This made sense—far more sense than giving the banks full discretion to say, Well, perhaps, if we hold them long enough, they really will be okay. The fact of the matter was

all the evidence suggested that more mortgages would be going into trouble—unless there was a massive bailout. The government's mortgage program was a help, but not enough, certainly not enough to justify the new system of marking to hope.

26. The mortgage servicers, who are responsible for managing the restructuring, have especially distorted incentives. By postponing foreclosure, they may be able to garner for themselves fees, money that in the end is at the expense of the holder of the first mortgage. See the discussion in chapter 4.

27. There are further problems: failing to use mark-to-market accounting exposes the economy to untold risks. Not marking to market provides an incentive for all banks to gamble. Assume a bank could keep assets on its books at the purchase price until it sold them, when it would record the price at which they were sold. A bank would have an incentive to buy high-risk assets, some of which would go up in value, some down. It could, then, easily artificially distort its apparent asset value by selling the assets that had gone up in value, and retaining those that had gone down as long as it could. If the bank is told that it only has to mark to market widely traded assets, then the bank has an incentive to buy assets that are not widely traded—which gives it more discretion to engage in non-transparent accounting. It is not simply that book value itself is a distorted measure of real value, but, consequently, flawed accounting systems distort lending and investment, encouraging excessive risk-taking and purchases of hard-to-value assets.

28. U.S. Government Accountability Office (GAO), "Cayman Islands: Business and Tax Advantages Attract US Persons and Enforcement Challenges Exist," Report to the Chairman and Ranking Member, Committee on Finance, U.S. Senate, GAO-08-778, July 2008.

29. There has been progress in curtailing bank secrecy in "off-shore" banking centers, and recent G-20 meetings suggest that there may be more. On one critical issue, the automatic exchange of information, too little has been done. And while the focus has been on tax evasion, little is being done about the other nefarious uses (like safe havens for money stolen by corrupt dictators) of bank secrecy. Moreover, while the focus of bank secrecy is on off-shore islands, the recent bank secrecy index constructed by the Tax Justice Network points out that the United States, United Kingdom, and Singapore are among the worst offenders. See Michael Peel, "Leading Economies Blamed for Fiscal Secrecy," *Financial Times online*, October 30, 2009, and Tax Justice Network, "Financial Secrecy Index," 2009, available at http://www.financialsecrecyindex.com.

30. The impossibility of a central planner performing such calculations was one of the main themes of my book *Whither Socialism* (Cambridge, MA: MIT Press, 1994), written at the time of the collapse of the Soviet system.

31. As chairman of the Council of Economic Advisers from 1995 to 1997, I had vigorously opposed the repeal of Glass-Steagall. As an economist, I certainly possessed a healthy degree of trust—trust in the power of economic incentives. I

pointed out that if those supporting repeal of the Glass-Steagall Act really constructed the Chinese walls, most of the "economies of scope," the alleged benefits of bringing the commercial and investment banks together, would be lost.

32. Federal Deposit Insurance Corporation, *Summary of Deposits*, October 15, 2009, available at http://www2.fdic.gov/SOD/sodSummary.asp?barItem=3.

33. Some, such as former SEC official Lee Pickard, put the 2004 change in the 1975 rule at the center of the failure. The SEC argued that its new rule "strengthened oversight." In retrospect, given the problems in so many of the investment banks, this claim seems unpersuasive. See Julie Satow, "Ex-SEC Official Blames Agency for Blow-up of Broker-Dealers," *New York Sun online*, September 18, 2008. For the contrary position, see the speech by Erik R. Sirri, Director of SEC Division of Trading and Markets, on April 9, 2009, available at http://www.sec.gov/news/speech/2009/spch040909ers.htm.

34. Some have argued for an extreme view of this called "narrow banking," where the depository institutions would be allowed to invest only in, say, T-bills. The functions of ordinary commercial banks—such as lending to small and medium-sized enterprises—are essential for the well-functioning of a market economy. There are, I believe, natural synergies arising from combining such lending with the payments system.

35. Speech of June 17, 2009, op. cit.

36. Group of Thirty, *Financial Reform: A Framework for Financial Stability*, January 15, 2009, available at http://www.group30.org/pubs/recommendations.pdf.

37. It does not make sense to force the banks that have been doing the job of real banking to pay for the costs of the losses of the too-big-to-fail banks. It is neither equitable nor efficient. With bonds guaranteed by the Federal Deposit Insurance Corporation (FDIC), all depositors, including those with their money in good banks, in effect are forced to bear at the very least some of the costs of the mistakes of the banks that engaged in excessive risk-taking. These too-big-to-fail banks should bear this cost, e.g., in the form of a special tax imposed on profits, dividend distributions, bonuses, and interest payments on bonds. (If we can make a credible commitment not to bail out bondholders—demonstrated by allowing the current bondholders to take a haircut—the latter should be exempted. Given the current stance, they should not be.)

As this book goes to press, the big banks are resisting imposing any extra charges. They claim that they will behave well, that they won't have to turn to the government for help, and that it would be unfair to make them pay for the mistakes of those that don't manage risk well. One proposal is to impose charges on the banks that have to be bailed out. But the point is that, typically, at the time the rescues occur, government has to put money in; there is seldom money left over for it to take out, as exemplified by the losses the government will experience in the current bailout. As I have noted, the government has had to repeatedly bail out the banks, and until it imposes regulations that are sufficiently strong that failures become a thing of the past, there must be charges against the too-big-to-fail banks. It is, evidently, part of the cost of running the financial system. Equity and efficiency require that the banks—not ordinary taxpayers—bear the costs.

38. None should be allowed to have any off-balance-sheet activities. Later in the chapter, I describe a particularly risky product, credit default swaps, and how they need to be regulated.

39. Proposals of "living wills," concrete plans of how the transactions should be unwound and the banks shut down, are a move in the right direction but are unlikely to suffice: the situation can change dramatically in a few hours, and a plan that might seem to have worked before the crisis won't during the crisis.

40. This book cannot go into detail on all of the complex instruments that the financial sector created—and what went wrong with them. One financial product that has received considerable attention is "auction-rated" securities, in which the rate of interest that is to be paid on the securities is determined each week in an auction. But in early 2008, the auctions stopped functioning, and the $330 billion market froze. While there is ample evidence of malfeasance by the Wall Street firms that sold them, getting redress through the legal system, especially in class-action suits, is, at best, slow and expensive, leaving individual investors to bear the losses. See Gretchen Morgenson, "A Way out of the Deep Freeze," *New York Times*, November 8, 2009, p. B1.

41. As I noted, this is not true for mortgage foreclosures. Insurance companies often exclude these kinds of correlated risks.

42. There is another fundamental difference between buying insurance on the death of a person and the death of a firm: the extent of information asymmetry. In the case of life insurance, both the insurance company and the insured have access to the same information about life expectancy. The person may have a slight informational advantage—he may know whether he engages in the kinds of risk-taking behaviors that might shorten his life expectancy. In the case of the death of a firm, the firm is likely to have far better information about its business prospects than the insurance company has, so it will not buy insurance if the insurance firm quotes a premium that reflects too large of an overestimate of the probability of bankruptcy. This is called the problem of adverse selection.

43. Like so much else that the financial markets did, their attempts at managing risk not only failed but were sometimes counterproductive; indeed by creating a complex web of conflicts of interest and legal entanglements, they increased risk. When the government provided money for one bank to buy another, it may have in fact been bailing out the first bank as much as the second, if the first bank would have had to have made large payments to third parties had the second bank gone bankrupt.

44. The financial markets—and government regulators—should have been aware of the risks, which were manifest in the East Asian crisis of a decade ago. Korea's banks thought they had managed a lot of the risks they faced, for instance, from

exchange rate changes; they thought they had obtained a cover, as it is called, against these risks from a firm in Hong Kong. However, the company that they had bought the insurance from went bankrupt, and they were left bearing the risk.

45. One can assess the likelihood of default, implicitly, from the price of the bond market. If capital markets were as efficient as their advocates claimed, there would be little need for credit default swaps, and it would be hard to justify the billions of dollars in fees reaped in by those issuing them. What the credit default swap market does is to allow those who want to focus on risk assessment to do that, without linking it to the task of providing funds. This, in itself, is potentially important, but, as we have seen, it is accompanied by considerable risk, especially as it invites speculation on differences in risk assessments.

46. So distrustful did Americans become of American meat after the publication of Upton Sinclair's scathing indictment of U.S. stockyards in his 1906 classic, *The Jungle*, that the industry begged the government to perform meat inspections. Customers didn't really trust certification that a private firm might provide. So too, it's impossible for ordinary citizens to evaluate the financial standing of a bank, to know whether it's safe enough to put their money in it. They have good reason not to believe any private-sector firm that is giving the bank a grade on its financial standing—especially one paid by the banks, such as a rating agency. This kind of information is what economists call a *public good*, underlying the strong case for government provision.

47. The Obama administration has proposed creating a financial products commission. As this book goes to press, it has not yet been passed by Congress, but the House Financial Services Committee has gutted key provisions and exempted the vast majority of banks.

48. In 1980, 56 percent of American adults had at least one credit card. In 2001, that number had grown to 76 percent. "Debt Nation," *NewsHour with Jim Lehrer*, PBS, April 18, 2001, available at http://www.pbs.org/newshour/extra/features/jan-june01/credit_debt.html.

49. Visa and MasterCard are different from other credit cards (like American Express and Diners Club) because they are effectively owned by the banks. Usage is also so widespread that stores hesitate not to accept them, lest they lose customers.

50. Of course, merchants can and do pass on the costs to their customers—but all customers pay, whether they use cash, a debit card, a credit card, or a premium credit card. The market for payment mechanisms (the choice among these alternatives) is totally distorted.

51. The key idea behind an efficient payment system is that efficiency requires separating out the payment function from the credit function—with individuals paying separately for each. Those who want a low-cost way of effecting a transaction should have that option, but there should also be an efficient and low-cost way of "adding" on a credit option. The cost of a pure "debit" transaction (com-

bining the charges to the customer and the charges to the merchant) would be a fraction of what is charged today.

Australia recently made a modest reform—allowing merchants to impose charges to reflect the costs to the merchant of the card and restricting the exploitive fees charged to merchants—with the beneficial outcomes that were much as predicted. See Reserve Bank of Australia, Media Release, "Reform of Credit Card Schemes in Australia," August 27, 2002, available at http://www.rba.gov.au/MediaReleases/2002/mr_02_15.html. For a review of the benefits, see Reserve Bank of Australia, "Reform of Australia's Payments System: Conclusions of the 2007/2008 Review," Sydney, Australia, September 2008.

52. World Bank, World Development Indicators 2008, GDP per capita, Purchasing Power Parity (that is, adjusted for differences in costs of living), revised edition, Washington, DC, April 16, 2008.

53. Only twenty-four states have set maximum check-cashing fees. See Matt Fellowes and Mia Mabanta, "Banking on Wealth: America's New Retail Banking Infrastructure and Its Wealth-Building Potential," Metropolitan Policy Program at Brookings Institute, Washington, DC, January 2008.

54. To get banks to lend in these underserved areas, Congress had to pass the Community Reinvestment Act. Once forced to lend, they found out that it could be profitable—with default rates, as I noted in chapter 1, that were comparable to those in other areas where they were lending.

55. See Congressional Budget Office, "Cost Estimate: H.R. 3221 Student Aid and Fiscal Responsibility Act of 2009," July 24, 2009, available at http://www.cbo.gov/ftpdocs/104xx/doc10479/hr3221.pdf.

56. Karen W. Arenson, "Columbia to Pay $1.1 Million to State Fund in Loan Scandal," New York Times, June 1, 2007, p. B1.

57. There is a large literature in economics and political science describing how regulators often get "captured" by those they are supposed to regulate. In the case of self-regulation, capture is obvious, and as we saw in the last chapter, regulation of the New York Federal Reserve Bank comes close to being self-regulation. But the problem is as much mindset as anything else ("cognitive capture"). Regulators are supposed to think differently from those they are regulating. They are supposed to think about what can go wrong. And they are supposed to act when things start to go awry—especially because they should know that it is others (and especially the taxpayers) who will have to pay for cleaning up any mess.

58. We have both private enforcement (through civil suits) and public enforcement; we have enforcement at the federal and state levels; and at the federal level, enforcement is the responsibility of both the Department of Justice and the Federal Trade Commission.

59. There are many other instances of financial markets resisting innovations: a few years earlier, some economists came up with a better way of selling Treasury bills through auctions that would lower transaction costs, make the sales more

transparent, and ensure that the government got a higher return for the bonds it was selling. Yet again, some on Wall Street resisted. The reason was obvious: Wall Street did not want to maximize government revenue. Instead, it wanted to maximize its revenue, and again, it could make more money out of the old non-transparent system.

Chapter 7 A NEW CAPITALIST ORDER

1. These numbers are for the ratio of publicly held debt to GDP. Under the most realistic scenarios provided by the Congressional Budget Office, the debt-to-GDP ratio is estimated to increase to 87 percent by 2019. If all debt (not just publicly held debt) is included, under the optimistic scenario of the Obama administration the debt-GDP ratio in 2019 exceeds 100 percent. See Office of Management and Budget, "Budget of the US Government, Fiscal Year 2010, Updated Summary Tables, May 2009"; Budget of the United States Government: Historical Tables Fiscal Year 2010, "Table 7.1—Federal Debt at the End of Year: 1940–2014," Washington, DC, available at http://www.gpoaccess.gov/USbudget/fy10/index.html; and Congressional Budget Office, "The Long-Term Budget Outlook," June 2009, http://www.cbo.gov/ftpdocs/102xx/doc10297/06-25-LTBO.pdf.

2. From 1950 to 1973, average per capita income increased by 59 percent, and median per capita income—the income of those in the middle—increased by 41 percent. U.S. Census Bureau, *Historical Income Tables—People*, "Table P-4. Race and Hispanic Origin of People (Both Sexes Combined) by Median and Mean Income: 1947 to 2007," available at http://www.census.gov/hhes/www/income/histinc/p04.html.

3. See Julia B. Isaacs, "Economic Mobility of Men and Women," in R. Haskins, J. Isaacs, and I. Sawhill (eds.), *Getting Ahead or Losing Ground: Economic Mobility in America* (Washington, DC: Brookings Institution, 2008).

4. Carmen DeNavas-Walt, Bernadette D. Proctor, and Jessica C. Smith, "Income, Poverty, and Health Insurance Coverage in the United States: 2008," U.S. Census Bureau, September 2009, available at http://www.census.gov/prod/2009pubs/p60-236.pdf.

5. Roy Walmsley, "World Prison Population List. 7th edition," International Centre for Prison Studies, School of Law, King's College London, 2007.

6. Fifteen-year-old students in the United States scored lower than the average for Organisation for Economic Co-operation and Development (OECD) members on the science literacy scale (22 of 57 countries had higher average scores) and on the mathematics literacy scale (31 countries had higher average scores and only 20 had lower). The United States had higher percentages of students who scored below the lowest level (Level 1) and at the lowest level than the OECD average in science literacy. Baldi, Jin, Skewer, Green, and Herget, *Highlights from PISA 2006*, op. cit.

7. The baby-boom generation consists of the 79 million Americans born between 1946 and 1964. The fraction of people in the United States ages sixty-five and over is expected to increase by more than 50 percent by 2030, growing from 13 percent of the population in 2010 to 20 percent in 2030, remaining above 20 percent for at least several decades. After 2010, the aging of the baby-boom generation will dramatically increase government outlays: annual Social Security spending is expected to accelerate from about 5.1 percent in 2008 to 6.4 percent by 2018. Spending for Medicare and Medicaid will increase even faster, in the range of 7 to 8 percent annually. Total outlays for Medicare and Medicaid are projected to more than double from 2009 to 2018, while GDP is projected to grow half as fast. U.S. Census Bureau, Population Division, "National Population Projections—Projections of the Population by Selected Age Groups and Sex for the United States: 2010 to 2050," August 14, 2008, and Peter Orszag, "The Budget and Economic Outlook: Fiscal Years 2008 to 2018," statement before the Committee on the Budget, U.S. Senate, Washington, DC, January 24, 2008.

8. Energy expenditures were 8.8 percent of GDP in 2006. See Energy Information Agency, "Annual Energy Review 2008, Table 1.5: Energy Consumption, Expenditures, and Emissions Indicators, 1949-2008," June 26, 2009, available at http://www.eia.doe.gov/emeu/aer/overview.html. Among America's largest companies are ExxonMobil (no. 1), Chevron (3), ConocoPhillips (4), and Valero Energy (10). "Fortune 500," *Fortune Magazine online*, 2009, available at http://money.cnn.com/magazines/fortune/fortune500/.

9. See Bureau of Economic Analysis, National Income and Product Accounts Table, "Table 6.16D. Corporate Profits by Industry," available at http://www.bea.gov/National/nipaweb/SelectTable.asp. In addition to these high profits, a very large amount was paid in bonuses (in the case of a few banks, the amounts are almost equal).

10. International Labour Organization, "Global Employment Trends Update, May 2009," International Labour Office, Geneva, Switzerland. 2009, available at http://www.ilo.org/wcmsp5/groups/public/---dgreports/---dcomm/documents/publication/wcms_106504.pdf.

11. The U.S. current account deficit was $804 billion in 2006. It has since declined slightly, to $727 billion and $706 billion in 2007 and 2008, respectively. Bureau of Economic Analysis, U.S. International Transactions Accounts Data, Table 1, September 14, 2009, available at http://www.bea.gov/international/xls/table1.xls.

12. Households went from net borrowing over $1 trillion in 2006 to saving $279 billion in the last quarter of 2008. Meanwhile, government borrowing has increased in the same period from $335 billion to nearly $2.2 trillion. Federal Reserve, Flow of Funds Accounts of the United States, Table F.1, Washington, DC, March 12, 2009, available at http://www.federalreserve.gov/releases/z1/Current/data.htm.

13. Encouraging China to consume more is misguided in another way: even if China were to increase its own consumption, there might result in little increase

in imports from the United States. High priority would and should be given to domestic services like education and health. The fallacy in thinking that increased Chinese consumption would easily deal with the huge U.S. trade deficit is akin to arguing that an appreciation of their currency would do the same. America wouldn't start producing apparel and textiles; the United States would simply shift purchases from China to other developing countries. The problem posed by global imbalances might be worsened: while China is willing to relend its surplus to the United States, other developing countries might not be so willing.

14. The effects in developed countries are self-evident: unskilled workers have to compete with the low-wage workers from the rest of the world. See Stiglitz, *Making Globalization Work*, op. cit.

15. For instance, a global commitment to a high price for carbon emissions (say, $80 a ton), now and in the future, would provide strong incentives for firms and households to make investments to increase their "carbon" efficiency.

16. The wage income shares of the top 1 percent and top 5 percent had already surpassed their previous peaks by the late 1980s and reached new all-time highs by 1998. Thomas Piketty and Emmanuel Saez, "Income Inequality in the United States, 1913–1998," *Quarterly Journal of Economics*, vol. 118, no. 1 (February 2003), pp. 1–39, figure IX.

17. In 2006, China overtook the United States as the largest emitter. See Elisabeth Rosenthal, "China Increases Lead as Biggest Carbon Dioxide Emitter," *New York Times*, June 14, 2008, p. A5.

18. See Wallace E. Tyner, "The US Ethanol and Biofuels Boom: Its Origins, Current Status, and Future Prospects," *BioScience*, vol. 58, no. 7 (July/August 2008), pp. 646–653. There is a broad consensus that there are little if any environmental benefits from corn-based ethanol. Critics also point out that subsidizing corn-based ethanol risks driving up the price of food grains.

19. Cuba has reduced its already low infant mortality rate to 7.2 deaths per 1,000 live births, which is the same as the U.S. average, and half the rate in Washington, DC. Molly Moore, "The Hemorrhaging of Cuba's Health Care; Doctors without Data, Patients without Drugs: U.S. Embargo, Economic Crisis Cripple a Showcase System," *Washington Post*, February 23, 1998, p. A12.

20. For instance, top fifteen-year-old students in Korea scored well above the OECD average on the OECD's PISA test, while students at the same level in the United States performed below the OECD average. Organisation for Economic Co-operation and Development, "OECD Briefing Note for the United States," *PISA 2006: Science Competencies for Tomorrow's World*, December 4, 2007, available at http://www.pisa.oecd.org/dataoecd/16/28/39722597.pdf. See also note 6, this chapter.

21. See Mamta Murthi, J. Michael Orszag, and Peter R. Orszag, "The Charge Ratio on Individual Accounts: Lessons from the U.K. Experience," Birkbeck College Working Paper 99-2, University of London, March 1999.

22. See Yao Li, John Whalley, Shunming Zhang, and Xiliang Zhao, "The Higher Educational Transformation of China and Its Global Implications," National Bureau of Economic Research Working Paper 13849, Cambridge, MA, March 2008, available at http://www.nber.org/papers/w13849.

23. The United Nations Development Programme's "human development indicator" (HDI) combines measures of per capita income with measures of education and health. According to the 2009 Human Development Report, Sweden ranked number 7 in HDI while the United States ranked number 13.

24. Herbert Simon, "Organizations and Markets," *Journal of Economic Perspectives*, vol. 5, no. 2 (1991), p. 28.

25. In both organizational forms, the management of the firm can be viewed as a public good, in the sense that all shareholders benefit if the firm is well managed. In both organizational forms, there is a risk of underprovision of oversight of this public good. Perhaps because the problem is more obvious in government-run enterprises, institutional arrangements to deal with the problem have often been created, preventing the worst abuses from occurring.

26. The for-profit schools, focusing on vocational training, have excelled in deceptive practices. Students graduating from these schools have often been sorely disappointed and have not wanted to pay back student loans. The Clinton administration tried to disqualify schools with high student loan default rates, but the private schools lobbied against this initiative—they knew that without access to government-guaranteed loans, they would be out of business.

27. See Environmental Working Group, "Farm Subsidy Database," available at http://farm.ewg.org/farm/progdetail.php?fips=00000&yr=2006&progcode=cotton&page=conc. In August 2009, a World Trade Organization appeals panel ruled that Brazil could impose up to $800 million worth of retaliatory trade barriers against the United States for its violations. See World Trade Organization, "WTO Issues Arbitration Reports in US-Brazil Cotton Dispute," August 31, 2009, available at http://www.wto.org/english/news_e/news09_e/267arb_e.htm.

28. "Statement of Senator McCain on the Energy Bill," November 19, 2003, http://mccain.senate.gov/public/index.cfm?FuseAction=PressOffice.Speeches&ContentRecord_id=9259EB94-5344-435F-B4D8-37F7BF6DAA77.

29. When I was a member and chairman of the Council of Economic Advisers, we compiled a list of corporate welfare programs, and compared our list with those compiled by others, including conservative think tanks. Interestingly, the assistance to banks through the IMF, which plays a major role in bank bailouts, was at or toward the top of many of the lists. This was even before the IMF provided big bank bailouts in Asia, Russia, and Latin America.

30. If the reason for market underpricing of risk has to do with distorted incentives, government can try to affect incentive structures, thereby indirectly affecting risk pricing.

31. That is why trying to get knowledge to be produced by markets may be highly

inefficient. In some cases, one can succeed in doing so (e.g., through the patent system), but the societal costs of using a market mechanism may be large.

32. Economists have devoted a great deal of attention to understanding the absence of key insurance markets. It has largely to do with information problems (in particular, information asymmetries). See M. Rothschild and J. E. Stiglitz, "Equilibrium in Competitive Insurance Markets: An Essay on the Economics of Imperfect Information," *Quarterly Journal of Economics*, vol. 90, no. 4 (November 1976), pp. 629–649.

33. The list of corporate exploitive behavior is long. One insurance firm sold life insurance policies against dreaded diseases—it knew that its salesmen, depicting the bereaved widow left helpless as a result of death by such a ghastly illness, could easily sell policies costing but a quarter a day—even though the actuarial risk was negligible. The former head of the Food and Drug Administration David Kessler provides instances from the food and beverage industry. See David Kessler, *The End of Overeating: Taking Control of the Insatiable North American Appetite* (Emmaus, PA: Rodale, 2009), and *A Question of Intent: A Great American Battle with a Deadly Industry* (New York: PublicAffairs, 2001).

34. Adam Smith recognized the dangers, and modern antitrust laws are designed to try to maintain a competitive marketplace and prevent abusive anticompetitive practices.

35. Claude Henry, *Patent Fever in Developed Countries and Its Fallout on the Developing World*, Prisme No. 6 (Paris: Centre Cournot for Economic Studies, May 2005), and Andrew Pollack, "Patent on Test for Cancer Is Revoked by Europe," *New York Times*, May 19, 2004, p. C3.

36. The patent system can even impede the pace of innovation. It raises, for instance, the price of the most important input into research (knowledge), and can create a patent thicket, with every innovator worried about trespassing on the patents of someone else. See chapter 4 in Stiglitz, *Making Globalization Work*, op. cit.

37. Bureau of Economic Analysis, Industry Economic Accounts, GDP by Industry Accounts, "Value Added by Industry as a Percentage of GDP," April 28, 2009, available at http://www.bea.gov/industry/xls/GDPbyInd_VA_NAICS_1998-2008.xls.

38. Were the government to require TV and radio stations to provide free time for candidates, it would reduce the need for campaign finance. Australia's system of required voting reduces the need for expenditures to get out the vote.

39. Data from the Federal Election Commission, compiled by the Center for Responsive Politics, revealed that political action committees and employees of securities and investment firms gave $156 million in political contributions in the 2008 election cycle. Goldman Sachs, Citigroup, JP Morgan Chase, Bank of America, and Credit Suisse gave $22.7 million and spent more than $25 million combined on lobbying in that period. Center for Responsive Politics, "Lobbying Database," available at http://www.opensecrets.org/lobby/index.php and "Heavy Hitters," available at http://www.opensecrets.org/orgs/list.php?order=A. Repre-

sentative Collin C. Peterson, chairman of the House Agriculture Committee, which normally has oversight over trading on futures markets (because of the origin of futures trading in agriculture commodities), put it bluntly: "The banks run the place. I will tell you what the problem is—they give three times more money than the next biggest group." Gretchen Morgenson and Don Van Natta Jr., "Even in Crisis, Banks Dig in for Battle against Regulation," *New York Times*, June 1, 2009, p. A1.

Chapter 8 FROM GLOBAL RECOVERY TO GLOBAL PROSPERITY

1. The idea for the meeting of the G-20 came from President Nicolas Sarkozy of France, and he had hoped to have the meeting in New York, under the auspices of the UN. President George W. Bush, presumably realizing that if he didn't act quickly Europe would take the initiative, called for the meeting in Washington, DC.

2. International Monetary Fund, *World Economic Outlook*, Washington, DC, April 2008, p. 24.

3. These are instances of externalities across countries. As I have repeatedly emphasized, externalities are pervasive and important, and when they are pervasive, markets, on their own, won't work well.

4. Ireland's defense minister said as much: "From Ireland's point of view, the best sort of fiscal stimulus are those being put in place by our trading partners. Ultimately these will boost demand for our exports without costing us anything. What we need to do is to ensure that we are well positioned to avail of the opportunities that result from our trading partners' actions." Willie O'Dea, Minister for Defense, "Why Our Response to Crisis Isn't Wrong," *Sunday Independent* (Ireland), January 4, 2009.

5. For a general discussion of these provisions, as well as the potentially distorting effect on trade of the assistance provided banks and other enterprises in the crisis, see Trade Policy Review Body, "Overview of Developments in the International Trading Environment—Annual Report by the Director-General," World Trade Organization, WT/TPR/OV/12, November 18, 2009, available at http://www.wto.org/english/thewto_e/minist_e/min09_e/official_doc_e.htm.

6. Elisa Gamberoni and Richard Newfarmer, "Trade Protection: Incipient but Worrisome Trends," Trade Notes No. 37, International Trade Department, World Bank, Washington, DC, March 2, 2009.

7. Capital market liberalization, allowing hot money that could come into a country overnight to flow out equally rapidly, leaving devastation in its wake, was a key factor contributing to the East Asian crisis of 1997–1998. I had been particularly critical of capital market liberalization because while the costs—the huge risks—were clear, there were no apparent benefits. One couldn't build factories with money that could flow in or out overnight. Eventually the IMF

reversed itself when its chief economist, Ken Rogoff, conceded that, at least in many cases, there was little evidence that capital market liberalization had led to more growth, and some evidence that it had led to more instability in some countries. See Prasad, Rogoff, Wei, and Kose, "Effects of Financial Globalization on Developing Countries," op. cit.

One of the key arguments for financial market liberalization, allowing foreign banks to operate freely within one's borders, was that U.S. banks would "teach" developing countries good banking practices and would bring greater growth and greater stability. It hasn't worked out that way. Ironically, until the era of liberalization hit, the United States had resisted even the notion of having *national* banks that stretched across the country. The worry was that the big banks from New York and the other money centers would drain all of the savings from the heartland, rather than reinvesting it locally. Lending is about information—good lenders know their borrowers, and if the lenders are in New York, they are more likely to lend to New York firms, not exclusively, but disproportionately. The restrictions led to the unique character of the U.S. financial system, marked by large numbers of local and community banks—even today, there are more than seven thousand. These banks not only lend to small and medium-sized local businesses; they are one of the sources of America's dynamism.

8. As a condition for giving money, the IMF insists that the recipient country do certain things. Every bank imposes certain conditions on borrowers to enhance the likelihood that the loan be repaid, but the conditions the IMF imposes sometimes reduce the likelihood of repayment, and often are only very loosely connected to the loan itself. There may be "macro-conditions" (for instance, requiring that the central bank raise its interest rates or that deficits be cut), structural conditions (for instance, requiring that the government privatize its banks), or political conditions (for instance, requiring that the government give full independence to the central bank). In total, the conditions reduce the scope for independent policy making. Many developing countries view the conditions as taking away their economic sovereignty.

9. Protests and riots against IMF policies also occurred in Argentina, Brazil, Colombia, Kenya, South Korea, and Zimbabwe. See Mark Ellis-Jones, "States of Unrest II: Resistance to IMF and World Bank Policies in Poor Countries," World Development Movement Report, London, April 2002, available at http://web .archive.org/web/20050130125648/www.wdm.org.uk/cambriefs/debt/Unrest2.pdf.

10. For instance, the IMF put pressure on Pakistan to raise interest rates and taxes (see James Melik, "Pakistan Business Fighting on All Fronts," BBC News, May 22, 2009). The IMF also set a target for Pakistan's budget deficit, which it was in danger of exceeding (see Khaleeq Ahmed and Khalid Qayum, "Pakistan's Budget Deficit May Exceed IMF Target, Tarin Says," *Bloomberg.com*, June 10, 2009). The IMF used its usual tactics for enforcing budget cuts in Latvia with a threat to delay the next installment of its loan, which might have pushed the

country into bankruptcy (see Aaron Eglitis, "Latvia Faces Bankruptcy by June If IMF Loan Delayed," *Bloomberg.com*, March 9, 2009). In each case, there is a debate about the appropriateness of IMF policies: Is the country able to have a more expansionary policy than it would have had without the IMF program? Is the IMF balancing trade-offs, say, between inflation and unemployment in an appropriate way? Still, the debate today is markedly different from what it was a decade ago.

11. I had called for this and many other reforms in my earlier book *Globalization and Its Discontents*, op. cit.

12. U.S. government assistance is only .18 percent of GDP, which is less than one-fourth of the contributions of Denmark (.82 percent), Netherlands (.8 percent), Norway (.88 percent), and Sweden (.99 percent). Organisation for Economic Co-operation and Development, *OECD.Stat*, "ODA by Donor," March 30, 2009, and "Gross Domestic Product," available at http://stats.oecd.org.

13. The United States was even reluctant to match Europe and Japan's support for the IMF. Its first response was to generously offer that the IMF invite China, Saudi Arabia, and others to lend more money to it, so it could lend the money to poorer countries. Eventually, the Obama administration did make a commitment to provide a $100 billion loan to the IMF—small in comparison to Japan's offer, relative to the size of the United States and relative to what the U.S. government had given its own banks, and especially small relative to its culpability for causing the crisis and the pain these countries felt. (And unlike much of the money given to the banks, this was a loan that would be repaid.) But Congress balked at even this sum, and the Obama administration, to its credit, expended considerable capital to do the right thing and get it passed.

14. The G-20 requested that the OECD publish lists categorizing countries where the authorities were considered fully committed to international standards of information exchange. The OECD put four countries (Uruguay, Costa Rica, Malaysia, and the Philippines) on a blacklist, more than thirty on a gray list, and about forty countries on a white list. All four countries blacklisted were upgraded to gray status within one week. See Organisation for Economic Co-operation and Development, "Four More Countries Commit to OECD Tax Standards," OECD press release, April 7, 2009, available at http://www.oecd.org/document/0/0,3343 ,en_2649_33745_42521280_1_1_1_1,00.html.

15. The issue of corruption was put on the agenda in the Pittsburgh meeting of the G-20.

16. Francis Fukuyama, *The End of History and the Last Man* (New York: Free Press, 1992).

17. Angus Maddison, *The World Economy: A Millennial Perspective* (Paris: Organisation for Economic Co-operation and Development, 2007).

18. Luc Laeven and Fabian Valencia, "Systemic Banking Crises: A New Database," op. cit.

19. Those in the advanced industrial countries (and especially in the United States) gave justifications for the seemingly hypocritical behavior. First, they said, America was rich enough to squander its resources on corporate welfare—the poor countries were not. Government officials might privately agree that it was wrong, but, they would add, we had no choice, we live in a democracy, and our political institutions demand it. They found it difficult to countenance the notion that democracies in the developing world might have equally strong views—and indeed, that the obvious hypocrisy was giving succor to those who opposed these international agreements.

20. These talented individuals play a key role in the advanced industrial countries—in the success, for instance, of Silicon Valley. The British National Health Service is now staffed in large part by doctors and nurses who trained abroad. The large movements of health professionals from developing countries to the United Kingdom, United States, and other advanced industrial countries contribute to the quality of health care in the advanced industrial countries, but deprive the health system in developing countries of essential personnel. Of course, other factors (such as underfunding) contribute to the problems in the health care sector in many developing countries. See Tikki Pang, Mary Ann Lansang, and Andy Haines, "Brain Drain and Health Professionals," *British Medical Journal*, vol. 324 (March 2, 2002), pp. 499–500, available at http://www.bmj.com/cgi/content/full/324/7336/499.

21. See also George Soros, *The New Paradigm for Financial Markets: The Credit Crisis of 2008 and What It Means* (New York: PublicAffairs, 2008).

22. At current exchange rates, China's GDP is $7,916 billion, and the United States' is $14,462 billion. The GDP per capita for China, at $5,962, is one-eighth that of the United States, which is $46,859. International Monetary Fund, *World Economic Outlook* database, April 2009, available at http://www.imf.org/external/pubs/ft/weo/2009/01/weodata/index.aspx.

23. See Peter Marsh, "China to Overtake US as Largest Manufacturer," *Financial Times online*, August 10, 2008, available at http://www.ft.com/cms/s/0/2aa7a12e-6709-11dd-808f-0000779fd18c.html, and "China to Surpass Japan in Auto Production in '09," iSuppli Corp press release, March 26, 2009.

24. See Rosenthal, "China Increases Lead as Biggest Carbon Dioxide Emitter," op. cit.

25. In November 2008, China announced a two-year stimulus package of $586 billion, approximately 14 percent of China's GDP. An equivalently sized U.S. stimulus would require $2 trillion. See Xinhua News Agency, "China's 4 Trillion Yuan Stimulus to Boost Economy, Domestic Demand," November 9, 2008, available at http://news.xinhuanet.com/english/2008-11/09/content_10331324.htm.

26. Two senators, Charles Schumer of New York and Lindsey Graham of South Carolina, had planned to introduce a bill imposing steep (27.5 percent) tariffs on Chinese goods unless China allowed its currency to appreciate, but in March

2009 they decided not to do so. The U.S.-China interdependence is reflected in the opposition of the National Association of Manufacturers, which estimated that a quarter of all manufactured goods from China come from subsidiaries of American companies. Edmund L. Andrews, "Trade Truce with China in the Senate," *New York Times*, March 29, 2006. The U.S. imposition of tariffs against China's low-grade tires in September 2009 provides an example of the curious way that trade tensions play out. The case was brought by the United Steel Workers but was not joined by the industry, which had long ago stopped producing these low-grade tires. China, like other latecomers to the World Trade Organization, had to accede to a set of demands to join that go well beyond those agreed to by old members—a practice Oxfam has called "extortion at the gate." China agreed that for a number of years after joining, America could protect its industries against a surge of China exports, even if China was simply playing by the rules of a market economy. China's sales had increased, but mainly at the expense of sales from other low-cost producers of these low-grade tires—it wasn't at the expense of American producers, since they didn't produce these tires. American consumers would surely be hurt through higher tire prices far more than any benefit that the producers received.

27. See speech by Zhou Xiaochuan, Governor of the People's Bank of China, "Reform the International Monetary System," March 23, 2009, available at http://www.pbc.gov.cn/english/detail.asp?col=6500&id=178.

28. For a description, see John Williamson, "Keynes and the Postwar International Economic Order," in Harold L. Wattel (ed.), *The Policy Consequences of John Maynard Keynes* (Armonk, NY: M. E. Sharpe, 1985).

29. *Report of the Commission of Experts of the United Nations President of the General Assembly on Reforms of the International Monetary and Financial System*, September 2009, available at http://www.un.org/ga/president/63/PDFs/reportof expters.pdf.

30. See Dani Rodrik, "The Social Cost of Foreign Exchange Reserves," *International Economic Journal*, vol. 20, no. 3 (September 2006), pp. 253–266, and Stiglitz, *Making Globalization Work*, op. cit.

31. Government offsets the trade deficit by running a fiscal deficit except in periods in which there is irrational investor exuberance—such as during the tech/dot.com bubble in the late 1990s.

32. In May 2008, finance ministers in ASEAN+3 (Association of Southeast Nations, plus three) agreed to a common fund of foreign exchange reserve of $80 billion. In December 2008, they proposed to increase the size to $120 billion. That proposal was confirmed in May 2009. See C. R. Henning, "The Future of the Chiang Mai Initiative: An Asian Monetary Fund?" Peterson Institute for International Economics Policy Brief 09-5, Washington, DC, February 2009, and "Asian Nations Unveil $120 Billion Liquidity Fund," *Wall Street Journal*, May 4, 2009, p. A10.

33. An example of a political event that might reverse the strengthening of

the euro might be some anti–European Union voter action in one of the major countries—or even in one of the smaller ones.

34. There is a natural solution: for the advanced industrial countries to transfer the special drawing right (SDR) allocations that they don't need to the developing countries that need them. The abuse of the exchange equalization fund by Secretary Robert Rubin to facilitate the Mexican bailout—in circumvention of Congress—so angered Congress that it has made it difficult for such transfers to be made. See J. Lawrence Broz, "Congressional Politics of International Financial Rescues," *American Journal of Political Science*, vol. 49, no. 3 (July 2005), pp. 479–496.

35. For a more extensive discussion of alternative ways in which the global reserve currency system might be designed and how the transition from the current system to the new system might be managed, see the *Report of the Commission of Experts of the United Nations President of the General Assembly on Reforms of the International Monetary and Financial System*, op. cit..

Chapter 9 REFORMING ECONOMICS

1. Most of this view that Franklin Roosevelt's New Deal made the economy worse is conservative journalism, like Amity Schlaes's book *The Forgotten Man: A New History of the Great Depression* (New York: HarperCollins, 2007). But some academic economists have provided support. As the current crisis brewed, the Council on Foreign Relations held a conference on March 30, 2009, celebrating the failure of Keynesian economics, called "A Second Look at the Great Depression and New Deal."

2. See E. Cary Brown, "Fiscal Policy in the Thirties: A Reappraisal," *American Economic Review*, vol. 46, no. 5 (December 1956), pp. 857–879, and Peter Temin, *Lessons from the Great Depression* (Lionel Robbins Lecture) (Cambridge, MA: MIT Press, 1989).

3. In 1936, total budget spending was 10.5 percent of GDP, but it dropped to 8.6 percent in 1937 and 7.7 percent in 1938. In the same period, the budget deficit was 5.5, 2.5, and 0.1 percent of GDP, respectively. Office of Management and Budget, Budget of the United States Government: Historical Tables Fiscal Year 2010, "Table 1.2: Summary of Receipts, Outlays, and Surpluses or Deficits (-) as Percentages of GDP: 1930–2014," available at http://www.gpoaccess.gov/USbudget/fy10/sheets/hist01z2.xls.

4. As Keynes put it forcefully, "The long run is a misleading guide to current affairs. In the long run we are all dead. Economists set themselves too easy, too useless a task if in tempestuous seasons they can only tell us that when the storm is past the ocean is flat again." From John Maynard Keynes, "The Theory of Money and the Foreign Exchanges," chapter 3, in *A Tract on Monetary Reform* (New York: Macmillan, 1923).

5. Charles Kindleberger, *Manias, Panics, and Crashes: A History of Financial Crises* (New York: Basic Books, 1978), and Carmen M. Reinhart and Kenneth S. Rogoff, *This Time Is Different: Eight Centuries of Financial Folly* (Princeton, NJ: Princeton University Press, 2009).

6. Franklin Allen and Douglas Gale, *Understanding Financial Crises* (Oxford: Oxford University Press, 2007).

7. Léon Walras, *Éléments d'économie politique pure, ou théorie de la richesse sociale (Elements of Pure Economics, or the Theory of Social Wealth)*, 1874.

8. Kenneth J. Arrow, "An Extension of the Basic Theorems of Classical Welfare Economics," in J. Neyman (ed.), *Proceedings of the Second Berkeley Symposium on Mathematical Statistics and Probability* (Berkeley: University of California Press, 1951), pp. 507-532, and Gerard Debreu, "Valuation Equilibrium and Pareto Optimum," *Proceedings of the National Academy of Sciences*, vol. 40, no. 7 (1954), pp. 588-592, and *The Theory of Value: An Axiomatic Analysis of Economic Equilibrium* (New Haven: Yale University Press, 1959).

9. This notion of efficiency is referred to as Pareto efficiency, after Vilfredo Pareto, the Italian economist who first articulated this view, in his book *Manual of Political Economy* in 1906.

10. Debreu, *The Theory of Value*, op. cit.

11. See, in particular, Bruce Greenwald and Joseph E. Stiglitz, "Externalities in Economies with Imperfect Information and Incomplete Markets," *Quarterly Journal of Economics*, vol. 101 (1986), pp. 229-264.

12. Such circumstances, where small changes in, say, parameter values can generate large changes in outcomes, arise frequently in physical sciences. Economists had simply assumed that that was not the case (as Alfred Marshall, one of the great economists of the late nineteenth and early twentieth century, put it, "*Natura non facit saltum*," or "Nature does not make a leap"). See *Principles of Economics* (London: Macmillan, 1920). This will be true under certain mathematical assumptions, but these assumptions are not usually satisfied when it comes to analyses of markets with endogenous information or innovation.

Indeed, even small information imperfections can affect conclusions about the existence of an equilibrium. See Michael Rothschild and Joseph E. Stiglitz, "Equilibrium in Competitive Insurance Markets: An Essay on the Economics of Imperfect Information," *Quarterly Journal of Economics*, vol. 90, no. 4 (November 1976), pp. 629-649.

13. The term *neoclassical economics* is used to distinguish it from the classical economics associated with David Ricardo and Adam Smith. It stresses the *marginal* valuations put on different commodities by individuals.

14. One of the problems I faced as chairman of the Council of Economic Advisers was hiring a macroeconomist. Macroeconomics is concerned with the broad movements in output and employment. As I explain later, the prevailing models taught in most graduate schools were based on neoclassical economics. I won-

dered how the president, who had been elected on a platform of "Jobs! Jobs! Jobs!" would respond to one of our brightest and best young economists, as he or she explained that there was no such thing as unemployment.

15. The assumption that individuals are easily able to borrow means, of course, that the pain inflicted by unemployment is less.

16. The classic paper by Franco Modigliani and Merton Miller was "The Cost of Capital, Corporation Finance and the Theory of Investment," *American Economic Review*, vol. 48, no. 3 (1958), pp. 261–297. They also argued that it made no difference whether firms paid out dividends or retained shares. Their original analysis ignored the impact of taxation, but later studies uncovered a "dividend paradox." Under the Modigliani-Miller theory, firms could reduce the combined corporate and individual taxes by buying back shares rather than paying out dividends. It seemed as if they voluntarily paid hundreds of billions in taxes beyond what was required. See Joseph E. Stiglitz, "Taxation, Corporate Financial Policy and the Cost of Capital," *Journal of Public Economics*, vol. 2 (1973), pp. 1–34. This dividend paradox has spawned a huge literature. I have not been convinced by any of the explanations based on models of rationality.

17. S&P 500 CEOs averaged $10.5 million in pay last year, 344 times the pay of typical American workers. Compensation levels for private investment fund managers soared even further out into the pay stratosphere. Last year, the top 50 hedge and private equity fund managers averaged $588 million each, more than 19,000 times as much as typical U.S. workers earned. Sarah Anderson et al., "Executive Excess 2007: How Average Taxpayers Subsidize Runaway Pay," 15th Annual CEO Compensation Survey, Institute for Policy Studies and United for a Fair Economy, Washington, DC, and Boston, MA, August 25, 2008, available at http://www.faireconomy.org/files/executive_excess_2008.pdf.

18. See, for instance, Gary Becker, *The Economics of Discrimination* (Chicago: University of Chicago Press, 1957). Becker received his Nobel Prize in 1992. Other Nobel Prize winners, Kenneth Arrow, Edmund Phelps, and I, provided strong critiques of Becker's theory. See, for instance, Joseph E. Stiglitz, "Approaches to the Economics of Discrimination," *American Economic Review*, vol. 63, no. 2 (1973), pp. 287-95, and "Theories of Discrimination and Economic Policy," in George M. von Furstenberg, Bennett Harrison, and Anne R. Horowitz (eds.), *Patterns of Racial Discrimination*, vol. II: *Employment and Income* (Lexington, MA: Lexington Books, 1974), pp. 5–26; Edmund S. Phelps, "The Statistical Theory of Racism and Sexism," *American Economic Review*, vol. 62, no. 4 (1972), pp. 659–661; and Kenneth Arrow, "The Theory of Discrimination," in Orley Ashenfelter and Albert Rees (eds.), *Discrimination in Labor Markets* (Princeton: Princeton University Press, 1973).

19. Particularly influential on me were my conversations with George Akerlof, who shared the 2001 Nobel Memorial Prize with me.

20. One of the main developments in modern economics is game theory, which

analyzes strategic interactions, especially among small groups of "players." Game theory has been especially helpful in analyzing noncompetitive markets. But it has also been useful in explaining the persistence of discrimination. Even those who may not have any racial prejudices can be punished by others if they deviate from the discriminatory norm, and those who fail to punish may themselves be punished. Such models can be used to explain the persistence of Jim Crow segregationist policies and other forms of discrimination. See Dilip Abreu, "On the Theory of Infinitely Repeated Games with Discounting," *Econometrica*, vol. 56, no. 2 (March 1988), pp. 383–396, and George A. Akerlof, "Discriminatory, Status-based Wages among Tradition-Oriented, Stochastically Trading Coconut Producers," *Journal of Political Economy*, vol. 93, no. 2 (April 1985), pp. 265–276.

21. See, for instance, Robert H. Frank, Thomas Gilovich, and Dennis T. Regan, "Does Studying Economics Inhibit Cooperation?" *Journal of Economic Perspectives*, vol. 7, no. 2 (Spring 1993), pp. 159–171. Interestingly, Adam Smith, in his other great book, *The Theory of Moral Sentiments* (1759), discussed all of these human qualities.

22. See the *Report by the Commission on the Measurement of Economic Performance and Social Progress*, available at http://www.stiglitz-sen-fitoussi.fr, as well as the "Overview" by Jean-Paul Fitoussi, Amartya Sen, and Joseph E. Stiglitz. The commission was appointed by President Nicolas Sarkozy of France, and I served as chair and Amartya Sen served as chief adviser.

23. Since the publication of *Bowling Alone: The Collapse and Revival of American Community* (New York: Simon and Schuster, 2000), Robert Putnam has begun an initiative called the Saguaro Seminar: Civic Engagement in America, in order to develop ideas to increase Americans' connectedness to one another and to community institutions. The thirty participants are from academia, the arts, clergy, business, and top policymakers from both major political parties. The resulting book, *Better Together*, and the Web site, www.bettertogether.org, put forth strategies to reengage America civically. See Lewis M. Feldstein, Don Cohen, and Robert Putnam, *Better Together: Restoring the American Community* (New York: Simon and Schuster, 2003).

24. There is, however, a large and growing literature on the subject. See, for instance, Richard Layard, *Happiness: Lessons from a New Science* (London: Penguin, 2005), and the *Report by the Commission on the Measurement of Economic Performance and Social Progress*, op. cit.

25. See Dan Ariely, *Predictably Irrational* (New York: HarperCollins, 2008).

26. See, for instance, Shiller, *Irrational Exuberance*, op. cit., and Robert J. Shiller, *The Subprime Solution: How Today's Global Financial Crisis Happened, and What to Do about It* (Princeton: Princeton University Press, 2008).

27. If it is known that a bubble will break, say, in twenty years, then it will never form; no one would want to hold the asset the moment before the collapse. But that would mean the collapse would occur then. But, by the same token, if that

was known, it would collapse the moment before that. It is easy to see how the bubble unravels. Interestingly, contrary to widespread belief, rational expectations do not suffice to rule out the possibility of bubbles. Bubbles can exist with rational expectations so long as different people have different information (obviously the case). When the market fundamentalists in the Federal Reserve assumed that with all wise-markets, there could not be a bubble, they were going well beyond what economic theory had established. See, for instance, Markus K. Brunnermeier, "Bubbles," in Steven N. Durlauf and Lawrence E. Blume (eds.), *The New Palgrave Dictionary of Economics*, 2d ed. (New York: Palgrave Macmillan, 2008); Dilip Abreu and Markus K. Brunnermeier, "Bubbles and Crashes," *Econometrica*, vol. 71, no. 1 (January 2003), pp. 173–204; and Roger Guesnerie, *Assessing Rational Expectations: Sunspot Multiplicity and Economic Fluctuations*, vol. 1 (Cambridge: MIT Press, 2001).

28. Though there can also exist models of "rational" herding, where individuals make inferences from others' behavior. See, for instance, Andrea Devenow and Ivo Welch, "Rational Herding in Financial Economics," *European Economic Review*, vol. 40, nos. 3–5 (1996), pp. 603–616.

29. Jared Diamond, *Collapse: How Societies Choose to Fail or Succeed* (New York: Viking Books, 2005).

30. The argument for government intervention has been strengthened by research showing the systematic ways in which individuals underestimate certain low-risk probabilities. Most individuals find it difficult making judgments about uncertain events, especially low-probability events. They will buy insurance—demonstrating high levels of risk aversion—at the same time that they will gamble—believing somehow that they have a chance of winning.

31. There are complex philosophical issues in assessing what one means by "better" in these contexts. At the very least, one wants to make sure that they have savings and investment policies that have a high probability of not forcing marked reductions in consumption levels/standards of living in later life. See Richard H. Thaler and Cass R. Sunstein, *Nudge: Improving Decisions about Health, Wealth, and Happiness* (New Haven: Yale University Press, 2008).

32. John Maynard Keynes, *The General Theory of Employment, Interest, and Money* (London: Macmillan, 1936).

33. The Obama administration may have also been motivated by an influential book, published contemporaneously, by George A. Akerlof and Robert J. Shiller: *Animal Spirits: How Human Psychology Drives the Economy, and Why It Matters for Global Capitalism* (Princeton: Princeton University Press, 2009).

34. See, for instance, Greenwald and Stiglitz, *Towards a New Paradigm of Monetary Economics*, op. cit.

35. George Soros, in his theory of reflexivity, emphasized the dependence of behavior and expectations on the expectations and beliefs of others. But this interdependence did not simply mean that one could move from one equilibrium

to another by announcing that there were "green shoots." See Soros, *The New Paradigm for Financial Markets*, op. cit.

36. Paul Samuelson was one of the greatest economists of the twentieth century. He played a central role in introducing Keynesian ideas into the United States, especially through his textbook, *Economics: An Introductory Analysis*, which was the bible for economics students for a quarter century beginning from 1948, when it was first published. He tried to reconcile the microeconomic and macroeconomic approaches through what he called the neoclassical synthesis: there were two regimes, an unemployment regime and a full employment regime. Once government restored the economy to full employment, the standard results about efficient markets applied. Samuelson's neoclassical synthesis was an assertion that believers took as an article of faith for years, but it did not rest on any theoretical foundations. See later discussion for a critique of this view.

37. Many economists at the University of Chicago do not subscribe to one or more tenets of the "Chicago School." As in any school of thought in economics, there are many variants. One of the more influential is called the "real business cycle" theory, because it sought to explain the ups and downs of the economy not in terms of monetary policy but as a result of "real" shocks to the economy, such as those associated with the developments of new technologies.

38. The assumption of perfect markets does, however, play an important role in many of the conclusions. It implies that there is no credit rationing and no unemployment. The representative agent assumption (living infinitely long) means that one cannot analyze the consequences of redistributing income from the young to the old or from the rich to the poor. It also means that the people enjoying the benefits of the government expenditure today are the same people who will have to pay the taxes tomorrow.

39. Critics of government spending to stimulate the economy focus on the supply-side effects—that taxes will induce less savings and less work. But in the short run, less savings means more consumption and is actually positive; while, with workers unable to find jobs, the reduced labor supply has no adverse consequence. The argument that *future* taxes discourage work and therefore society is worse off is another example of the intellectual inconsistencies that mark the Chicago School's work: if everyone were identical, then the government would impose lump sum taxes (taxes that did not depend on income or any other action of workers). These taxes would be totally non-distortionary, and work would actually be encouraged.

40. See, in particular, Bruce Greenwald and Joseph E. Stiglitz, "Keynesian, New Keynesian and New Classical Economics," *Oxford Economic Papers*, vol. 39 (March 1987), pp. 119–133.

41. This view, which traces its origins back to John Hicks, an Oxford economist (one of my predecessors as Drummond Professorship of Political Economy at All

Souls College), who received his Nobel Prize in 1972, has, in fact, been the prevailing view for most of the second half of the twentieth century.

42. The intellectual godfather of this second strand is Irving Fisher, with his classic 1933 article, "The Debt Deflation Theory of Great Depressions" (*Econometrica*, vol. 1, pp. 337–357), and in the more modern reincarnation, it has been developed further by Hyman Minsky (*John Maynard Keynes* [New York: Columbia University Press, 1975], *Can It Happen Again?* [Armonk, NY: M. E. Sharpe, 1982], *Stabilizing an Unstable Economy* [New Haven: Yale University Press, 1986]), and by Bruce Greenwald and myself in a series of papers beginning in the early 1980s, including "Financial Market Imperfections and Business Cycles," *Quarterly Journal of Economics*, vol. 108, no. 1 (February 1993), pp. 77–114, and culminating in *Towards a New Paradigm of Monetary Economics*, op. cit.

43. The view was that there was a "natural" rate of unemployment and so attempts to lower unemployment by lowering interest rates were doomed to failure—they only led to ever-increasing inflation. There is a grain of truth in the theory: people's expectations about future inflation can depend on their experiences, and those expectations can affect future wage demands and inflation rates. But whether there is a stable relationship between rates of change in inflation and the unemployment rate remains more controversial; there is even uncertainty about the level of unemployment below which inflation starts to increase, as we noted earlier. See, for instance, J. E. Stiglitz, "Reflections on the Natural Rate Hypothesis," *Journal of Economic Perspectives*, vol. 11, no. 1 (Winter 1997), pp. 3–10.

44. The exact level of inflation at which problems start to rise is a matter of debate, and may change from time to time. There is a broad consensus that inflation rates below 8 to 10 percent do not have significantly negative effects, and some countries, like Turkey, managed to continue to grow with much higher rates. At the same time, because of downward rigidities of prices, when the inflation rate is too low, there may be problems in adjustment. See George A. Akerlof, William R. Dickens, and George L. Perry, "The Macroeconomics of Low Inflation," *Brookings Papers on Economic Activity*, vol. 27, no. 1 (1996), pp. 1–76.

45. I joke that the Fed was determined to show that there was such a significant adverse effect of low to moderate inflation on economic growth, but in spite of having a large staff of excellent econometricians, none could claim the obvious rewards that would be extended to anyone who could demonstrate this.

46. There was another criticism of inflation: because of it, people hold less money than would be "efficient," less than they would hold in a world with stable prices. Even if it had some relevance in the past, in the modern world where most money is interest bearing, this concern is no longer valid. As inflation increases, so too does the (nominal) interest they receive. The focus on how low levels of inflation might cause a loss of economic efficiency by inducing people to hold a little less currency than they otherwise would—but ignoring how an asset

price bubble might bring down the entire economy—is illustrative of the extent to which some strands of academic economics had lost touch with the real world.

47. If one focuses on one thing, there is a risk that other things get short shrift. Indeed, there is a general proposition: stabilizing prices leads to instability in quantities, and vice versa. Not only did the focus on inflation not ensure real stability, but also it impaired long-term growth—contrary to the advocates of inflation targeting. The experience of most other countries in crises is that they almost never regain the lost time. Growth will eventually resume. But even fifteen years later, output will be lower than it would have been had there not been a crisis.

48. An even simpler example, often quoted, is that the price of a 32-ounce bottle of ketchup in a fully efficient market is twice that of a 16-ounce bottle. There are transaction (bottling and shipping) costs, so in reality, a 32-ounce bottle will often cost less than twice the cost of a 16-ounce bottle.

49. Under the efficient markets theory, the value of a stock is supposed to equal the expected present discounted value of future dividends. Thus a 20 percent decline in market value would imply that somehow, expectations of future dividends had suddenly declined by that amount. There is simply no news that could explain "rationally" such a change in expectations. For an excellent popular discussion of the view that one can't beat the market, see Burton G. Malkiel, *A Random Walk Down Wall Street: The Best and Latest Investment Advice Money Can Buy* (New York: W. W. Norton, 2003). For a powerful argument against the efficient markets hypothesis, see Shiller, *Irrational Exuberance*, op. cit.

50. The billions made by some investment banks and hedge funds from having advance information concerning order flow ("flash trading") is another example. Of course, if the losers were rational, they would realize that it was an unfair game, and they would drop out. Some of the profits of these investment banks are at the expense of these irrational market participants who want to believe that they too are at the top of the class; but some of the profits may be at the expense of governments when they intervene in markets, for instance, when they try to stabilize exchange rates in a currency crisis, as I noted in *Globalization and Its Discontents*, op. cit.

51. There is another way to *seem* to beat the market: to undertake more risk, in ways that are not fully apparent. See the earlier discussion in chapter 6.

52. See Sanford Grossman and Joseph E. Stiglitz, "On the Impossibility of Informationally Efficient Markets," *American Economic Review*, vol. 70, no. 3 (June 1980), pp. 393–408. We also showed that markets could not perfectly aggregate fully the disparate information of different market participants. See Grossman and Stiglitz, "Information and Competitive Price Systems," *American Economic Review*, vol. 66, no. 2 (May 1976), pp. 246–253.

53. This distinction between the social and private return to information was made forcefully by Jack Hirshleifer, in "The Private and Social Value of Information and the Reward to Inventive Activity," *American Economic Review*, vol. 61,

no. 4 (September 1971), pp. 561–574, and by Joseph E. Stiglitz, "The Theory of Screening, Education and the Distribution of Income," *American Economic Review*, vol. 65, no. 3 (June 1975), pp. 283–300.

54. The reason why the Federal Reserve disingenuously pretended that it did not have the instruments with which it could deflate a bubble—or even that it could not detect a bubble—is perhaps that it did not want to do anything. It viewed that as interfering with the market—though obviously, as we have seen, setting interest rates is interfering with markets.

55. Alan Greenspan admitted as much in his famous "mea culpa," before the House Oversight Committee chaired by Henry Waxman, on October 23, 2008. See the discussion in earlier text.

56. By some estimates, more than 80 percent of the increase in per capita income was due to innovation, as opposed to capital accumulation or the improvement in skills of workers. Other estimates place somewhat more emphasis on capital accumulation. See Robert M. Solow, "Technical Change and the Aggregate Production Function," *Review of Economics and Statistics*, vol. 39, no. 3 (1957), pp. 312–320.

57. These theories were called "endogenous" because the explanations of innovation were within the theory, as opposed to "exogenous," outside the theory. Endogenous growth theory goes back to the work of Hirofumi Uzawa, Ken Arrow, Nicholas Kaldor, and Richard Nelson, and a host of their students (including William Nordhaus, Karl Shell, and myself) in the late 1950s and 1960s. See, for instance, Hirofumi Uzawa, "Optimum Technical Change in an Aggregate Model of Economic Growth," *International Economic Review*, vol. 6, no. 1 (1965), pp. 18–31; Kenneth J. Arrow, "The Economic Implications of Learning by Doing," *Review of Economic Studies*, vol. 29 (1962), pp. 155–173; Nicholas Kaldor, "A Model of Economic Growth," *Economic Journal*, vol. 67 (1957), pp. 591–624; and Richard R. Nelson and Edmond S. Phelps, "Investment in Humans, Technological Diffusion and Economic Growth," *American Economic Review*, vol. 56, no. 1/2 (March–May 1966), pp. 69–75. In collaboration with Sir Partha Dasgupta of Cambridge, I extended this work and integrated it with the modern theory of industrial organization in the late 1970s. See, for instance, Partha Dasgupta and Joseph E. Stiglitz, "Industrial Structure and the Nature of Innovative Activity," *Economic Journal*, Royal Economic Society, vol. 90, no. 358 (June 1980), pp. 266–293. In more recent years, Paul Romer further explored these ideas: Paul Romer, "Increasing Returns and Long-Run Growth," *Journal of Political Economy*, vol. 94, no. 5 (1986), pp. 1002–1037.

58. Joseph A. Schumpeter, *Capitalism, Socialism and Democracy* (New York: Harper and Brothers, 1942).

59. Natural selection doesn't work well, especially when capital markets are imperfect—which they always are. See J. E. Stiglitz, "Information and Economic Analysis," in J. M. Parkin and A. R. Nobay (eds.), *Current Economic Problems:*

The Proceedings of the Association of University Teachers of Economics, Manchester, 1974 (Cambridge: Cambridge University Press, 1975), pp. 27–52.

60. Friedrich Hayek, *Constitution of Liberty* (Chicago: University of Chicago Press, 1960), pp. 502–503.

61. Though in his later work, he seemed to have some misgivings about the role of central banks.

Chapter 10 TOWARD A NEW SOCIETY

1. If Angelo Mozilo had kept the dirty secrets to himself, he might have been spared; self-deception is no crime, nor is persuading others to share in that self-deception. In 2002, several investment analysts were caught in a similar deception: the crime was not that they were paid more for their ability to recruit new business than on the basis of the accuracy of their analyses, or that their grading was skewed so that almost all stocks were graded a "buy." They were caught in a rare moment of honesty, in sending e-mails that described the stocks they were publicly touting as "dogs," "toast," and "junk." The lesson for future financiers is simple: don't share your innermost doubts. See SEC Press Release, "SEC Charges Former Countrywide Executives with Fraud," June 4, 2009; Deborah Lohse, "Probe Finds Analysts Pushing Stocks They Privately Bad-Mouthed," *San Jose Mercury News*, April 12, 2002; and Stiglitz, *Roaring Nineties*, op. cit.

2. To avoid the even weak limitations on interest and fees, rent-a-center companies sell furniture on "time payment plans." But contractually, they describe themselves as renting the furniture until it is paid off. With late fees and hidden charges, the amounts paid are often a multiple of the original price—in one case I looked at, a $150 couch was still not paid for after the purchaser had given the company $2,000 in the span of a few years. Many states have outlawed these firms, but they have tried to use federal preemption to stave off state regulation. To help this along, the most prominent of these firms even had a former very senior congressman on its board.

3. Just as there is nothing wrong with financing slavery—so long as it is legal (as the predecessors to J.P. Morgan did; "JP Morgan Admits US Slavery Links," BBC News, January 21, 2005) or providing support to apartheid South Africa (as Citibank did; Barnaby J. Feder, "Citibank Is Leaving South Africa; Foes of Apartheid See Major Gain," *New York Times*, June 17, 1987, p. A1).

4. Some might argue that economists should stick to their knitting—and a discussion of morals takes them beyond their arena of competence. We should remember that Adam Smith was a professor of moral philosophy. The discipline of economics is concerned with how we make decisions about the use of resources—and about how those decisions affect others. Any inquiry into actions that have impacts on others quickly brings us into a moral discourse.

5. John Donne, "Meditation XVII," in *Devotions upon Emergent Occasions*, 1624.

6. Another example of cognitive dissonance is the visceral reaction against mark-to-market accounting, which, as I noted in chapter 6, many in the financial sector blame for much of the industry's problems. For years they praised the importance of the "price discovery" function of markets (see chapter 9). But now that the prices of real estate are lower than they like, they have temporarily lost faith in market pricing. They say there is irrational pessimism. But irrational pessimism is just the mirror of the irrational exuberance in the years before the bubble broke. If prices are wrong, it means that the bonuses they got, based on the false reading of returns, were excessive. If bankers were acting in an intellectually coherent way, they should be offering to give back part of those bonuses, as a sign of good faith that they really don't believe in mark-to-market pricing. But to date, I have not heard a single critic of mark-to-market accounting follow through on this, the logical import of his or her critique.

7. As I noted earlier, there are many heroes who, realizing what they were doing, said they couldn't continue. They took responsibility for their actions. But many more did not.

8. This section draws heavily on the *Report by the Commission on the Measurement of Economic Performance and Social Progress*, op. cit. See also Layard, *Happiness*, op. cit.

9. This is not the first time problems using GDP as a measure of well-being have arisen. In the late 1990s, Argentina looked, according to GDP indicators, as though it was doing marvelously. The IMF praised the country, bringing its soon-to-be-discredited president, Carlos Menem, to its annual meeting in Washington, parading him as an example for other countries. But Argentina's performance, like America's, was built on a house of cards. There were many similarities: both were based on a consumption boom feeding off of massive foreign borrowing. A good measure would have shown this increased indebtedness—providing a clear indication that future growth was at risk.

10. America is not alone in these problems with the use of GDP to measure well-being. In countries that are heavily dependent on mining, oil, timber, or other natural resources, much of today's consumption is at the expense of the well-being of future generations. The result is that current living standards may not be sustainable. The United Kingdom, for instance, has depleted its treasure of North Sea oil at the same time that it allowed its manufacturing base to weaken, and bet its future on a vibrant financial system. A few countries, like Chile and Norway, have recognized this problem and have been setting aside funds. As their wealth below the ground diminishes, they have used the revenues to increase their wealth above the ground.

11. If our society becomes more dysfunctional—with more spending on prisons—then our GDP goes up, but it is hardly a mark of success. Such spending is referred to as "defensive spending." See, e.g., William D. Nordhaus and

James Tobin, "Is Growth Obsolete?" *Economic Research: Retrospect and Prospect*, vol. 5: *Economic Growth* (New York: Columbia University Press, for the National Bureau of Economic Research, 1972).

12. Bureau of Economic Analysis, National Income and Product Acccounts Table, "Table 7.1. Selected Per Capita Product and Income Series in Current and Chained Dollars," August 27, 2009, release, available at http://www.bea.gov/national/nipaweb/TableView.asp?SelectedTable=264&Freq=Qtr&FirstYear=2007&LastYear=2009, and U.S. Census Bureau, Current Population Survey, "Table P-7. Regions—People (Both Sexes Combined) by Median and Mean Income," available at http://www.census.gov/hhes/www/income/histinc/incpertoc.html.

13. United Nations Development Programme, Human Development Index, 2008. Iceland ranked number one in 2008—before the financial crisis—with Norway at number two, Sweden at number seven, and Finland at number twelve.

14. Putnam, *Bowling Alone*, op. cit.

15. The number of houses for which the value of the mortgage exceeds the value of the property could rise even further if prices decline further. There is considerable uncertainty about how much further prices will decline, but one estimate suggests that the percentage of underwater mortgages will rise to 48 percent, or 25 million homes, as prices drop through the first quarter of 2011. Jody Shenn, "'Underwater' Mortgages to Hit 48 Percent, Deutsche Bank Says," *Bloomberg .com*, August 5, 2009.

16. Nayla Kazzi, "More Americans Are Losing Health Insurance Every Day: An Analysis of Health Coverage Losses during the Recession," Center for American Progress, May 4, 2009, available at http://www.americanprogress.org/issues/2009/05/pdf/healthinsurancelosses.pdf.

17. As I have argued elsewhere in this book, most Americans want to work; the problem was not that they were lazy but that there were too few jobs. Most Americans will do what they can to avoid losing their homes; the problem was that they were sold mortgages that were beyond their ability to pay. They have learned the lesson—at great pain to themselves—and most are not likely to repeat the mistake.

18. I am indebted to Professor David Kennedy of Harvard University for discussions on these issues of "rights."

19. The Universal Declaration of Human Rights was adopted in the General Assembly on December 10, 1948.

20. "Economic Possibilities for Our Grandchildren (1930)," in John Maynard Keynes, *Essays in Persuasion* (Harcourt, Brace and Company, 1932), pp. 358–373. A recent book, *Revisiting Keynes: Economic Possibilities for Our Grandchildren*, edited by Lorenzo Pecchi and Gustavo Piga (Cambridge, MA: MIT Press, 2008), provides a discussion of alternative interpretations of why Keynes's prediction didn't come true. See, in particular, my chapter, "Toward a General Theory of Consumerism: Reflections on Keynes's Economic Possibilities for Our Grandchildren" (pp. 41–87).

21. Olivier Blanchard, "The Economic Future of Europe," National Bureau of Economic Research Working Paper 10310, February 2004, available at http://www.nber.org/papers/w10310.

22. Americans know they should be saving more—for their children's education, against the risk of a layoff, in case of a medical emergency—but the immediate "need" for goods is overwhelming. In a materialistic society, one judges oneself by comparison with the goods owned and consumed by one's neighbors and friends. It's a friendly rat race. To keep up with the Joneses—let alone to be them—one has to have more income. In this milieu, the choices are clear. This is another way in which the standard "neoclassical" model may be flawed: it assumes that each individual's sense of well-being depends only on his own consumption, not that of others. There is considerable evidence, however, that individuals do care about their relative position. See, for instance, Robert H. Frank and Cass R. Sunstein, "Cost-Benefit Analysis and Relative Position," *University of Chicago Law Review*, vol. 68, no. 2 (2001), pp. 323–374, and Erzo F. P. Luttmer, "Neighbors as Negatives: Relative Earnings and Well-Being," *Quarterly Journal of Economics*, vol. 120, no. 3 (August 2005), pp. 963–1002.

23. The political scientist Elinor Ostrom, who received the 2009 Nobel Memorial Prize in Economics, has studied how social and economic sanctions in small communities can be an important instrument of social control.

24. See Avner Greif, "Contract Enforceability and Economic Institutions in Early Trade: The Maghribi Traders' Coalition," *American Economic Review*, vol. 83, no. 3 (June 1993), pp. 525–548, and Avner Greif, Paul Milgrom, and Barry Weingast, "Coordination, Commitment, and Enforcement: The Case of the Merchant Guild," *Journal of Political Economy*, vol. 102, no. 4 (August 1994), pp. 745–776.

25. There is good reason for the lack of trust: there are clear conflicts of interest, worsened when the service provider is owned by the holder of the second mortgage. Then, different ways of restructuring the debt have differential effects on the holders of the first and second mortgages. It is remarkable how unaware of these potential conflicts of interest many in the financial sector seemed to be.

26. Dieter Helm, "Britain Must Save and Rebuild to Prosper," *Financial Times*, June 4, 2009, p. 9.

27. Quoted in Peggy Hollinger, "Dirigisme de rigueur," *Financial Times*, June 4, 2009, p. 7.

28. In Eisenhower's "Farewell Address to the Nation," on January 17, 1961, he said, "This conjunction of an immense military establishment and a large arms industry is new in the American experience. The total influence—economic, political, even spiritual—is felt in every city, every Statehouse, every office of the Federal government. We recognize the imperative need for this development. Yet we must not fail to comprehend its grave implications. Our toil, resources and livelihood are all involved; so is the very structure of our society."

Afterword

1. In chapter 3 I explain why the problems in the housing market might, for instance, spill over to impede the smooth working of the labor market. Individuals would find it more difficult to relocate to take on a new job. Another reason why growth rates might be lower in coming years relates to cutbacks on spending on research and development.

2. A structural deficit is a deficit that persists even when the economy is at full employment, as opposed to a cyclical deficit, which arises only because the economy is in a recession.

3. See chapters 7 to 10 for a discussion of those issues.

4. Recall from the discussion in chapter 3 that individuals are called unemployed only if they are actively seeking work. Those who have stopped looking, because they have become so discouraged by job prospects, or who have taken a part-time job because there are no full-time jobs available, are *not* called unemployed.

5. See http://www.bls.gov/opub/ils/pdf/opbils82.pdf.

6. See http://www.nelp.org/page/-/UI/2010/july.2010.exhaustions.pdf.

7. For example, one analysis of the impact of layoffs during the 1982 recession found that workers suffered an immediate loss of 30 percent in annual earnings; even 15 to 20 years later, their earnings were still 20 percent lower than people who had not been laid off. See Till von Wachter, Jae Song, and Joyce Manchester, "Long-Term Earnings Losses due to Mass Layoffs during the 1982 Recession: An Analysis Using U.S. Administrative Data from 1974 to 2004," Working Paper, Columbia University, April 2009, available at http://www.columbia.edu/~vw2112/papers/mass_layoffs_1982.pdf.

8. See U.S. Census data on "New Privately Owned Houses Started," available at http://www.census.gov/const/startssa.pdf.

9. Congressional Oversight Panel, "Commercial Real Estate Losses and the Risk to Financial Stability," February 10, 2010.

10. The contrast between the "forbearance" of the accounting rules and the strictness of the supervisors might seem odd. But without the lax accounting rules, the banks would have to come up with more money *now*. (Tighter accounting rules would show that the banks had more losses than they were willing to own up to, and thus had less capital—insufficient to meet bank regulations. When that happens, if banks can't improve their "capital adequacy," for instance by raising additional funds, they are shut down.) Banks have used their political muscle to avoid this.

By contrast, tight supervision has meant that banks are not allowed to make risky loans (or have to have much more capital if they do make such loans.) Supervisors consider loans to small businesses with insufficient collateral highly risky. Much of the cost of this tough supervision is thus borne by the small and medium-sized firms that do not, as a result, get access to credit.

11. See chapter 4.

12. In residential real estate there were typically no more than two claimants, the first and second mortgage holders. In commercial real estate, there could be many more claimants, with different (and often ambiguous) "seniority." Senior claimants get fully paid before junior claimants can get anything. Thus, in the case of first and second mortgages, in the event of a default, proceeds from the sale of the asset first go to the first mortgage holder, and only if there is something left over do the second mortgage holders get anything.

13. Of course, there will always be *some* demand for new houses, as parts of the country expand and others contract.

14. Based on comparison of Federal Reserve Statistical Releases from 2005 (http://www.federalreserve.gov/releases/e2/200504/default.htm) and 2010 (http://www.federalreserve.gov/releases/e2/200504/default.htm).

15. By July 20, 2010, ninety-six banks had gone bankrupt. See FDIC, Failed Bank List, available at http://www.fdic.gov/bank/individual/failed/banklist.html.

16. For 2009 as a whole, net exports of goods and services improved dramatically, but it was because imports fell almost a quarter; exports (in nominal terms) fell 15 percent. See www.census.gov/foreign-trade/statistics/highlights/annual.html.

17. Sixteen countries of the European Union share a common currency, the euro. Several countries within the EU, including the United Kingdom and Sweden, decided not to, for some of the reasons discussed here. I use the term *Eurozone* to refer to the countries of the EU that share the euro.

18. Eurostat, News Release, Euro Indicators, April 22, 2010, available at http://epp.eurostat.ec.europa.eu/cache/ITY_PUBLIC/2-22042010-BP/EN/2-22042010-BP-EN.PDF.

19. U.S. Government Accountability Office (GAO), Report to the Congress, "Recovery Act: One Year Later, States' and Localities' Uses of Funds and Opportunities to Strengthen Accountability," March 2010, available at http://www.gao.gov/new.items/d10437.pdf.

20. The new jobs bill includes provisions for exempting employers from paying Social Security taxes on new hires who have been unemployed for more than two months, and a $1,000 tax credit for each new hire who remains on the job for more than one year. It encourages small businesses to invest by providing an immediate write-off of up to $250,000 of investment. The bill is so modest that the total number of jobs expected to be created is, by some estimates, only 200,000. See Timothy Bartik, Economic Policy Institute, http://www.epi.org/analysis_and_opinion/entry/not_all_job_creation_tax_credits_are_created_equal/, and Carl Huse, "Senate Approves $15 Billion Jobs Bill," *New York Times*, February 24, 2010, available at http://www.nytimes.com/2010/02/25/us/politics/25jobs.html.

21. Some of the best financial journalists were quick to point this out. See, for instance, Gretchen Morgenson, "This Bailout Is a Bargain? Think Again," *New York*

Times, April 18, 2010, p. BU1, available at http://www.nytimes.com/2010/04/18/business/economy/18gret.html. Some financial journalists seemed more willing to repeat the administration's interpretation. See, e.g., Andrew Ross Sorkin, "Imagine the Bailouts Are Working," *New York Times*, April 13, 2010, p. B1, available at http://www.nytimes.com/2010/04/13/business/13sorkin.html.

22. See Gretchen Morgenson, "Behind Insurer's Crisis, Blind Eye to a Web of Risk," *New York Times*, September 27, 2008, p. A1, available at http://www.nytimes.com/2008/09/28/business/28melt.html?scp=2&sq=Gretchen%20Morgenstern%20goldman%20sachs%202008&st=cse. For our purposes, what is important is not whether or not particular institutions engaged in the scurrilous practices of which they have been accused; rather, it is the patterns of behavior and deceit, and the consequent loss in confidence and trust.

23. Lynnley Browning, "A.I.G. Sues U.S. for Return of $306 Million in Tax Payments," *New York Times*, March 19, 2009, available at http://www.nytimes.com/2009/03/20/business/20aig.html?em. This is not the only court case involving AIG. AIG was sued by, among others, the attorney general of Ohio, alleging deceptive practices. In an out of court settlement, AIG agreed in July 2010 to pay this one state alone more than a half billion dollars—raising further doubts about whether the US government would ever get its money back.

24. The most notorious example of the use of derivatives as an instrument of budgetary deception involves Goldman Sachs, the largest beneficiary of the AIG bailout. Goldman Sachs is accused of using derivatives to help Greece hide its true fiscal position, so that it could meet the conditions for joining the European Union. In honor of this, a provision of the financial reform bill aimed at reducing the scope for such abusive uses of derivatives was referred to as the "Greece Fraud" provision. The details of how derivatives do any of this need not concern us here. The basic idea, though, is simple: a derivative can be structured as a payment today by one party to another ("buying a bet"), in return for a payment at a later date in the event that certain contingencies occur. If the risks are small (they can even be negligible), then the derivative is nothing more than a loan, in which the interest payment is masked as an insurance premium.

25. For an analysis of the role of automatic stabilizers in the increase in debt, see Mark Horton, Manmohan Kumar, and Paolo Mauro, "The State of Public Finances: A Cross-Country Fiscal Monitor," IMF Staff Position Note, 09/21, Washington, DC, International Monetary Fund, July 30, 2009, available at http://www.imf.org/external/pubs/ft/spn/2009/spn0921.pdf.

26. The Fed normally sets only the short-term interest rate; the "market" determines other interest rates. In the midst of the crisis, the Fed intervened to try to dampen long-term interest rates, but it has since exited from these programs. As this paperback edition goes to press, the market concerns about future inflation have been overshadowed by other worries—such as those concerning Europe, which I discuss later in the afterword.

There is a concern that worries about inflation might set in before the economy is firmly on the road to recovery. Then, the cutbacks in spending or increases in interest rates that might follow would dampen aggregate demand and weaken the recovery.

27. Deflation increases the "real interest rate," the interest rate adjusted for deflation. This illustrates how economies are not automatically self-adjusting. Once nominal interest rates reach zero, if unemployment persists, downward pressure on wages and then prices leads to an increase in *real* interest rates, dampening the economy further.

28. One of the standard arguments put forward by conservative critics of the stimulus program is that government spending crowds out private investment. The mechanism by which this occurs is that interest rates increase (as government borrowing competes with private borrowing). It is remarkable that these conservatives continue to espouse such ideas when interest rates (both short and long term) remain at record low levels, when there is no way by which this crowding out will occur.

29. China's growth in 2009 was 8.7 percent, and it is expected to be 10 percent in 2010.

30. This is especially true for small countries. Small countries like Greece face a problem that is different from that confronting the United States: they may find it difficult to finance the deficit. In a world of turbulence, America looks *relatively* safe. But, as we note shortly, even the United States can face problems.

31. See the discussion in chapter 3.

32. In 2010, China and India are expected to account for some 40 percent of global GDP growth, which is projected to be 4.2 percent. Even in 2009, when global GDP fell 0.9 percent, growth in China and India gave the measure a 1.4 percentage point boost.

33. Consumption contributed significantly to China's 11.9 percent expansion in the first quarter of 2010, and was predicted to grow by 9.5 percent over the course of 2010. See World Bank, "China Quarterly Update—June 2010," available at http://siteresources.worldbank.org/CHINAEXTN/Resources/318949-1268688634523/Quarterly_June_2010.pdf.

34. European Commission, Eurostat, Government Finance Statistics, Public Finance (tsieb080), April 2010, available at http://epp.eurostat.ec.europa.eu/portal/page/portal/government_finance_statistics/data/main_tables.

35. Economic modeling has failed to substantiate the "Hooverite" approach; in almost all models, cutbacks in spending to reduce deficits lead to lower growth. One of the few instances where spending failed to restore growth was Japan in the 1990s, but its policies were not consistent. For instance, taxes were raised in 1997, undermining a fragile recovery.

36. Selling a bond short entails, in effect, promising to deliver a bond, say, in three months, but receiving the current price up front. If the price falls from

$100 to $80, one can buy the bond at $80, pocketing the $20 difference. The more the price falls, the higher the return.

37. In some ways, the attack was similar to the famous Hong Kong double play during the East Asia crisis, when speculators mounted a concerted attack against Hong Kong's currency and stock market. As speculators attacked its currency, they reasoned that Hong Kong would try to save its currency. The conventional way of doing so is to raise interest rates, which depresses stock prices. So they sold stocks short (i.e., bet that stocks would fall in price). If the government did raise interest rates, they would make money on the stock market; if they didn't, and the currency fell, they would make money on the foreign exchange market. Either way, they were guaranteed a profit. Or so they thought. Governments are not powerless, even against the might of the financial markets. The Hong Kong government raised interest rates *and* intervened in the stock market, buying up shares. The speculators lost on both accounts. The markets were furious. Even U.S. Treasury officials, reflecting the objections of Wall Street, raised concerns. This is not how governments are supposed to respond to an attack, they claimed. They are supposed to shovel out the money; they are not supposed to counterattack. Hong Kong had violated the basic principles of capitalism! But Hong Kong had not only stabilized its economy. It had also made a pretty profit on the deal. In the current case, speculators were attacking both Greek bonds and the euro, perhaps reasoning that no matter how Europe responded, confidence in the euro would weaken. And they were right, especially because Europe's response did not inspire confidence.

38. For a description of the way that Greek debt was masked, see Louise Story, Landon Thomas, Jr., and Nelson D. Schwartz, "Wall St. Helped to Mask Debt Fueling Europe's Crisis," *New York Times*, February 13, 2010, Page A1, available at http://www.nytimes.com/2010/02/14/business/global/14debt.html.

39. One needs to put some perspective on the size of what Greece needed: its financing needs for 2010 were, for instance, a fraction (less than a third) of the amount that went to *one* financial corporation (AIG).

40. The Icelandic debacle is described in greater detail in chapter 1. Subsequent events have highlighted the inadequacy of the European response. The United Kingdom and the Netherlands had advanced depositors' money, which they wanted Iceland to refund. Iceland did not feel legally obligated to do so but wanted to work out a solution that was fair and equitable to all parties. But the UK wanted to charge Iceland an interest rate considerably in excess of the rate at which it could borrow funds—making, in effect, a profit out of the deal. This was unacceptable to the people of Iceland, who would have been burdened for a generation by these debts, the result of the failure not just of Icelandic banks, but also of UK and Dutch regulators. Again, not surprisingly, Icelanders rejected the deal, by a vote of more than 90 percent.

41. A trade surplus is the excess of exports over imports. The current account

surplus is a broader measure, which includes "invisible" exports, like expenditures by foreigners on education and health, and tourism in the country.

42. I explain this at greater length in chapter 8.

43. The European Exchange Rate Mechanism was an exchange rate system created in 1979 as a way to reduce the volatility of the various European currencies and to create a stable monetary system. The ERM created fixed margins in which a country's currency could operate.

44. The figure is for 2009. Historical figures can be found at http://www.census .gov/foreign-trade/balance/c5700.html#2009.

45. However, there is considerable disagreement about the extent of China's exchange rate "misalignment"—from those who believe that it is not misaligned to those who think China still needs to appreciate its currency by some 30 percent. Part of the problem is that "equilibrium" exchange rates are affected by a host of policies. If, for instance, China allowed Chinese citizens to invest freely in the United States, it is possible that the flow of funds out of China might even lead to a depreciation of the currency. Inflows could be discouraged by taxes on capital gains, especially short-term capital gains associated with speculation, and these taxes too could lead to a depreciation of the currency. Some critics argue that America has been artificially depressing its exchange rate through its abnormal interest rate policies.

46. America's and Europe's huge agricultural subsidies complicate China's currency appreciation. They lead to lower prices for China's poor farmers, undermining that country's efforts to reduce poverty. Spending money to offset these effects through distorting agricultural policies uses scarce funds that could be used for improving health and education or promoting growth. See chapter 8 and Stiglitz, *Making Globalization Work,* op. cit.

47. Reuters, "Piraeus Port Sees Return to Full-Year Profit," December 3, 2008. Chinese companies have further invested in Greece in the wake of the crisis. See Reuters, "China, Greece Sign Deals, Want Stronger Business Ties," June 15, 2010.

48. Nominal expenditure on national defense from 2000 to 2009 was $4.7 trillion. See Office of Management and Budget, "Table 3.2—Outlays by Function and Subfunction: 1962–2015," Historical Tables, President's Budget, available at http://www.whitehouse.gov/omb/budget/historicals/.

49. John Arlidge, "I'm Doing 'God's Work'. Meet Mr Goldman Sachs," *Sunday Times,* November 8, 2009, available at http://www.timesonline.co.uk/tol/news/ world/us_and_americas/article6907681.ece.

50. A "repo" is nothing more than a sale of an asset (a bond) with a promise to buy it back ("repurchase"). It is, in that sense, little different from a collateralized loan. This allowed Lehman Brothers to pretend that it had more cash and fewer assets on its books. The amounts were large: "Lehman undertook $38.6 billion, $49.1 billion, and $50.38 billion of repo 105 transactions at quarter

end fourth quarter 2007, first quarter 2008, and second quarter 2008, respec-tively," according to the Report of the Examiner in the Chapter 11 proceedings of Lehman Brothers Holdings Inc, available at http://lehmanreport.jenner.com/VOLUME%203.pdf.

51. The SEC's suit against Goldman alleged that John Paulson "played an influ-ential role in selecting the reference portfolio" while shorting that portfolio by entering into credit default swaps. The SEC complaint is available at http://www.sec.gov/litigation/complaints/2010/comp-pr2010-59.pdf. On July 15, Goldman Sachs finally agreed that it had made a "mistake," and paid a record fine for a Wall Street firm. See SEC announcement at http://www.sec.gov/news/press/2010/2010-123.htm.

52. Goldman Sachs made a big deal of the fact that the investors were sophis-ticated, that they knew there was someone on the other side of the transaction taking the opposite bet, and that as a matter of practice, Goldman never discloses the party taking the opposite side. But all of this is disingenuous. It was of crucial relevance that the mortgages had been chosen not randomly, but with an eye to lose money if the bubble broke.

53. Speculators benefited too from a story in a leading financial newspaper that Greece had approached China for assistance. Senior government officials have told me that that story was not true; though one of its Wall Street financial advi-sors had recommended that they do so, Greece rejected that idea. Confidence in financial markets' integrity was further undermined by rumors that the story had been planted by some of those who had been speculating against Greece and stood to gain by a decline in the value of its bonds.

54. Uri Dadush et al., "Paradigm Lost: The Euro in Crisis," Carnegie Endow-ment for International Peace, Washington, DC, 2010, available at http://carnegie endowment.org/files/Paradigm_Lost.pdf.

55. Nonetheless, some of its banks have needed a bailout, and others appear fragile.

56. It is remarkable that, in spite of 2,000 pages of text, so much of the financial reform is left to the discretion of regulators. As the *New York Times* points out, "It is notably short on specifics, giving regulators significant power to determine its impact—and giving partisans on both sides a second chance to influence the outcome." See also Binyamin Appelbaum, "On Finance Bill, Lobbying Shifts to Regulations," *New York Times*, June 26, 2010, available at http://www.nytimes.com/2010/06/27/business/27regulate.html.

57. The role of the Obama administration in all of this has been confusing and ambiguous. While it finally supported actions to reduce some of the conflicts of interest that had become commonplace since the repeal of the Glass-Steagall Act, it sometimes seemed to be doing so reluctantly. It seems to have opposed key provisions aimed at encouraging banks to go back to focusing on lending— and at stopping them from writing credit default swaps, with taxpayers, in effect, bearing part of the risk.

58. Can be found online here: http://frwebgate.access.gpo.gov/cgi-bin/getdoc .cgi?dbname=111_cong_bills&docid=f:h4173enr.txt.pdf.

59. In particular, the credit card rules that require any merchant who accepts, say, any Visa or MasterCard to honor all cards *and not charge the user* mean that the worst practices will continue: premium credit cards will give rewards, for which the merchants are charged high fees, but the costs are borne by merchants and partially passed on to consumers, including those not using premium cards (who on average have lower incomes).

60. Another important provision intended to protect ordinary citizens gives the Securities and Exchange Commission the right—after six more months of study—to impose a fiduciary responsibility on brokers that give investment advice. (Imposing fiduciary responsibility says that the brokers must act in the best interests of those that they are supposed to be representing—they can't just blatantly try to rip them off.)

61. Bankruptcy law effectively encourages derivatives: they are given priority over other elements of the capital structure when a firm fails. And when derivatives are written by government-insured banks, they are effectively underwritten by taxpayers, a form of hidden subsidy. Buyers of derivatives sometimes complain that eliminating the subsidy (requiring higher capital, as is required by other forms of insurance) will increase costs; but that is as it should be. There is no argument for why taxpayers should be subsidizing this particular form of insurance (if that is what it is), and an even weaker argument for subsidizing this particular form of gambling, if that is what these derivatives are.

62. The Fed opposed this provision, suggesting that it was important for banks and borrowers to be able to hedge their risks. The argument was bogus: The proposed provision didn't even affect a bank's ability to offer a commercial customer a swap in connection with originating a loan. It only said that such "insurance" shouldn't effectively be subsidized by taxpayers. When banks make a housing loan, for example, they often demand, and facilitate, borrowers buying property insurance. But that doesn't mean that banks should be in the business of providing fire insurance. The Fed and Treasury's opposition to the curbs on derivatives became symbolic of where they stood on regulatory reform.

63. As in the case of so many other provisions, we should say "probably" or "hopefully" since so much is left up to the regulators.

64. Chapter 1 documents U.S. officials' persistently rosy predictions in the early stages of the crisis. The administration repeatedly referred to "green shoots" in the spring of 2009. But the Federal Reserve too was persistently overly optimistic, just as it had been in the run-up to the crisis. It could not, however, totally ignore what was going on; its projections for the 2010 and 2011 unemployment rates were raised each time they met during the first half of 2009, indicating they were repeatedly underestimating the economy's problems. Still, in May 2009, Ben Bernanke said, "We don't think [unemployment] will get to 10 percent," only to see it reach that level in October and stay there for three months. It is one

thing for a president not well versed in economics to exude excessive confidence in the economy—that, in a sense, is part of the job description—but when the Fed badly misdiagnoses the economy's situation, it has long-term effects on its credibility, even more so when others are simultaneously providing a far more accurate interpretation of the data.

65. Indeed, this was one of the important theses in my previous book, written with Linda Bilmes, *The Three Trillion Dollar War: The True Cost of the Iraq Conflict*, op. cit.

66. There is a particular example of rewriting history in which I was a participant. In April 2009, President Obama invited a group of economists (including me) who had been critical of some aspects of his programs, including the adequacy of his stimulus and the design of his bank rescue, to a White House dinner. The dinner was portrayed as the beginning of a dialogue—but in fact appears to have been a one-off event, and because of its uniqueness has received excessive attention in the press. Some press accounts describe those in the Treasury and administration as claiming that the critics were given the opportunity to defend nationalization of the banks, but the critics failed to persuade the President. But in fact, the critical decisions about what to do with the failing banks had already been made, and the issue was not nationalization, but following the standard rules, which require putting banks that have inadequate capital into receivership (or conservatorship, as "bankruptcy" is called in the case of banks). Most of those at the dinner agreed with the view presented in this book that not following these rules had been a mistake. But no one urged the President to reverse that decision. It was too late. However, several of the participants forcefully argued that, should the banks once again need more capital, the standard rules of capitalism should be followed. Fortunately for the too-big-to-fail banks, additional government capital was not required, but in the case of the smaller banks, the standard procedures did apply. Moreover, I (and others) argued that it was likely that a second round of stimulus would be required. It now appears clear that that view was correct.

67. This book focuses on economic leadership. There are other equally important issues. The fact that the United States has expanded an unpopular war in Afghanistan, supporting a government widely criticized for its corruption, has not helped. The failure to close Guantánamo Bay serves as a constant reminder of U.S. abuses of human rights, and its violation of the Geneva Convention and the United Nations Convention Against Torture. But there have been positive developments as well, including the U.S.-Russia agreement to reduce their nuclear arsenals, signed in April 2010.

INDEX

Penguin Politics

GLOBALIZATION AND ITS DISCONTENTS
JOSEPH STIGLITZ

'A massively important political as well as economic document ... we should listen to him urgently' Will Hutton, *Guardian*

Our world is changing. Globalization is not working. It is hurting those it was meant to help. And now, the tide is turning ...

Explosive and shocking, *Globalization and Its Discontents* is the bestselling exposé of the all-powerful organizations that control our lives – from the man who has seen them at work first hand.

As Chief Economist at the World Bank, Nobel Prize-winner Joseph Stiglitz had a unique insider's view into the management of globalization. Now he speaks out against it: how the IMF and WTO preach fair trade yet impose crippling economic policies on developing nations; how free market 'shock therapy' made millions in East Asia and Russia worse off than they were before; and how the West has driven the global agenda to further its own financial interests.

Globalization *can* still be a force for good, Stiglitz argues. But the balance of power has to change. Here he offers real, tough solutions for the future.

'Compelling ... This book is everyone's guide to the misgovernment of globalization' J. K. Galbraith

'Stiglitz is a rare breed, an heretical economist who has ruffled the self-satisfied global establishment that once fed him. *Globalization and Its Discontents* declares war on the entire Washington financial and economic establishment' Ian Fraser, *Sunday Tribune*

'Gripping ... this landmark book ... shows him to be a worthy successor to Keynes' Robin Blackburn, *Independent*

Penguin Politics

THE ROARING NINETIES: WHY WE'RE PAYING THE PRICE FOR THE GREEDIEST DECADE IN HISTORY
JOSEPH STIGLITZ

'One of the most important economic and political thinkers of our time'
Independent on Sunday

His previous book revealed the shocking truth about globalization. Now, Joseph Stiglitz blows the whistle on the devastation wrought by the free market mantra in the nineties – and shows how Bush is ignoring the lessons from what happened.

This is the explosive story of how capitalism US-style got its comeuppance: how excessive deregulation, government pandering to big business and exorbitant CEO salaries all fed the bubble that burst so dramatically amid corporate scandal and anti-globalization protest.

As Chief Economic Advisor to the President at the time, Stiglitz exposes the inside story of what went wrong, but also reveals how Bush's administration is now making things worse – much worse – for the economy, the US and the rest of the world. Stiglitz takes us one step further, showing how a more balanced approach to the market and government can lead not only to a better economy, but a better society.

'Stiglitz's dissection of the follies of the "Roaring Nineties" is as good as it gets' Will Hutton

'An iconic figure ... Stiglitz's book will encourage those who wish to halt the partial Americanization that has already taken place in Europe' *Daily Telegraph*

'Stiglitz has become a hero to the anti-globalization movement' *Economist*

PENGUIN ECONOMICS

THE RETURN OF DEPRESSION ECONOMICS
PAUL KRUGMAN

'Essential reading' *Economist*

At the end of the 1990s, seven economies experienced slumps eerily reminiscent of the Great Depression. A botched devaluation in Thailand set off ripples all the way from Indonesia to South Korea. Russian debt default triggered disaster in Brazil. Hedge funds seemingly unaccountable to any government nearly succeeded in their aim of forcing up interest rates in Hong Kong. And almost no one had predicted these developments. Perhaps, argues Paul Krugman in his dazzling polemic, that is because we are trapped by a cosy free-market orthodoxy which cannot accept that 'bad things happen to good economies'. Yet if we truly hope to confront the immense challenges which lie ahead, we had better start facing up to reality right now.

'A lucid and punchy analysis of the dangers posed by global financial markets and a wake-up call for complacent or economically ignorant policymakers' *Economist*

'One of the world's most talented economists...his combination of wit and clarity makes him a true heir to Keynes' *Independent*

'An account of the Asian crisis that is unlikely to be rivalled in its lucidity...a rattling good read' *Financial Times*

PENGUIN POLITICS

THE SPIRIT LEVEL
RICHARD WILKINSON AND KATE PICKETT

'A book with a big idea, big enough to change political thinking' *Sunday Times*

Why do we mistrust people more in the UK than in Japan? Why do Americans have higher rates of teenage pregnancy than the French? What makes the Swedish thinner than Australians? The answer: inequality.

This groundbreaking book, based on years of research, provides hard evidence to show:

• How almost everything – from life expectancy to depression levels, violence to illiteracy – is affected not by how wealthy a society is, but how equal it is

• That societies with a bigger gap between rich and poor are bad for everyone in them – including the well-off

• How we can find positive solutions and move towards a happier, fairer future

Urgent, provocative and genuinely uplifting, *The Spirit Level* has been heralded as providing a new way of thinking about ourselves and our communities, and could change the way you see the world.

'A remarkable new book ... the implications are profound' Will Hutton, *Observer*

'Profound ... brave ... transformative ... its conclusion is simple: we do better when we're equal' Lynsey Hanley, *Guardian*

He just wanted a decent book to read ...

Not too much to ask, is it? It was in 1935 when Allen Lane, Managing
Director of Bodley Head Publishers, stood on a platform at Exeter railway
station looking for something good to read on his journey back to London.
His choice was limited to popular magazines and poor-quality paperbacks –
the same choice faced every day by the vast majority of readers, few of
whom could afford hardbacks. Lane's disappointment and subsequent anger
at the range of books generally available led him to found a company – and
change the world.

'We believed in the existence in this country of a vast reading public for intelligent
books at a low price, and staked everything on it'
Sir Allen Lane, 1902–1970, founder of Penguin Books

The quality paperback had arrived – and not just in bookshops. Lane was
adamant that his Penguins should appear in chain stores and tobacconists,
and should cost no more than a packet of cigarettes.

Reading habits (and cigarette prices) have changed since 1935, but
Penguin still believes in publishing the best books for everybody to
enjoy. We still believe that good design costs no more than bad design,
and we still believe that quality books published passionately and responsibly
make the world a better place.

So wherever you see the little bird – whether it's on a piece of
prize-winning literary fiction or a celebrity autobiography, political tour
de force or historical masterpiece, a serial-killer thriller, reference book,
world classic or a piece of pure escapism – you can bet that it represents
the very best that the genre has to offer.

Whatever you like to read – trust Penguin.